P9-DMH-348

The American Political Economy

The American Political Economy

Macroeconomics and Electoral Politics

Douglas A. Hibbs, Jr.

Harvard University Press
Cambridge, Massachusetts, and London, England   1987

Library of Congress Cataloging-in-Publication Data

Hibbs, Douglas A., 1944–
    The American political economy.

    Bibliography: p.
    Includes index.
    1. Business cycles—Political aspects—United States.
2. Elections—United States.   3. United States—
Economic policy—1981–   4. United States—
Economic conditions—1981–   I. Title.
HB3743.H52   1987   338.973   87-155
ISBN 0-674-02735-3 (alk. paper)

In memory of my father and my mother—
Douglas A. Hibbs, Sr., and Lillian C. Hibbs

Acknowledgments

I began writing first drafts of the early chapters of this book late in the summer of 1981, and I worked on the manuscript intermittently over the following four years. Along the way I was helped by many people.

It is no trouble at all for me to decide whom to thank first. Nearly the entire quantitative data base and a large portion of the statistical analyses appearing in this volume were managed by Nicholas Vasilatos. Nick is a programmer of rare ability and a man of equally rare equanimity. How he put up with me—an impossibly demanding person at the best of times—I still do not understand. Without his help the research for this book, which dragged on much too long as it was, still would not be finished.

Also assisting with computer and data analysis tasks were several Harvard University undergraduates. During the early stages of the work I was helped by David Golden and Danny Ertel, each of whom wrote a brilliant Harvard College thesis on politics and economics in the United States, which I had the pleasure of supervising and from which I learned much. Jonathan Nagler, a Harvard College government major, also assisted with data processing during early phases of the research. Toward the end of the project George Tsibouris assisted with data analysis and preparation of graphics. Under great pressure from his impatient employer, George calmly went about helping me, in the process displaying unusual skill and maturity for someone so young.

It is a genuine pleasure for me to acknowledge the contribution of Doug Rivers, once a graduate student and teaching fellow of mine at Harvard and then, for all too brief a time, a faculty colleague at the same institution. Before Doug left to join the faculty of the California Institute of Technology, he and I collaborated on a number of articles on macroeconomic performance and mass political support; Chapter 5 draws on this work.

Several skilled technical typists have wrestled with the manuscript over the last couple of years. Two deserve special mention. Joy Mundy, one of the smartest people I met at Harvard among the ranks of students, staff, or faculty, typed (or "text edited") the early drafts of the first half of the book. Joanne Klys, another person of exceptional intelligence, typed most of the final draft of the book. Joanne also served as an indispensable research assistant, maintaining complex computer data bases and running many a nonlinear regression.

A great many colleagues in economics and political science have commented on one or more chapters of this book. The late Otto Eckstein of Harvard, one of the great applied macroeconomists of the postwar era, on several occasions forcefully conveyed to me his views about politics, economic policy, and political business cycles (Chapter 8). Alan Blinder of Princeton University's economics department carefully reviewed Chapter 3 and a very early version of Chapter 5. I also received detailed comments on Chapter 3 from Lawrence Summers of the Harvard economics department. Robert J. Gordon of Northwestern University, another leading macroeconomist from whom I have learned a great deal, commented on early versions of the Introduction and Chapter 5. Robert Hall of Stanford University gave me a vigorous critique of a previous version of Chapter 4 and generously shared his wide-ranging knowledge of macroeconomics during the year we were both fellows at the Center for Advanced Study in the Behavioral Sciences at Palo Alto, California. I also benefited from the comments of economist Carl Christ of The Johns Hopkins University on an earlier version of Chapter 4. While he was a visiting professor in the Harvard economics department, Thomas Sargent of the University of Minnesota helped me sort out some of the subtler aspects of discrete time dynamics, which are used extensively in Chapters 7 and 8. Johan Lybeck, a leading Swedish macroeconomist and a good friend, gave me the benefit of his comments on the entire manuscript. Mark Watson, a young econometrician at Harvard, was always available to talk with me about time series statistical estimation issues.

Two leading scholars of politics and economics, Edward Tufte and David Cameron of the Yale University political science department, gave me insightful comments on and criticisms of early versions of Chapters 4, 5, and 6. William Keech of the University of North Carolina political science department pushed me to extend the discussion of the behavioral implications of the class of political support models appearing in Chapter 5. Richard Neustadt of Harvard, an expert on the American presidency, helped clarify my thinking in that chapter about the connections between presidential approval ratings and economic conditions. Doug Price, a former colleague in the Harvard government department who knows more about the history of American party politics and policy than anyone else I ever met, saved me from going into print with several embarrassing factual errors in Chapter 1. Doug also was a continual source of items of fact and interpretation, which are scattered throughout the book. Leon Lindberg, a political economy specialist in the University of Wisconsin political science department, provided many useful comments, both editorial and substantive, on Chapters 4, 5, and 9. And Michael Cornfield, a graduate student in the Harvard government department, read the entire manuscript with great care. Mike called to my attention many instances of muddled thinking, identified numerous awkward constructions, and—to the extent possible with this style of work—helped anchor the book in the "real world" of politics.

Money is as important to the conduct of social science research as it is to the functioning of an exchange economy and a competitive political system. From 1975 to 1982, when I was engaged in projects that form the foundations of this study, my research was continuously funded by the National Science Foundation. Although I like to believe that the foundation (and the taxpayers) got their money's worth, I am very grateful for the NSF sponsorship. During my years at Harvard, the Center for International Affairs financed released time from my usual teaching obligations and covered the costs of running political economy seminars for specialists, which greatly enhanced the local environment for research and writing on politics and economics. I am grateful to my former colleagues on the CFIA executive committee and to the CFIA director, Samuel P. Huntington, for the support.

I would not have had the time to write this book without a generous grant from the Alfred P. Sloan Foundation, which supported my work during 1983–1985. I thank in particular Arthur L. Singer at Sloan for his confidence that an award to me would turn out to be a productive investment of the foundation's resources. The last chapter of this book was written and the others were edited while I was a fellow at the Institute for Advanced Study in Berlin during the spring term of 1985. The helpfulness of the staff made the institute one of the most comfortable places I know of for thinking and writing.

Finally, I want to express thanks to my wife, Eva Bernbro-Hibbs. Eva made no contribution at all to the mechanics of researching and writing the volume. Her role was more fundamental. She stood behind me, without flinching, in the face of enormous pressure during a profound personal and professional crisis when I came very close to abandoning the work. This book would never have been completed had she not been there.

I ask those whom I have forgotten to thank—and I expect that there are several—to understand. I write these acknowledgments in Europe without benefit of files or records.

Contents

The American Political Economy

Introduction: A Framework for the Analysis of Macroeconomics and Electoral Politics

From one important point of view, indeed, the avoidance of inflation and the maintenance of full employment can be most usefully regarded as conflicting class interests of the bourgeoisie and proletariat, respectively, the conflict being resolvable only by the test of relative political power in society and its resolution involving no reference to an overriding concept of the social welfare.

—Harry G. Johnson

The American political economy is, one hardly need say, a very broad and rich topic. This book deals with only part of the terrain, though I think it is a very important part: the connections between public opinion and electoral behavior, and macroeconomic policies and outcomes. This volume was conceived on the assumption, amply demonstrated by casual observation as well as by systematic research, that the macroeconomic policies pursued by political administrations operating in a democratic setting rarely originate with idealized, apolitical "golden rule" norms. Rather, macroeconomic policies, which critically affect economic outcomes, are responsive to and are constrained by the electorate's reactions to economic events. In a democratic society, then, macroeconomic policies and outcomes reflect the intersection of both economic and political forces. This interdependence is usefully thought of in terms of a political-economic system of the *demand for* and *supply of* economic outcomes.[1] The main features of this framework are illustrated in Figure I.1.

Containing inflation at politically acceptable rates of growth and unemployment has been the most important economic problem confronted by American policy authorities for almost two decades. Although there is no stable, long-run (traditional Phillips-curve) trade-off between inflation and unemployment in the American macroeconomy, by and large economists and politicians alike understand that achieving low unemployment levels (and high growth rates) and stabilizing inflation are often conflicting goals. It is frequently difficult to make substantial progress on one without running great risks with respect to the other.[2] Faced with demand shifts, supply shocks, labor-cost push, and other inflationary events, political administrations repeatedly have been forced to choose between accommodating inflationary pressures by pursuing expansive monetary and fiscal policies, thereby forgoing leverage on the pace of price rises in order to preserve aggregate demand and employment, and leaning against such pressures by tightening spending and the supply of money and credit, thereby slowing the inflation rate, at the cost of higher unemployment and lower growth.

An important political-economic issue, then, is why the fiscal and monetary "discipline" exhibited by policy authorities varies over time and presidential administrations, especially during major episodes of inflationary pressure. Put another way, why are policy authorities less inclined to "supply" unemployment and more inclined to "supply" inflation (and conversely) at some times than at others? The choices implied by this question have important class-linked distributional consequences affecting the relative and absolute economic well-being of socioeconomic groups, and important electoral consequences affecting the political well-being of politicians and parties. Not surprisingly, therefore, these choices have been the focus of intense controversy and conflict among key actors in American political and economic life.

The economic interests at stake during inflations and recessions, the ways in which class-related political constituencies perceive their interests and respond in the opinion polls and in the voting booth to macroeconomic fluctuations, and the ways in which the economic interests, preferences, and priorities of political constituencies are transmitted to macroeconomic policies and outcomes observed under the parties are the main themes of this book.

I.1   Macroeconomic and Institutional Background

Part I begins with an account of postwar American macroeconomic performance in historical perspective. Chapter 1 identifies three striking features of the postwar macroeconomy that stand in sharp contrast to the prewar experience: comparatively high rates of growth, stabilization of macroeconomic fluctuations, and near-continuous inflation (though at widely varying rates). Special attention is given to the institutional changes and policy innovations enhancing macroeconomic stability and individual security in the decades after the Great Depression of the 1930s, which in turn increased the inflationary expectations and behavior of firms, unions, workers, and consumers.

Understanding the electorate's reactions to economic outcomes, which are treated in Part II, requires knowledge of the aggregate costs and distributional consequences of macroeconomic fluctuations. Accordingly, Chapters 2 and 3 are devoted to detailed analyses of the costs of unemployment and inflation, respectively. The costs of unemployment are unambiguous and therefore are easily established. After reviewing the aggregate costs—which amount to at least 2 percent of a year's Gross National Product (GNP) per extra percentage point of annual unemployment—Chapter 2 deals with the livelier question of how those costs are distributed across individuals. As one would expect from the sociological incidence of unemployment, the main losers from recessions tend to be located at the lower ends of the income and occupational-class hierarchies. Although the tax and transfer system succeeds, as intended, in offsetting an important fraction of the income losses of those directly affected by a rise in the aggregate rate of unemployment, recessions nevertheless have pronounced class-linked distributional consequences.

The costs of inflation, which are covered in Chapter 3, are much more controversial than those of unemployment. For decades inflation has been a *bête noire* of affluent conservatives, although, as Part II shows, many citizens of modest means and status also view rapidly rising prices as a significant problem. Yet there is little or no evidence that postwar inflations have adversely affected the American economy's aggregate real output or income performance. Relative to those of unemployment, the distributional consequences of inflation also appear to be rather small; and, if anything, they seem to disadvantage the rich rather than the poor. The lengthy analysis in Chapter 3 suggests that public aversion to inflation is based largely on difficult-to-measure psychological factors. It is also based on confusion, sometimes abetted by policy authorities, of the real income losses imposed by international energy price increases, with the rate of inflation per se.

I.2   The Demand for Economic Outcomes

As Figure I.1 indicates, mass political support for the president and his party—as reflected by votes on election day and by poll ratings during interelection periods—depends on, among other things, cur-

Supply of Economic Outcomes

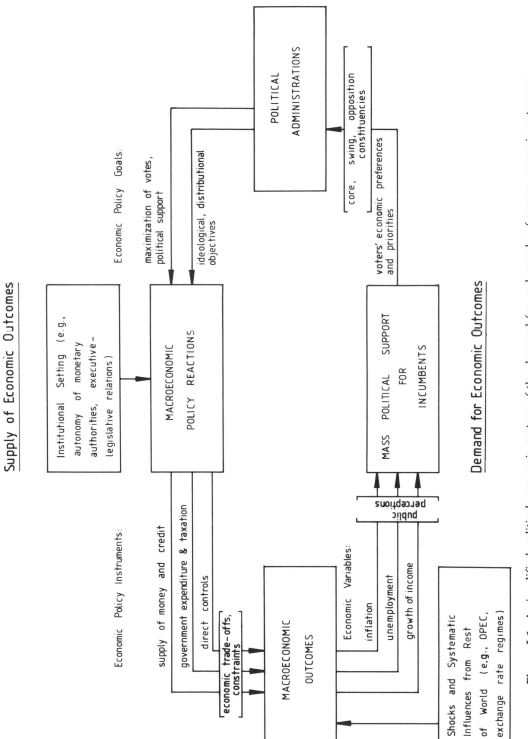

Demand for Economic Outcomes

Figure I.1 A simplified political-economic system of the demand for and supply of macroeconomic outcomes.

rent, past, and perhaps anticipated future economic performance.[3] The response of mass political support for incumbents to economic conditions reveals information about the electorate's economic priorities and relative preferences (as between, most importantly, higher inflation and higher unemployment) and constitutes voters' *demand* for economic outcomes. These issues are taken up in Part II.

In Chapter 4 I analyze opinion survey data that assess the public's relative concern about inflation and unemployment during the 1970s and 1980s. Analyses of the aggregate survey responses, presented in the first half of that chapter, yield a reasonably good picture of the combinations of inflation, unemployment, and real income growth in the economy that typically give rise to anti-inflation-oriented versus anti-unemployment-oriented majorities in the electorate. Because the costs of unemployment fall most heavily on down-scale groups (which make up the core constituency of the Democratic party) and the costs of inflation are distribution neutral except at the highest income levels, relative concern about inflation and unemployment varies across electoral groups. Disaggregated opinion data, discussed in the last section of Chapter 4, show that Democratic partisans, blue-collar workers, and low-income classes are in all situations less inflation averse (more unemployment averse) than are Republicans, white-collar workers, and high-income classes.

Direct evidence on the political consequences of macroeconomic events is presented in Chapter 5. In this chapter the impact of economic (and noneconomic) performance over time on mass political support for presidents among partisan groups in the electorate, as registered in Gallup polls, is investigated. The analyses are embedded in a dynamic nonlinear model of political choice, which is derived from the theory of utility maximization and is based on the idea that voters evaluate a president's performance relatively rather than absolutely. The complexity of the model makes this one of the most technically demanding chapters of the book. Yet the analytic setup allows me to address some very important issues concerning the structure and formation of the electorate's implicit demands for economic outcomes. Among these are (1) the rate at which past as opposed to current performance is discounted when the electorate makes contemporaneous political evaluations of the president; (2) the weight that voters, when making current political judgments about the president, appear to give the cumulative economic and noneconomic record of political parties in comparison to that given to the performance of discrete administrations and to the unique appeal of particular incumbents; and, most significantly, (3) the relative weights voters place on inflation and unemployment outcomes. Estimation results for the political support equations show that the implicit preference (or demand) for low inflation is pronounced among all voter groups. However, as one would anticipate from the distributional analyses in Chapters 2 and 3 and the public opinion data in Chapter 4, Democratic partisans in the electorate have greater sensitivity to unemployment relative to inflation than do Republicans or Independents.

Chapter 6 rounds out Part II by demonstrating the decisive contribution of economic performance to recent presidential election outcomes. In this chapter I show that Ronald Reagan's back-to-back victories in 1980 and 1984 had little or nothing to do with conservative tides or ideological shifts to the right in the electorate. Rather, voters (predictably) punished Carter and the Democrats in the 1980 elections for the poor economic performance of 1979–1980, and rewarded Reagan and the Republicans in the 1984 contests for the vigorous economic expansion of 1983–1984. The cyclical timing of macroeconomic events in relation to the 1980 and 1984 elections, as well as the contrasting priorities placed on unemployment and inflation (and redistribution) by the Carter and Reagan administrations, leads naturally to the analysis of the politically motivated supply of economic outcomes in Part III.

I.3   The Supply of Economic Outcomes

Political administrations may attempt to maintain a comfortable level of mass political support over the electoral term, to maximize votes on election day, and also to pursue ideological and distributional goals reflecting the distinctive preferences of their core electoral constituencies (Figure I.1). The economic policy reactions of administrations to voters' economic preferences and priorities (or demands) determine the politically driven *supply* of economic outcomes. The impact of political forces on the formulation and implementation of macroeconomic policies is subject to institutional arrangements, which include the degree of autonomy of monetary authorities from elected political officials, executive-legislative relations, federalism, and so on. Furthermore, the impact of macroeconomic policies on macroeconomic outcomes is constrained by the structure of economic relations (for example, short-run Phillips curves) and international economic influences (for example, OPEC oil supply shocks). Therefore, domestic politics and policy strongly influence but do not completely shape macroeconomic outcomes.

Domestic macroeconomic policy includes monetary policy (the money supply and credit conditions), fiscal policy (taxation and expenditure), direct controls (principally wage and price controls), and occasionally rhetoric and persuasion ("jawboning"). The monetary and fiscal policy instruments have been much more significant than the others in the United States because they account for most of the policy-induced movements in the major macroeconomic variables—the inflation rate, the unemployment rate, and the rate of growth of income and output.

The relative importance of monetary policy—in particular, expansions and contractions of the money supply—has been acknowledged widely only during the last dozen years. Today most economists concur with Milton Friedman's long-held view that sustained expansions of the money supply are the most important proximate source of sustained inflations, accepting what Robert J. Gordon described as the "abundant empirical evidence . . . that the major historical accelerations and decelerations of inflation—not only during wars and hyper-inflations but also during peacetime—have been accompanied by accelerations and decelerations of the rate of growth of the supply of money."[4] Moreover, many economists are now skeptical that discretionary tax and expenditure manipulations can decisively influence real output and employment levels without a cooperative monetary policy. The conclusion of Ray Fair's econometric study reflects a strong version of this thinking: "when the Fed keeps the money supply unchanged, the fiscal authority has little room to maneuver . . . the fiscal authority can do little about changing the output path once the money supply is fixed."[5] Hence, the Keynesian-activist position that government can (and should) stabilize the macroeconomy now rests heavily on the case for demand management via monetary as well as fiscal policy activism.[6]

The conclusion that macroeconomic outcomes are largely governed by the course of monetary policy is only the starting point for analysis, however, because the causes of monetary growth rates are not obvious. Although under American institutional arrangements the monetary authority has considerable formal autonomy,[7] the Federal Reserve's insulation from political direction is largely illusory. The popular myth of Federal Reserve independence endures primarily because incumbent politicians often use it as a scapegoat when the economy is going badly.

Federal Reserve authorities are drawn from, or have intimate connections with the financial community, and it is fair to say that by and large they are reluctant to sacrifice control of inflation in order to expand employment, preferring instead to maintain a steady control over the money supply. But in the end the Fed cannot resist accommodating vigorous pressure from elected political officials (most important of whom is the president), which is often conveyed tangibly by fiscal deficits that administrations want covered by money creation. If the Federal Reserve did lean too long and too hard against political pressures, its statutory insulation from direct political control could be stripped away. In 1982 the Reagan administration quite openly threatened to do just this when it announced the need for a reevaluation of the Federal Reserve's relationship to the Treasury in the face of the Fed's initial resistance to the administration's desire to abandon disinflationary monetary policy and launch a recovery for the last half of Reagan's first term.[8] Therefore, although in principle the (elected) fiscal authority's leverage on the path of output and employment may be diminished substantially "once the money supply is fixed," in practice monetary policy is quite responsive to the political climate, especially as represented by the preferences of the president.

This conclusion is supported by virtually every careful analysis of Federal Reserve policy behavior (in contrast to Federal Reserve policy rhetoric). In his historical review of the Fed's relations with Congress and the executive, Robert Weintraub, a leading congressional staff expert on the Federal Reserve, summarized the matter this way: "Congressional oversight cannot be said to have significantly affected the course of monetary policy. What the Administration wants or is perceived to want continues to dominate the Federal Reserve's conduct as it is manifested in the money supply, as it has ever since the Accord."[9] Similarly, in a subsequent study of the Fed, Robert J. Shapiro concluded: "Throughout the Reserve's history, its formal independence was substantively compromised whenever it tried to resist specific directions from any administration."[10] Economist and Fed watcher Robert J. Samuelson put the same idea even more bluntly: "To think that the Fed is the economy's nerve center is to misunderstand politics and economics."[11] Perhaps the strongest statement that can be made about the Federal Reserve's autonomy in the American system is that the Reserve authorities act to preserve their nominal independence from explicit political direction by typically choosing "independently" to pursue monetary policies accommodating strongly articulated preferences of presidential administrations.[12]

In Chapters 7 and 8 of Part III, the two most significant potential sources of political influence on macroeconomic policies and outcomes are investigated: the differing economic priorities of the political parties and the election-year policy incentives of incumbent politicians. To the degree that presidential administrations have economic goals consistent with the objective interests and revealed preferences of their parties' class-related core political constituencies, we should observe, other things being equal, persistent partisan variations in macroeconomic policy thrusts and macroeconomic outcome configurations. In Chapter 7 I introduce a "party cleavage" model that embodies such partisan-based differences in the supply of macroeconomic policies and outcomes. Empirical results for suitably specified equations show that Democratic presidential administrations typically pursue more expansive policies yielding lower unemployment and higher real output and growth (which tend to produce higher rates of inflation) than do Republican administrations. I also argue in this chapter that the parties have contrasting distributional objectives that are consistent with the locations of their core constituencies in the hierarchy of income classes. Empirical analyses are presented which indicate that most of the modest growth in the equalization of after-tax, after-transfer incomes during the postwar period occurred under Democratic administrations.

The special political pressures on macroeconomic policies that may build up during election years are evaluated in Chapter 8. The so-called political business cycle—the idea that economic activity vibrates with the election calendar as a result of the tendency of incumbents to create unsustainable booms just prior to elections and to postpone the inevitable austerity measures until just after elections—has received more attention than any other topic in the contemporary macropolitical economy literature. The historical and statistical evidence reviewed in Chapter 8 provides two clear examples of electorally well-timed economic expansions that plausibly can be traced to political motives: the 1971–1972 recovery under Nixon and the 1983–1984 recovery under Reagan. On the other hand, economic policy and performance over the Carter years looks like a political business cycle run in reverse. Expansive policies fueling brisk growth rates and falling unemployment during 1977–1978 were followed by restrictive policies and a sharp deterioration of the economy in 1979–1980. Looking at the postwar experience as a whole, I argue that election-oriented economic policy and output cycles have not been a pronounced feature of the American political economy.

It is appropriate that this book concludes, in Chapter 9, with an analysis of the political economy of "Reaganomics," for economic events during Ronald Reagan's first term sharply illustrate both the political business cycle in action and the macroeconomic and distributional consequences of a shift from a Democratic to a Republican presidential administration. President Reagan pushed through Congress the largest package of tax and social spending cuts in postwar American history, achieving as a result an enormous redistribution of after-tax, after-transfer income in favor of the affluent. At the same time, his administration supported a Draconian disinflationary monetary policy during 1981–1982, which created the highest rates of unemployment since the last years of the Great Depression. Yet the combination of monetary relaxation and big deficits during the last half of the term produced a surge in real income growth rates perfectly timed to yield a vote harvest in 1984. President Reagan, therefore, pursued redistributive policies that served the economic interests of the Republican party's prosperous core constituency exceedingly well and also presided over a late-term economic recovery that led to a resounding reelection victory. Judged on the basis of partisan economic interest as well as electoral success, a more impressive performance is difficult to imagine.

I Macroeconomic and Institutional Background

1 Postwar American Macroeconomic Performance in Historical Perspective

[The business cycle's impact] on the lives and fortunes of individuals has been substantially reduced in our generation . . . There is no parallel for such a sequence of mild or such a sequence of brief contractions, at least during the past hundred years in our own country.

—Arthur Burns, 1959 presidential address to the American Economics Association

What goes up no longer comes down. I suppose that's because everybody nowadays guesses that recessions will be short. And because American bosses have bank deposit insurance, while American workers have unemployment compensation, nobody feels desperately he must accept price and wage cuts.

—An economic adviser in the Carter administration

When postwar American macroeconomic performance is viewed in historical perspective, three facts stand out. First, the remarkable historical record of American capitalism in delivering increasing real income has been sustained. Indeed, on a per capita basis, the real output growth rate during the post–World War II period has been more favorable than in earlier eras of comparatively unfettered capitalism. This is worth underscoring, because the government's postwar and economic policies have been assailed in recent years as having perverse effects on incentives and productivity, on saving and investment, and therefore on growth.

Second, macroeconomic stability and individual security have increased dramatically since World War II. Although recessions have been an all-too-familiar feature of our postwar economic life, the historical cycle of sensational booms and crushing busts appears to have expired more than forty years ago. Really wild oscillations in output and employment no longer occur. Moreover, firms and employers, as well as workers and citizens, are now sheltered from economic misfortunes to an unprecedented degree.

Third, the general price level falls only rarely, and never by much or for prolonged periods. Until World War II, American capitalism was characterized by great deflations as well as by great inflations; consequently, over the long run the price level tended to be flat. By contrast, since 1950 the general price level has risen almost continuously, though by varying rates. As we shall see in later sections of this chapter, enhanced economic security and macroeconomic stability are important structural sources of the postwar inflations.

1.1 Growth and Unemployment

Perhaps the single most impressive feature of the historical performance of American capitalism is the enormous expansion of the aggregate production of goods and services. Between 1890 (the first year for which we have reasonably accurate data) and 1980, real (constant dollar) Gross National Product increased about nineteenfold. The average annual percentage rate of growth of real GNP during this period was more than 3 percent. Prior to 1930 the annual real growth rate averaged about 3.5 percent, and after 1949 it averaged about 3.6 percent. Of course, the population and the labor force also expanded dramatically over the last near-century, and therefore it is more revealing to examine growth on a per capita basis.

Figures 1.1 and 1.2 show the relevant data. Constant dollar GNP per capita (shown in 1967 prices) grew just over fivefold between 1890 and 1980: from 1000 (1967) dollars per head in 1890 to about 5100 (1967) dollars per head in 1980 (Figure 1.1).[1] The average percentage rate of growth was 1.8 percent per annum over the entire ninety-year period, but it was somewhat higher in the post–World War II years (2.17 percent per year) than in earlier eras (see Figure 1.2). Real output and unemployment (see Figures 1.3 and 1.4), however, have fluctuated widely.

The really major catastrophies in output and employment all predate the postwar "Keynesian" era.[2] The rate of unemployment rose by more than 5 percentage points, and the annual growth rate of per capita real GNP declined by more than 10 percent during the great contractions of 1907–1908, 1920–1921, and 1929–1932. Serious depressions of employment and real output also occurred during 1893–1894, 1913–1914, and 1937–1938. The 1890s and 1930s are perhaps best viewed as entire decades of sustained depression.[3] Real output

Figure 1.1 Gross National Product per capita 1890–1980 (1967 dollars). *Sources:* U.S. Department of Commerce, *Historical Statistics of the United States, Colonial Times to 1970*, Series F 1-5, 1971; and TROLL-Citibank Economic Database, Series NBER-GNPP72.

per capita was below trend and the unemployment rate stood at 10 percent or more *every year* between 1892 and 1899 and between 1930 and 1941. Indeed, the prewar unemployment data probably understate the magnitude of the problem. The rate of unemployment is conventionally measured as the number of people unemployed as a percentage of the civilian labor force.[4] But during the nineteenth century and first part of the twentieth century, a large fraction of the labor force comprised farmers and small proprietors who, though frequently immiserated, rarely joined the ranks of the officially unemployed.

The post–World War II era stands in sharp contrast to this previous experience. Although the postwar growth rate of real output per head compares favorably to that of previous periods (Figure 1.2), as does the average rate of unemployment (Figure 1.3), the most significant change was the *stabilization* of growth and unemployment. Prior to the 1950s, fluctuations in real per capita GNP of plus or minus 10 percent, and oscillations in the unemployment rate of plus or minus 4 to 5 percent, were common occurrences. American capitalism was

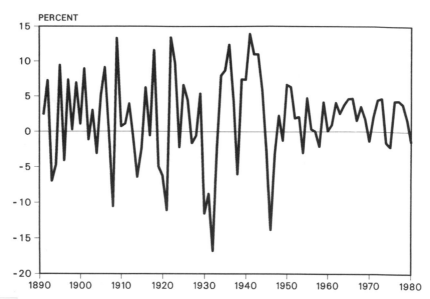

Figure 1.2 Real output stability over time: real GNP per capita growth rates (percent per annum), 1891–1980. *Sources:* U.S. Department of Commerce, *Historical Statistics of the United States, Colonial Times to 1970,* Series F 1-5, 1971; and TROLL-Citibank Economic Database, Series NBER-GNPP72.

	1891–1929	1930–1949	1950–1980
Mean ($\bar{x}$)	1.78	1.32	2.17
Standard deviation (σ)	6.28	9.22	2.65
Coefficient of variation ($\sigma/\bar{x}$)	3.54	6.99	1.22

relatively unrestrained by forces outside the market, and the system revealed a chronic tendency to produce great booms and busts along its long-run average growth paths. Between 1950 and 1980 real GNP per capita rose from one year to the next by more than 5 percent only once (in 1951, as a result of the Korean War boom), and it never declined by more than 3 percent. The standard deviation statistics and coefficients of variation reported at the bottom of Figure 1.2 summarize the story. Both quantities show that the cyclical variability of real output growth rates (both absolutely, as measured by the standard deviations, and relative to the means, as measured by coefficients of variation) has been much lower during the postwar era than it was previously.

The rate of unemployment displays the same secular pattern. In contrast to the situation in earlier decades, between 1950 and 1980 the average annual unemployment rate never exceeded 8.5 percent or fell below 2.9 percent (Figure 1.3).[5] As Figure 1.4 indicates, year-to-year changes in unemployment have not exceeded 3 percent since 1950, and typically they have been much smaller. The standard deviation of annual changes in the unemployment rate is only about 1.2 for 1950–1980, as compared to 3.2 and 3.9, respectively, for the 1891–1929 and 1930–1949 periods.

By historical standards, then, the post–World War II era of government regulations, controls, cyclical interventions, and relatively high taxes and public expenditures has been characterized by compara-

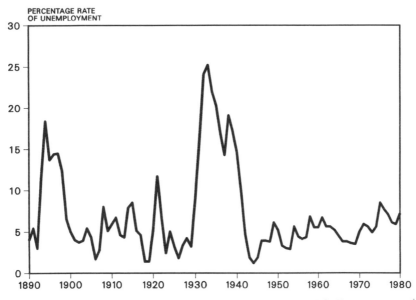

Figure 1.3 The unemployment rate, 1890–1980. *Sources:* U.S. Department of Commerce, *Historical Statistics of the United States, Colonial Times to 1970,* Series D 1-10, 1971; and TROLL-Citibank Economic Database, Series NBER12-LHUR.

	1890–1929	1930–1949	1950–1980
Mean ($\bar{x}$)	6.12	11.81	5.23
Standard deviation (σ)	4.07	8.10	1.39
Coefficient of variation ($\sigma/\bar{x}$)	0.66	0.69	0.27

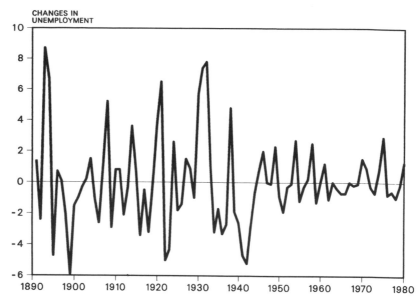

Figure 1.4 Year-to-year changes in the unemployment rate, 1891–1980. *Note:* Standard deviation (σ) for 1891–1929 is 3.24; 1930–1949, 3.85; 1950–1980, 1.18.

tively high growth, low unemployment, and, most significantly, great macroeconomic stability. Of course, stability, growth, and un-employment all deteriorated after the first great OPEC oil supply shock of 1973. And this economic deterioration increased the number and strengthened the hands of those pressing for a reversal of the upward trend in the government's fiscal, monetary, and regulatory powers and activities. It is difficult, however, to blame "government" for our post-OPEC economic problems. Virtually all energy-depen-dent countries experienced adverse changes in growth and unem-ployment after 1973, and the post-OPEC real economic performance of the United States has not been poor compared to that of other industrial nations with both large and small public sectors. Moreover, our average real GNP per capita growth rate for 1973–1980 was about the same as the 1891–1949 mean growth rate (1.6 percent per year), and our average unemployment rate over the same period was actu-ally more favorable than the 1891–1949 mean (6.8 versus 8.0 percent). Reagan's first term excepted, the economic performance of even the worst postwar years does not seem so unappealing when compared to the prewar experience.

The overall postwar record for price inflation, however, is less attractive.

1.2 Inflation

Inflation, as Robert Solow defined it in his influential essay on the topic, is "a substantial, sustained increase in the general level of prices," where the general price level describes "the terms on which some representative bundle of goods and services exchanges for money."[6] The important thing to remember is that inflation is a monetary phenomenon involving a decline in the purchasing power of money. In principle it tells us nothing whatsoever about the quantity of goods and services produced or about people's standard of living.

There are many measures of the general price level. Throughout most of this book I shall focus on the Consumer Price Index (CPI)—a weighted average of the prices of a "representative" bundle of goods and services purchased by a "representative" group of people—because that is the price index that government benefits and private contracts are usually tied to and that citizens and voters (and the media) appear to be most concerned about.[7] In any case, the choice of a particular measure of the price level is not very important; except in the 1970s, all price level indexes have moved together rather closely. Figure 1.5 graphs the behavior of the CPI since 1860; the base year is 1967 = 100. The annual percentage rates of change are shown in Figure 1.6.

It is obvious from these data that the big inflationary surges occurred during and just after the major wars. Between 1860 and 1864 and between 1940 and 1948, the price level increased by 170 percent. Between 1914 and 1920 it doubled. Prices also rose during the Korean and Vietnamese conflicts, but the association between inflation and these wars is not as noticeable because the CPI increased in every year after 1949 except 1955, when it decreased by a whisker from 80.5 to 80.2.

The persistent inflation of the post–World War II years is the most striking feature of the price-level data. In earlier decades bursts of inflation were eventually followed by deflations, and so the price level showed little sign of the uninterrupted secular increases we are now so accustomed to. From 1884 to 1893 the price level was flat, and by 1910 it stood only slightly higher than it had in 1860, before the big Civil War inflation. Between the late 1860s and the late 1930s, price deflations just about canceled the price inflations: the price level in

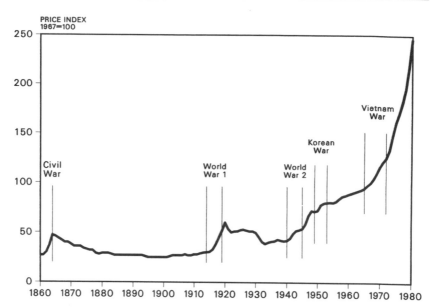

Figure 1.5 The Consumer Price Index, 1860–1980. *Sources:* U.S. Department of Labor, *Handbook of Labor Statistics, 1978*, Table 116; and TROLL-Citibank Economic Database, Series NBER12-PU.

1939 was nearly the same as the price level in 1869. Since 1950, however, the price level has moved upward, by varying rates, almost continuously. Obviously there has been a strong bias toward price (and wage) inflation during the postwar era.

1.3   The Bias toward Inflation

What explains this inertia or downward inflexibility of wages and prices since World War II? The underlying reason that the American economy is now so resistant to deflation, and even to disinflation,[8] is that it is virtually depression-proof—a development that has fundamentally altered the expectations and hence the behavior of economic and political actors.

During the nineteenth century and the first part of the twentieth century, periodic, prolonged contractions of output and employment acted as a brake on sustained upward movements in the price level. The market imposed a harsh discipline on the wage-setting behavior of unions and workers and on the price-setting behavior of firms and employers. Workers were relatively unorganized both politically and

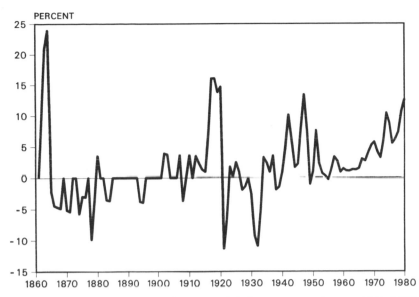

Figure 1.6 Consumer price inflation and deflation, annual rates, 1861–1980.

	1861–1929	1930–1949	1950–1980
Mean ($\bar{x}$)	0.93	1.65	4.00
Standard deviation (σ)	6.27	6.04	3.39
Coefficient of variation ($\sigma/\bar{x}$)	6.74	3.66	0.85

industrially, and they knew that when markets eventually softened and demand showed signs of contracting, prolonged unemployment might follow. And they were right. In such an environment workers were deterred from pushing too long and too aggressively for wage increases when economic conditions worsened, and employers were more inclined to resist wage demands. The typical nineteenth-century firm was smaller and more exposed to competitive pressures than are firms today, and prices therefore were reduced with a frequency and readiness ("cutthroat competition") that is difficult to imagine now.[9] The costs of price inflexibility were high: forgone profits, reduced market shares, of bankruptcy.

All this had changed substantially by the 1950s. Recessions had lost much of their terror, and as a result the need and the inclination to lower wages *and* prices declined. As we shall see in subsequent sections, today large firms and their workers are significantly sheltered against the consequences of market mistakes, individuals are cushioned against economic misfortune, and governments have the knowledge, the institutional flexibility, and the policy tools to prevent economic contractions of the scale experienced in the 1870s, the 1890s, the early 1920s, and the 1930s. Moreover, no administration could weather the political storm that would follow if it presided over a major depression; indeed, relatively small economic contractions often produce electoral shifts large enough to defeat sitting presidents and to push the governing party into opposition. By 1950 the cumulative effect of these developments had led workers and employers to believe, correctly, that major depressions were next to impossible and that less catastrophic hardships were unlikely to be experienced for very long. Firms and unions therefore drew no strong expectations about the future demand for labor and products from contemporaneous market conditions. Hence, even when conditions slackened during postwar recessions, workers and employers were slower to reduce their wage and price claims than they had been earlier.

THE RESPONSIVENESS OF PRICES TO RECESSIONS:
QUANTITATIVE EVIDENCE

Some quantitative evidence on the responsiveness of inflation to economic contractions appears in Tables 1.1 and 1.2. Table 1.1 shows the changes in the CPI inflation rate accompanying contractions of real output per capita (deviations of the logarithm of per capita real GNP from trend, which measures the severity of recessions and depressions over the period 1890–1980). The table distinguishes price response to mild and moderate contractions from price behavior during strong contractions. As one would expect, the strong contractions—defined as a gap of 10 percent or more between actual and trend per capita real output—generally produced the greatest disinflations. We have not experienced a 10-percent contraction since the depression of 1929–1932, but mild and moderate contractions have occurred with some regularity over the entire 1890–1980 period. The data in Table 1.1 show that, with the exception of the 1895–1896 recession, prior to the 1950s the smaller contractions produced significant decelerations of prices. Beginning with the 1953–1954 recession, however, the inflation rate seemed to respond modestly, and sometimes hardly at all, to contractions of real output. Thus the flexible downward response of consumer prices to recessions weakened after World War II; certainly there was noticeably less downward price and wage flexibility by the early 1960s.[10]

Table 1.1 Response of inflation to business cycle contractions,
1890–1980

Response to—	Change in the CPI inflation rate	Change in the gap between actual and trend log per capita Real GNP (× 100)
Mild and moderate contractions		
1895–1896	+3.92	−5.46
1903–1904	−3.77	−4.56
1923–1924	−1.58	−3.67
1926–1927	−2.85	−3.05
1937 1938	−5.43	−7.51
1953–1954	−0.25	5.19
1957–1958	−0.81	−3.95
1959–1961	+0.20	−3.09
1969–1970	+0.52	−3.47
1973–1975	+2.71	−8.29
1979–1980	+2.05	−4.37
Strong contractions		
1892–1894	−3.77	−14.6
1907–1908	−7.27	−12.0
1919–1921	−25.1	−20.4
1929–1933	−5.27	−45.4
(1929–1932)	(−10.9)	(−41.4)

Note: The gap between actual and trend log (base *e*) real GNP per capita measures the severity of cyclical contractions. Trend values are the fitted values from the regression $\ln Y_t = a + bT +$ error, where Y is real GNP per capita and T is a time index. Trend values are obtained from regressions applied to two separate time periods: 1890–1949 and 1950–1980. Mild contractions refer to cycles in which the change in the gap (× 100) between actual and trend real GNP per capita was less than 5.0; moderate contractions designate cycles in which the change in the gap fell between 5.0 and 10.0; strong contractions denote cycles where the change in the gap was greater than 10.0.

Additional evidence on the relative inflexibility of postwar prices appears in Table 1.2. The table reports results of Phillips curve–like regressions of the CPI inflation rate on lagged inflation rates and the real output gap described in Table 1.1. The estimates reveal two clear patterns.

Table 1.2 Regression of consumer price inflation rate on lagged inflation and deviations of ln per capita real GNP from trend, 1890–1929 and 1950–1980

Model: $DCPI_t = a_0 + \sum_{i=1}^{3} a_i(DCPI_{t-i}) + a_4[\ln Y_t - (\ln Y_t)^*] + u_t$

Time period	Coefficients			
	a_0	$\sum a_i$	a_4	$\bar{R}^2$
1890–1949	0.07	0.54	30.4	0.38
	(0.09)	(3.21)	(2.92)	
1950–1980	0.32	1.01	9.00	0.69
	(0.51)	(5.97)	(0.83)	

Notes: The t statistics appear in parentheses; $DCPI_t = \ln (CPI_t/CPI_{t-1}) \cdot 100$, the annual percentage rate of change of the Consumer Price Index; $\ln Y$ = natural logarithm of per capita real GNP; and $\ln Y^*$ = trend $\ln Y$ as predicted from regressions performed separately in each period of $\ln Y$ on linear-time trend terms.

First, between the prewar 1891–1929 period (the exceptional depression and World War II years are excluded from the regression intentionally) and the postwar 1950–1980 period, there is a large increase in the magnitude of the sum of the lagged inflation coefficients. During the prewar period there was only a modest dependence of contemporaneous inflation rates on past inflation rates, and so inflationary impulses tended not to persist very long. By contrast, during the 1950–1980 period inflation exhibited very strong persistence: indeed, the sum of the lag coefficients in this regression is for all practical purposes unity (1.0), indicating that inflationary impulses tend to persist indefinitely unless the authorities depress real output and employment or take other actions to offset price shocks.

Second, the magnitude of the output gap coefficients is much smaller in the 1950–1980 regression than in the 1890–1949 equation. Interpreted at face value, this means that in the postwar era prices have been less responsive to movements in real output (and unemployment) than they were earlier, which implies that the cost of consumer price deceleration, in terms of forgone real output, is higher than it was earlier.[11] Also, the t-ratio of the real output gap variable in the postwar regression is small (that is, the standard error of the regression coefficient is relatively large), indicating that the response of consumer prices to declines in real output (and employment) during the postwar period may have been more uncertain as well as more sluggish than before.[12] It is not surprising, then, that political authorities often have been reluctant to pursue restrictive, anti-inflationary policies for very long, although ironically, such reluctance itself probably strengthened expectations about the persistence of inflation and thereby raised the output and employment costs of reducing inflation.

POSTWAR LABOR BARGAINING ARRANGEMENTS AND INFLATION

An important proximate cause of the postwar inertia in wage and price inflation reflected in Tables 1.1 and 1.2 is the staggered, multiyear wage contract system, which spread rapidly throughout the unionized sector of the labor market in the 1950s. As late as 1948 only about one-quarter of the major labor contracts were multiyear agreements, and most of these had wage reopening clauses and hence did not fully specify wage increases in advance.[13] Prior to the passage of the Wagner Act in 1935, such multiyear assignments were virtually nonexistent. By the mid 1950s, however, the incidence of long-term contracts fixing wage increases several years in advance—and often providing cost-of-living escalators as well—had increased dramatically. This substantially reduced the short-run flexibility of nominal wages and hence of prices. Moreover, because the expiration dates of multiyear contracts are staggered across industries, negotiated wage increases in a given industry may be conditioned by earlier settlements in other industries as unions attempt to preserve the traditional structure of relative wages, which further reduces the sensitivity of wage (and price) inflation to current market conditions.[14]

Joseph Garbarino marked 1955 as the watershed year for the spread of the multiyear wage contract. He noted that by the end of that decade between 70 and 85 percent of the major labor agreements had set wage increases for future years.[15] It was obvious to employers by the mid-1950s that unions were here to stay, at least in the manufacturing sector. The Taft Hartley Act of 1947 had not significantly weakened existing trade unions, and the Eisenhower administration (the first Republican government since the Hoover years) showed no signs of attempting to alter fundamentally the union-management balance of power established during the New Deal and World War II. Therefore big business at last became resigned to dealing with entrenched unions and saw the long-term contract as a way of reducing the frequency of bargaining confrontations and potentially disruptive labor strikes.

Perhaps even more important for the evolution of the overlapping, multiyear contract system was the emergence of a relatively stable, predictable macroeconomic environment. In the early 1950s, as Garbarino observed, "employees as a whole became convinced that the deflationary collapses that had followed the major wars in the past would not be repeated."[16] And in 1952 Clark Kerr wrote of industry's faith that "neither fiscal and monetary policies will be so restrictive nor price ceiling so inflexible that added costs [of wage increases scheduled in advance] cannot largely be offset by higher prices with unreduced volume . . . Their vision of industrial peace at the cost of wage increases is not today daunted by the terrors of bankruptcy; and *their faith in government is a faith that moves wage levels.*"[17]

This line of reasoning, however, should not be taken too far. Union membership in the United States has slowly declined over the last thirty years, from about a third to under a fifth of the labor force, with a shift from manufacturing to difficult-to-organize service industries. And the penetration of imports into the domestic manufacturing markets (particularly steel and automobiles) combined with back-to-back recessions in 1979–1980 and 1981–1982, produced in some union firms a flexibility (wage cutting) not seen for more than a quarter-century.[18] Still, looking at the postwar American political economy as a whole, one finds that prices and nominal incomes rarely fell. Shifts in the relative price (economic value) of commodities, as well as redistributions of income between labor and capital or between sectors of economic activity, usually have taken place through differential inflation rates, rather than by means of actual decline in some prices or money incomes.[19] The sources of the growth in the security of workers and firms and of the stabilization of the macroeconomy, which have so fundamentally altered wage and price behavior, lie in the torrent of New Deal social and economic legislation as well as in the impact of Keynes on macroeconomic theory and practice. These developments in the American political economy, which first appeared (haltingly) in the 1930s and reached maturity only well after World War II,[20] are worth reviewing in some detail.

1.4   Monetary Policy, the Financial System, and Economic Stabilization

A major cause of the postwar stability of output and employment has been the dramatic increase in the year-to-year stability of the economy's monetary mechanism. As Figure 1.7 shows, before World War II the money supply exhibited wild oscillations, which very likely

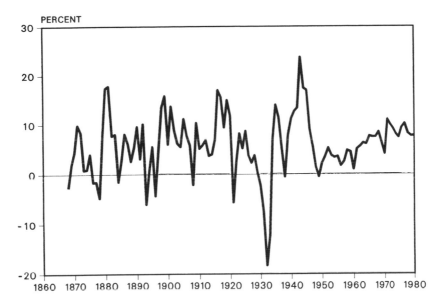

Figure 1.7 Monetary stability over time: M2 growth rates (percent per annum), 1868–1980. *Sources:* U.S. Department of Commerce, *Long Term Economic Growth 1860–1965*, Series B112, 1966; and TROLL-Citibank Economic Database, Series NBER12-FMM2X.

	1868–1929	1930–1949	1950–1980
Mean ($\bar{x}$)	5.78	5.80	6.08
Standard deviation (σ)	5.69	10.47	2.68
Coefficient of variation ($\sigma/\bar{x}$)	0.99	1.81	0.44

were a significant source of the wide swings in real output and unemployment (Figures 1.2 and 1.4).[21] There is little doubt that the dramatic reduction in short-run variance of money played a critical role in the stabilization of the real economy. Although the Federal Reserve System (America's first central bank since the 1830s) was created by Congress in 1913, the most important changes in monetary arrangements and banking practices contributing to monetary stabilization were initiated during the New Deal in response to the great depression of the 1930s.

GOVERNMENT AS INSURER, GUARANTOR OF CREDIT, AND LENDER OF LAST RESORT

One crucial New Deal innovation was the establishment of federal deposit insurance—in particular, the creation of the Federal Deposit

Insurance Corporation (FDIC) and the Federal Savings and Loan Insurance Corporation (FSLIC) in 1934. The FDIC and the FSLIC essentially converted to the deposit liabilities of commercial banks and thrift institutions into liabilities of the federal government. Consequently, the principal cause of bank runs and financial collapses that periodically drained money and credit from the economy was eliminated.[22]

By 1978 deposits insured by the FDIC and the FSLIC totaled about 1162 billion dollars.[23] The addition of the insurance activities of more recently established federal institutions (such as the Federal Crop Insurance Corporation, the Pension Benefit Guaranty Corporation, and the Federal Emergency Management Agency) brings the total dollar value of risks covered by the federal government in 1982 to 2000 billion.[24] The scale of federal insurance operations now far exceeds that of the largest private companies.

Since the FDIC and the FSLIC were formed, the federal government has also become a major supplier and guarantor, directly and indirectly, of credit through such agencies as the Commodity Credit Corporation Export-Import Bank, the Federal Home Loan Bank System, the Farmers Home Administration, the Federal Intermediate Credit Bank, the Veterans Administration, the Federal Housing Administration, the Overseas Investors Protection Corporation, the Government National Marketing Association, the Federal National Mortgage Association, the Federal Home Loan Mortgage Corporation, the Rural Electrification Administration, the Small Business Administration, and the Student Loan Mortgage Association. Benjamin Friedman reported that the stock of direct, guaranteed, and sponsored federal credit grew from minuscule proportions in the 1930s and 1940s to 440 billion dollars in 1978.[25] According to David Stockman, director of the Office Management and Budget under the Reagan administration, this amount would have exceeded 800 billion dollars in 1982 if the administration had not curtailed federal credit activities, which accounted for as much as 30 percent of all borrowing and lending in 1980.[26] Much of the federal credit activity takes place "off-budget" (is not recorded by the official unified budget) through the Federal Financing Bank, established by Congress in 1973 to coordinate federal lending.

The activities discussed above represent only part of the picture; they exclude the underwriting performed by nonfederal public authorities, as well as federal participation in emergency boards and other adhoc arrangements established to protect investors and creditors. Such activities have secured the credit needs of, for example, the Franklin National Bank (1970), the Penn Central Transportation Company (1970), the Lockheed Corporation (1971), the City of New York (1975 and after), the First Pennsylvania Bank (1980), the Chrysler Corporation (1980–1984), and, in the largest federal rescue package ever implemented for private enterprise, the Continental Illinois National Bank and Trust Company (1984). This massive socialization of lenders' risks has eased the flow of private credit to a diverse constituency of students, home buyers, small businesses, farmers, hard-pressed giant corporations, and the nation's largest municipality. And, more fundamentally, the regularity of federal bailouts and rescue operations have so reduced the American public's expectations of major corporate and banking failures that fears of a widespread financial collapse have all but disappeared. As the First Boston Corporation's Albert Wojnilower put it: "[By the mid-1970s] both central banks and market participants came to regard such rescues as reliably institutionalized responsibilities. It is now everywhere taken for granted that no monetary authority will allow any key financial actor to fail."[27]

DECOUPLING THE MONEY SUPPLY FROM GOLD

Another change in the monetary system reduced the sensitivity of the supply of money and credit to external conditions: the decoupling of money and gold, which permitted the evolution of today's fiat money standard administered by the Federal Reserve. The classical gold standard tied the supply of money to gold by defining the value of each form of currency as a fixed weight in gold and by requiring central banks to hold proportionate gold reserves against currency and deposit liabilities. The supply of money and credit, and therefore the price level, hinged on gold discoveries, mining technologies, and other sources of gold inflows and outflows. This contributed to recurrent liquidity crises and financial panics, which typically occurred during vigorous economic expansions, when the money-creating capacity of the gold system was unable to meet the demand for currency and credit. In these periods prices plunged, interest rates soared, and firms were forced into bankruptcy.[28] The great contractions of 1882–1884, 1893–1894, and 1907–1908 illustrate the pattern well. All took place during the gold standard era of 1879–1914 and were ushered in by severe financial panics.

Not surprisingly, the gold standard system was the source of great political agitation. The controversy peaked during the long post–Civil

War deflation with William Jennings Bryan's famous "cross of gold" speech at the 1896 Democratic convention. The populist movement for a bimetallic monetary standard articulated the demand of debt-burdened farmers and the unemployed (and the silver-mine owners) for increased liquidity[29]—the equivalent of contemporary pressures on the Federal Reserve to expand the supply of today's fiat money.

The classical gold-standard system survived the agitation of the 1890s largely because gold discoveries in South Africa and in the Klondike-Yukon area of Alaska, as well as the development of the cyanide mining process, greatly increased the supply of gold, which in turn boosted domestic liquidity and the price level. In addition, the development of checking-account practices increased the velocity (turnover) of money, relieving strains on the available gold reserves during expansions. Inflationary pressures generated by World War I prompted a suspension of the gold standard (as had the pressure on prices created by the Civil War, during which the term *inflation* first appeared). Most countries resumed the gold standard sometime after the war (the United States in 1919 and Britain in 1925, for example), but the large central banks, including the newly established Federal Reserve System, assumed a more active posture and attempted to offset and at least partially neutralize the internal monetary effects of gold inflows and outflows.[30]

The biggest step in freeing the U.S. money supply from gold, however, followed the great contraction of 1929–1933, which was exacerbated by an excessive exchange–rate rigidity imposed by the interwar international gold regime. In 1933–1934 President Franklin Roosevelt inflated the official dollar price of gold from $20.67 to $35.00 an ounce, removed gold from public circulation, and limited currency redemption in gold to foreign governments and central banks. Subsequently fractional gold reserve requirements were periodically relaxed to meet liquidity needs, until finally, in March 1968, they were removed altogether. At this time the fixed price for gold was also abandoned. Money was divorced totally from a commodity standard in August 1971, when President Nixon formally abandoned international gold convertibility. The gold anchor on the monetary system had been feeble since World War II; with the demise of the gold exchange system after 1971, it vanished completely.

Combined with the knowledge gained from the painful mistakes of the 1930s—for we now realize that perverse monetary policy exacerbated the 1929–1933 depression and probably was a major cause of the 1937–1938 contraction—these changes in the monetary system mean that destabilizing credit crunches and money shortages are now just about impossible, unless they are engineered *deliberately* by the authorities. As the data on growth rates of the M2 money supply from 1868 to 1980 show (Figure 1.7), monetary policy since the 1950s has been much more stable than it was previously. And, despite the upward trend in the velocity of money brought on by the development of electronic transfers of funds, the annual rate of growth of the nominal M2 money supply has not been negative since 1949.

MONETARY POLICY ACTIVISM

Another important development in the evolution of postwar monetary practices was the Treasury–Federal Reserve Accord of 1951. The accord freed the central bank of its obligation to support the prices of Treasury securities, which had been viewed as necessary to protect investors who helped finance World War II. Along with the other changes noted previously—not the least of which was the enhanced understanding of the effects of the Federal Reserve's open-market operations that was gained during the 1930s and 1940s—the 1951 accord made it possible for the Fed to pursue short-run countercyclic policies designed to reverse contractions of output and employment. Put differently, since the accord it has been possible (though, in the view of many analysts, not entirely desirable) for the Federal Reserve to implement Congress's original instruction in the 1913 Federal Reserve Act "to furnish an elastic currency."

The money supply feedback equations in Table 1.3 estimate the response of the growth rate of M2 in the 1891–1929 and 1951–1979 periods to prior movements of inflation and to the proportional gap between actual and trend per capita real output. The figures clearly reveal the emergence of countercyclical monetary policy during the postwar era.[31] The regression results for 1891–1929 (as well as parallel results for 1930–1950, not shown in the table) indicate that in the earlier period there was no systematic connection between the inflation rate or the real output gap and subsequent monetary growth. Monetary expansions and contractions therefore did not respond systematically to the state of either the nominal or of the real economy; with respect to the variables in the feedback equation, these changes appear essentially to have been random variations about trend.

The pattern of monetary fluctuations in the postwar period contrasts sharply with the earlier pattern. The regression results for the 1951–1979 subperiod show that inflationary trends were generally accommodated, but only partly in the short run: each percentage

Table 1.3   Postwar monetary activism: feedback equations for the money supply growth rate, 1891–1949 and 1951–1979

$$\text{Model: } DM2_t = c_0 + c_1(DM2_{t-1}) + c_2(DM2_{t-2}) + c_3(DCPI_{t-1})$$
$$+ c_4[\ln Y_{t-1} - (\ln Y_{t-1})^*] + u_t$$

Time period	Coefficients					
	c_0	c_1	c_2	c_3	c_4	$\bar{R}^2$
1891–1929	4.85	0.25	−0.01	0.06	−10.9	0.0
	(2.43)	(1.19)	(−0.05)	(0.24)	(−0.72)	
1951–1979	1.62	0.52	0.072	0.29	−19.0	0.55
	(1.91)	(2.88)	(0.41)	(2.01)	(−1.79)	

Notes: The t statistics appear in parentheses; $DM2_t = \ln (M2_t/M2_{t-1}) \cdot 100$, the annual percentage rate of change of M2 money supply. For definitions of ln Y, ln Y*, and DCPI, see Tables 1.1 and 1.2.

point increase in the inflation rate typically led to an increase above trend of about 0.3 percentage point in the M2 growth rate during the following year. Gaps between actual and trend log real output per capita also show a systematic association with subsequent monetary expansions and contractions. The regression estimates indicate that a 5-percent real output shortfall from trend generated, on average, a 0.95-percentage-point increase above trend in the money supply growth rate (0.05×19) in the next year and, by virtue of the significant lag-one autoregressive term in the equation, more in subsequent periods.

Whether short-run countercyclical monetary (or fiscal) policy activism has actually made a *direct* contribution to the stabilization of postwar real output and employment remains controversial. Given the magnitudes involved and the lags between policy actions and economic effects, the views of the skeptics must be taken seriously. It is likely, however, that policy activism at least *indirectly* contributed to the stability of the real macroeconomy by fundamentally altering the expectations and, as a result, the behavior of the private sector. Because firms believed that the policy authorities were likely to respond to downturns in demand in order to prevent deep and prolonged contractions, they hesitated to reduce production and employment at the first sign of recession. Therefore, as Martin Neal Baily has argued, modern stabilization policy may influence private-sector behavior itself to become more stabilizing.[32]

The behavioral consequences of these stabilizing forces are relevant to the issue of inflation. Because recessions during most of the postwar period were expected to be temporary, prices were not restrained by the fear of prolonged contractions. And this belief was reinforced repeatedly by experience. Hence, even though countercyclical monetary policy tends to restrain unsustainable upward deviations of real output from trend, private sector actors nonetheless sensibly anticipated that wage and price increases would be accommodated by the authorities. Clearly this contributed to the inflation-prone structure of postwar economic relations, in which, as noted earlier, relative price changes and redistribution tended to occur via differential upward movements in prices and wages.

1.5   Fiscal Policy and Economic Stabilization

The second great institutional source of macroeconomic stabilization, and an important contributor to the enhanced security of individuals, is the expansion of government expenditures. As the data in Table 1.4 show, over the half-century from 1929 to 1979 total government expenditures in percent of GNP increased more than threefold (from 10 percent to about 33 percent), and the federal expenditure in relation to GNP increased nearly ninefold (from 2.5 percent to about 22 percent).

One important feature of these fiscal developments was the growth in government purchases of goods and services in GNP, which created a sizable share of total output—about 20 percent by the late 1950s—that is relatively unresponsive to cyclical fluctuations in private spending. A relatively high fraction of total economic activity, therefore, now either depends directly on government purchases that are not affected by multiplier-accelerator interactions and other destabilizing forces in the private market economy or else depends indirectly on income-contingent and employment-contingent transfers designed explicitly to shelter people from the consequences of cyclical fluctuations in the private economy.

THE EVOLUTION OF THE TAX-AND-TRANSFER SYSTEM
The way to the modern income tax was paved by ratification in 1913 of the Sixteenth Amendment to the Constitution, which overrode the Supreme Court decision of 1895 declaring federal income taxes unconstitutional because they were not levied among the states according to population. Although a federal personal income tax was im-

Table 1.4 Growth of government expenditure as a percentage of GNP, in ten-year intervals

Year	Total government (federal, state, local)	Federal government (includes grants-in-aid to state and local governments)	Total government purchases of goods and services	Government transfer payments to persons (retirement, disability, unemployment, and low-income assistance)
1929	10.0	2.5	8.5	1.1
1939	19.4	9.8	14.9	2.8
1949	23.0	16.0	14.9	4.3
1959	26.9	18.7	20.3	5.1
1969	30.5	20.1	22.3	6.5
1979	32.6	21.5	19.9	9.9

Source: Economic Report of the President, January 1980, January 1981; tables B1, B18, B72, B73, B74.

posed between 1862 and 1871 and financed the North's victory in the Civil War, federal revenues traditionally were derived primarily from tariff receipts, the sale of public lands, and selected excise taxes. Not until World War II did personal and corporate income taxes, which at the federal level are based on progressive nominal schedules, constitute a very large share of total tax receipts on a sustained basis. Moreover, prior to the War, income taxes for any year were collected in the following year. During the war pay-as-you-go current tax withholding at the source was introduced for wages and salaries; just after the war similar changes were made for corporate taxes. As a result, the lag between tax payments and tax liabilities was sharply reduced, and consequently tax payments and liabilities now respond more quickly to movements in national income.

The expansion of government transfer payments also helped raise the sensitivity of net tax revenues to changes in income. Prior to the New Deal government transfers to individuals in the form of retirement, disability, unemployment, medical, and low-income assistance payments were negligible. By 1949 they constituted only about a fifth of total public expenditures and less than 5 percent of GNP (Table 1.4). By 1979, however, transfer payments to individuals had risen to just about 10 percent of GNP and made up nearly one-third of total government expenditures. At the federal budget level, outlays for transfer payments exceeded purchases of goods and services by the mid 1970s. Indeed, nearly all the growth in federal spending since the early 1950s is accounted for by the expansion of transfers to persons. By the late 1970s more than 40 percent of American households were receiving cash transfers.[33]

A great part of these transfers are age-contingent retirement benefits rather than welfare and unemployment payments, which are income-contingent benefits. This distinction is significant, because although the former help maintain aggregate demand during contractions, the latter increase the sensitivity of net revenues to short-run output fluctuations by raising private purchasing power when the economy goes into recession. Income-contingent transfers, which are triggered automatically by declines in employment and output, undoubtedly have made a much greater contribution to the postwar stability of the macroeconomy than have such discretionary fiscal actions as legislated tax cuts, speedups of government construction projects or defense purchases, and temporary increases and extensions of transfer benefits.[34]

The transfer program with the greatest implications for macroeconomic stability and the inflation process is unemployment insurance. As the late Arthur Okun pointed out, unemployment benefits alone did more to increase private purchasing power during postwar recessions than all the discretionary fiscal stimulations together.[35] Prior to the Social Security Act of 1935, which among other things established our national unemployment insurance system, only a tiny fraction of the labor force was covered by some form of private or state insurance. By 1940 just about half of the labor force was insured, and coverage has fluctuated around that level since then, though not all spells of unemployment were covered.[36] Unemployment insurance wage replacement apparently has increased over time. Joseph Hight's estimates indicate that the ratio of average weekly unemployment benefits to average net-of-tax weekly wages in covered employment grew from 35–36 percent in 1953–1954 to 44–45 percent in 1976–1977.[37] Together with other income and employment-related programs, the unemployment insurance system has helped to shelter individuals from personal economic catastrophies, and by increasing individual security it also has helped to stabilize the macroeconomy.[38]

THE STYLIZED ANALYTICS OF FISCAL STABILIZATION

To get a more precise idea of the contribution of government fiscal activities to macroeconomic stabilization, imagine a world without government purchases of goods and services, government transfers, or taxation. On the assumption that trade is in balance, national income or output (Q) in such a hypothetical economy is simply the sum of consumption (C) and investment (I),

$$Q = C + I \tag{1.1a}$$

and changes in output are equal to

$$\Delta Q = \Delta C + \Delta I \tag{1.1b}$$

For simplicity, let us assume that investment changes are autonomous (that is, independent of income changes) and that changes in consumption depend solely on movements of income, all of which in principle is available for consumption because taxes and government expenditure do not exist:

$$\Delta C = c' \Delta Q \tag{1.2}$$

where c' is the marginal propensity to consume increments to (disposable) income. It follows that

$$\Delta Q = c'\Delta Q + \Delta I \qquad (1.3)$$

$$\Delta Q(1 - c') = \Delta I$$

$$\Delta Q = \Delta I/(1 - c')$$

Changes in output generated by exogenous fluctuations in investment (or consumption, if some variable part of consumption is independent of income) are therefore proportional to $1/(1 - c')$—the output *multiplier*. If, for example, the marginal propensity to consume is 0.80, the output multiplier is $1/(1 - 0.80) = 5.0$. In other words, output fluctuations magnify changes in autonomous spending by a factor of 5.0 (or more if the marginal propensity to consume is greater than 0.80). Small changes in exogenous spending therefore would tend to generate large oscillations in national income.

Output fluctuations caused by movements in autonomous spending are stabilized by the presence of government. If we let G denote government purchases of goods and services, the income/output identity (equation 1.1b) for an economy with a government sector is

$$\Delta Q = \Delta C + \Delta I + \Delta G \qquad (1.4)$$

But consumption now must be written explicitly as a function of disposable income (Q_d)—that is, income available for private spending, rather than aggregate income (Q).

$$\Delta C = c'\Delta Q_d \qquad (1.5)$$

Disposable income is simply aggregate income (Q) less taxes paid to government (T) plus transfers received from government (R).

$$\Delta Q_d = \Delta Q - \Delta T + \Delta R, \quad \text{or} \quad \Delta Q_d = \Delta Q - \Delta T_n \qquad (1.6)$$

where T_n denotes net tax receipts and $T_n = (T - R)$, because transfer payments are usefully viewed as negative taxes.

Changes in taxes net of transfers (T_n) depend on changes in income times the net-of-transfer marginal rate of taxation of income (t') and on changes in autonomous taxes (T_a) less changes in autonomous transfers (R_a), which are independent of income fluctuations in the short to medium run.

$$\Delta T_n = t'\Delta Q + \Delta T_a - \Delta R_a \tag{1.7}$$

Substituting equations (1.5), (1.6) and (1.7) into the national income identity in (1.4) gives

$$\begin{aligned}
\Delta Q &= c'\Delta Q_d + \Delta I + \Delta G \tag{1.8}\\
&= c'(\Delta Q - \Delta T_n) + \Delta I + \Delta G\\
&= c'(\Delta Q - t'\Delta Q - \Delta T_a + \Delta R_a) + \Delta I + \Delta G\\
&= c'(1 - t')\Delta Q - c'\Delta T_a + c'\Delta R_a + \Delta I + \Delta G
\end{aligned}$$

or

$$\Delta Q = \frac{1}{1 - c'(1-t')}(- c'\Delta T_a + c'\Delta R_a + \Delta I + \Delta G)$$

In a highly stylized economy with government activity, then, the output multiplier is $1/[1 - c'(1 - t')]$ as opposed to $1/(1 - c')$ in an economy without government activity. The former is smaller than the latter because the tax-and-transfer system reduces the fluctuations in consumption that are induced by changes in aggregate income. For example, if the marginal propensity to consume (c') takes the plausible value 0.80 and the transfer-adjusted marginal rate of income taxation (t') is 0.3, the output multiplier is $1/[1 - 0.80(1 - 0.3)] = 2.27$. Without taxes, transfers, and government purchases (that is, in an economy in which $t' = 0$), the multiplier would be, as noted earlier, $1/(1 - 0.80) = 5.0$. Therefore, the presence of income taxes and income-contingent transfers insulates the economy from adverse changes in exogenous spending behavior. The process is symmetric, so taxes also dampen the magnitude of output expansions generated by surges in autonomous spending.

The degree of this government fiscal stabilization depends on the magnitude of the net marginal income tax rate, t', which, as line 3 of equation (1.8) indicates, comprises that fraction of a decline in output restored by the automatic reduction in government tax revenues. This is readily seen from another point of view by remembering that the change in the government budget surplus/deficit (S/D) is simply the difference between the change in tax revenues adjusted for transfers (T_n) and government purchases of goods and services (G):

$$\Delta(S/D) = \Delta T_n - \Delta G \qquad (1.9)$$

or, in view of equation (1.7),

$$\Delta(S/D) = t'\Delta Q + \Delta T_a - \Delta R_a - \Delta G$$

Thus, even if the government takes no *discretionary* action by increasing G, increasing R_a, reducing T_a, or altering the income tax schedule, the budget surplus *automatically* decreases (the deficit increases) as output falls. The presence of government purchases and the tax-and-transfer system offsets declines in Q and stimulates aggregate demand. This will be true even if the income tax is proportional—that is, the same rate applies to all income levels. If the direct tax schedule is progressive, with rates increasing with income, and/or if transfers (negative taxes) are sensitive to changes in output (and employment), then t' will be relatively large, and changes in the government budget surplus will be even more sensitive to output changes.

A NUMERICAL ILLUSTRATION

The quantitative importance of the growth in the size of government and the progressivity of the tax system as sources of macroeconomic stabilization can be evaluated in terms of the simple framework introduced above by rewriting the transfer-adjusted marginal income tax rate, t', as the product of two components:

$$t' = \Delta T_n/\Delta Q \qquad (1.10)$$

$$= \frac{T_n}{Q} \cdot \frac{\Delta T_n/T_n}{\Delta Q/Q}$$

The first term in the second line of equation (1.10) is the share of government tax revenues minus transfer payments in national income. Over the long run it is roughly equal to the share of government purchases of goods and services in GNP (the direct contribution of government to GNP in the national accounts); that is, $\bar{T}_n/\bar{Q} = \bar{G}/\bar{Q}$. T_n/Q therefore represents the effect of the *size* of government on the transfer-adjusted marginal tax rate. As the data in Table 1.4 on government purchases as a share of GNP indicate, T_n/Q grew from 8 to 9 percent of GNP in the late 1920s to about 20 percent of GNP in the 1960s.

The second term in the second line of equation (1.10) is the government revenue elasticity—that is, the proportional change in government net tax receipts following a proportional change in aggregate income. The magnitude of the elasticity component reflects the progressivity of the tax-and-transfer system. If tax liabilities and transfer payments are progressive and hence sensitive to changes in income, the net revenue elasticity will exceed 1.0. If the tax-and-transfer system is proportional, the elasticity will equal 1.0. If the system, on average, is regressive, the elasticity will be less than 1.0.

The growth in the size of government and the establishment of progressive personal and corporate income tax rates (primarily by the federal government), as well as the changes in tax collection methods and the expansion of income-related transfers discussed in previous sections, have all contributed to raising the aggregate marginal tax rate t'. The net marginal rate increased from about 0.05 in the early 1930s to about 0.30 by the late 1970s.[39] This implies (via equation 1.10) the following about the growth in the net marginal tax rate from the late 1920s and early 1930s to the late 1970s:

Period	Marginal transfer-adjusted tax rate, t'		Transfer-adjusted size of government, T_n/Q		Transfer-adjusted revenue elasticity, $\dfrac{\Delta T_n/T_n}{\Delta Q/Q}$
Late 1920s or early 1930s	0.05	=	0.085	×	0.60
Late 1970s	0.30	=	0.20	×	1.50

In the late 1920s and early 1930s, t' was on the order of 0.05, so a 1.0-billion-dollar decline in GNP would be offset automatically by only a 5.0-million-dollar reduction in government taxation. By the late 1970s the marginal tax rate had increased sixfold, to about 0.30, which meant that each billion-dollar decline in aggregate income or output automatically triggered an offsetting decline of approximately 300 million dollars in tax liabilities.[40] Notice that the growth in automatic fiscal stabilization appears to stem about equally from the expansion of the *size* of government and the increase in the *progressivity* of the tax-and-transfer system.[41]

Given that the marginal propensity to consume out of total disposable income (c') has been in the vicinity of 0.80 during the last half-century, this increase in the marginal tax rate means that the output multiplier (equation 1.8) has declined[42] from approximately $1/[1 - 0.80(1 - 0.05)] = 4.2$ to approximately $1/[1 - 0.80(1 - 0.30)] = 2.3$. The economy is therefore less volatile today than it was fifty years ago, partly because output fluctuations now magnify changes in autonomous spending by a factor in the neighborhood of 2.3 rather than by a factor that is closer to 4.2. Put another way, a decline of only 240 million dollars or so in exogenous private demand was enough to reduce aggregate real output by 1 billion dollars in the early 1930s, whereas today autonomous spending probably would have to decline by more than 400 million dollars to generate the same decline in aggregate output. Surely the last great depression of 1929-1932 would have been considerably less severe had the postwar regime of higher marginal tax rates and associated lower multipliers been in place during those years.

Changes in the scope and progressivity of the fiscal system have made, then, a substantial contribution to macroeconomic stabilization. But as pointed out earlier, economic stability and security have also contributed to the inflationary bias of the postwar American political economy.

1.6   The Security-Inflation Trade-Off

We no longer experience the great deflations that in the past tended to keep the price level flat over the long run, because we no longer suffer from the great crashes and decade-long contractions that helped force down wages and prices throughout most of our history. Even contractions of a more modest scale, a recurrent feature of postwar American economic life, appear to bring less disinflation than they once did, partly because wage and price claimants generally expect that recessions will be short-lived and do not signal the onset of really severe busts. The institutional changes and public policy innovations that contributed so dramatically to postwar macroeconomic stability and individual security have also fundamentally altered wage-price expectations and behavior. Because unintended economy-wide depressions are now virtually impossible and intended, policy-induced depressions are not politically feasible, and because so many of us are now partly sheltered from the consequences of economic misfortunes, the historical effectiveness of the market as a disciplinary force inducing noninflationary behavior has been significantly weakened. As the early Reagan years remind us, though, the disinflationary impact of market slack has by no means been eliminated. Nonetheless, we have experienced persistent inflation of varying degree during the postwar era.

Notwithstanding the free enterprise rhetoric of the right, there is little evidence that many economic actors—workers, managers, unions, or firms—really have much desire to bring back the unrestrained market capitalism of the nineteenth and early twentieth centuries. Indeed, the evolution of the American political economy since the 1930s rather clearly reveals a pronounced national aversion to risk and a social preference for economic security, even though this security contributed to the continuous upward drift of the price level. Certainly no group has come forward demanding to be stripped of its economic security in order to help lower the inertia of prices and wages and restore fully the disciplinary powers of the market.[43]

After the strong surge of inflation following the first OPEC supply shock in 1973, public concern about inflation increased sharply, however. The Reagan administration seemed to be convinced, at least initially, that the 1980 election outcome had given the new government a mandate to strip away much of our insulation from free market forces in order, among other things, to facilitate disinflation. Yet the principal agent of Reagan administration–induced disinflation was severe unemployment. It is therefore important to explore the objective costs of unemployment and inflation before turning to an investigation of the public's perceptions of and political reactions to macroeconomic outcomes.

2 The Costs of Unemployment

> A very large increase in unemployment may be justifiably incurred to achieve a small permanent reduction in inflation.
>
> —Martin Feldstein

Understanding the public's preferences about and political responses to macroeconomic events requires knowledge of the aggregate costs and distributional consequences of various economic configurations. Fortunately, there has been a great deal of solid empirical research on these matters, and it shows that the rewards and penalties associated with postwar economic fluctuations are typically large and quite unevenly distributed within the electorate. Because fluctuations in unemployment and real output (or real income) are intimately connected, this chapter focuses primarily on the incidence and costs of unemployment. Chapter 3 analyzes the costs of inflation.

2.1 Defining, Interpreting, and Measuring Unemployment

An unemployment rate measures the degree of underutilization of available labor resources in the economy. Because unemployment is almost universally recognized as among the most significant indicators of the health of the macroeconomy, and because it is generally taken to be a useful index of individual hardship as well, its definition, measurement, and interpretation are economically controversial and politically divisive.[1] This was especially true during the post-OPEC years of high unemployment and high inflation—a doubly unpleasant situation imposing correspondingly tough choices on political officials. For although there is no fixed, stable trade-off between unemployment and inflation in the American macroeconomy, policy makers recognize that they pose conflicting goals in the short to medium run.[2] In fact, policy authorities frequently have responded to surges of inflation by using monetary and/or fiscal policy to increase unemployment.

The main problem in measuring unemployment is to translate the responses of approximately 56,000 households to a long series of questions in the monthly Current Population Survey into judgments about whether a person is employed, unemployed, or outside the available work force. The conventional or "official" unemployment rate compiled by the Bureau of Labor Statistics from the Current Population Survey data is defined as the number of people sixteen years and older who were without work during the past week, were available for a job, and actively sought work during the preceding four weeks as a percentage of the total civilian labor force (employed and unemployed).[3] Some economists have been quick to point out that the official unemployment rate conveys a misleading impression of the state of the economy and the extent of individual hardship because many people designated as "unemployed" are not workers who have lost a job and are looking for another. For example, Milton Friedman remarked, "The report that eight million persons are unemployed [in 1975] conjures up the image of eight million persons fruitlessly tramping the streets looking for a job. That is a false picture. Most people recorded as unemployed are between jobs or between entering the labor force and finding a job."[4]

There is some truth to Friedman's observation. But only some. Data on the components of the official unemployment rate in Table 2.1 show that generally one-third or less of the unemployed are people who have been fired from their jobs (job losers). Usually less than one-half of the officially unemployed have been either laid off or permanently terminated by their employers.[5] Almost as many of the unemployed either have left their previous jobs voluntarily and are searching for others (job leavers) or fall into the residual "other" category. This category includes reentrants to the labor force (people who left or lost jobs but who in the recent past were defined to be out of the labor force because they reported no efforts during the preceding four weeks to find work) and new entrants into the labor market who are well past school-leaving age (often women who are no longer fully occupied with child rearing and are seeking paid work for the first time).

The data indicate, then, that the unemployed are not overwhelmingly people recently thrown out of work and searching for a new job, even though job losers do contribute more to official unemployment than does any other single group without work. Instead, unemployment has many sources. Very few of the unemployed, however, can be accurately described as being in the painless process of making a

Table 2.1 Components of the official unemployment rate, 1967–1983

Year	Total official unemployment rate (percent)	Percentage of those unemployed who are—					
		On layoff[a]	Job losers	Job leavers	Seeking temporary work	School leavers	Other
1967	3.8	13.2	29.0	15.8	15.8	7.9	23.7
1968	3.6	11.1	25.0	16.7	19.4	5.6	22.2
1969	3.5	11.4	22.9	14.3	20.0	5.7	22.9
1970	4.9	16.3	28.6	14.3	16.3	6.12	28.6
1971	5.9	15.3	32.2	11.9	15.3	6.8	32.2
1972	5.6	8.9	25.0	14.3	14.3	8.2	19.6
1973	4.9	10.2	28.6	16.2	16.2	8.2	22.5
1974	5.6	14.3	28.6	14.3	18.1	8.9	19.6
1975	8.5	21.2	34.1	10.6	12.9	5.9	15.3
1976	7.7	14.3	35.1	11.7	13.0	6.5	19.5
1977	7.0	12.9	32.9	12.9	12.9	7.1	21.4
1978	6.1	11.5	30.0	14.1	NA	NA	
1979	5.8	14.0	28.8	14.3	NA	NA	
1980	7.1	19.8	32.1	11.6	NA	NA	
1981	7.6	17.5	34.2	11.1	NA	NA	
1982	9.7	19.9	38.8	7.9	NA	NA	
1983	9.6	16.6	41.8	7.7	NA	NA	

Sources: The figures for 1966–1977 are based on unpublished BLS data reported in Robert E. Hall, "The Nature and Measurement of Unemployment," National Bureau of Economic Research, Working Paper no. 252, July 1978. The figures for 1978–1983 are based on data from the Bureau of Labor Statistics, Handbook of Labor Statistics, December 1983, table 24; and idem, Employment and Earnings, January 1984, table 10.
a. Temporary and indefinite.

normal career transition from one job to another. On the contrary, as Robert E. Hall noted fifteen years ago, many job leavers and labor-force reentrants drift from one unpleasant job to another without career advancement, spending spells between employment either out of the labor force or unemployed.[6]

In some ways the official unemployment rate understates the dimensions of the unemployment problem. For example, "discouraged workers"—people who say they want a job but are not actively looking for work because they believe there are no jobs available for them—are not included in the official figures. Similarly, workers who are involuntarily employed part-time because they cannot find full-time work make no contribution to the official unemployment rate. If the official figures were adjusted upward in proportion to the magnitude of involuntary unemployment and if discouraged workers were also included in the computations, the conventional unemployment rate would be increased by between one-third and one-half. Data available since the late 1960s on discouraged and involuntarily underemployed workers permit precise calculations. In 1977, for example, the official unemployment rate was 7 percent. Adjusting this figure to take into account involuntary underemployment by counting as one-half an unemployed person each part-time worker who wants full-time work, as well as each person who is voluntarily employed part-time or is seeking only part-time work, yields an unemployment rate of 8.6 percent. Adding the discouraged workers to the pool of unemployed and to the labor force raises the unemployment rate to 9.7 percent, which is 39 percent higher than the 1977 official rate.

Figure 2.1 shows time plots of a range of unemployment concepts spanning several points of view.[7] Reflecting the argument that only long-term unemployment generally imposes real financial hardship, U-1 is defined as the percentage of the civilian labor force unem-

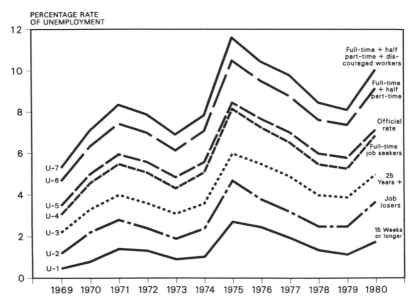

Figure 2.1 Range of unemployment concepts, 1969–1980. *Sources:* Bureau of Labor Statistics, *Handbook of Labor Statistics*, December 1980; and idem, *Employment and Earnings*, August 1981.

ployed 15 weeks or more. The number of job losers (permanently terminated or on layoff) as a percentage of the civilian labor force is U-2. This series represents the view that unemployment among recent job holders, which imposes actual income losses, is more serious than joblessness among reentrants or new entrants to the labor force. The idea that unemployment among teenagers and young adults is a relatively unimportant matter underlies the U-3 series, which measures the number of unemployed people 25 years and older as a percentage of the civilian labor force 25 years and older. The number of full-time job seekers as a percentage of the full-time labor force is U-4. The assumption here is that the part-time labor force includes many people without a strong commitment to work and that unemployment in this group should therefore be discounted (in this case, completely). The official unemployment rate for all civilian workers age 16 years and older is U-5. It is a useful benchmark for the evaluation of the other series. The unemployment rate obtained by weighting part-time workers in the official labor force by only one-half and adjusting the official rate upward to include involuntary (part-time) underemployment is U-6. Finally, U-7 is the series obtained by adding "discouraged workers" to the numerator and the denominator of the U-6 unemployment rate.

The degree of socioeconomic distress implied by the different rates obviously varies enormously. In 1969, a boom year, long-duration unemployment (U-1) was only 0.5 percent, the official rate (U-5) was 3.5 percent, and the rate including underemployed and discouraged workers (U-7) was 5.3 percent. During the terrible recession of 1975, the rates were of course higher: 2.7 percent, 8.5 percent, and 11.6 percent for U-1, U-5, and U-7, respectively. Despite the differences in these percentages, it is clear from Figure 2.1 that the various unemployment concepts are very strongly correlated. The official series, U-5, is therefore a useful indicator of cyclical activity in the labor market.

Observant readers may have noticed that the official rate of unemployment and other measures of the excess supply of labor appear to have drifted upward. In fact, there is widespread agreement among specialists that today's unemployment rates are not strictly comparable to those of twenty or thirty years ago. An official unemployment rate of, say, 6 percent in the late 1970s would be equivalent to a somewhat lower rate in the 1950s.

Many factors have contributed to the upward trend of measured unemployment, which has weakened the comparability over time of the unemployment rates.[8] Some of the increase has been traced to changes in the system of transfer payments. Extensions of the coverage and benefit periods of unemployment insurance can raise both the frequency of unemployment episodes per worker and the duration of an average episode, thereby raising the measured unemployment rate. Workers on temporary layoff receiving unemployment compensation may find it more advantageous simply to wait until they are recalled rather than to seek temporary work or to find a new job. Extended benefits make it easier for unemployed workers looking for a new job to prolong the search in hopes of landing a really attractive position rather than taking the first thing to come along. For these reasons it is estimated that steady increases since the mid-1950s in the percentage of workers covered by unemployment insurance (UI) and the extension of UI benefits, particularly during the 1970s, have added between 0.3 and 0.4 percent to the noncyclical rate of unemployment.[9] The requirement, enacted by Congress in 1972, that some food-stamp beneficiaries and mothers receiving Aid for Dependent Children (AFDC) register for work also expanded the pool of unemployed. Experts put the increase in the official unemployment rate associated with these work-registration requirements at between 0.2 and 0.4 percent.

Changes in the composition of the labor force also have affected the comparability over time of unemployment statistics. In particular, the maturation of the large post–World War II baby cohort (the postwar "baby boom" generation) substantially increased the proportion of young workers in the labor force. Between 1960 and 1980 the fraction of the labor force made up of teenagers and young adults (workers under 25 years old) grew by about 7 percentage points—from 16.6 to 23.5 percent (see Table 2.4 in the next section). This generated considerable pressure on the supply of entry-level jobs and hence has pushed up the overall unemployment rate. Similar pressures accompanied the sharp increase in the labor-force participation of inexperienced females. (The female fraction of the labor force grew by almost 10 percent from 1960 to 1980; see Table 2.4.) Specialists estimate that the increase in the official rate of unemployment due to these changes in the composition of the labor force lies between 0.6 and 1.0 percent. The precise magnitude of the increase depends on the assumptions made about the impact of the rise in the proportions of inexperienced workers in the work force on the gap between the demand for and the supply of entry-level employment opportunities.[10]

Altogether, changes in social welfare legislation and employment-related transfer programs, as well as demographic changes in the

composition of the labor force, have raised noncyclical unemployment between 1.0 and 2.0 percentage points. An official unemployment rate of, say, 5.0 percent in the 1950s would therefore be comparable to a rate of between 6.0 and 7.0 percent today. As a result, the
capacity of conventional monetary and fiscal policies to sustain (without generating extra inflation) noncyclical unemployment rates that
were feasible twenty or thirty years ago has been weakened commensurately.

2.2   The Aggregate Costs of Unemployment

Unemployment represents underutilized human resources and lost
real output. Information about the former is conveyed by aggregate
unemployment rates, such as those illustrated in Figure 2.1. Remember, however, that unemployment rates are just that—*rates*—and a
far larger fraction of the labor force experiences bouts of actual unemployment during any given time interval than the percentage rate
numbers might suggest. The data in Table 2.2 show that over a full
calendar year the fraction of the labor force experiencing one or more
spells of official unemployment is likely to be 2.5 to 3.0 times larger
than the annual average official rate (U-5). An even bigger fraction of
the labor force (or the electorate) is touched indirectly by unemployment through the experiences of relatives, friends, neighbors, and
workmates. Such vicarious experiences do not impose measurable
economic costs, but they do help explain the extent of public anxiety

Table 2.2   Official unemployment experience, five-year averages of annual
data for 1961–1980

Period averages	Official unemployment rate (percent) (1)	Percentage of labor force experiencing one or more spells of unemployment during a calendar year (2)	Ratio of (2) to (1) (3)
1961–1965	5.5	16.1	2.9
1966–1970	3.9	13.2	3.4
1971–1975	6.1	16.8	2.8
1976–1980	6.7	17.3	2.6

Sources: Bureau of Labor Statistics, *Handbook of Labor Statistics,* December 1980, table
49; and idem, *The Employment Situation,* News Release, USDL 81-413.

about unemployment, which, as the analyses in subsequent chapters show, has important political consequences.

Unemployment also appears to have important social, psychological, and even medical costs, though these are difficult to measure or document precisely. Schlozman and Verba's analysis of survey data suggests that the experience of unemployment adversely affects the level of family tension, people's satisfaction with their accomplishments and income, and their sense of job security.[11] Moreover, the Schlozman and Verba data indicate that these various forms of psychological anxiety and distress do not appear to be relieved appreciably by unemployment insurance benefits. M. Harvey Brenner's research, which reports strong aggregate associations between unemployment fluctuations and mental hospital admission rates and suicide rates, reinforces the picture emerging from the survey data. Brenner's investigations also show strong connections between changes in unemployment and variations in cardiovascular-renal disease mortality rates, homicide mortality rates, and crime and imprisonment rates in virtually all age groups, among whites and non-whites, and for women as well as men. Brenner estimated that a sustained 1-percentage-point increase in the unemployment rate ultimately produces 30,000 extra fatalities each year.[12]

More easily quantified than the social and psychological effects of unemployment are the real output, or income, costs. About twenty years ago the late Arthur Okun, chairman of the Council of Economic Advisers during the Johnson administration and subsequently a leading macroeconomist at the Brookings Institution, identified an empirical relationship between changes in the unemployment rate and real output, which is now known as Okun's Law.[13] Thanks to his work, revealing estimates of the real output costs of cyclical increases in unemployment may be obtained by regressing the proportional rate of change of real GNP (Q) on changes in the official rate of unemployment (U). For annual data over the period 1950–1983, the results are as follows (standard errors appear in parentheses):[14]

$$(\ln Q_t - \ln Q_{t-1}) = 0.036 - 0.021 \, (U_t - U_{t-1}) \qquad (2.1)$$
$$\qquad\qquad (0.002) \quad (0.002)$$

$$R^2 = 0.82, \qquad SER = 0.012, \qquad DW = 1.77$$

A more sophisticated way of estimating the real output cost of unemployment fluctuations[15] involves regressing the proportional shortfall of Q from Q^N on the deviation of U from U^N, where U^N is the minimum sustainable level of unemployment below which inflation tends to escalate and Q^N is the economy's real output capacity when U equals U^N. Again for annual data over the period 1950–1983, we obtain

$$(\ln Q_t - \ln Q_t^N) = 0.0008 - 0.022 \ (U_t - U_t^N) \qquad (2.2)$$
$$(0.002) \quad (0.001)$$

$$R^2 = 0.94, \quad SER = 0.009, \quad DW = 1.24$$

Equations (2.1) and (2.2) tell essentially the same story: a 1-percentage-point increase in the official rate of unemployment lasting a year is accompanied by a decline in real output of about 2 percent.[16] In a 3.75-trillion-dollar economy (the end-of-1984 GNP in current dollars), this means that each extra percentage point of unemployment costs at least 75 billion dollars in unproduced output (0.02×3750 billion dollars), which amounts to $880 per household. But postwar U.S. recessions have typically been more severe than this. The cumulative shortfall of real GNP from potential (the proportional deviation of Q from Q^N) has averaged about 9 percent during cyclical downturns, which in a 3.75-trillion-dollar economy means 338 billion dollars in lost output, or almost $4,000 per household.

Converting this real output loss into a "social loss" requires a number of adjustments. A rise in unemployment and underemployment increases the time available for leisure and other activities (searching for more attractive and productive jobs, making home repairs, and so on) that are not designated as "work" and make no contribution to measured GNP. Although the value of extra free time resulting from involuntary joblessness cannot be equated to that of nonwork activities pursued voluntarily, free time undoubtedly does have some social utility and hence partially offsets the output and real income losses from recessions.[17] Economic slack also reduces the depletion of nonrenewable natural resources (by slowing the rate at which they are exploited), decreases wear and tear on capital goods (because plant and equipment are idled), and eases the problem of shortages (because labor and products are in excess supply). Recessions also may help to enhance economic efficiency by providing occasions for desirable management shake-ups and the shedding of inefficient employees.

Although these possibly ameliorating factors have defied realistic measurement, they almost certainly are offset by the adverse effects of recession and unemployment on the formation of new physical capital and, especially, on the accumulation of human capital in the form of on-the-job training and work experience. It is very likely, therefore, that if we were able to quantify reliably the social disutility of extra unemployment, the monetized social costs would closely approximate the real output dollar losses discussed earlier.[18]

Thus the aggregate costs of cyclical increases in unemployment are high—very high. But who bears the burden?

2.3   The Incidence of Unemployment

The best way to begin an assessment of the distribution of the aggregate social and economic costs imposed by higher unemployment is to examine the incidence of unemployment in various demographic groups. Tables 2.3 and 2.4 present some relevant data on unemployment rates (and associated fractions of the labor force) prevailing among groups defined by occupation, age, race, and gender in selected years.

The magnitudes of the intergroup differences are obviously large. For example, the official unemployment rates experienced by blue-collar and service workers are typically between two and three times larger than the rates of white-collar workers. The differentials between the least skilled blue-collar classes and the highest status white-collar groups are much greater. Nonfarm laborers normally experience unemployment rates between four and nine times greater than those of managers or professionals. The complete postwar time-series record (not reported here) shows that such interoccupational inequalities in exposure to unemployment have typically risen during recessions and fallen during sustained booms. Blue-collar workers (especially unskilled blue-collar workers) have borne the heaviest burdens during macroeconomic contractions, therefore, and have also enjoyed the greatest rewards during economic recoveries.

In addition to the pattern in the sensitivity of occupational unemployment differentials to cyclical movements in the macroeconomy, time-series data also show a downward trend in such differentials between the late 1950s (when the relevant data were first published) and the early 1970s.[19] The reasons for this trend are unclear, although the pressure on available jobs associated with the expansion of the proportion of the labor force in white-collar occupations and the decline of the proportion in blue-collar occupations (see Table 2.4) are

Table 2.3 Unemployment rates for demographic groups in
selected years (percent)

Demographic group	1960	1970	1980
Total labor force	5.5	4.9	7.1
Occupation			
Total white collar	2.7	2.8	3.7
Professional and technical	1.7	2.0	2.5
Managers and administrators	1.4	1.3	2.4
Sales workers	3.8	3.9	4.4
Clerical workers	3.8	4.0	5.3
Total blue collar	7.8	6.2	10.0
Craftspeople and kindred	5.3	3.8	6.6
Operatives	8.0	7.1	11.4
Laborers (excluding farm)	12.6	9.5	14.6
Service workers	5.8	5.3	7.9
Farmers and farm laborers	2.7	2.6	4.4
Gender			
Males	5.4	4.4	6.9
Females	5.9	5.9	7.4
Race			
Whites	4.9	4.5	6.3
Nonwhites	10.2	8.2	13.2
Age			
16 to 19	14.7	15.3	17.7
20 to 24	8.7	8.2	11.5
25 to 54	4.5	3.4	5.4
55 and older	4.1	2.9	3.3

Sources: Bureau of Labor Statistics, *Handbook of Labor Statistics,* December 1980; and idem, *Employment and Earnings,* August 1981, various tables.

probably significant factors. Another reason may be that the jobs of government employees, who are disproportionately white-collar professionals, are much less secure now than they were earlier. In any case, cyclical movements aside, this means that a high-status white-collar job no longer provides quite the same relative insulation from unemployment that it once did. Economic downturns still fall more heavily on blue-collar workers, but the blue-collar/white-collar gap

Table 2.4 Demographic distribution of the civilian labor force in selected years (percent)

Demographic group	1960	1970	1980
Total labor force	100	100	100
Occupation			
Total white collar	42.0	47.6	50.8
Professional and technical	10.8	13.8	15.4
Managers and administrators	10.2	10.2	10.8
Sales workers	6.5	6.1	6.2
Clerical workers	14.5	17.4	18.4
Total blue collar	37.5	36.0	33.0
Craftspeople and kindred	12.9	12.8	12.9
Operatives	18.6	18.2	15.0
Laborers (excluding farm)	6.0	5.0	5.0
Service workers	12.6	12.5	13.5
Farmers and farm laborers	7.9	3.9	2.7
Gender			
Males	66.6	61.9	57.4
Females	33.4	38.1	42.6
Race			
Whites	88.9	88.9	88.0
Nonwhites	11.1	11.1	12.0
Age			
16 to 19	7.0	8.8	8.8
20 to 24	9.6	12.8	14.7
25 to 54	65.4	60.9	62.4
55 and older	18.1	17.5	14.1

Sources: Bureau of Labor Statistics, *Handbook of Labor Statistics*, December 1980; and idem, *Employment and Earnings*, August 1981, various tables.

has closed somewhat—from perhaps a 3-to-1 "normal" unemployment differential in the late 1950s to a differential closer to 2.5 to 1 in the 1970s.

The data on unemployment by gender in Table 2.3 clearly indicate that women have traditionally suffered higher jobless rates than men. More extensive time-series data would show, however, that the gender-related differential has declined in recent periods despite the fact that female labor-force participation has grown enormously during the last twenty to thirty years (Table 2.4). In fact, in September 1980 a record that had stood for thirty years was broken when unemployment among adult men briefly exceeded that among adult women. This was not a fluke. For 1982 and 1983 as a whole, the average unemployment rate for males was more than half a percentage point higher than the rate for females. (For 1984 the rate for females was 7.6 percent, as opposed to 7.4 percent for males.) In any case, the unequal distribution of unemployment experience across the sexes always was quite small in comparison to the inequalities across occupational classes and, as the data in the lower part of Table 2.3 show, in comparison to the situation prevailing among race and age groups. Nonwhites who are officially counted as part of the labor force generally suffer unemployment rates approximately twice as high as those of whites. This situation is much worse for teenagers; their proportionate share of unemployment varies between about three and five times that of "prime age" workers (those aged 25 to 55). The gaps become even more dramatic if one examines groups sharing several demographic characteristics associated with relatively high unemployment. For example, when the national official unemployment rate is 7 percent, in some large cities unemployment among black teenagers can reach a staggering 85 percent.

2.4 The Costs of Unemployment to Individuals

Unskilled workers, women, nonwhites, and teenages have historically experienced higher unemployment rates than have professionals, men, whites, and older workers. But the economic (and presumably the social) costs absorbed by groups during economic downturns are not strictly proportional to the increase in their unemployment rates. Unemployment compensation, food stamps, low-income assistance, and other features of the postwar American tax-and-transfer system distribute the aggregate costs of unemployment more widely throughout the society than would be the case in a purely market-driven economy. Individuals (and firms) most directly affected by increased unemployment (decreased product demand) are sheltered from the full economic impact of recessions. The rest of us share the aggregate losses through higher current and future taxes that finance unemployment-related transfers to individuals (and bailouts of firms). Consequently, in some cases the economic losses absorbed by individuals directly affected by unemployment may be small.

Martin Feldstein illustrated how the interaction of just the tax and unemployment compensation systems alone can minimize the individual costs of unemployment with the following (atypical) example, involving an unemployed male worker in Massachusetts in 1977 with a working wife and two children:

> His gross earnings are $140 per week while hers are $100 per week. If he is unemployed for ten weeks, he loses $1400 in gross earnings but only $279 in net income. Why does this occur? A fall in gross earnings of $1400 reduces his federal income tax by $226, his social security tax by $82, and his Massachusetts income tax by $75. Thus, total taxes fall by $383, implying that net wages are reduced by $1017.
>
> Unemployment benefits are 50 percent of his wage plus a dependents' allowance of $6 per child per week. The benefit is thus $82 a week. Since there is an annual one week "waiting period" before benefits begin, nine weeks of benefits are paid for the ten week unemployment spell. Total benefits are thus $738. The loss in net income is only the $279 difference between these benefits and the fall in after-tax wages. The $279 private net income loss *is less than 20 percent of the loss in output* as measured by the gross wage.
>
> Because of the one week waiting period, the private cost of unemployment is even lower for an additional week of unemployment. If he stays unemployed for eleven weeks instead of ten, he loses an additional $140 in gross earnings but only $16 in net income. The private net income loss *is less than 12 percent of the loss in output* as measured by the gross wage. If the individual values his leisure and nonmarket work activities at even 50 cents an hour, there is no net private cost of unemployment![20]

However, as Feldstein acknowledges, this hypothetical case is extreme. For instance, in three very populous states—New York, California, and Texas—as recently as the end of 1981 there was an unemployment benefit ceiling of $130 a week or less, although blue-collar workers in manufacturing were earning a national average of $320 a week. Feldstein's own analysis of the March 1981 *Current Population Survey* data shows that for prime-age (25 to 55 years), nonfarm, private-sector, experienced workers on temporary layoff, the average unemployment benefit was 55 percent of previous net-of-tax wage income.[21] This is a considerably smaller net wage replacement ratio than in the Massachusetts example. Had younger workers, agricultural workers, public-sector workers, inexperienced workers, and the long-duration unemployed not been excluded from Feldstein's analysis, the average unemployment insurance replacement percentage would have been considerably lower, and the implied average net private cost of unemployment would have been correspondingly higher. For individuals experiencing long periods of unemployment without assistance from unemployment compensation or other transfer payments, the costs of joblessness may be nothing short of catastrophic.

A balanced assessment of the individual costs and distributional consequences of unemployment requires broadly based, systematic empirical analysis, not unusual examples or anecdotal evidence. The best systematic studies are by Gramlich and by Gramlich and Laren, who analyzed the distributional effects of higher unemployment in the 1970–1971 and 1980–1981 recessions by gender, race, and normal family income.[22] Using data for 1967–1980 on 3124 households from the (national) Michigan Longitudinal Panel Study on Income Dynamics, Gramlich and Laren were able to estimate the average income losses absorbed by various types of families from increased aggregate unemployment, and they were also able to assess the effectiveness of the tax-and-transfer system in offsetting those income losses. As one would guess from the demographic correlates of unemployment, Gramlich and Laren found cyclical unemployment experience to have a pronounced inverse relationship with family income (cyclical increases in unemployment fall most heavily on low-income families),[23] so it is natural to report some of their results by families' relative income.

Table 2.5 shows Gramlich and Laren's estimates of the percentage decline in family earned personal income from the actual loss of jobs, decreases in hours worked, and reductions in the income of secondary earners induced by a 1-percentage-point increase in the aggregate official rate of unemployment in 1980–1981. The losses are averages based on the experience of all households of each type, only small factions of which were directly affected by unemployment or underemployment. This should be kept in mind when one is interpreting the percentage declines in income, which otherwise might appear to be "small." The average percentage losses of pretransfer and posttransfer income are shown separately for families headed by black males, by white males, and by females at different relative income levels (multiples of poverty-line income). In these data the overall average loss of pretransfer income due to a 1-percent increase in the unemployment rate is 1.3 percent.[24] This serves as a benchmark against which the estimated pretransfer losses for various family types should be compared.

Table 2.5 Changes in pre– and post-tax-and-transfer income due to a 1-percentage-point rise in the aggregate unemployment rate

Average normal family income as multiple of poverty line (1967–1980)	Average probability that primary earner will experience unemployment during a year (1967–1980)	Pre–tax-and-transfer income loss as percent of normal income	Post–tax-and-transfer income loss as percent of normal income	Replacement rate of tax-and-transfer system as percent of pre–tax-and-transfer loss
Families in which primary earner is a white male				
<1.0	0.32	−5.8	−2.6	56
1.5–2.0	0.23	−2.1	−1.3	40
2.5–3.0	0.16	−1.4	−0.9	37
>5.0	0.04	−0.7	−0.5	31
Overall weighted average	0.13	−1.2	−0.8	37
Families in which primary earner is a nonwhite male				
<1.0	0.35	−5.9	−3.5	40
1.5–2.0	0.25	−2.1	−1.3	37
2.5–3.0	0.17	−1.4	−1.0	32
>5.0	0.04	−1.0	−0.7	31
Overall weighted average	0.20	−2.0	−1.3	37
Families in which primary earner is a female				
<1.0	0.27	−2.2	−1.6	27
1.5–2.0	0.21	−1.2	−0.7	20
2.5–3.0	0.14	−0.6	−0.5	22
>5.0	0.02	−0.6	−0.4	21
Overall weighted average	0.13	−0.9	−0.7	22

Source: Edward Gramlich and Deborah Laren, "How Widespread Are Income Losses in a Recession?" in D. Lee Bawden, ed., The Social Contract Revisited (Washington, D.C.: Urban Institute, 1984), tables 1, 3.
Note: Figures are based on computations for 1980–1981.

For all families in which the primary earners are males with normal incomes below the poverty line, Table 2.5 indicates that the average reduction of *pre*–tax-and-transfer income induced by an extra percentage point of aggregate unemployment is 5.8–5.9 percent. This is more than four times the average loss for all families (1.3 percent). The corresponding loss of pre–tax-and-transfer income for male-headed families with normal family incomes equal to more than five times the poverty-line income is 0.7–1 percent. This, of course, reflects the fact that low-income families are more exposed to unemployment and therefore absorb higher income losses when the economy goes into recession. The probability of experiencing unemployment, however, is higher for households headed by nonwhite males than for households headed by white males. Therefore the typical pre–tax-and-transfer income loss experienced by these male-headed black families is larger (2.0 versus 1.2 percent).

The average income losses are smaller for families headed by females than for those headed by males, although here too the losses decline as normal income rises. The reason is that a much smaller fraction of the income of female heads of household typically comes from labor-market activities. A higher proportion of female-headed families are AFDC recipients, widows, and others who for one reason or another are outside the labor market.

The post–tax-and-transfer data in Table 2.5 reveal the effectiveness of the tax system, unemployment-insurance payments, the AFDC program, the AFDC–Unemployed Parent program, food-stamp benefits, Social Security benefits, and other income transfers in offsetting the income losses from extra unemployment. Remember, however, that the post–tax-and-transfer data also represent averages for all families of each type sampled by the national surveys, and there is considerable dispersion around these average experiences. Only some of the households were directly affected by the cyclical unemployment or underemployment, and the coverage and benefit levels of the transfer programs are not uniform. The cushioning effects of transfer programs are, therefore, overstated by the averages for some households and understated by the averages for others.

Nonetheless, in conjunction with the pre–tax-and-transfer data, the post–tax-and-transfer losses convey useful information about the distributional effects of recessions across important demographic groups in American society. The difference between the pre–tax-and-transfer income losses and the post–tax-and-transfer income losses, expressed as a percentage of the pre–tax-and-transfer losses, yields an estimate of the so-called replacement rate: the typical proportion of each group's private income losses restored by the tax-and-transfer system. For example, the tax-and-transfer system reduced the average income loss experienced by below-poverty-line households headed by nonwhite males from approximately 5.9 percent to 3.5 percent. The cushioning effect of transfer programs was therefore about 40 percent of the average gross pretransfer loss [(5.9 − 3.5)/ 5.9]. This represents the share of the economic pain due to an increase of 1 percentage point in aggregate unemployment that the tax-and-transfer system distributed away from male-headed nonwhite families to the rest of society during the 1980–1981 recession. The remaining fraction of the average gross loss—about 60 percent—is the net private loss ultimately absorbed by the nonwhite families directly affected by the increased unemployment.

The tax-and-transfer system was more successful in offsetting the gross income losses experienced by male-headed white families at below-poverty-line incomes. For these households, transfers reduced the average loss induced by an extra percentage point of unemployment from 5.8 percent to 2.6 percent—that is, by a factor of 56 percent. The net private cost, therefore, was equal to about 44 percent of the gross loss. As would be expected, the income-loss replacement percentages tend to decline as household income rises. A range of typical replacement percentages is shown in the last column of Table 2.5.

For male-headed households, the replacement ratios declined from the 40 and 56 percent levels just discussed for those below the poverty line, to around 31 percent for families with normal incomes equal to more than five times the poverty line. This means that families in this category affected directly by a 1-percentage-point increase in the overall unemployment rate—because the family head actually lost a job or experienced a reduction in hours or because the earned income of secondary family earners declined—absorbed approximately 70 percent of the gross costs.

Although the tax-and-transfer system neutralizes a smaller fraction of the gross private costs of recession to higher-income families (or, equivalently, after taxes and transfers such families experience higher net private losses), it must be remembered that low-income households are more exposed to increased unemployment to begin with. Therefore they are typically hit with much larger economic losses in relation to their normal incomes than are higher-income households. As a result, even though the tax-and-transfer system responds more effectively to the plight of the poor (as it is intended to do), recessions still exacerbate inequalities in the distribution of post–tax-and-transfer income. I shall return to this important point in Chapters 3 and 9.

Table 2.5 shows that the tax-and-transfer system has generally been much less successful in sheltering female-headed households than male-headed households from the private costs of higher unemployment. At below-poverty-line income levels, transfers replaced about 27 cents of every dollar of lost income for families headed by females. At normal income levels of 1.5 or more times the poverty line, transfers restored 20 to 22 percent of the gross income loss. Female heads receive less cyclical protection than male heads because, when working, they are more likely to hold jobs not covered by unemployment insurance. On the other hand, female-headed families absorb smaller losses to begin with from recessions, because female family heads are less likely to be in the labor force. Their economic well-being is more dependent on AFDC benefits, and unemployment compensation and other transfer programs aiding all types of families have less complete coverage than does AFDC.

The success of the transfer system in cushioning families from the full economic impact of increased unemployment may well have been somewhat greater than Table 2.5 implies, because transfer income was probably underreported to some degree by the survey respondents.[25] For the years after 1981, however, the reverse is undoubtedly true. Cuts made by the Reagan administration in the unemployment and food-stamp programs (which, as Chapter 9 will make clear, fell most heavily on the working poor) dramatically increased the net private costs of recessions. As pointed out in the earlier section on the aggregate costs of unemployment, the quantifiable losses of recessions, such as those reported in Table 2.5, do not include the value of work experience and on-the-job training (and, of course, psychological well-being) sacrificed by extra unemployment. These unmeasured costs are probably especially high—indeed, they doubtless reach tragic proportions—in the case of younger and minority workers attempting to break into or keep a grip on the world of steady jobs and career advancement.

Even if the estimates in Table 2.5 of the effectiveness of the tax-and-transfer system in replacing unemployment-induced income losses are increased substantially, say by a factor of one-quarter, the implied net private costs are much greater than anecdotal evidence often suggests. Although in our mixed political economy the tax-and-transfer system manages to shift a significant share of the costs of extra unemployment away from those affected directly to a wider range of the society, the net private costs remain high and inequitably distributed.[26] Yet the extra inflation that might accompany activist government policies designed to minimize unemployment also may have high aggregate costs and important distributional consequences. I turn to these issues next.

3 The Costs of Inflation

A change in the value of money, that is to say in the level of prices, is important only insofar as its incidence is unequal.

—John Maynard Keynes

There can be little doubt that poor people, or people of modest means generally, are the chief sufferers of inflation.

—Arthur F. Burns, former chairman of the Board of Governors of the Federal Reserve

3.1 Defining and Measuring Inflation

Inflation refers to a pervasive rise in the money prices of goods and services, and therefore it involves a decline in the purchasing power of the currency. But as emphasized in Chapter 1, inflation tells us nothing whatever about changes in people's standard of living—an important distinction frequently missed in opinion surveys that equate "rising prices" with a "high cost of living." (See Chapter 4.)

Measuring inflation requires construction of an overall price index, and that has become a major statistical enterprise with political as well as economic implications. Devising a general price index requires decisions about what items to include, how much weight to give each item, and whether to use fixed (base–period) or variable (current–period) weights. There are about as many price indexes and associated measures of the inflation rate as there are conceptions of the unemployment rate, though the various indexes do not exhibit nearly as much dispersion as do the unemployment indicators discussed in Chapter 2. Year-on-year inflation rates of the most important price indexes in postwar periods up to the big disinflation of 1982–1984 are shown in Table 3.1. (Chapter 9 analyzes the course of inflation and other macroeconomic events during President Reagan's first term.)

The first four columns of Table 3.1 are measures of the inflation rates experienced by consumers: the percentage rates of change in the traditional Consumer Price Index (CPI), in the revised CPI, and in the

Table 3.1 Annual inflation rates of various price indexes by period, 1950–1981

Time period	Traditional CPI (1)	Revised CPI (2)	PCE deflator (current weights) (3)	PCE deflator (fixed 1972 weights) (4)	GNP deflator (current weights) (5)	GNP deflator (fixed 1972 weights) (6)	Underlying consumer price rate (PCE nonfood, nonenergy, current-weights deflator) (7)
1950–1954	2.42	NA	2.68	NA	2.52	NA	NA
1955–1959	1.63	NA	2.03	NA	2.54	NA	NA
1960–1964	1.26	NA	1.46	1.09	1.47	1.20	1.48
1965–1969	3.33	NA	3.06	2.79	3.53	3.26	2.93
1970–1974	5.93	5.54	5.51	5.56	5.65	5.69	4.62
1975–1979	7.74	7.08	6.66	7.01	7.01	7.38	6.41
1980	12.67	10.59	9.78	10.59	8.92	9.43	8.61
1981	9.84	9.10	8.22	8.90	9.03	9.18	8.26
Statistics, 1960–1981							
Cumulative price rise	207%	NA	171%	173%	185%	185%	152%
Mean of annual compound rates	5.17	NA	4.61	4.62	4.83	4.83	4.28

Source: Computed from price index data in the Citibank Economic Database.
Notes: NA means not available; annual percentage rates of change are computed as $\ln(X_t/X_{t-1}) \cdot 100$; cumulative inflation is computed as $X_{81}/X_{60} - 1$.

current- and fixed-weight deflators of Personal Consumption Expenditures (PCE). The rates of change of the current- and fixed-weights GNP deflators, shown to the right of the CPI and PCE rates in Table 3.1, yield measures of the inflation of all goods and services produced and sold in the marketplace. The inflation rate most directly relevant to voters is the rise in prices of goods and services purchased by consumers (which make up about two-thirds of total output), as distinguished from the behavior of prices for capital goods, office buildings, the services of public employees, and so on, which are purchased by firms and governments and are included in the GNP price deflators. Historically, however, the consumer-oriented price index to which citizens have been most sensitive, to which the media have paid most attention, and to which cost-of-living wage escalators and transfer payments have most often been linked is the Consumer Price Index, or the CPI.

First published by the Bureau of Labor Statistics in 1919 to facilitate adjustment of the wage levels of workers in shipbuilding yards, the CPI has been expanded and revised many times since then. It is one of the most closely watched statistics produced by the federal government,[1] and for good reason. By the late 1970s, increases in the wage rates of nearly 10 million private-sector workers were based in some fashion on rises in the CPI through a variety of cost-of-living adjustments (COLAs) written into labor contracts.[2] And the resulting trends in these workers' wages have influenced wage settlements involving many millions of others in unorganized firms. Moreover, benefit payments from numerous government transfer programs are now tied to the CPI. In President Reagan's fiscal year 1983 budget, about one-third of total federal expenditures ($244 billion of $757.6 billion) was slated for indexed programs. The most important is the Social Security program, which by 1982 had about 36 million beneficiaries. Until 1972, Social Security benefits were adjusted informally (but more than adequately) for inflation through periodic special acts of Congress. In 1972, however, Congress mandated that starting in 1975 benefits would be automatically and fully indexed. Each June, therefore, Social Security benefit payments are now increased by the full percentage rise in the CPI over the four quarters ending in the previous March.[3] As a result of the June 1980 adjustment, for example, July 1 payments to 32 million recipients rose 14.3 percent, for an increase of 17 (1980) billion dollars in Social Security outlays. Had a different price index been used—say, the implicit-price deflator for Personal Consumption Expenditures, which will be discussed shortly—the benefit adjustment would have been about 10 percent and about 6 billion dollars in Social Security payments would have been saved.

The pensions of nearly 3 million retired military and federal civil service employees and survivors are now fully indexed to the CPI. The pension benefits of the retired employees of twenty-one state governments are also indexed, although for these pensioners the CPI-based adjustments are typically fractional rather than total. Inflation adjustments of other transfer payments are based on components of the CPI. Groups affected significantly include about 22 million food-stamp recipients and about 25 million school children receiving federally subsidized lunches, whose benefits are increased by a rise in the CPI food items. Finally, payments received by an unknown, though surely large, number of child-support, alimony, rent, and royalty recipients are linked contractually to rises in the CPI. Altogether it is likely that more than half of the American population (including dependents) is affected, through public laws or private contracts, by changes in the CPI. This estimate does not include those people affected by the indexing of federal tax rates to inflation, which under the Economic Recovery Taxation Act of 1981 began in 1985.

The CPI is a "Laspeyres" type index, giving the current (period t) cost of a fixed market basket of goods and services relative to the cost in some reference period (period 0):

$$\text{CPI}_t = \frac{\sum_i q_{i0} P_{it}}{\sum_i q_{i0} P_{i0}}$$

where i denotes items in the CPI consumption bundle of goods and services and q_i and P_i denote the associated quantities and prices.[4] The "fixed basket" or commodity consumption bundle used to construct the CPI is not held constant indefinitely. It has been updated about once every twelve years to allow for changes in spending patterns accompanying the appearance of new products and the disappearance of old ones, shifts in consumer tastes, and changes in relative prices. Since 1978 the index had been based on expenditure weights derived from the 1972–1973 Survey of Consumer Expenditures, which involved a sample of about 40,000 households from the population of all urban residents (about 80 percent of the national population).[5] The latest 1972–1973 commodity basket includes about 400 items priced monthly from more than 60,000 sources in 85 urban areas across the country. Roughly a million and a half price quotations are obtained annually for the index.

The CPI is not a "true" cost-of-living index (though it is often thought of in this way), because it makes no allowance for shifts in consumption expenditures away from commodities with rising relative prices toward commodities with falling relative prices in ways that yield no loss of consumer satisfaction (utility). For example, if the price of steak doubles and the price of chicken remains stable, I may shift my expenditures toward the latter in order to offset the shift in relative prices. I will experience no decline in utility by doing so if I find eating beef and eating poultry equally satisfying (that is, if I am indifferent between the two). The CPI makes no provision for such behavior, and it therefore tends to exaggerate increases in the "true" cost of living in periods of major relative price changes where opportunities exist for some substitution among commodities without loss of consumer utility. No price index is able to overcome the source of this difficulty, however, because doing so requires unavailable knowledge about the combinations of goods and services yielding constant satisfaction to representative consumers (in other words, knowledge of consumers' indifference curves).[6] In any case, the principal problem with the CPI resides not so much in the fact that the commodity basket is fixed for long intervals as in the way in which certain components have been weighted, particularly the home ownership component of the index.[7]

Owner-occupied housing has been one of the most important investment goods for the middle class in recent decades. Yet until recently the CPI treated home prices like any other item: the index for current sale prices of new houses relative to base period prices was multiplied by the expenditure weight for new house purchases established by the latest consumer survey. This procedure clearly mixes the cost of owned shelter with the return on a significant investment asset. The weighting of home mortgage interest costs was even more bizarre. Essentially the CPI treated mortgage interest payments as if they were totally unrelated to home purchases. One-half of the lifetime (undiscounted) home mortgage interest costs appeared as an *additional* item in the index.[8] Hence both interest payments and purchase prices contributed to the expenditure weight and prices of the CPI overall home ownership component, even though interest expense obviously represents the cost of financing home purchases (the discounted present value of house prices less down payments). The CPI, therefore, greatly overstated the contribution of home ownership to inflation by counting house prices once through the weight assigned to changes in home prices and then, indirectly, a second time through the weight assigned to changes in mortgage interest. As a result, the rate and the variability of inflation were clearly exaggerated by the CPI in periods of sharply increasing real property values and volatile interest rates, such as the late 1960s and the 1970s.[9] Conversely, the conventional CPI may have understated inflation during periods of sluggish and falling real estate prices, such as 1981–1982, when the housing market collapsed (along with other interest-rate-sensitive industries) in the wake of restrictive monetary policy.

The CPI's distortion of inflation historically has been on the up side. The magnitude of the exaggeration can be assessed by comparing the behavior of the traditional CPI to that of the revised CPI or its nearest cousin, the fixed weights deflator of Personal Consumption Expenditures (see the fixed-weights PCE deflator in column 4 of Table 3.1). The PCE fixed-weights deflator is a Laspeyres price index that is conceptually equivalent to the CPI, giving the current cost of base-year consumption goods and services relative to base-year prices. (Currently, the fixed weights are based on 115 components priced in 1972.) The PCE, however, covers all personal consumption expenditures in the national accounts (about two-thirds of the GNP) rather than the type of survey-based, urban market basket used for the CPI. But more important, the PCE treats home ownership costs more realistically than does the traditional CPI. Home ownership costs in the PCE deflator, as well as in the revised CPI, are assumed to change as rented shelter prices do, and both are measured by the CPI rent index. This "rental equivalence" method avoids the overcounting of home ownership costs (by excluding mortgage interest) as well as the confusion of home owners' actual shelter costs with the home asset appreciations that are built into the traditional CPI. Comparison of columns 1 and 4 of Table 3.1 shows that the traditional CPI inflation rate exceeded the PCE fixed-weights rate on average by less than a fifth of a percentage point per year in the first half of the 1960s, by four- to five-tenths of a percentage point per year in the late 1960s and first part of the 1970s, and by a more sizable seven-tenths of a percentage point per year in the last half of the 1970s. With the explosion of housing and mortgage costs, the CPI-PCE inflation gap ballooned to 2 percentage points in 1980 and stood at about 1 percentage point during 1981.

As the means at the bottom of Table 3.1 show, the average difference between the traditional CPI and the PCE fixed-weights deflator inflation rates over the entire 1960–1981 period was 0.55 percent per year (5.17% − 4.62%). With compounding, this yields a gap between the cumulative price rises implied by the traditional CPI and the PCE fixed-weights index of about 34 percentage points (207% − 173%), most of which was built up after the late 1960s. Over a fairly long period, then, the traditional CPI's peculiar treatment of home ownership produced significant exaggeration of the rise in prices experienced by consumers.[10] And, because so many monetary payments were linked to rises in the traditional CPI, its exaggeration of inflation in turn helped perpetuate the wage-price spiral. At the same time, indexation to the traditional CPI *improved* (rather than just preserved) the real standard of living of Social Security and federal civil service pensioners, and it pushed privileged union members enjoying generous CPI-based wage escalation up the relative income ladder at the expense of other blue-collar and white-collar workers.

Political pressure from the self-interested, in combination with pure bureaucratic inertia, helps explain why it proved so difficult to modify the CPI. Naturally, the advantaged groups, which tend to be well organized and politically influential (especially the Social Security recipients), resisted tying wage and transfer payments to more accurate measures of inflation. The upward bias of the CPI resulting from the treatment of home ownership had been obvious for a decade; dozens of technical analyses had identified the sources of the problem, and staff support within the Bureau of Labor Statistics for corrective action had been unanimous since the mid-1970s. Yet not until October 1981 did the bureau announce its intention of introducing a rental equivalence method of measuring housing costs, which yields the revised CPI in column 2 of Table 3.1. Even then, the change from the traditional to the revised CPI as the official measure of consumer price inflation was deferred until January 1983 in the all-urban consumers index (CPI-U) and until January 1985 in the wage and clerical earners index (CPI-W). Inasmuch as housing prices actually were falling by the end of 1981 (because extremely tight monetary policies from 1979 onward eventually crippled the housing industry), those who had historically benefited from the traditional CPI's overweighting of home ownership costs had little reason to oppose the innovation when it was finally announced.

The other major index of consumer prices shown in Table 3.1 is the current-weights deflator for Personal Consumption Expenditures, also known as the PCE implicit-price deflator. The PCE current-weights deflator is a "Paasche" type index, giving the current cost (P_{it}) relative to the cost in the (1972) reference period (P_{i0}):

$$\text{PCE}_t \text{ (current weights)} \equiv \frac{\sum_i q_{it}P_{it}}{\sum_i q_{it}P_{i0}}$$

The consumption bundle and the expenditure weights of the PCE implicit-price deflator change every period.[11] Therefore, unlike the CPI and the fixed-weights PCE deflator—which tend to exaggerate cost-of-living rises because allowances are not made for product substitutions that entail no loss of consumer satisfaction—the current-weights PCE deflator tends to understate the true cost of living (in periods *after* the reference period), because all product substitutions are treated as if they involved no decline in consumer utility. For example, the great increase in the relative price of energy after 1973 prompted many of us to substitute, say, wool sweaters for home heating oil in order to escape part of the burden of higher fuel bills. Very few of us were indifferent to this chilling substitution, but the current-weights PCE deflator does not register the decline in satisfaction (and, hence, the increase in true cost of living) associated with the change in energy consumption patterns.

Because consumers typically make commodity substitutions in ways that minimize the cost-of-living *level* they experience each period, the PCE current-weights deflator will yield higher inflation rates than will a fixed-weights deflator in periods prior to the reference date.[12] Consequently, the cumulative inflation from 1960 to 1981 implied by the commonly used PCE implicit-price deflator is essentially the same as that implied by the fixed-weights PCE deflator: 171–173 percent. For the same reasons the GNP fixed- and current-weights deflators show almost identical cumulative inflation between 1960 and 1981 (185 percent), even though the implicit GNP deflator should only be used to gauge cumulative price rises since the reference year 1972. Inasmuch as the GNP price indexes cover all goods and services produced and sold and nonconsumer commodities have been inflating at a slightly higher rate than consumer commodities, the GNP indexes show slightly higher cumulative and average annual price rises than do the PCE price indexes.

3.2   Recent Trends and Fluctuations in the Underlying Inflation Rate

The last inflation measure in Table 3.1, shown in the far-right column, is based on the PCE current-weights index exclusive of food and energy prices. Rises in this index reflect the so-called underlying, or core, rate of consumer price inflation—that is, the inflation rate that would tend to be perpetuated at full employment in the absence of large changes in volatile food and energy prices, which are more difficult to influence through monetary and fiscal policies than are wages. This index yields a good indication of fundamental inflationary trends embedded in the wage bargaining–price setting process. Year-on-year changes in the underlying rate (vertical axis) are plotted against the actual PCE current-weights inflation rates (horizontal axis) in Figure 3.1. Vertical deviations from the 45-degree line indicate the contribution to inflation of food and energy shocks. (Plotting the revised CPI against the same index stripped of food and energy would yield the same pattern.)

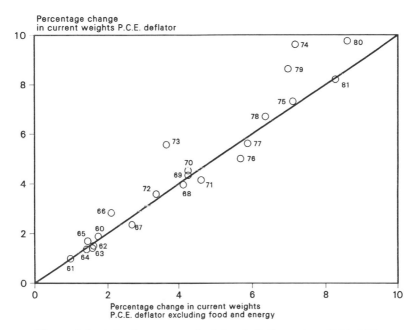

Figure 3.1 Actual versus underlying inflation rates, 1960–1981.

The data in Table 3.1 and Figure 3.1 show that the underlying inflation rate escalated about sixfold from the early 1960s to the early 1980s. When President Kennedy took office, the underlying rate was only 1.5 percent. Since that time it has increased in three great jumps. One jump can be unambiguously attributed to policy mismanagement; as Figure 3.1 shows, the other two were due in large part to very bad luck in the form of adverse food and energy supply shocks.

The first great jump represents a textbook example of the inflationary consequences of excess aggregate demand. To avoid drawing attention to the cost of an unpopular war, President Johnson attempted to finance both the large increases in military expenditures for our Vietnam involvement and the rises in social outlays for the Great Society programs without raising taxes. The resulting growth in the government deficit and an associated rise in the money supply subjected the economy, which by mid-1965 was already at full employment, to large, expansionary fiscal and monetary thrusts. During 1965–1968 the natural-employment, or high-employment, federal deficit[13] averaged 1.65 percent of the natural, or high-employment, GNP, having peaked in 1967 at 2.5 percent (about 48 billion 1981 dollars), a postwar record at the time. This represented a dramatic and expansionary change from the fiscal policy of the first half of the 1960s, when the natural-employment budget on average showed a surplus approximately equal to 0.48 percent of the natural GNP. The real money supply growth rate, deflated M1-B, doubled over the same period, rising from an average of 1 percent per year during 1960–1964 to about 2 percent per year during 1965–1968.[14]

The Johnson policy of (hidden) deficit finance was abandoned in July 1968 with a 10-percent income tax surcharge. By early 1969 unemployment had been driven more than 1.5 percentage points below the so-called natural rate, and the excess demand pressures had pushed up the underlying inflation rate from 1 percent to over 4 percent. Indeed, because this first big jump in core inflation was a classic demand-push episode not fueled by unusual food or energy supply shocks, it is well mapped by almost any measure of the trend of prices. (Notice that the points in Figure 3.1 for the 1960s fall close to the 45-degree line.)

The incoming Republican administration of President Nixon reacted to the acceleration of prices by pursuing orthodox contractional policies. In 1969 the natural-employment budget deficit as a percentage of the natural GNP was almost 2 points lower than it had been the preceding year. Arthur Burns, Nixon's appointee as chairman of the

Federal Reserve Board of Governors, accommodated the administration's fiscal policy, and the real money supply (deflated M1-B) increased by only 0.5 percent in 1969 and decreased by more than 2 percent in 1970. The policy worked, producing the 1970–1971 recession, which pushed unemployment to 6 percent—about three-quarters of a percentage point above the natural rate. But the underlying inflation rate was affected very little by the short-lived recession and hence remained way above the 1-percent annual rate of the early 1960s. For the reasons developed in Chapter 1, economic slack is slow to produce disinflation in the postwar American economy, and a year of less than 1-percentage-point extra unemployment in 1971 simply could not roll back the rise in the core inflation rate that had accumulated from 1965 to 1969.[15]

In August of 1971 the Nixon administration imposed wage and price controls, and the policy of fiscal and monetary restraint was jettisoned in a successful attempt to stimulate an election-year boom. President Nixon apparently was determined not to let the economy cost him the White House in 1972, as he believed it had in 1960 when the economy was flagging and Eisenhower, as a matter of (anti-inflationary) principle, declined to take stimulative actions. (See Chapter 8 on political business cycles.) The natural-employment budget, which essentially was in balance in 1969, went into deficit to the tune of about 1.5 percent of the natural GNP in 1971 (28 billion 1981 dollars) and 1.7 percent of the natural GNP in 1972 (39 billion 1981 dollars). Perhaps more important, the real M1-B money supply grew by 2.4 percent in 1971 and by a whopping 3.7 percent in 1972. This combination of fiscal and monetary stimulation ensured that as soon as the wage-price controls were lifted, as they were by stages in late 1973 and early 1974, inflation would bounce right back, wiping out the transitory disinflationary impact of the nation's first serious experiment with an incomes policy since the Korean War.

The second big jump in the core inflation rate was fueled less by the relaxation of the controls policies (or by the devaluation of the dollar and rise in import prices following President Nixon's abandonment of international gold convertibility of the dollar in August 1971) than by two major exogenous supply shocks. First came the dramatic increases in the world price of food in late 1972 and early 1973, which originated in the worldwide crop failure in grains. A much more damaging event soon followed: the quadrupling of world petroleum prices by the OPEC cartel in October 1973. Despite controls on the price of domestically produced oil (which meant that initially the average price per barrel of oil in the U.S. market only doubled), the combination of these supply shocks helped push the rate of inflation, measured by any conventional means, to double-digit or near-double-digit levels throughout 1974. The increases in the relative prices of food and energy represented a direct transfer of real resources from consumers to farmers and to OPEC and other energy producers. Workers naturally sought to offset the transfer through increased incomes, and the higher food and energy prices gradually worked their way into the wage bargaining–price setting process. Consequently, although real wages declined in this period, the core (non-food, nonenergy) inflation rate also rose sharply—from the 4.0-percent-per-year rate prevailing in 1971–1972 to about 7.0 percent per year in 1974–1975.

Gerald Ford, who became president after Nixon's near-impeachment and resignation in August 1974, responded to this big jump in inflation by launching the "Whip Inflation Now" media campaign and, more tangibly, by cutting back the natural-employment deficit as a percentage of natural GNP, making the 1974 deficit nearly 1 percent (or 20 billion 1981 dollars) lower than the average for the preceding two years. Burns again accommodated the fiscal authority's policy of restraint, proclaiming that the shortage was "of oil not money,"[16] and real M1-B declined by a crushing 5.6 percent in 1974 and by 4.2 percent in 1975. The consequence was the most severe contraction since the Great Depression of the 1930s. Unemployment averaged 8.5 percent for 1975 (fully 2.5 percentage points above the natural, nonaccelerating inflation rate) and remained high—at 7.7 percent—throughout 1976, when the recovery began. A recession of this magnitude did yield significant disinflation, and the underlying rate declined about 1.5 percentage points between 1974 and 1976 to an annual rate of less than 6 percent.[17] The severity of the recession, pressure from the Democrat-controlled Congress and, perhaps, the fact that the presidential election year was approaching prompted the Ford administration to abandon contractional policies in mid-1975. President Ford, however, apparently remained committed, at least rhetorically, to his earlier anti-inflation priorities, declaring to a cheering Wall Street audience during the campaign that "after all, unemployment affects only 8 percent of the people while inflation affects 100 percent."

These priorities were reversed during the first years of the Carter administration, which emphasized the traditional Democratic party goal of moving the economy toward full employment. At a postelection press conference in November 1976, President-elect Carter announced his administration's intention of reducing unemployment to the 4.0–4.5 percent range, an ambitious goal that later was modified upward to 4.75 percent. Policy actions early in the term were consistent with this goal. Real M1-B grew at a rate of 1.1 percent in 1977, and for that year the natural-employment deficit remained at about 2 percent of the natural GNP, peaking at 68 billion 1981 dollars in the fourth quarter, after Congress in May 1977 passed the modest tax cuts proposed by the administration to stimulate the economy. Responding to these policy actions and also to the economy's endogenous recuperative capability, the rate of unemployment declined continuously, falling by 2 percentage points between the end of 1976 and the beginning of 1979.

Because the unemployment rate was not pushed below the natural, nonaccelerating inflation rate of about 6 percent, the core inflation rate remained stable in the vicinity of 6.0 to 6.5 percent per year during 1977–1978. Nonetheless, the consumer price inflation rate began to creep upward in 1978 with the acceleration in food costs (this time beef prices). Along with the coincident depreciation of the dollar against the major international currencies, the increase in the consumer price inflation rate led the Carter administration to back off from its expansionary policies by the end of the year. The administration's policy reversal became more pronounced after the second great OPEC price increase of 1979–1980, which doubled the cost of imported oil from about $15 a barrel at the end of 1978 to $35 a barrel at the close of 1980 and produced the third big jump in inflation. President Carter implicitly acknowledged that his voluntary wage-price guidelines policy announced on October 24, 1978 was unlikely alone to affect inflation significantly, and his earlier commitment to achieving a sustained low rate of unemployment was for practical purposes abandoned. In 1979 the natural-employment deficit as a percentage of the natural GNP was reduced by about 1 percent (27 billion 1981 dollars), and in 1980 the deficit stood at only 0.7 percent of the natural GNP. On two occasions (November 1, 1978 and October 6, 1979) the discount rate was increased by a full percentage point, and, more important, monetary policy refused to accommodate the surge in inflation. Real M1-B declined by more than 3 percent in 1979 and by more than 6.5 percent in 1980, thanks in part to President Carter's naming Paul Volcker, the anti-inflationist president of the New York Federal Reserve bank, to the chairmanship of the Federal Reserve Board.

The policy shift succeeded in creating an election-year recession, but the contraction came too late to put significant downward pressure on prices. Carter and the Democrats therefore faced the electorate in 1980 with the worst of all possible situations—increased unemployment, falling real income and output, and high inflation. (The 1980 election and the economy are analyzed in Chapter 6.) The CPI year-on-year inflation rate was 13 percent in 1980—higher than it had been following the first OPEC price shock in 1974. Increased energy prices quickly worked their way into wages and prices generally, and, as Figure 3.1 indicates, the underlying inflation rate stood at more than 8.5 percent per annum in 1980.

The incoming Reagan administration was committed to large increases in defense spending and large reductions in federal tax rates. Fiscal policy, therefore, was expansionary, but the potentially stimulative effects on output and employment were neutralized by the continuation of a truly Draconian monetary policy launched during the Carter administration by Paul Volcker, who was still chairman of the Federal Reserve. ("Reaganomics" is evaluated in Chapter 9.) Yet Volcker's Fed acted with the support and encouragement of the Reagan administration—the first American government to give advocates of a "monetarist" solution to inflation full and open reign over the nation's money and credit policies.[18] Monetary policy under Reagan and Volcker leaned hard against inflation during 1981–1982, producing a large decline in real money supply growth rates. (See Chapter 9.) The problem for the administration (and the country) was, as historical experience suggested and neo-Keynesian theory predicted, that prices responded to the monetary deceleration (here as in Prime Minister Thatcher's Britain) only after the creation of considerable economic slack. Reagan-Volcker monetary stringency therefore aborted the recovery from the 1980 recession and yielded a renewed decline in output and employment over 1981–1982, surpassing the 1974–1975 recession to assume the dubious distinction of being the deepest contraction since the last years of the Great Depression. Such a large contraction did put substantial downward pressure on prices. The CPI inflation rate fell by more than 9 percentage points between 1980–1984, though much of the decline was due to the "pass through" of the 1979–1980 OPEC oil price rise. But core inflation—a more accurate guide to fundamental price trends in the economy— also declined by a sizable 4 percentage points over the same period. By 1984, after four years of tight money and three years of excessive unemployment, the underlying annual inflation rate was down to less than 5 percent per annum.

The most striking feature of the data in Figure 3.1, however, is the fact that after each of the three big inflationary episodes the underlying inflation rate did not decline to its earlier level, despite large sacrifices in real output and employment that were made on behalf of disinflation. Until the Reagan period, therefore, the trend of core inflation was persistently upward. There was of course *some* level of unemployment, idle capacity, and depressed real output prior to the experience of 1981–1983 that would have forced inflation down to previous rates. But given the structure of the postwar American political economy described in Chapter 1, the policy-induced contractions of 1970–1971, 1974–1975, and 1979–1980 were not severe enough to neutralize the inflationary impact of policy mismanagement in the late 1960s or the food and (far more damaging) energy price shocks of the 1970s. The costs of completely reversing the associated big jumps in inflation using orthodox policies clearly would have been extremely high (see Chapter 2), a painful conclusion that is one of the principal lessons of "Reaganomics."

But what were the costs of the secular rise in inflation?

3.3   Inflation and the Distribution of Personal Income

Few topics have stimulated more public rhetoric during the last fifteen years than the alleged impact of inflation on lower income groups, particularly the poor. The image regularly conjured up in public debate, most commonly by conservatives mobilizing support for disinflationary policies, is one of inflation's eroding the purchasing power and in general adversely affecting the absolute and relative economic well-being of low-income households. Little or no empirical evidence supports this view, however.

By any measure the price level has more than quadrupled since the Second World War, yet the distribution of personal income shows no persistent postwar trend, as the data in Table 3.2 on family income shares by quintiles show.[19] Despite decades of continuous inflation, families in the lowest fifth of the income distribution commanded essentially the same share of total personal income in 1980 as in 1947, although their share in 1980 was somewhat lower than it had been in the late 1960s and early 1970s. Families in the highest income quintile, on the other hand, received a smaller share of money income in 1980

Table 3.2 The percentage distribution of money income among families by quintiles, five-year intervals, 1947–1980

Year	Lowest fifth	Second fifth	Third fifth	Fourth fifth	Highest fifth
1947	5.0	11.9	17.0	23.1	43.0
1952	4.9	12.3	17.4	23.4	41.6
1957	5.1	12.7	18.1	23.8	40.4
1962	5.0	12.1	17.6	24.0	41.3
1967	5.5	12.4	17.9	23.9	40.4
1972	5.4	11.9	17.5	23.9	41.4
1977	5.2	11.6	17.5	24.2	41.5
1980	5.1	11.6	17.5	24.3	41.6
Mean share (1947–1980)	5.1	12.1	17.6	23.8	41.3
Income range in 1980 (in thousands of 1980 dollars)	0–10.3	10.3–17.4	17.4–24.6	24.6–34.5	34.5–

Sources: U.S. Bureau of the Census, Current Population Reports, Series P-60, No. 123, table 13, June 1980; and No. 127, table 5, August 1981.

Notes: Families are households of two or more related people. Income includes employment income; interest, dividends, rents, and royalties; cash transfers from the government; private and government pension payments; and regular cash receipts from other private sources. Taxes are not deducted, and in-kind transfers are not included.

than in 1947, but a larger share in 1980 than, for example, in 1967.[20] Specialists have concluded that the absence of strong trends in overall postwar income inequality is the result of two powerful offsetting groups of factors.[21] Various demographic trends were pushing inequality higher. These trends included the shift in the age distribution; the breakup of extended families, which created more younger and older (and, hence, lower income) households; and the rise in the incidence of female-headed families. Offsetting these forces were the rapid growth of government income transfers and of other government policies (affirmative action regulations, equal opportunity and anti-discrimination laws) that exerted powerful equalizing effects on the income distribution. Disequalizing demographic forces, then, were successfully neutralized by activist government policies designed to improve the economic well-being of low-income groups.[22] The point to be emphasized here, however, is that there appears to be no broad, obvious connection between income inequality and the upward postwar trend in the price level.

Although the relative position of the lower income classes appears not to have been eroded in a major way by postwar inflation, it is possible that the relatively small variations in distribution of annual incomes have moved with fluctuations in the inflation rate. Following Blinder and Esaki,[23] the impact of inflation on income shares, net of variations in unemployment and latent trends, can be evaluated by estimating the regression model

$$\text{Share}_{it} = a_{0i} + b_{1i}\,\text{Unemployment}_t + b_{2i}\,\text{Inflation}_t \qquad (3.1)$$
$$+ c_{1i}\text{Time} + a_{1i}\text{Dum58} + c_{2i}(\text{Dum58} \cdot \text{Time}) + e_{it}$$

where Share_{it} is the percentage share of the ith quintile (i = 1, 2, . . . , 5) in the distribution of annual money income among families in the tth year (t = 1947, . . . , 1980), Unemployment is the conventional percentage rate, Inflation is based on the annual percentage rate of change of the traditional CPI, Time is a linear trend beginning with 1.0 in 1947, Dum58 equals 1.0 for the period 1958–1980 and 0 earlier, and Dum58 and (Dum58 · Time) reflect intercept and trend shift terms, respectively, corresponding to the change in the Census Department's method of calculating income shares in 1958.

Ordinary least-squares estimates of equation (3.1) for each quintile of the income distribution appear in Table 3.3.[24] It is immediately apparent from these estimates that, net of unemployment movements and latent trends, the size distribution of family income has not been influenced greatly by postwar variations in the inflation rate. And, although the effects of inflation have been small, the pattern of the coefficients runs exactly contrary to the claim that the poor have been the "chief sufferers of inflation."[25] The only inflation coefficient approaching statistical significance appears in the equation for the lowest income quintile (the poor), and it suggests that each 1-percentage-point rise in the rate of change of consumer prices has been associated with an *increase* on the order of 0.024 percentage point in the share of income going to the bottom fifth of the income distribution. The inflation coefficient is smaller but still positive for the second quintile (the working poor?), it is essentially zero for the middle quintile, and it is negative for the top two quintiles of the income distribution. Although these coefficients are small and not significant, the conclusion suggested by the results is unmistakable: at worst, postwar surges of inflation have been neutral with respect to the

Table 3.3 The impact of inflation and unemployment fluctuations on the distribution of money income among families by quintiles, 1947–1980

Variable	Lowest fifth	Second fifth	Third fifth	Fourth fifth	Highest fifth
Constant (a_0)	5.04**	12.20**	17.14**	23.00	42.44**
	(0.200)	(0.149)	(0.128)	(0.140)	(0.370)
Unemployment	−0.114**	−0.104**	−0.026	0.049*	0.201**
rate (U)	(0.027)	(0.020)	(0.017)	(0.019)	(0.051)
Inflation	0.024	0.013	−0.000016	−0.010	−0.017
rate (DCPI)	(0.013)	(0.010)	(0.008)	(0.009)	(0.024)
Dummy 1958–1980	0.440	1.09**	0.968**	0.322	−2.58**
(Dum58)	(0.246)	(0.184)	(0.157)	(0.173)	(0.457)
Time	0.030	0.073**	0.094**	0.062**	−0.241**
	(0.020)	(0.015)	(0.012)	(0.014)	(0.036)
Dum58 × Time	−0.016	−0.105**	−0.108**	−0.045**	0.250**
	(0.024)	(0.018)	(0.015)	(0.017)	(0.044)
R^2	0.74	0.82	0.78	0.83	0.78
Standard error of regression	0.180	0.135	0.115	0.126	0.334
Durbin-Watson	0.89	1.00	1.95	1.48	1.40

Note: Standard errors appear in parentheses.
 * Significant at 0.05 level, two-tail test.
** Significant at 0.01 level, two-tail test.

money income distribution; at best, they have made a minor contribution to enhancing the relative income position of the poor.

The impact of unemployment on the income distribution is less ambiguous statistically and stronger substantively. Movements into recessions clearly disadvantage the bottom 40 percent of the income distribution, to the relative advantage of the top 40 percent—particularly the top 20 percent (the upper middle class and the rich).[26] The regression estimates in Table 3.3 indicate that each extra percentage point of unemployment yields a decline of about a tenth of a percentage point in the shares of both the lowest and the second lowest quintiles of the distribution. Because the average income share of the bottom quintile is only about 5 percent, as compared to 12 percent for the second quintile (see Table 3.2), the proportional income losses absorbed by families in the lowest quintiles are of course higher. A visual impression of the response of the lowest two quintiles' income share to recessions is given by Figure 3.2, which graphs the time

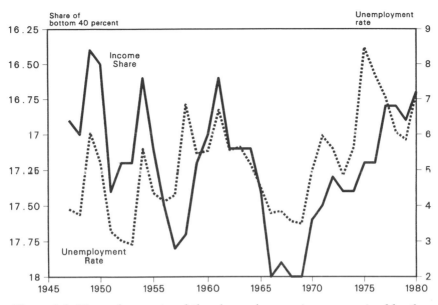

Figure 3.2 Unemployment and the share of money income received by the bottom 40 percent of the family distribution, 1947–1980.

paths of the income shares and aggregate unemployment rates between 1947 and 1980. Fluctuations in the group's income share (shown on an inverted scale) are not dramatic, but they do broadly track major changes in unemployment. Notice in Figure 3.2 that the decline in the share accompanying the high unemployment rates of the late 1970s appears smaller that what might have been expected from the earlier record. Perhaps this is because government programs were more effective in the 1970s than they had been ten years earlier (before the "Great Society" legislation) in creating income floors for the poor and near-poor. The decline also may reflect in part the modest equalization of intergroup differences in the incidence of unemployment mentioned in Chapter 2.

As noted above, the main relative gainers from recessions are the upper quintiles of the distribution—principally the highest quintile, whose income share rises by one-fifth of a percentage point for each additional point of unemployment. Taken at face value, the unemployment and inflation coefficient estimates in Table 3.3 imply that the likely outcome of a year-long contraction that raised the unemployment rate, say, from 6 to 10 percent and generated a decline in the inflation rate of 2.0 percentage points[27] would be to shift about

0.95 percentage point of income from the bottom two-fifths of the income distribution to the top two-fifths. The biggest loser would be the poor (the bottom quintile), who would suffer a decline of about one-half a percentage point in their income share, or a proportional loss of about 10 percent given the lowest quintile's mean postwar income share of 5.1 percent. The biggest winner would be the upper middle class and the rich (the top quintile), who would enjoy an increase of 0.84 percentage point in their share, which represents a proportional gain of only 2 percent given the highest quintile's average income share of over 41 percent. Most of these relative income shifts are due to the rise in unemployment rather than the associated decline in inflation. Yet the estimated distributional effects of even a major recession involving a 4-point increase in the unemployment rate are not dramatic. Again, this reflects the overall success of employment- and income-related government transfers in sheltering lower income groups from the full impact of recessions. As data in Chapter 2 suggested, without transfers the absolute and proportional burdens on the poor from higher unemployment would be much greater. Moreover, it must be remembered that there is mobility of families among quintiles (though the bulk of such movements occur between adjacent quintiles), and so there is some variation over time in the particular households affected by unemployment fluctuations.

Although it is clear from the evidence presented above that the distribution of *money* income has not been altered substantially by inflation, rising prices may nonetheless have affected the distribution of *real* income if there have been persistent differences in the cost-of-living changes actually experienced by various income classes. For example, by virtue of their modest resources the lower income classes have limited discretion in their consumption patterns and therefore must devote a comparatively large fraction of their expenditures to the "basic necessities" (food, shelter, clothing, medical care, and fuel and utilities). Consequently, if the prices of so-called necessary goods and services chronically rise faster than the prices of "nonnecessary" commodities, low-income groups will experience higher inflation rates than will other income classes and their relative real income position will deteriorate even though, as we have seen, their share of total money income is quite stable.[28]

Hollister and Palmer have quite firmly established that from the 1950s through the mid-1960s the effective rate of consumer price inflation experienced by the poor as a whole was essentially the same as that experienced by other income groups.[29] By constructing income group–specific price indexes based on the income-specific consumption patterns in the 1960-1961 Consumer Expenditure Survey, Hollister and Palmer were able to show that whereas the "poor" (households with incomes below the official poverty line[30]) experienced a cumulative rise in prices of 39 percent between 1950 and 1967 and the "near poor" (households with incomes of up to 1.2 times the poverty line) experienced a cumulative price inflation of 39.4 percent over the same period, the goods and services consumed by "high income" households (those with 1960 incomes in excess of $10,000; about $30,000 and above in 1981 prices) rose by 39.5 percent from 1950 to 1967.[31] The reason for these patterns was that the prices of necessary and nonnecessary goods and services increased at about the same rate. Consequently, income class–specific consumer price indexes inflated at essentially the same rate.

As Figure 3.1 indicated, however, sustained high rates of inflation really commenced in the late 1960s. Perhaps, then, rhetoric about the calamitous price rises faced by the poor more accurately describes the situation during the last decade or so. Computations from the most recent Consumer Expenditure Survey (1972–1973) give a good idea of just how much of the budgets of various income classes are absorbed by the basic necessities. The data in Table 3.4 for selected income classes indicate that the poorest households spend fully 55 percent or more of their income on necessities, that middle-income households devote about 40 percent of their expenditures to the necessities, and that this percentage falls to 30 percent or less for the higher-income households.[32]

Yet contrary to the impression given by many treatments of the great inflation of the late 1960s and the 1970s,[33] prices of the so-called necessities actually rose less over the 1967–1981 period than did prices of nonnecessities. Table 3.5 gives the relevant price indexes and associated year-on-year and cumulative percentage rates of change. During the entire fourteen years from 1967 to 1981, the cumulative inflation in prices was 152.2 percent for necessities as compared to 161.1 percent for nonnecessities. Of course necessities prices did not run behind nonnecessities prices in every year. Largely because of the enormous bulge in food prices in 1973, necessities prices inflated by more than 8 percent—over 4 percentage points more than did nonnecessities prices. Although food prices continued to rise at a rate well above the overall CPI in 1974, the big shock to the necessities that year was in the fuel-and-utilities sector, as a result of the OPEC oil price hike of October 1973. In 1974 fuel and utilities inflated by

Table 3.4 Distribution of household expenditures between necessities and nonnecessities in the 1972–1973 Consumer Expenditure Survey for selected income classes (percent)

Type of expenditure	All households (N = 67,477 reporting)	Low income (0–19.3%)		Middle income (39.4–58.5%)		High income (85.8–100%)	
		<$3000	$3000–$4999	$8000–$9999	$10,000–$11,999	$20,000–$24,999	> $25,000
Necessities	37.3	55.2	52.5	41.9	38.3	31.3	29.0
Nonnecessities	62.7	44.8	47.5	58 1	61.7	68.7	71.0

Source: Computed by the author from Bureau of Labor Statistics, *Consumer Expenditure Survey: Interview Diary and Interview Survey Data, 1972–73,* Bulletin 1992, 1978.

Notes: Household incomes are for 1972–1973; sample percentiles appear in parentheses. "Necessities" include food at home, rented shelter, fuel and utilities, clothing, and medical care. "Nonnecessities" include food away from home, alcohol, home ownership, household furnishings, transportation, educational expenses, personal care, tobacco, and entertainment.

Table 3.5 Price indexes and inflation rates for necessity and nonnecessity components of the Consumer Price Index, 1967–1981

Year	Necessities		Nonnecessities	
	Index	Year-on-year inflation rate	Index	Year-on-year inflation rate
1967	1.000	—	1.000	—
1968	1.037	3.7%	1.043	4.3%
1969	1.086	4.8	1.095	5.0
1970	1.139	4.8	1.157	5.6
1971	1.186	4.1	1.210	4.6
1972	1.228	3.6	1.243	2.7
1973	1.330	8.3	1.290	3.9
1974	1.480	11.3	1.423	10.3
1975	1.600	8.1	1.563	9.8
1976	1.680	5.0	1.672	7.0
1977	1.797	7.0	1.777	6.2
1978	1.939	7.9	1.893	6.5
1979	2.112	9.0	2.096	10.7
1980	2.318	9.7	2.370	13.1
1981	2.522	8.8	2.611	10.2
Cumulative inflation (1967–1981)	152.2%		161.1%	

Source: Computed by the author from Bureau of Labor Statistics data, based on the most recently available Consumer Expenditure Survey, for 1972–1973.

Notes: "Necessities" include food at home, rented shelter, fuel and utilities, clothing, and medical care. "Nonnecessities" include food away from home, alcohol, home ownership, household furnishings, transportation, educational expenses, personal care, tobacco, and entertainment.

more than 18 percent as compared to 11 percent for the total CPI, and necessities prices continued to run ahead of nonnecessities prices. Despite another acceleration of food prices in 1978 and the second great shock to energy prices in 1979–1980, however, soft prices of other items had put the nonnecessities index well above the necessities index by 1980–1981.

These patterns in relative prices underlie the inflation rates actually experienced by different income classes that are reported in Table 3.6.[34] The computations in the table indicate that the cumulative rise in prices faced by the poor during this long stretch of comparatively

Table 3.6 Consumer Price Indexes and inflation rates experienced by selected income classes, 1967–1981

| | Low income (0–19.3%) | | | | Middle income (39.4–58.5%) | | | | High income (85.8–100%) | | | |
| | <$3000 | | $3000–$4999 | | $8000–$9999 | | $10,000–11,999 | | $20,000–24,999 | | >$25,000 | |
Year	Index	Year-on-year inflation rate	Index	Year-on-year inflation rate	Index	Year-on-year inflation rate	Index	Year-on-year inflation rate	Index	Year-on-year inflation rate	Index	Year-on-year inflation rate
1967	1.000	—	1.000	—	1.000	—	1.000	—	1.000	—	1.000	—
1968	1.037	3.7	1.038	3.8	1.040	4.0	1.040	4.0	1.042	4.2	1.043	4.3
1969	1.085	4.6	1.087	4.7	1.090	4.8	1.090	4.8	1.095	5.0	1.097	5.1
1970	1.141	5.2	1.143	5.2	1.147	5.2	1.148	5.3	1.154	5.4	1.157	5.5
1971	1.191	4.4	1.193	4.4	1.197	4.4	1.198	4.4	1.205	4.4	1.209	4.5
1972	1.230	3.2	1.231	3.2	1.233	3.0	1.234	3.0	1.240	3.0	1.245	3.0
1973	1.306	6.2	1.306	6.1	1.303	5.7	1.302	5.5	1.306	5.3	1.308	5.1
1974	1.444	10.6	1.445	10.6	1.442	10.6	1.442	10.7	1.445	10.7	1.446	10.5
1975	1.571	8.8	1.563	8.9	1.572	9.1	1.574	9.1	1.580	9.3	1.580	9.3
1976	1.664	5.9	1.667	5.9	1.670	6.2	1.673	6.3	1.680	6.3	1.680	6.3
1977	1.774	6.6	1.776	6.5	1.779	6.5	1.782	6.5	1.788	6.5	1.788	6.4
1978	1.904	7.3	1.905	7.3	1.904	7.1	1.906	7.0	1.913	7.0	1.913	7.0
1979	2.090	9.8	2.092	9.8	2.095	10.0	2.099	10.1	2.107	10.1	2.105	10.0
1980	2.325	11.2	2.326	11.2	2.338	11.6	2.347	11.8	2.359	12.0	2.356	12.0
1981	2.546	9.5	2.545	9.4	2.562	9.6	2.574	9.7	2.588	9.7	2.585	9.7
Cumulative inflation (1967–1981)	154.6%		154.5%		156.2%		157.4%		158.8%		158.5%	

Source: Computed by the author from Bureau of Statistics data, based on the most recently available consumption bundles, for 1972–1973.
Notes: Household incomes are for 1972–1973; sample percentiles appear in parentheses.

high overall inflation rates was on the order of 154 to 155 percent. Middle-income groups absorbed a cumulative inflation rate a couple of percentage points higher, from about 156 to 157 percent; and the highest income classes experienced the greatest inflation, between 158 and 159 percent. Interpreted at face value and in conjunction with earlier analyses, these results imply that inflation, although essentially neutral in its impact on money income distribution, may actually have improved somewhat the relative real income position of low-income households. But the dispersion of inflation rates across income classes is neither large enough nor sufficiently uniform to justify carrying this line of reasoning very far.[35] After all, the year-on-year percentage increases in prices of the consumption bundles of lower income households exceeded (by a small margin) the increases in the bundles of higher income households in 1972-1974 and again in 1977-1978 (Table 3.6).[36] Yet these episodes in which income class–specific inflation rates diverged to the relative disadvantage of the poor were never important enough to push, even for a single year, the low-income-class Consumer Price Index values above the high-income household values.[37]

The above-mentioned consequences of inflation for the distribution of real income, implied by both the response of the money income distribution to rising prices and the evidence on price level changes actually experienced by various income classes, are reinforced by the results of simulation studies using more complicated methodologies and large micro–data sets. The most impressive of such studies was undertaken in the late 1970s by Joseph Minarik of the Brookings Institution.[38] Minarik's analysis was based on the Brookings MERGE data file—a statistical match between the Census Bureau's March 1971 Current Population Survey of about 50,000 American households and the Internal Revenue Service's 1970 Individual Income Tax Model File, containing a statistical sample of 100,000 personal income tax returns. Given detailed information about the social characteristics, tax liabilities, assets, and other income sources of a very large sample of households, Minarik was able to simulate the impact of inflations on the "accrued comprehensive income" of households, where comprehensive income includes consumption plus change in net worth.[39]

Figure 3.3 illustrates the results for two representative situations. The solid line shows the effects after one year of a 2 percentage-point increase in the inflation rate over the actual rate in 1970 (from about 6 to 8 percent per annum). The results are displayed in terms of the

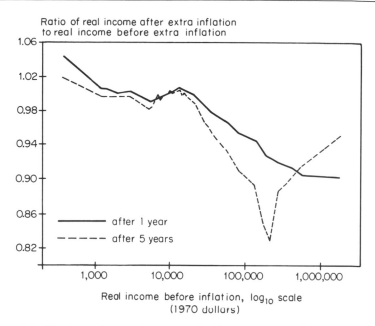

Figure 3.3 The impact on real income of a 2-percentage-point increase in the inflation rate. *Source:* J. Minarik, "The Size Distribution of Income during Inflation," *Review of Income and Wealth* (December 1979), figure 4, reproduced with permission.

ratio of comprehensive real income with the extra inflation to comprehensive real income without the extra inflation. The data indicate that, on average, low-income households are typically better off or unaffected after a year of increased inflation, though households in the 27th to 39th percentiles of the preinflation distribution (5000–7000 1970 dollars) do appear to suffer small postinflation real income declines of between 1 and 2 percent. Most of the real income loss is absorbed by the upper middle class and, especially, the very rich. The average losses due to extra inflation grow steadily as preinflation 1970 household incomes rise above $20,000 (above the 80th percentile, or about $45,000 in 1981 prices) and peak at an income of $200,000 (the top 0.01 percent of the distribution, or approximately $448,000 in 1981 prices). For the latter income class—a small and extremely affluent group—postinflation real comprehensive income is eroded by 17 percent or more. The reason upper income households do so badly under the extra inflation is that real income tax liabilities grow, after-tax corporate retained earnings decline, and dollar-denominated interest-bearing securities depreciate. (See the discussion later in this chapter of corporate profits and inflation.)

The dashed line in Figure 3.3 shows the simulated effects of a 2-percentage-point increase above the prevailing inflation rates, sustained for five years (over 1965–1970). Comprehensive real incomes in the final year are measured relative to incomes in the same year without the extra 2 points of inflation. In this experiment households with 1970 incomes of up to $20,000 fare just slightly better than they did after a single year of extra inflation. In the $20,000 to $500,000 range (from the 80th percentile up to all but the top few households in the income distribution), incomes are higher after five years of increased inflation than they were after one year, largely because interest receipts and the market values of debt securities—an important source of income for the upper quintile of the distribution—are adapting to the sustained acceleration of prices. Nonetheless, real incomes for these households remain below preinflation levels. Figure 3.3 indicates that households with 1970 incomes above $500,000 (1.12 million 1981 dollars) are worse off with a persistent bout of extra inflation than with a transitory acceleration of prices. It is probably hazardous to draw firm conclusions about this tiny group of super-rich households, however.[40]

Taken as a whole, then, recent evidence on the impact of inflation on the distribution of economic well-being supports conclusions scarcely different from those drawn by Hollister and Palmer a decade ago from their analyses of data for the 1950s and early 1960s: "Nothing in these results suggests that the poor would gain from a reduction in inflationary pressure . . . they suggest that a policy to reduce inflation, especially if coupled with even a 'slight' rise in unemployment, could result in serious losses for the poor."[41]

3.4   Inflation and Personal Income Growth Rates

The evidence just discussed shows that postwar inflations have not had pronounced effects on the distribution of money income or real income across the great majority of American households—that is, on the relative position of broad income groups. Yet the notion that rapid price rises during the 1970s contributed to a general deterioration of living standards is widespread. The mass media, including the highbrow press, were filled with stories about inflation's "wiping out" the gains of higher money wages and benefits achieved during the 1970s, leaving American families no better off, and by the end of the 1970s worse off, than before.[42] So it is not surprising that many ordinary citizens believe that inflation *per se* somehow robs them of the higher real standards of living they otherwise might enjoy, even though such a conclusion is supported neither by theoretical reasoning nor by empirical analysis.

There is of course some factual basis for the perception that rapidly rising prices have adversely affected standards of living, as the data on per capita real personal disposable income growth rates and CPI inflation rates indicate (see columns 1 and 7 of Table 4.7). Viewed by five-year periods, the per capita real income growth rate declined steadily (in step with the escalation of inflation) from the postwar peak achieved during the long boom of the late 1960s. Indeed, after negative growth rates in 1979–1980 and 1980–1981, constant dollar disposable income per person was lower in 1981 (3240 1967 dollars) than it had been in 1973 (3243 1967 dollars). Even though the disposable income concept and the CPI-based cost-of-living measure used to deflate the money income series tend to exaggerate the negative association implied in Table 3.7 between rising prices and changes in economic well-being,[43] there is no doubt that the growth rate of average standards of living did deteriorate substantially during the post-Vietnam decade of comparatively high and rising inflation rates.

Yet, as the subperiod data on the GNP gap (the percentage deviation of actual from natural real output) in Table 3.7 remind us, the latter part of the 1970s and the early 1980s was also an era of repeated, largely policy-induced recessions. Rather than reflecting some mysterious structural tendency for personal incomes to lag behind prices during high-inflation periods—an idea prominently featured in the media—the slowdown of real personal income growth may in large part simply mirror the painful sequence of business cycle contractions in 1970, 1974–1975, 1980, and 1981–1982. Unless one believes that accelerations in the general level of prices were a direct cause of these contractions—a belief not supported by any widely accepted economic theory—there are only three main channels through which inflation might have contributed to the real income growth slowdown.

One channel is *the interaction of inflation with the tax system.* Federal income tax rates (and many state income tax systems) are progressive and are based on nominal, money income tax brackets. As nominal incomes rise with inflation, taxpayers are pushed into higher rate brackets and the proportion of income absorbed by personal taxation rises, even when real incomes are not changed.[44] This phenomenon,

Table 3.7 Real income per capita growth rates, personal tax rates, the business cycle, and inflation by period, 1950–1981 (percent)

Time period	Real personal disposable income per capita growth rate, $[\Delta\ln(GYDPC/PU)]\cdot100$ (1)	Personal taxes (including social insurance contributions) as a percentage of personal income, $[(GPTX + GPSIN)/GPY]\cdot100$ (2)	Personal taxes (including social insurance contributions) less transfers as a percentage of personal income less transfers, $[(GPTX + GPSIN - GPT)/(GPY - GPT)]\cdot100$ (3)	GNP gap: percentage deviation of actual from natural real GNP,[a] $[\ln(GNP72/RGNPPOT)]\cdot100$ (4)	Labor share: compensation of employees as a percentage of domestic income of corporate business, $[(GCOomp/GKY)]\cdot100$ (5)	Shift in relative price of energy: energy price inflation rate less total consumer price inflation rate,[b] $(\Delta[\ln(PU803/PU)])\cdot100$ (6)	Consumer Price Index inflation rate, $[\Delta(\ln PU)]\cdot100$ (7)
1950–1954	2.15	12.7	7.7	1.39	78.0	0.03	2.42
1955–1959	2.14	13.7	7.8	0.28	79.9	0.24	1.63
1960–1964	2.41	14.9	7.9	-0.85	79.9	-0.67	1.26
1965–1969	3.01	16.5	9.1	4.04	78.9	-1.39	3.33
1970–1974	1.92	18.0	7.8	0.43	83.8	2.60	5.93
1975–1979	1.29	18.5	5.9	-2.05	83.1	3.20	7.74
1980	-3.77	19.7	6.9	-3.12	85.1	14.9	12.7
1981	-0.15	20.3	7.5	-3.86		2.9	9.8

Sources: Computed from Citibank Economic Database unless otherwise indicated. Bracketed expressions give Citibank variable names.
a. Natural real GNP, 1972 dollars, is from Robert G. Gordon, "Inflation, Flexible Exchange Rates and the Natural Rate of Unemployment," National Bureau of Economic Research, Discussion Paper No. 708, July 1981, plus extensions.
b. Set equal to PU821 for 1953–1956 and to PU for 1950–1952.

known as "bracket creep," unambiguously lowers average after-tax, disposable personal incomes, unless the authorities take compensatory action by adjusting tax schedules.

Although the personal tax system was clearly designed for noninflationary times, the political process has responded to the bracket creep phenomenon: between 1964 and 1981 (a period of more than 110 percent inflation) Congress legislated nine changes of the federal income tax system to offset inflation-induced increases in tax rates. Prior to the 1981 tax law revisions initiated by the Reagan administration, these efforts were focused largely on raising personal exemptions and the standard deduction, leaving the basic structure of tax schedules essentially unchanged. (See Chapter 9.) As a result of these actions, the effective federal personal tax rates faced by lower income groups actually fell, and the federal income tax system became more progressive during the 1970s.[45]

Table 3.8 provides some illustrative data on how effective federal tax rates on adjusted gross income[46] changed under inflation between 1970 and 1979. The first two columns show constant dollar levels of adjusted gross incomes; because prices rose about 90 percent over the period, incomes in 1979 dollars are 190 percent of incomes in 1970 dollars. Comparison of columns 4 and 5 of the table shows how effective tax rates would have increased at all constant-dollar income levels had 1970 tax law prevailed in 1979. The escalation of effective tax rates reflects the movement of taxpayers into higher rate brackets as a result of inflation. Without any increase in real income, taxpayers with a constant adjusted gross income of 5000 1970 dollars (equal to 1.9 × 5000, or 9500, 1979 dollars) would have experienced a rate increase from 9.8 percent to 13.2 percent between 1970 and 1979. The average effective tax rates applied to adjusted gross incomes of 10,000 1970 dollars would have increased more moderately from 13.3 percent to 13.7 percent, but the rise in the tax burden would have been much sharper at the higher income levels.

As noted earlier, however, the income tax laws did not remain unaltered during the 1970s. Small downward adjustments were made directly to the scheduled rates; much larger upward adjustments were made to exemptions and deductions, which favored low- and middle-income groups. Under 1979 law the effective tax rates of all income groups were lower at the end of the period than they would have been under 1970 law, but the effective-rate relief was much greater for the $5000 and $10,000 (1970 dollars) income groups in Table 3.8, corresponding to the lower 60 percent of the distribution.

Table 3.8 Changes in effective federal income tax rates with inflation, 1970–1979

Constant adjusted gross incomes		Percentile of 1970 income distribution (approximate)	Effective tax rate (percent) on 1970 adjusted gross income (actual)	Effective tax rate (percent) on 1979 adjusted gross income	
1970 dollars	1979 dollars			Under 1970 law (hypothetical)	Under 1979 law (actual)
5,000	9,500	28	9.8	13.2	6.5
10,000	19,000	60	13.3	13.7	12.6
25,000	47,500	96	15.3	21.2	19.7
50,000	95,000	99	21.8	29.9	29.0
100,000	190,000	—	30.9	38.3	37.9

Source: Richard A. Musgrave and Peggy E. Musgrave, *Public Finance in Theory and Practice*, 3rd ed. (New York: McGraw-Hill, 1980), table 17-9, p. 387. Income distribution percentiles are from Bureau of the Census, *Current Population Reports*, Series P-60, No. 80, October 4, 1971, table 19, p. 41 (two-person, husband-wife families).

Notes: Calculations are based on a joint return, with no dependents and with deductions in excess of the standard deduction amounting to 23 percent of adjusted gross income. Adjusted gross income is approximately equal to personal income plus employee Social Security contributions and capital gains less untaxed cash transfers and other income, indirect labor compensation, and other exclusions. 1979 income equals 190 percent of 1970 income, keeping real income constant over the period.

For these groups effective income tax rates were lower in 1979 than they had been in 1970, despite the great rise in money incomes and prices. Hence, although our progressive income tax system based on nominal brackets was not formally indexed to inflation until 1985, in practice it was (differentially) indexed earlier through the political mechanism of inflation-induced discretionary adjustments by Congress. And during the 1970s, when Congress was firmly under the control of the Democratic party, such adjustments produced a more progressive system of federal income taxation. In view of the superior resources of well-heeled groups, this progress probably would not have been feasible politically under an inflation-neutral, indexed tax system requiring direct realignment of rates in order to change the distribution of tax burdens. As we shall see in Chapter 9, this pattern was reversed in 1982–1984 under President Reagan.

Despite partial "political indexing" of federal income tax rates, total personal taxes as a percentage of gross personal income rose substantially between 1950 and 1981. The subperiod data in column 2 of Table 3.7 show that the average effective rate of taxation of personal income increased from 12.7 percent in 1950–1954 to 20 percent in 1980–1981.[47] Yet much of the rise occurred prior to the big inflationary episodes during 1974–1981, implying that inflation played little or no role. This observation, based on visual inspection of personal tax rate and consumer price inflation rate data in Table 3.7, is readily confirmed by time-series regression analysis.

Regressing the average effective tax rate on personal incomes,[48] (Tax Rate) on the logarithms of nominal and real personal income per capita (GPYPC and RGPYPC, respectively) yields (with an appropriate specification for autoregressive time dependence in the residuals, e_t)

$$Tax\ Rate_t = \begin{array}{cc} -0.588^{**} & +\quad 0.013\ \ln GPYPC_t \\ (0.114) & (0.009) \end{array} \qquad (3.2)$$

$$\begin{array}{c} +\ 0.080^{**}\ \ln RGPYPC_t \\ (0.023) \end{array}$$

$$\begin{array}{cc} +\ 0.613^{**}e_t & -\ 0.403^{*}e_{t-1} \\ (0.170) & (0.168) \end{array}$$

where $\bar{R}^2 = 0.943$; standard error of regression = 0.006; Durbin-Watson = 2.25; * = significant at 0.05 level, two-tail test; and ** = significant at 0.01 level, two-tail test; for annual data, 1947–1981.

The results demonstrate clearly that the postwar growth in average personal tax rates responded little, if at all, to the inflation-fueled expansion of nominal money per capita personal income (GPYPC), but rather increased with the upward trend in *real* per capita income (RGPYPC). Over the postwar period as a whole, each 1-percent increase in real per capita personal income was accompanied, on average, by a 0.08-percentage-point increase in the effective personal income tax rate. The increase of nearly 8 percentage points in the tax burden on personal incomes, then, proceeded in step with the doubling of real per capita personal income between the late 1940s and the late 1970s.[49]

The regression of log *gross* tax revenues from personal income (ln Tax Revenues) on log *gross* nominal and log *gross* real personal income (ln GPY and ln RGPY, respectively) yields elasticity estimates supporting the same conclusion:

$$\text{ln Tax Revenues}_t \qquad\qquad (3.3)$$
$$= -10.9 + 1.017^{**} \text{ ln GPY}_t + 0.432^{**} \text{ ln RGPY}_t$$
$$\quad (1.19)\ (0.059) \qquad\qquad (0.116)$$
$$+ 0.730^{**}e_t - 0.543^{**}e_{t-1}$$
$$\quad (0.150) \qquad (0.146)$$

where $\bar{R}^2 = 0.998$; standard error of regression = 0.042; Durbin-Watson = 2.30; and ** = significant at 0.01 level, two-tail test; for annual data, 1947–1981.

These results show that the elasticity of personal tax revenues to nominal personal income (GPY) is essentially 1.0, implying a negligible long-run escalation of real tax burdens due to inflation. Instead, the postwar expansion of government revenue out of personal income was raised out of increments to real income (RGPY). The parameter estimate for RGPY means that about 0.43 of each 1-percent increase in real personal income went to taxes[50]—in other words, that the elasticity of real tax revenues with respect to real personal income was on the order of 1.43.

A look at postwar trends in transfer-adjusted tax burdens confirms conclusion that average disposable incomes have not been adversely affected by the interaction of inflation and our unindexed tax system. As noted in Chapter 1, transfers are usefully viewed as negative taxes, and therefore the relevant tax rate for economic analysis is personal taxes less transfers as a percentage of personal income less transfers.[51] Data by subperiod on transfer-adjusted personal tax rates are reported in column 3 of Table 3.7. Clearly, the postwar time path of the net-of-transfer tax burden on net-of-transfer personal incomes bears no systematic connection to the escalation of inflation. Indeed, despite an increase of many hundred percent in prices and money incomes during the last thirty years, the average transfer-adjusted tax burden was lower at the end of the period than it had been during the early 1950s.

Income from employment comprises about 70 percent of total personal income, and so variations in the former are an important determinant of economic well-being. A second channel through which inflation might have influenced the slowdown of real disposable income growth, then, is via *the connection of price rises to the distribution of income between labor and capital,* known as the "functional" income distribution.

It was once believed that during inflations wages lagged and profits swelled, yielding declines in the income share of labor.[52] Yet the postwar experience suggests that, if anything, just the opposite has been true. The most reliable and comparable data are for corporate businesses,[53] and the fifth column of Table 3.7 shows trends in the labor share of income for that sector. Clearly, there was no tendency for the employee share of corporate domestic income to fall in step with the great acceleration of prices in the 1970s and early 1980s. On the contrary, given that the labor and capital shares of corporate income move inversely, the data in Table 3.7 suggest that the share of profits rather than the share of wages may have been the victim of escalating postwar inflation. (This important point is pursued further in the next section.)

A third way in which inflation may be connected directly to erosion of real disposable income growth rates is through *relative price effects.* To the extent that upward surges in the general price level originate with sharp shifts in relative prices, disadvantaging the broad mass of American consumers, inflation will have an adverse association with real income performance. The most important instances of such relative price changes have been the OPEC-induced upward shifts in the international price of energy, which imposed large international redistributions of income away from energy importers to energy exporters. The dominant figures in column 6 of Table 3.7, showing the average increases in energy prices relative to the total CPI for five-year subperiods, are those for the years in which the big OPEC shocks occurred: energy price inflation was 15 percentage points higher than the total CPI inflation rate in 1974, and 12 and 14 points higher in 1979 and 1980, respectively. Although the averages shown in Table 3.7 obscure year-to-year fluctuations, the subperiod data nonetheless suggest that the real income slowdown of the 1970s and early 1980s may have had less to do with inflation *per se* than with the redistributions of income away from energy consumers generated by the underlying bulges in energy prices.

This and earlier observations are evaluated more rigorously by regressing the annual growth rate of per capita real personal disposable income, denoted RGYDPC, on the energy-price-shift term, the current and lagged inflation rate, and the current and lagged state of the business cycle (measured by GNP gap terms):[54]

$$RGYDPC_t \qquad\qquad\qquad\qquad\qquad\qquad\qquad (3.4)$$

$$= 2.29^{**} \quad -0.015 \text{ Inflation}_t \quad -0.049 \text{ Inflation}_{t-1}$$
$$\;\;(0.437) \quad\;\; (0.149) \qquad\qquad\;\; (0.167)$$

$$+ \; 0.031 \text{ Inflation}_{t-2} - 0.193^{**} \text{ Energy Price Shift}_t$$
$$\quad (0.124) \qquad\qquad\qquad (0.065)$$

$$+ \; 0.714^{**} \text{ GNP Gap}_t - 0.536^{**} \text{ GNP Gap}_{t-1}$$
$$\quad (0.110) \qquad\qquad\quad (0.160)$$

$$+ \; 0.214e_t - 0.115e_{t-1}$$
$$\quad (0.187) \quad\;\; (0.160)$$

where $\bar{R}^2 = 0.786$; standard error of regression $= 1.04$; Durbin-Watson $= 2.11$; and ** = significant at 0.01 level, two-tail test; for annual data, 1950–1981.

The regression results indicate clearly that general consumer price inflation had negligible influence on per capita real disposable income growth rates. The main source of inflation-induced real income declines was the international redistribution of income from energy consumers to energy producers following the OPEC oil supply shocks. On average, each 1-percent change in the relative price of energy (in the CPI) generated a decline in the per capita real personal disposable income growth rate of almost one-fifth of a percentage point.[55] The other important source of real income slowdowns was general contractions of output: each sustained 1-percentage-point shortfall of actual from natural real output produced a decline of about 0.18 percent in the per capita real disposable income growth rate (0.714 − 0.536).

In view of these results, the collapse of real disposable income performance in 1980–1981 and earlier comes as no surprise. On top of the second great oil shock of 1979–1980, back-to-back policy-induced recessions at the end of the Carter administration and the beginning of the Reagan administration produced GNP gaps of −3.1 and −3.9 percent in 1980 and 1981, respectively. These contractions alone depressed the average real income growth rates during 1980–1981 by about 1.65 percent. The effects of the recessions amount to nearly four-tenths of the mean 1980–1981 growth rate decline of 1.96 percent, or (−3.77 − 0.15)/2 (see Table 3.7), calculated net of the trend growth rate of 2.3 percent per annum implied by the constant in equation (3.4): −1.65/(−1.96 − 2.3) = 0.39. The remaining six-tenths of the real personal income slowdown in this period is accounted for largely by energy price shocks. As in the 1974-1975 episode of major real income erosion, inflation of the overall price level played no significant role.[56]

External energy price shocks and the largely intentional, policy-induced output contractions designed to fight inflation are, then, the keys to understanding the real personal income growth rate slowdowns of the 1970s and early 1980s. Contrary to political rhetoric and popular perceptions (about which more will be said later), inflation *per se* had almost nothing to do with the average real income experiences of American households.

But what about the impact of inflation on corporate incomes?

3.5   Inflation and Corporate Profitability

In the previous section we saw that the labor share of domestic corporate income rose by 5 to 6 percentage points from the late 1960s to the early 1980s (see Table 3.7, column 5). Implied in the increase is a corresponding fall in capital's share during this period of high and rising inflation rates. The impact of inflation on corporate incomes and on rates of return is worth examining in some detail.

Table 3.9 reports data on the two most revealing measures of pretax and posttax corporate profitability: (1) the share of profits in the domestic income of American private corporations and (2) the rate of return on private capital (that is, profits as a percentage of the net value of fixed, nonresidential corporate capital stock).[57] The profits data are inclusive of net interest payments[58] and have been adjusted for true capital depreciation (using the Commerce Department's replacement cost basis) and for artificial "inventory profits" recorded by firms during periods of rapidly rising prices (by converting all inventory valuations to a last in/first out, or LIFO, basis). These standard

Table 3.9 Profit shares, rates of return, corporate tax rates, real stock prices, and the business cycle by period, 1950–1981

Time period	Pretax profit share (profits with inventory valuation and capital consumption adjustments plus net interest as percentage of corporate domestic income), [(GKJVA + GKINT)/GKY] · 100 (1)	After-tax profit share (profits with inventory valuation and capital consumption adjustments plus net interest less taxes as percentage of corporate domestic income), [(GKJVA + GKINT − GPTAX)/GKY] · 100 (2)	Pretax rate of return (profits with inventory valuation and capital consumption adjustments plus net interest as percentage of net stock of fixed nonresidential private corporate capital, [(GKJVA + GKINT)/K2] · 100 (3)	After-tax rate of return (profits with inventory valuation and capital consumption adjustments plus net interest less taxes as a percentage of net stock of fixed nonresidential private corporate capital, [(GKJVA + GKINT − GPTAX)/K2] · 100] (4)	Corporate tax rate (percent), [GPTAX/(GKJVA + GKINT)] · 100 (5)	Percent idle capacity in manufacturing, Federal Reserve Board Index, 100 − IPXCA (6)	Real stock prices (500 common stocks, 1967 = 100) FPS6US/PU (7)
1950–1954	22.0	9.3	19.7	8.3	57.8	15.3	33.2
1955–1959	20.1	9.5	16.9	8.0	52.8	17.3	60.8
1960–1964	20.0	10.7	18.0	9.7	45.7	18.4	80.4
1965–1969	21.1	12.3	19.8	11.5	42.0	11.8	99.4
1970–1974	16.2	8.8	13.1	7.1	43.8	17.5	81.9
1975–1979	16.9	9.5	12.6	7.1	43.7	19.1	57.4
1980	14.7	8.2	NA	NA	44.3	20.9	52.3
1981	15.2	9.6	NA	NA	36.9	21.6	51.1

Sources: Computed from Citibank Economic Data Base unless otherwise indicated. Bracketed expressions give Citibank variable names. K2 (net capital stock) is from John P. Musgrave, "Fixed Capital Stock in the U.S.: Revised Estimates," *Survey of Current Business* 61 (February 1981), 58.

adjustments put the profits data on a comparable footing by ironing out variations in corporate accounting practices. The resulting series yield good estimates of the genuine economic income of private corporate capital.[59]

Columns 1 and 3 of Table 3.9 show that the pretax profit share and pretax rate of return declined sharply between the 1960s and the 1970s. The aggregate corporate profit share dropped from 20-to-22-percent range prevailing in the 1950s and 1960s to the 15-to-17-percent range of the 1970s and early 1980s. The slide in the aggregate pretax rate of return was also 5 to 6 percentage points—from the 17-to-20-point range in the 1950s and 1960s to the 12-to-13-point range in the 1970s. (At the time of this writing, data on the net capital stocks necessary to compute rates of return after 1979 were not available.) In view of the adjustments made to the raw profits data, such declines almost certainly are indicators of genuine squeeze on corporate profitability, rather than a statistical artifact of shifts in corporate accounting procedures.

The sources of the profit erosion since the 1960s have been a topic of intense analysis and considerable speculation.[60] Our concern here, however, is connections between the profits dive and inflation. Although the deterioration of corporate profitability clearly does correspond in time to the big acceleration of prices, in principle there are no persuasive reasons why an inflationary environment should favor labor in wage bargaining, hinder firms from passing increased costs onto prices, or otherwise squeeze profit margins *before tax*. Moreover, as the data on capacity utilization in the next-to-last column of Table 3.9 show, the profits slide also corresponds to the deterioration of the real macroeconomy following the peak achieved during the long boom of the 1960s.[61]

Indeed the regression results in Table 3.10 indicate that after adjustments are made for business cycle fluctuations—movements in idle capacity and the growth rate of labor productivity—inflation bears essentially no connection to either the pretax profit share or the pretax rate of return in the private corporate sector of the American economy. Instead, the dive in profits since the 1960s (and hence the corresponding rise in the aggregate labor income share) was driven largely by low capacity utilization and the associated slowdown in labor productivity. Profits fell relative to labor income during this period of repeated recessions because, as Walter Oi observed more than twenty years ago,[62] firms treat their skilled, experienced workers, in whom much training is invested, as a quasi-fixed factor, or near-capital good, in the production process. Consequently, when demand contracts, idle (physical) capacity rises, and corporate income falls, firms tend to be slow to shed labor ("labor hoarding"), and as a result labor costs fall at a slower rate than corporate income. This produces a decline in labor productivity (output per labor hour) and a squeeze on the share of profits.[63] The process is reversed during the first phases of expansions. As the utilization of physical capacity rises, firms are slow to take on new workers (given the high fixed costs associated with hiring and training), and the utilization rate of the existing labor force increases, thereby generating rapid productivity increases and a surge in the share of profits and the rate of return.[64]

The erosion of pretax profits since the 1960s, then, had little to do with mysterious exogenous trends or, more importantly, with escalating inflation. Rather, to the extent to which it reflects identifiable, systematic economic forces, the profits dive was the consequence of repeated recessions and generally sluggish real macroeconomic activity throughout the 1970s and into the 1980s.[65]

The role of inflation in the behavior of *after-tax* corporate profitability, however, is a different story. The interaction of inflation and the corporate tax structure can have a powerful impact on the after-tax profit share and rate of return experienced by firms. First, depreciation expenses traditionally allowed by corporate tax law were based on the historical cost valuation of capital assets, and the value of such tax deductions is continually eroded by inflation.[66] As corporate revenues rise with inflation, depreciation deductions fixed in historical dollars shelter an ever-declining fraction of revenue from taxation. Second, most firms traditionally used first in/first out (FIFO) inventory accounting methods, by which materials used in current production are assumed to have been acquired at the prices of the oldest items in the inventory stock. During inflations, materials costs are therefore understated and book profits rise by a corresponding amount. The book profits are taxed at full rates, thereby raising the corporate tax bite and lowering the after-tax corporate income. Firms are permitted by the Internal Revenue Service to use last in/first out (LIFO) accounting, in which the recording of inventory appreciation as profit is avoided by pricing all materials at the costs of the newest items in stock; one of the great mysteries of corporate behavior during the inflationary 1970s is why the movement from FIFO to LIFO bookkeeping methods was so slow.[67] In any case, the impact of inflation through this channel on the corporate tax burden, and hence on after-

Table 3.10 Response of corporate profitability and real stock prices to inflation and the business cycle, annual 1949–1979/1981

Variable	Pretax profit share (1)	After-tax profit share (2)	Pretax rate of return (3)	After-tax rate of return (4)	In real stock prices (5)
Constant	23.247**	10.707**	22.173**	10.377**	-0.755*
	(1.726)	(1.447)	(2.991)	(2.586)	(0.290)
Inflation rate					
t	0.017	-0.298**	-0.002	-0.302*	-0.013
	(0.107)	(0.093)	(0.153)	(0.140)	(0.010)
$t-1$	-0.0101	0.037	0.029	0.057	-0.005
	(0.120)	(0.118)	(0.138)	(0.162)	(0.009)
Percent idle capacity					
t	-0.162**	-0.080	-0.239**	-0.120*	
	(0.056)	(0.050)	(0.065)	(0.059)	
$t-1$	-0.056	-0.141*	-0.076	-0.140	
	(0.078)	(0.068)	(0.097)	(0.104)	

Labor productivity, percentage rate of change [ln(LOUTB$_t$/LOUTB$_{t-1}$) · 100]

t	0.519**	0.396*	0.597**	0.377
	(0.180)	(0.171)	(0.200)	(0.194)
$t-1$	0.160	0.115	0.243	0.149
	(0.123)	(0.114)	(0.141)	(0.122)
Trend (1948 = 1, 1981 = 34)	−0.123	0.147	−0.163	0.107
	(0.069)	(0.051)	(0.133)	(0.081)
After-tax rate of return				
t				0.045*
				(0.019)
$t-1$				0.020
				(0.019)
GLS autoregressive coefficients				
ρ_1	0.588**	0.469*	0.760**	0.636*
	(0.199)	(0.202)	(0.190)	(0.302)
$\bar{R}^2$	0.861	0.659	0.870	0.735
Standard error of regression	1.016	0.912	1.243	1.024
Durbin-Watson	1.638	1.635	1.608	1.607

Notes: See earlier tables for sources and definitions of variables. Standard errors appear in parentheses.
* Significant at 0.05 level, two-tail test.
** Significant at 0.01 level, two-tail test.

tax profits, has been large. As late as 1979, for example, "unnecessary" FIFO inventory profits artificially raised the corporate tax base
by 43.1 billion dollars and the corporate tax bill by about 19.8 billion
dollars, assuming the statutory marginal corporate tax rate of 46 percent. Looked at in isolation, this factor alone lowered the after-tax
corporate profit share by 1.6 percentage points and the rate of return
by 1.2 points.

On the other hand, there are countervailing forces associated with
inflation. Higher inflation leads to higher nominal interest rates,
which, because nominal interest payments are tax deductible, lowers
the after-tax burden of corporate debt and the effective corporate tax
rate, thereby offsetting some of the inflation-induced drain on after-
tax profits.[68] Firms were not slow to exploit the attractiveness of debt
financing of new investment in an inflationary environment. By the
mid-1970s interest deductibility had reduced effective corporate tax
rates below what they would have been by 15 to 20 percentage points,
as compared to 6 to 7 points a decade earlier. Moreover, purposeful
government actions, many taken in response to and in anticipation of
sustained inflation, also softened the corporate tax bite. Prior to President Reagan's big corporate tax reduction package of 1981, depreciation allowances were liberalized by legislation enacted in 1954, 1962,
and again in 1971. The basic marginal corporate rate was reduced in
1964 from 52 to 48 percent. After increasing as a result of the temporary Vietnam surcharge in 1968–1970, this rate had been reduced
further to 46 percent by the end of the 1970s. The investment tax
credit was introduced in 1962, liberalized in 1964, and made even
more generous in 1975.

The impact of these contrasting forces—inflation-induced tax increases caused by depreciation erosion and nominal inventory profits
on the one hand, and interest deductibility, liberalized depreciation
schedules, investment credits, and rate reductions on the other—are
summarized by the data on average effective corporate tax rates in
column 5 of Table 3.9. The data show that effective corporate rates
generally declined over the 1950s and 1960s. In other words, tax
policy during this period of moderate inflation more than offset the
upward pressure of rising prices on effective rates and actually succeeded in driving rates sharply downward. Because effective rates are
given by the proportional difference between pretax and posttax
profit shares or rates of return, trends in the former are a convenient
summary of relative trends in the latter. Hence, policy-induced reductions in the effective rate of corporate taxation during an era of

moderate inflation are the primary reason that after-tax profit shares and rates of return rose between the 1950s and the 1960s while pretax profitability was comparatively stable. (Compare columns 2 and 4 of Table 3.9 to columns 1 and 3.)

By the end of the 1960s, however, inflation was escalating fast enough to swamp the value of interest deductions, investment credits, and depreciation liberalizations, and effective corporate rates floated upward until the big corporate tax relief legislation was pushed through Congress by the Reagan administration in 1981.[69] Consequently, after-tax corporate profitability deteriorated more rapidly than pretax profitability. This observation is reinforced by the regression results in Table 3.10, suggesting that the after-tax profit share and rate of return, in contrast with the pretax indicators, were adversely affected by extra inflation as well as by falling productivity and capacity utilization. Given an increase of about 6 percentage points in prevailing inflation rates between the late 1960s and the late 1970s, the regression results suggest that perhaps as much as 1.8 percentage points of the decade-long slide of 6 points in corporate profitability might be tied to accelerating prices ($-0.3 \cdot 6 = -1.8$). The remaining, and larger, fraction of the profits dive was largely the consequence of rising idle capacity and falling labor productivity—that is, poor real macroeconomic performance. Ironically, much of the slowdown in real activity was intentionally created by contractive monetary and fiscal policies designed to defeat inflation. It seems obvious that assaulting the corporate tax code rather than the macroeconomy would have been a more effective and less painful way to boost after-tax corporate profitability.

The behavior of real stock prices over the postwar period, shown in the last column of Table 3.9, loosely parallels the movements in after-tax profitability, but the trends are substantially more pronounced. Between 1949 and 1968, when the market peaked, real (CPI-deflated) stock prices more than tripled, growing at an average compounded annual rate of 7.8 percent, compared to a corresponding growth rate of about 4 percent for the real GNP. It was during this era that common stocks acquired the reputation of being an ideal hedge against inflation. A portfolio of common stocks clearly was much more than this; in retrospect it is hard to imagine a better passive investment vehicle.

At the end of the 1960s, however, the market began a long decline, which lasted until the onset of the great bull market of 1982–1987. Between 1968 and 1981 real stock prices plunged at an average compounded annual rate of 5.4 percent; this decline far exceeded the corresponding slowdown of from 4 to 2.4 percent in the average annual real output growth rate. By the end of the 1970s the price-deflated market value of a diversified portfolio of 500 common stocks was no higher than it had been in the mid-1950s. Over no comparable period, including the Great Depression, had stock prices performed so dismally. The market's performance during this period and over the subsequent years of stock price rises has mystified academic economists and Wall Street financial analysts; no one has devised a convincing story to explain it.[70]

It has been known for some time that the inflation rate and stock market performance are negatively correlated.[71] Martin Feldstein and his students have traced this correlation to the post-1960s erosion of after-tax corporate profitability induced in part by the interaction of inflation and the corporate tax structure.[72] The last regression in Table 3.10 shows that the negative association between real stock prices and inflation does indeed vanish in the presence of the after-tax rate of return.[73] Yet the slide of 5 to 6 percentage points in after-tax corporate profitability explains only four-tenths or so of the observed decline of 60 to 70 percent in real stock prices between 1968 and 1979.[74] And, as the regressions discussed previously suggest, less than 2 percentage points (that is, less than one-third) of the after-tax profits dive is attributable to inflation. It follows that the contribution of escalating inflation to the poor stock market performance of the 1970s was comparatively minor, probably accounting for not much more than one-seventh of the great plunge in real share prices.

How one views levels of corporate profitability, or even stock market prices, prevailing after the great inflations of the 1970s partly depends on which past period is taken as a point of reference. Compared to those of the 1950s, after-tax profit shares at the end of the 1970s were not unusual, and after-tax corporate rates of return were off only a percentage point or so. By 1979 the price-deflated market value of a diversified portfolio of common stocks purchased in 1949 had grown by more than 120 percent, which represents an average compounded annual growth rate of 2.7 percent. An investor who made a one-time purchase in the late 1940s would have little to cheer about thirty years later, but little cause to despair either. By contrast, investors entering the stock market in the latter half of the 1960s— and that includes a great many institutional, pension-fund investors whose decisions affected the subsequent economic well-being of a large number of middle-income citizens—typically experienced a genuine catastrophe during the ensuing dozen years. Corporate profitability also deteriorated after the 1960s, but the decline, though substantial, was much less dramatic in magnitude than the corresponding collapse of the stock market.

It now seems clear that the recipe for the high after-tax corporate profitability and rapidly rising real equity share prices realized during the 1960s was the conjunction of brisk growth, little idle capacity, and moderate inflation rates that did not undermine pro-investment tax policies legislated by Congress. We have seen that the contribution of inflation to the erosion of after-tax profit margins and real stock prices was channeled indirectly through the corporate tax structure, and that it was relatively small in magnitude. Nonetheless, these effects were not negligible and must be listed among the tangible consequences of inflation.

But have inflation-induced declines in profitability and equity share returns been translated into a decline in saving and investment? I turn to this important question next.

3.6   Saving, Investment, and Inflation

Since the onset of stagflation in the mid-1970s, a great deal of attention has been given to the impact of inflation on saving and investment, which in turn affects the capital intensity of production and, therefore, the rate of economic growth. Because nominal interest receipts are taxable and nominal interest payments are tax deductible, at high inflation rates the federal income tax system would appear to discourage household saving for future consumption and to encourage current consumption and consumer borrowing.[75] And for a fixed tax rate these (dis)incentive effects become stronger as the inflation rate rises.

Consider the following simple example of a middle-income family[76] facing a marginal income tax rate, τ, of 0.3. The net-of-tax nominal yield on extra saving is equal to the nominal interest rate, i, times 1 minus the marginal tax rate: $i(1 - \tau)$, or $i(1 - 0.3)$ in the example. Subtracting the inflation rate, $\dot{p}$, gives the net-of-tax real return to extra saving: $i(1 - \tau) - \dot{p}$. As Table 3.11 illustrates, even if nominal interest rates fully reflect inflation and the pretax real interest rate holds at, say, 3 percent, the after-tax marginal real return to savers falls as inflation rises.[77] Indeed, at the effective tax rates faced by many middle-income households, posttax real interest rate costs for borrowers and yields for savers actually are *negative* at higher rates of

Table 3.11 Interest costs and yields (percent) at various
inflation rates for households facing a marginal tax rate,
τ of 0.3

Inflation rate, $\dot{p}$	Nominal interest cost/yield, $i = \dot{p} + 3\%$	Real net-of-tax interest cost/yield, $i(1 - \tau) - \dot{p}$
2.5	5.5	1.35
5	8	0.60
7.5	10.5	−0.15
10	13	−0.90

inflation (see the figures in Table 3.11 for inflation rates of 7.5% and 10%). Conventional saving, which can be viewed as an expenditure for future consumption, therefore would appear to be discouraged in favor of current consumption by the interaction of inflation and the tax system. Moreover, inflation induced declines in the after-tax cost of borrowed funds would appear to encourage debt financing of consumer durables and especially the mortgage debt financing of residential housing. Although durable goods and housing are both forms of "saving" in that they are "consumed" for many periods after the date of purchase, and although housing is an important asset in the portfolios of middle- and upper-income households, neither durable goods nor housing investments add to the pool of loanable funds available to finance expansions of America's productive capital.

For these reasons some economists, most prominently Martin Feldstein,[78] advocated abandoning the conventional pro-investment prescription of "easy money" (designed to lower interest rates and reduce the cost of funds to investors, thereby encouraging the accumulation of plant and equipment) and a "tight fiscal position" (designed to reduce deficits and limit consumer demand). Instead, Feldstein urged a policy of "tight money" that would lean hard against inflation and substantially increase real net-of-tax interest rates, combined with tax concessions to business borrowers that would offset the higher cost of funds. This mix would discourage housing construction and the credit-financed purchase of consumer durables while increasing the flow of investment funds into new plant and equipment.[79]

These policy prescriptions and the associated assumptions about the connections among inflation, taxation, saving, and investment bear a marked resemblance to the macroeconomic policies pursued (*de facto*) by the Reagan administration during 1981–1982 and the less euphoric economic rationalizations offered on their behalf.[80] Although both inflation and effective tax rates on personal income did increase considerably after the mid-1960s (see Table 3.7 and the earlier discussion), empirical data on savings and investment rates presented later in this chapter give little or no support to the behavioral assumptions underlying these policy views.[81]

Surprisingly, the data on personal saving as a percentage of disposable personal income in the first column of Table 3.12 show that household savings rates have not exhibited much variation around the postwar (1949–1981) mean of 6.76 percent. (Nor did savings rates respond to the Reagan tax cuts and disinflation after 1981, but discussion of the 1982–1984 experience is deferred to Chapter 9.) Personal saving out of disposable income in 1980–1981, when inflation averaged 11.3 percent per annum and the average effective income tax rate had reached a post-war high of 13.8 percent, was almost identical to the household savings rate in 1960–1964, when inflation averaged only 1.3 percent per annum and the effective income tax rate averaged about 10.9 percent.[82] During 1970–1974, when the inflation and personal income tax rates were also relatively high, the savings rate was more than a percentage point higher than during 1950–1954, when, by later standards, inflation and tax rates were relatively low (and after-tax savings yields were comparatively high). The main lesson to be learned from these data, however, is that savings rates (and, hence, propensities to consume) are remarkably stable in the face of postwar variations in inflation, taxes, interest rates, and so on.[83]

More systematic evidence supporting this conclusion appears in the first column of Table 3.13, which reports the regression of the personal savings rate on the current and lagged inflation rate and on the current and lagged state of the business cycle as measured by the percentage deviation of actual real output from natural real output (the so-called GNP gap).[84] The regression results reinforce the point that savings behavior has not been adversely affected by inflation.[85] Both current and lagged inflation are statistically insignificant and have positive estimated coefficients. Nor does household saving appear to respond strongly to the business cycle, although saving does show signs of having risen after expansions and having fallen after contractions (with a 1-period lag). This result is consistent with Milton Friedman's "permanent income" hypothesis that households maintain a steady consumption level by reducing saving when there

Table 3.12   Personal saving rates and private investment rates, by period, 1950–1981

Time period	Personal saving as a percentage of personal disposable income, (GPSAV/GYD) · 100 (1)	Gross real private nonfarm residential investment as a percentage of real GNP, (GIRU72/GNP72) · 100 (2)	Net real private nonfarm residential investment as a percentage of real GNP, ([net investment/ (GDIRU/100)]/GNP72) · 100 (3)	Gross real private nonresidential fixed investment as a percentage of real GNP, (GIN72/GNP72) · 100 (4)	Net real private nonresidential fixed investment as a percentage of real GNP, ([net investment/ (GDIN/100)]/GNP72) · 100 (5)
1950–1954	6.80	4.66	3.06	9.04	2.83
1955–1959	6.81	4.56	2.88	9.25	2.52
1960–1964	6.00	4.60	2.88	9.07	2.46
1965–1969	7.12	3.88	2.25	10.6	4.14
1970–1974	7.95	4.36	2.65	10.5	3.36
1975–1979	6.67	3.83	2.10	10.4	2.61
1980	5.82	3.01	1.27	11.3	3.00
1981	6.42	2.80	1.05	11.4	3.14

Sources: Computed from Citibank Economic Database, unless otherwise indicated. Bracketed expressions give Citibank variable names. Net investment data are from *Economic Report of the President*, February 1982 and February 1984, table B-16; and *Survey of Current Business* 62 (July 1982), table 5.2.

are transitory income shortfalls and increasing saving when there are transitory rises in income.[86]

Although the interaction of inflation and the personal income tax system unquestionably affects after-tax interest costs and yields, thereby reducing the rate at which households can substitute future for current consumption, aggregate personal saving has not responded to these forces. The reasons are not difficult to understand. To the extent that inflation erodes the real value of savings accounts and other forms of wealth, rising prices actually may stimulate households to increase their savings rates as they attempt to restore the value of their net worth. For example, among people who have target levels of retirement income, an inflation-induced decline in the net real rate of return to saving (or for that matter a decline in the return to savings from any source) will tend to raise the propensity to save. Conversely, a rise in the net rate of return to saving caused, say, by a substantial decline in inflation may actually stimulate households to reduce the fraction of disposable income saved, because retirement income goals can then be met with less current saving effort. In other words, the so-called income effect of decreased savings yields, which makes greater saving necessary to finance a given level of future consumption, is opposite in sign to the so-called substitution effect, which, as noted earlier, increases the attractiveness of current consumption relative to future consumption. The empirical evidence in Tables 3.12 and 3.13 indicates strongly that the forces favoring personal consumption and the forces favoring personal saving have offset each other in the postwar United States, leaving a null association between inflation and aggregate personal savings rates.[87] The interaction of inflation and our tax system has indeed penalized savers, especially small savers, and on equity grounds it is correct to argue that we should tax only real savings yields or, for that matter, increments to inflation-adjusted, real income from any source.[88] But such changes are not likely to increase substantially household savings rates.

Given that the National Income and Product Account (NIPA) concept of personal savings includes net investment in owner-occupied dwellings, it remains possible that the interaction of inflation and the personal income tax system (in particular, the tax deductibility of mortgage interest payments) has nonetheless increased the flow of resources into the residential sector at the expense of investment to enchance the stock of plant and equipment. Columns 2 and 3 of Table 3.13 show postwar data on gross and net[89] real private nonfarm resi-

Table 3.13 Response of savings and investment rates to inflation and the business cycle, Annual 1949–1981

Variable	Personal savings as a percentage of disposable personal income (1)	Gross real private nonfarm residential investment as a percentage of real GNP (2)	Net real private nonfarm residential investment as a percentage of real GNP (3)	Gross real private nonfarm nonresidential fixed investment as a percentage of real GNP (4)	Net real private nonfarm nonresidential fixed investment as a percentage of real GNP (5)	Ratio of net investment in nonfarm residential capital to net investment in plants and equipment [(column 3/column 5) · 100] (6)
Constant	6.670**	4.796**	3.137**	8.227**	2.041**	136.0**
	(0.356)	(0.344)	(0.352)	(0.135)	(0.131)	(8.46)
Inflation rate						
t	0.034	−0.083*	−0.084*	0.073*	0.028	−5.36**
	(0.067)	(0.034)	(0.034)	(0.027)	(0.020)	(1.64)
$t − 1$	0.013	−0.102**	−0.099**	0.037	−0.012	−1.68
	(0.069)	(0.030)	(0.030)	(0.026)	(0.022)	(1.48)

Percentage GNP gap

t	−0.023	0.031	0.051	0.148**	0.228**	−6.00**
	(0.376)	(0.030)	(0.029)	(0.021)	(0.017)	(1.45)
$t-1$	0.122	−0.093**	−0.094**	0.056*	0.080**	−3.82*
	(0.372)	(0.029)	(0.029)	(0.021)	(0.017)	(1.39)
Trend (1948 = 1, 1981 = 34)		0.0086	0.0064	0.063**	0.040**	−0.75
		(0.021)	(0.021)	(0.012)	(0.010)	(0.63)
GLS autoregressive coefficients						
ρ_1	0.350	0.574**	0.585**	0.600**	0.640**	0.491*
	(0.192)	(0.196)	(0.198)	(0.139)	(0.124)	(0.20)
ρ_2				−0.499**	−0.362**	−0.353*
				(0.107)	(0.089)	(0.14)
R^2	0.257	0.766	0.784	0.933	0.948	0.852
Standard error of regression	0.790	0.317	0.313	0.230	0.171	14.1
Durbin-Watson	1.765	1.725	1.765	1.306	1.749	1.83

Notes: See earlier tables for sources and definitions of variables. Standard errors appear in parentheses. Percentage GNP gap is positive during expansions, negative during contractions.
* Significant at 0.05 level, two-tail test.
** Significant at 0.01 level, two-tail test.

dential investment as a percentage of real GNP. Obviously there is no clear association between the residential investment share of GNP and inflation. In fact, despite a secular increase in inflation rates from the mid-1960s to 1980, both gross and net investment rates in the housing sector declined steadily, with but a brief interruption in 1970–1974.[90]

The decline is even more striking when viewed in comparison to trends in nonresidential fixed investment rates (new plant and equipment), which are shown in columns 4 and 5 of Table 3.12. During the first subperiod in Table 3.12, 1950–1954, gross real residential investment expenditure was just over half of gross real nonresidential investment expenditure ($0.52 = 4.66/9.04$). By the early 1980s this ratio had fallen to about one-quarter ($0.25 = 2.9/11.4$). The decline of housing relative to net investment expenditures is still sharper. Net real nonfarm residential investment actually exceeded net investment in plant and equipment from the first half of the 1950s through the mid-1960s. But with the escalation of inflation thereafter the ratio began to fall, and it stood at 0.4 ($1.16/2.78$) by 1980–1981.

The regression results in columns 2 and 3 of Table 3.13 indicate that the fall in the share of resources allocated to the housing sector does not simply reflect an exogenous trend, but rather was conditioned by the business cycle and, more strongly, by inflation. The share of GNP invested in housing appears to have risen with initial expansions of actual (relative to natural) real output, with a more than compensating bounceback the following year. The response of residential investment to inflation was much greater and indicates unambiguously that price accelerations depressed the flow of resources into housing construction. After two years each extra percentage point of inflation tended to lower the gross residential investment share of GNP by about 0.185 percent ($-0.083 - 0.102$) and to lower the net investment share by approximately the same magnitude ($-0.084 - 0.099$).

The bias in favor of homebuilding written into our tax structure, therefore, was not strengthened in practice by inflation. Although inflation-induced high nominal interest rates reduced the net real cost of mortgage financing, other factors overrode this incentive to invest in housing. During high-inflation years interest rate ceilings on deposits imposed by banking regulations (in particular, the Federal Reserve System's Regulation Q) stimulated an enormous flight of funds from the savings and loan institutions that finance the bulk of American residential mortgages (disintermediation), thereby reducing the supply of mortgage funds. During many high-inflation periods mortgages were simply unobtainable, even at officially quoted (and very high) mortgage interest rates. Moreover, the convention prevailing until recently that home mortgage contracts be written with *level* nominal payments meant that the real payback on mortgage debt was heavily "front loaded" in periods of high inflation. As a result, great numbers of potential homebuyers were discouraged from entering the housing market, and others were dissuaded from taking on new mortgages to upgrade their housing.[91] Finally, because much of the extra inflation of the late 1970s and early 1980s originated in the dramatic upward movements in the relative price of energy, an increasing fraction of new housing construction during these high-inflation years was in the form of smaller, more fuel efficient, and relatively cheaper dwellings. As a result of these factors, inflation was a powerful force in reducing the gross and net share of residential investment in GNP.

As we saw earlier, inflation erodes the real value of depreciation allowances under an unindexed tax system and, because of inventory accounting practices, raises nominal "book" profits, which together increase the corporate tax burden and lower the after-tax rate of return on corporate investments. Yet inflation also lowers the net-of-tax real cost of borrowed investment funds to firms, and, as the regression results just discussed indicate, on balance has depressed the flow of investment to housing. Therefore it is difficult to say a priori what impact inflation has had on the rate of investment in new plant and equipment.[92] Empirical evidence in columns 4 and 5 of Tables 3.12 and 3.13 on gross and net real private nonresidential fixed investment as a percentage of real GNP gives no support to the view that inflation lowered the capital intensity of production in the United States during the postwar period. The data in Table 3.12 show that the gross real nonresidential investment share of GNP grew by 1.5 percentage points between the early 1950s and the late 1960s (from 9 to 10.6 percent) and had grown by almost another full percentage point (to 11.4 percent) by 1980–1981. The pattern for net nonresidential investment—that is, investment above that necessary to offset deterioration of the existing capital stock—exhibits no such upward trend, but it also appears not to have been adversely affected by rising inflation rates. The net nonresidential investment share of GNP peaked at over 4 percent during the 1964–1969 boom years, and it stood no lower during the high-inflation late 1970s and early 1980s than it had during the low-inflation late 1950s and early 1960s.[93]

These patterns are perhaps more convincingly demonstrated by the regression results in columns 4 and 5 of Table 3.13. Net of (upward) trend, gross nonresidential investment expenditure as a percentage of GNP has a moderately positive association with the contemporaneous inflation rate, whereas neither current nor lagged inflation shows any association with the net nonresidential investment share of GNP. More important, expenditures on new plant and equipment are strongly procyclical, rising during expansions and falling during contractions. After two years the gross nonresidential investment share of GNP falls more than one-fifth of a percentage point for each 1 percent that actual real GNP lies below natural real GNP (0.148 + 0.056). The net nonresidential investment estimates imply an even stronger procyclical response: a 0.31-percentage-point decline in the investment share of GNP for every negative percentage point in the GNP gap that is sustained for two years (0.23 + 0.08).

The regression results in the last column of Table 3.13 summarize and reinforce the main message of the earlier analyses. This regression assesses the systematic postwar connection of inflation and business cycle fluctuations to the *ratio* of net real housing investment to net real investment in new plants and equipment. The estimates indicate unambiguously that both output expansions and inflations are strongly associated with declines in residential investment relative to nonresidential investment. Contrary to the widely held idea (forcefully promoted by Martin Feldstein and his colleagues) that inflation has distorted investment decisions in favor of housing, the last regression in Table 3.13 shows that each extra percentage point on the inflation rate *lowered* net housing investment relative to net investment in plants and equipment by more than 5 percent.

Thus, although inflation, in conjunction with an unindexed tax system that exempts interest payments but taxes interest receipts, frequently has been implicated as a source of low personal savings in the United States and as a force diverting investment resources into housing at the expense of new plant and equipment, the empirical record clearly points to quite different conclusions. Postwar variations in the rate of inflation, which are substantial, exhibit no connection to household savings rates and are associated with shrinkages rather than expansions in the absolute and relative shares of GNP going to residential investment. The main sources of adverse fluctuations in nonresidential investment expenditures, which weakened the capital intensity of production and hence lowered subsequent rates of growth, were recessions, not inflations. This means that a restrictive monetary policy that sharply raises real interest rates may succeed in crippling the housing sector, but it will have even more crushing effects on investment to enchance the nonresidential capital stock. The mechanisms are the policy-induced declines in aggregate demand and capacity utilization and the ensuing rises in unemployment, which, no matter how generous the accompanying tax concessions for business investment, make expenditures for additional plant and equipment pointless. Reinforcing this conclusion is the ample evidence supplied by the first two years of the Reagan administration.

3.7   Inflation's True Costs

The inventory of inflation's true costs surely is much shorter and less significant than is alleged in conservative political rhetoric, in many media accounts, and, alas, in some academic writings. First, on the personal income side of the economy, the extensive evidence reported in this chapter shows that inflation has had little systematic connection with the distribution of either money or real incomes. Indeed, contrary to the usual assertions, the small impact on relative income (and wealth) positions that can be traced to inflation appears to have disadvantaged the rich, not the poor. By contrast, upward movements in unemployment unambiguously create significant pain for low- and middle-income groups, further skewing the income distribution away from the bottom two quintiles toward the top one.

Second, analyses of postwar per capita real personal disposable income growth rates indicate that similar conclusions apply to trends and fluctuations in absolute standards of economic well-being. Movements into and out of recessions had large effects on the growth of real personal incomes; the corresponding impact of fluctuations in inflation was essentially nil. Shifts in the terms of trade favoring energy producers and exporters, brought on by the two big oil supply shocks of 1973–1974 and 1979–1980, did of course have major impact on the real incomes of American households. But these painful changes in relative prices were the causes rather than the consequences of inflationary bursts.

Third, on the corporate side of the economy, the principal causes of falling profit shares and rates of return were the all-too-frequent policy-induced economic contractions of the 1970s and early 1980s. It is true that the interaction of inflation with corporate accounting practices and the tax system made a significant contribution to the poor performance of profits. Perhaps as much as one-third of the 6-percentage-point slide in after-tax corporate profitability since the late 1960s can be attributed through this mechanism to inflation. And because after-tax profitability affects real stock prices, some of the decade-long decline in price-deflated equity share values (about one-seventh or so of the 70-percent market plunge) can also be traced to inflation. Although the rich were most heavily affected by the stock market dive, many middle-income citizens were also hurt by the erosion of their pension reserves.

Yet despite the modest adverse impact of price accelerations on after-tax corporate profitability and the stock market, postwar empirical evidence does not support the view of some economists that inflation lowers personal savings rates or, more important, shifts investment away from new plant and equipment to the housing sector. On the contrary, postwar savings rates exhibited no response to the great fluctuations in inflation, and the principal source of downward movements in investment in new plant and equipment was recessions, not price accelerations. In fact, inflationary bursts appear to have lowered both absolute and relative investment in residential capital, which no doubt has been viewed as a significant cost of inflation by ordinary citizens who were squeezed out of the housing market.

It is unlikely that the measurable consequences of inflation are important enough to explain satisfactorily the common belief that rising prices pose a serious problem. (Public opinion about inflation is analyzed in Chapter 4.) Therefore, less tangible and partly psychological factors are probably more significant in accounting for concern about inflation than are easily identified objective costs. One source of anxiety about inflation stems from its association with the variability of rising prices.

In Chapter 1 we saw that the structure of the postwar American political economy imparts a strong bias toward inflation. Realignments of the relative prices of goods and services—that is, changes in their relative market economic value—typically occur by means of differential inflation rates. Major relative price adjustments are registered infrequently by steep declines in some prices and money incomes. Consequently, the variability of relative prices—the variance of changes in the prices of particular goods and services about the total inflation rate—tends to be positively correlated with the total inflation rate. Put more strongly, in recent decades large shifts in relative prices have been an important proximate source of upward surges in the rate of change of the general price level.

The association between the overall consumer price inflation rate and the variability of relative prices (as measured by the standard deviation) is illustrated in Figure 3.4, which is based on the data for fifteen commodity groups used earlier to construct income class–specific price indexes.[94] Of course an empirical association between these variables is not by itself persuasive evidence that major relative price realignments, increasing the dispersion of commodity-specific price movements, are a leading source of general inflation. In principle a causal relation, if one exists at all, could go the other way—from general inflation to relative price variability.[95] The characterization of the postwar inflationary process developed earlier, however, strongly favors the former interpretation. So do the events underlying the big surges of inflation and relative price variability during the past fifteen years, graphed in Figure 3.4.

The big dispersions of relative prices in Figure 3.4 occur during 1973–1975 and 1979–1980. They reflect the sharp upward relative movement in food prices in 1973 and the wrenching increases in the relative price of energy in 1973–1974 and again in 1979–1980. If wages and prices were completely flexible—or were "forced" to be flexible by policies creating very high rates of unemployment, as during Ronald Reagan's first years in office—such realignments could have produced the same widening of individual prices without substantially affecting the mean rate of change of all prices. But prices during the postwar period have not been flexible. On the contrary, as we saw in Chapter 1, they exhibit considerable downward inflexibility.[96] For this reason the great relative shifts in food and energy prices during the early and late 1970s contributed to high rates of inflation in the general price level. And because of the stubborn persistence of inflation once underway, such major relative price disturbances generated increases in the average rate of change of prices that lasted many subsequent periods, until the new relative price alignments became more or less firmly embedded in economic relationships.[97] Indeed only part of the second great OPEC-induced rise in oil prices in 1979–1980 represented an additional increase in oil's relative price. Some of the rise merely restored the 1973–1974 relative price level that had eroded during 1975–1978, when prices of imported oil were almost flat but the dollar price of other commodities continued to inflate at a brisk pace. From the oil producing countries' point of view, it was as if energy-consuming nations were attempting to inflate their way out of the painful shift in the terms of trade imposed by the OPEC cartel in October 1973.

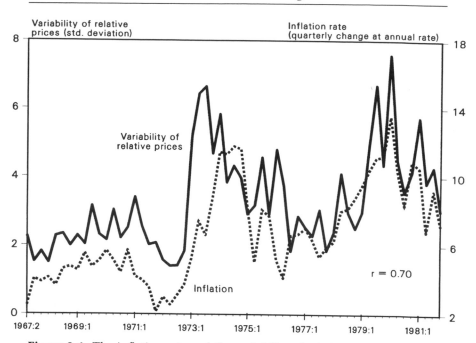

Figure 3.4 The inflation rate and the variability of relative prices, quarterly, 1967:2–1981:4. *Note:* The overall inflation rate (Divisia index formulation) is

$$DP_t = \sum_{i=1}^{15} w_{it} DP_{it}$$

where w_{it} is the average expenditure share on the ith commodity in periods $t - 1$ and t, and

$$DP_{it} = \ln(P_{it}/P_{it-1}) \cdot 400$$

where P_{it} is the price index of the ith commodity in period t. Commodity groups $i = 1, 2, \ldots , 15$ are given in Table 3.4. The variability (standard deviation) of relative prices is

$$\sigma(DP_{it}) = \left[\sum_{i=1}^{15} w_{it} (DP_{it} - DP_t)^2 \right]^{1/2}$$

But why discuss the connection between the rate of inflation and the dispersion of relative prices among the "costs" of inflation? After all, as I have argued, big relative price shifts have been important sources of inflationary bursts and, as James Tobin observed, "Relative distributional changes are always occurring, inflation or no inflation."[98] One of the costs is informational. Because relative price changes yield upward movements in the general price level, households and firms must devote time and resources to distinguishing the former from the latter. In a political economy in which relative shifts were not obscured by the veil of inflation, these efforts might go into more productive activity. Such information costs also have a psychological dimension. Price increases and price dispersions may, as the late Arthur Okun put it, "undermine the foundations of habit and custom," forcing people "to compile more information and to try to predict the future—costly and risky activities that they are poorly qualified to execute and bound to view with anxiety . . . After generations of keeping score in terms of the dollar, society cannot shift smoothly to a new system denominated in real units."[99] Perhaps this is why Lipset and Schneider found that inflation seems to lower the public's expectations about their own and the country's future well-being.[100]

Habits, however, are adaptable. Though the costs of adapting may be high initially, they are presumably transitory. The negative impact of inflation on households and firms extends beyond the discomfort associated with the disruption of habitual ways of making economic decisions and measuring economic performance, habits contingent on stable or slowly rising prices and a stable or slowly evolving relative price structure. As I emphasized earlier in this chapter, the price variability and price inflation of the 1970s brought sizable *real* income losses to a broad segment of the public. Because the major relative price disturbances of the 1970s represented shifts in the terms of trade in favor of the producers of food and, especially, of energy, the rest of us—the consumers of food and energy—experienced substantial declines in our standards of living.

For example, following the first big increase in petroleum prices in 1974, per capita real personal disposable income fell by more than 2.5 percent and inflation was running at double-digit levels. The vast majority of the public saw inflation as the nation's most important problem. (See Chapter 4.) It is likely that many people blamed rapidly rising prices for the shrinkage of their standard of living, even though the immediate post-OPEC burst of extra inflation was to a large extent merely the mechanism of a dramatic (and, for energy consumers, painful) change in relative prices. If the real loss absorbed by energy consumers had taken place about a stable overall price level, the experience would not have been any less unpleasant, but inflation would not have been held responsible. Painful relative price realignments typically do yield some extra inflation of the general price level; to the degree that people attribute the pain to rising prices *per se*, inflation is costly psychologically and, as we shall see in subsequent chapters, politically. If people have been confused about inflation, however, it is understandable. As James Tobin pointed out, after the first OPEC energy shock neither President Ford nor his economic advisers nor the Federal Reserve authorities nor the majority of outside economists explained to the public that anti-inflationary policies could not restore the former terms of trade and the associated real income loss.[101]

Beyond the tangible losses imposed on the consuming public by sharp upward movements in the relative price of food, energy, and other essential commodities noticeably correlated with higher overall inflation, inflation also involves psychological and hence political costs if people perceive its effects on their assets and liabilities or on their receipts and expenditures to be asymmetrical. The public may fail to credit unanticipated inflation-induced windfall gains—for example, on fixed interest liabilities such as home mortgages—against the unanticipated losses incurred on such money-valued assets as pension and life insurance reserves. Perhaps more important, the connection between rising prices and rising wages and salaries may not be fully understood by many ordinary citizens.[102] Although there is no solid empirical evidence supporting this conjecture, it is quite possible that inflation tends to be viewed as an arbitrary tax chipping away the purchasing power of money income increases that people believe they deserve to enjoy fully. For example, between the last quarter of 1975 and the last quarter of 1976, nominal personal disposable income per capita rose by about 7.5 percent, but prices increased by about 4.9 percent, leaving a more modest 2.6 percent real income gain. Perhaps some people entertained the mistaken idea that their standard of living could have risen by 7.5 percent or so were it not for the "evil" of inflation.[103] Of course, economists would be quick to point out that the increase in the quantity of goods and services produced between 1975 and 1976 simply could not have supported anything like a 7.5 percent rise in the nation's average standard of living. But what is obvious to the professional gives little comfort to the less well informed citizen who may be unaccustomed to thinking in real terms and whose aspirations and expectations may be strongly conditioned by money income standards.[104]

The biggest costs of inflation probably do not stem from the uncertainty, anxiety, and frustration experienced by so many citizens, however. The biggest costs are *indirect* costs, flowing from the consequences of monetary and fiscal policy reactions to inflation, rather than the direct effects of rising prices *per se*. Policy authorities in the United States have repeatedly responded to price accelerations with contractive monetary and fiscal actions, sacrificing employment and output in order to put downward pressure on the inflation rate. Looked at in this way, the indirect costs of inflation—via anti-inflation policy reactions—are equivalent to the direct output costs of increased unemployment discussed in Chapter 2. The cumulative costs since the first oil supply shock of October 1973 are truly staggering, as from data in Figure 3.5 on the gap between potential and actual GNP from 1973 to 1982 illustrate.[105]

During 1973, in the aftermath of President Nixon's successful attempt to create an election-year boom, actual GNP stood almost 80 billion (1982:4) dollars above potential GNP. Left unchecked, this

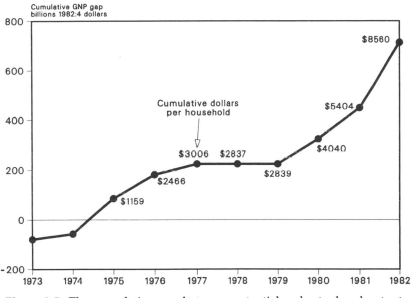

Figure 3.5 The cumulative gap between potential and actual real output.

situation would have led to rising inflation rates. But President Ford (who replaced Nixon in August 1974) did much more than trim economic activity back to the sustainable ("natural") output level and growth rate. As described earlier in this chapter, the Ford administration, along with a cooperative Federal Reserve, responded to the first OPEC shock with contractive, disinflationary policies that by 1976 had created more than 180 billion (1982:4) dollars of lost output. Weighting real output growth and employment more heavily than inflation, the Carter administration from 1977 through the first part of 1979 pursued expansionary policies, which at first slowed and then began to reverse the cumulative gap between potential and actual output. Stimulative policies were abandoned completely in response to the second great OPEC oil price rise of 1979–1980, however, and by the last year of Carter's presidency the cumulative cost of attempts to contain inflation stood at over 320 billion (1982:4) dollars of forgone output.

The Reagan administration continued the battle against inflation with a vengeance, giving "hardline monetarists" full reign over the Federal Reserve during 1981–1982. The Fed assaulted inflation vigorously, which meant that output and employment were assaulted vigorously. Not surprisingly, significant disinflation was indeed achieved as soaring real interest rates pushed the economy into the deepest recession since the 1930s. But, as Figure 3.5 indicates, the cost was enormous. At the end of Reagan's second year, the cumulative shortfall of potential from actual GNP had reached 715 billion (1982:4) dollars,[106] which represents 21 percent of total 1982 potential GNP (3.37 trillion dollars), or nearly $8600 per household.

The most important costs of inflation, then, have been indirect in the sense that they have flowed from the consequences of "fighting inflation" in a political economy in which the chief disinflationary weapons have been policy-induced contractions. Do the distributions of opinion and preferences in the electorate help to explain or justify the heavy sacrifices in terms of output and employment imposed by disinflationary monetary and fiscal policies? I turn to this question in the chapters ahead, which analyze the public's demand for macroeconomic outcomes.

II The Demand for Economic Outcomes

4 Public Concern about Inflation and Unemployment

One hundred percent of the people have been hit by inflation, only ten percent really worry about unemployment.

—an economic adviser to President Gerald Ford

4.1 The Salience of the Economy as a Public Issue

For more than a decade economic issues (principally inflation, the energy crisis, and unemployment) have overshadowed other problems as sources of public concern. Indeed, not since the Great Depression of the 1930s and the immediate post–World War II reconversion scare has the state of the economy occupied such a salient place on the American public agenda.

The Gallup poll time-series data in Figure 4.1 track the relative prominence of economic, domestic political and social, and international and defense issues over the last forty years. When the Second World War was successfully concluded, many feared that another Great Depression was at hand. It had happened before: the end of the First World War brought one of the biggest contractions in U.S. history, with real output falling by more than 17 percent between 1918 and 1921. In 1946 it looked as if the pessimists were right. Real output fell by a whopping 16 percent in that year, as the economy moved from a wartime to a peacetime footing. On top of that there was a burst of inflation following the relaxation of World War II price controls; in 1946 the GNP price deflator rose by 15 percent. Consequently, in the first few years after the war the economy overshadowed other issues as source of public concern.

But the economy bounced right back and adjusted with remarkable ease to the massive conversion from defense to civilian production. For the next fifteen years international tensions and foreign policy crises dominated the public agenda on a fairly continuous basis, as relations with the Soviet Union deteriorated and the cold war deep-

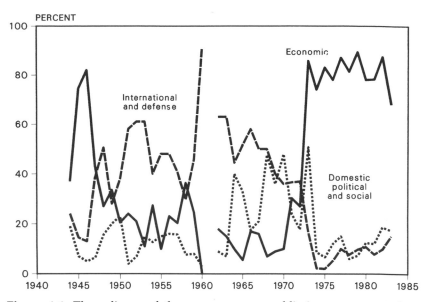

Figure 4.1 The salience of the economy as a public issue: aggregated responses to the question "What is the most important problem facing this country today?" (annual, 1944–1983). *Sources:* George Gallup, *The Gallup Poll, Public Opinion: 1935–1971*, vol. I–III (New York: Random House, 1972); and American Institute for Public Opinion, *The Gallup Opinion Index*, various issues. Responses coded by the author. *Note:* Question wording varied slightly over time.

ened. Sustaining the salience of international issues among voters were the Berlin blockade in 1948, the Korean War from 1950 to mid1953, a long stretch of essentially "institutionalized" antagonistic relations with the Soviet Union under John Foster Dulles's bellicose stewardship of American foreign policy during the Eisenhower years, the U2 spy plane incident in 1960, the Berlin Wall crisis and the Bay of Pigs fiasco in 1961, and the Cuban missile crisis in 1962.

In the latter half of the 1960s, the domestic issues of poverty and, especially, race relations finally achieved a degree of prominence, after lurking in the background for decades. Mass mobilization of blacks and sympathetic whites by the civil rights movement and large-scale race riots in more than a half-dozen major cities were the main causes of the shift. But a significant decline in Soviet-American tensions, symbolized by the 1967 Glassboro summit, also contributed to the heightened concern about domestic social issues revealed by the Gallup data in Figure 4.1. The Vietnam War soon competed with the race question for the attention of activists and the general public; in fact, during most of the latter half of the 1960s this "international" problem was more salient to voters than were either social or economic issues. The main reason was probably the intensity of the war, rather than any amelioration of poverty and racial discrimination through the war-on-poverty programs and the civil rights acts.

When Richard Nixon entered the White House in 1969, he inherited gradually accelerating inflation, as well as the Vietnam War, from Lyndon Johnson. The Nixon administration dealt with what by subsequent standards was a relatively mild inflation by inducing a moderate recession in 1970–1971. Although Vietnam was still a major issue, the salience of the economy, as the Gallup data in Figure 4.1 indicate, ratchetted upward. The economy did not dominate the public agenda, however, until after the Vietnam War was resolved (by American withdrawal and the defeat of our South Vietnamese allies) and the first OPEC energy price shock hit in late 1973. In every year since the completion of the American withdrawal from Vietnam and the first OPEC shock, more than two-thirds of the electorate identified an economic issue as "the most important problem facing the country today."

In view of the history of macroeconomic events during the last dozen years, this comes as no surprise. (Macroeconomic events were reviewed systematically in conjunction with trends in core inflation in Chapter 3. Also see Figure 4.3.) Of course there were also noneconomic events of major importance during this period. Some prominent examples are the Watergate scandal, which drove Nixon from office; the Soviet invasion of Afghanistan and the seizure of American hostages in Tehran during the Carter administration; and the loss of hundreds of marines in Lebanon and the KE 007 airliner affair during Reagan's presidency. But the severe inflation and contraction of 1974–1975, a second big OPEC oil price hike and recession in 1979–1980, and the crushing contraction of 1981–1982 all helped ensure that economic issues remained at the forefront of the public's attention.

4.2   The Distribution of Concern about Inflation and Unemployment in the General Electorate

The Gallup poll data in Figure 4.1 show that the "economy" became the dominant issue in the early 1970s. Unfortunately, the Gallup organization chronically confuses the "high cost of living" with "rising

prices"—that is, the price level and standards of living with the inflation rate.[1] Consequently, responses to the Gallup poll "most important problem" question cannot be used to assess the public's relative
concern about inflation and unemployment, two problems that have
preoccupied both policy makers and the mass public on a sustained
basis.

However, at intermittent periods between the third quarter of 1971
and the fourth quarter of 1974 and at least once a quarter thereafter,
the Surveys of Consumer Sentiment taken by the Survey Research
Center at the University of Michigan have asked national samples of
American households the following question:[2]

> Which of the two problems—inflation or unemployment—do you
> think will cause the more serious economic hardship for people [may
> have the more serious consequences for the country] during the next
> year or so?

Notice that the question refers to "people" generally (or to "the
country") and not to the respondent personally. Questions pertaining to personal economic concerns invariably yield more mentions of
inflation and fewer mentions of unemployment than do questions
pertaining to respondents' assessments of national economic problems. For example, in February 1980 the Harris survey asked a national cross section:[3]

> If you had to choose, which do you think is a more serious problem
> (1) for you and your family today—
> (2) for the country today—
> rising prices or high unemployment?

Responses were as follows:

	Rising prices	High unemployment	Both
(1) Problem for you and your family	82%	10%	7%
(2) Problem for the country	46%	44%	17%

Source: Harris Survey, March 20, 1980.

Research indicates that national economic concerns have greater
influence on political behavior than do personal economic concerns,[4]
undoubtedly because, as Gerald Kramer has argued, government
typically has more responsibility for economic problems seen as na-

tional rather than personal in scope. Voters rationally make this connection and hold politicians accountable accordingly.[5] The wording of the University of Michigan survey question, then, suits my purposes well. Although the Michigan question embodies a degree of projection into the near future ("during the next year or so"), it encourages people to acknowledge (implicitly) the difficult choice that has been at the heart of macroeconomic policy debates[6] and thus provides the best available time-series evidence on the public's relative concern about inflation and unemployment over the critical 1971–1984 period.[7]

Figure 4.2 shows the time series of aggregate responses to the Michigan inflation/unemployment question, and Figure 4.3 shows the actual rates of inflation, unemployment, and growth of real personal disposable income per capita in the macroeconomy. It is difficult to explain the frequently high levels of public concern about inflation revealed in Figure 4.2 by the concrete economic costs of inflation discussed in Chapter 3. After all, what matters from a purely economic point of view is real quantities such as output and employment, not movements of the nominal price level, and previous analy

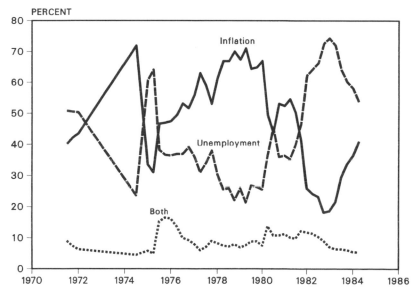

Figure 4.2 Public concern about inflation and unemployment, 1971:3–1984:2. *Source:* Surveys of Consumer Sentiment, University of Michigan. *Note:* See text for question wording.

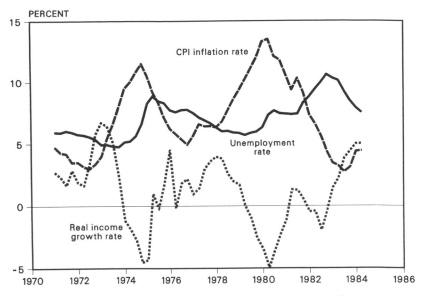

Figure 4.3 Macroeconomic outcomes, 1971:1–1984:2. *Note:* Inflation and real income growth rates are four-quarter changes.

ses indicated that any adverse direct effects of inflations on quantities are quite modest. The costs of unemployment are, by comparison, enormous. As I argued earlier, however, anxiety, uncertainty about the future and other subjective or psychological factors associated with price rises and fluctuations almost certainly play a significant role in accounting for popular aversion to inflation as opposed to unemployment.

It is obvious from Figures 4.2 and 4.3 that the public's relative concern about inflation and unemployment responds to the prevailing macroeconomic situation.[8] In late 1971 and early 1972 the conjunction of (modestly) recessionary levels of unemployment and comparatively low and falling inflation rates produced popular majorities more concerned about unemployment than about inflation. By the summer of 1974, however, after the first OPEC oil price shock, inflation was raging at more than 10 percent per annum, real personal income was falling by nearly 3 percent on an annual basis, and almost three-quarters of the public viewed inflation as the more serious problem. The situation was reversed just six months later. The Ford administration's policy response to the OPEC price hike had helped push unemployment to the highest level since the Great Depression, and the inflation rate had begun to fall; consequently, nearly two persons out of three expressed greater concern about unemployment than about inflation. As the economy moved from severe recession into "stagflation" during the last half of 1975 and into 1976, popular aversion to inflation increased sharply and hovered in the vicinity of 50 percent for the remainder of Ford's presidency.

During the first year of the Carter administration unemployment fell dramatically, but prices began to accelerate and the public's relative concern about inflation drifted upward. Over the next two years unemployment stabilized at just under 6 percent, and, as the data in Figure 4.3 indicate, the consumer price inflation rate increased *every* quarter from the first quarter of 1978 until the third quarter of 1980. With such a steady acceleration of prices and the associated decline of real incomes, both of which were fueled by the second OPEC oil supply shock of 1979–1980, the public's concern about inflation shot upward. Throughout 1978 and 1979 and into the first part of 1980, only about one person in four was more concerned about unemployment than about inflation, and two-thirds or more of the public typically identified inflation as the more serious economic problem. Predictably, the situation changed with the onset of the 1980 recession. Public concern about unemployment rose with the rate of unemployment, although the Michigan data show that it never exceeded concern about inflation, as prices continued to rise at double-digit rates during the rest of Carter's term.

Stringent disinflationary policy under Reagan, however, produced the longest run of double-digit and near-double-digit rates of unemployment since the 1930s, and the public's assessment of which was the more serious problem shifted accordingly. By Reagan's second year six to seven out of every ten Americans viewed unemployment as a more serious problem than inflation. The long-awaited recovery that began at the end of 1982 diminished relative concern about unemployment somewhat, but by mid 1984, the face of historically low inflation and high unemployment, a solid majority of the public continued to be more concerned about unemployment than about inflation.

A more precise picture of the response of public concern about inflation versus unemployment can be obtained by statistical analysis of the association of the index of Inflation Concern based on the Michigan data (equal to the percentage more concerned about inflation plus one-half the percentage responding "Both are equally serious") with the actual rates of inflation, unemployment, and growth of per capita real personal disposable income.[9] The results for an appropriately specified linear regression equation are

$$\text{Inflation Concern}_t = \underset{(6.16)}{45.4^{**}} - \underset{(1.15)}{6.88^{**}}\text{Ugap}_t \tag{4.1}$$

$$\underset{(3.14)}{-6.72^{*}}(\text{Ugap}_t - \text{Ugap}_{t-1}) + \underset{(0.62)}{2.36^{**}}p_t$$

$$\underset{(1.61)}{+1.39}(p_t - p_{t-1}) - \underset{(0.77)}{0.569}r_t$$

where R^2 adjusted $= 0.81$; standard error of the regression $= 6.76$, for sample range 1971:3–1984:2 (with gaps; see Figure 4.2); Ugap denotes the deviation of the unemployment rate (U) from Gordon's calculation of the "natural" or benchmark rate[10] (U^N); p denotes the rate of inflation of consumer prices; r is the percentage rate of change of per capita real personal disposable income (nominal income deflated by the CPI);** and * denote statistical significance at the 0.01 and 0.05 levels, respectively (two-tail tests); standard errors appear in parentheses, and all rates of change are calculated using the formula $\ln(X_t/X_{t-4}) \cdot 100$.

Reestimating the equation after dropping the last two (statistically insignificant) variables yields

$$\text{Inflation Concern}_t = \underset{(4.38)}{48.9^{**}} - \underset{(0.91)}{7.64^{**}}\text{Ugap}_t \tag{4.2}$$

$$\underset{(2.67)}{-8.36^{**}}(\text{Ugap}_t - \text{Ugap}_{t-1}) + \underset{(0.46)}{2.09^{**}}p_t$$

The Ugap terms on the right side of equations (4.1) and (4.2), the level and change of the so-called unemployment gap, measure the severity of unemployment (the degree of slack in the labor market) relative to the changing demographic structure of the workforce. Over the regression sample range, the unemployment gap varied within the interval −0.5 to +5.0, which, inasmuch as the "natural" rate was around 6.0 percent throughout this period, reflects "raw" unemployment rates ranging between 5.5 and 11 percent. Despite the substantial aversion to inflation revealed by the surveys, the impact of the Ugap variables on fluctuations in the aggregate distribution of concern about inflation and unemployment clearly is based on more than the experiences of people actually jobless at the time of the surveys. For people who were employed at the time of the interviews, the Ugap variables undoubtedly pick up encounters with unemployment in the recent past and anticipated bouts of joblessness in the near future.[11] The incidence of past, current, and anticipated future *indirect* encounters with unemployment via the experiences of respondents' children, relatives, neighbors, and workmates probably also shows up in the impact of Ugap terms on public concern about inflation as opposed to unemployment.[12] The response of the distribution of opinion to the Ugap variables, then, most likely represents the impact of both direct and vicarious exposure to unemployment in the electorate.

The coefficient estimates for equation (4.2) indicate that, other things being equal, each 1-percentage-point increase in the unemployment gap yields an enduring shift in popular concern of between 7 and 8 percentage points away from inflation and toward unemployment.[13] Beyond such permanent shifts in public concern associated with (stable) unemployment gaps, there are additional transitory shifts of 8 percentage points or so per unit change in the unemployment gap. Transitory effects of this magnitude are not surprising given that *changes* in the unemployment rate are more likely to generate feelings of anxiety or reassurance among the citizenry than is any *stable* rate. Great fluctuations in the public's fear of inflation versus unemployment are associated, then, with movements of the economy into and out of recessions.

The parameter estimates for the inflation terms in equation (4.1) show that only the rate of inflation, p, has sizable and significant influence on public concern about rising prices. The coefficient estimate for accelerations (and decelerations) of prices, $p_t - p_{t-1}$, though large and properly signed, has a standard error that is much too big to permit any sensible conclusions to be drawn about the response of public concern about inflation and unemployment to the second derivative (with respect to time) of the price level. Nonetheless, it is clear from the equations that each 1-point increase in the consumer price inflation rate raises aggregate public concern about inflation as opposed to unemployment by about 2 percentage points. Because the impact of the inflation rate on the distribution of public concern was estimated (in equation 4.1) in the presence of the real income growth rate, r, this result implies that people find sustained price rises distasteful even when, on average, money incomes are adjusting fully to upward movements in the cost of living.

The real income growth rate per se appears to have no systematic impact one way or the other on the distribution of public concern between unemployment and inflation. This probably means that people have no uniform tendency to perceive either inflation or unemployment as the more important threat to the real income stream.[14] If this is so, public perceptions are inconsistent with standard macroeconomic facts. Economists know that movements in unemployment and real output (real income) are intimately connected (Okun's Law) but that, in principle, inflations do not adversely affect output and employment. (See Chapters 2 and 3.) On the other hand, the opinion data span the period of the two major external supply shocks of the postwar era—the OPEC oil price hikes of 1974 and 1979–1980, which imposed large redistributions of income from consumers to producers of oil and other energy commodities. The income loss attributable directly to the oil shocks was on each occasion equal to about 2 percent of GNP.[15] In 1984, when the GNP was 3.75 trillion dollars, this would have amounted to about 75 billion dollars per shock, or over $850 per household. Inasmuch as inflation was the mechanism registering the shifts in the terms of trade in favor of oil, these episodes created a statistical association between poor real income growth and high inflation rates. The null relation between real income growth rates and concern about inflation versus unemployment may reflect the public's understandable inability to distinguish causal or structural relations in the macroeconomy from a noncausal statistical relation induced by the OPEC shocks.

The most striking and significant feature of the statistical results (which, it should be remembered, merely convey in quantitative terms the associations among the public opinion and the economic time series shown in Figures 4.2 and 4.3) is the extent and durability of anti-inflation sentiment among the American public. This is grasped more readily with the help of Figure 4.4, which graphs the distribution of public concern about inflation versus unemployment implied by the regression estimates for equation (4.2) at various stable combinations of unemployment and inflation rates. Figure 4.4 makes clear that for unemployment rates in the vicinity of 5 to 6 percent (that is, unemployment gaps of −1 and 0, because the computations are normed to a "natural" unemployment rate of 6 percent) solid majorities of the public are likely to be more concerned about the problem of rising prices at almost any sustained rate of inflation. At unemployment rates associated with the typical modern recession—say, joblessness rates of 7 to 8 percent—the opinion distribution changes. In these situations inflation must be at or near double-digit rates to

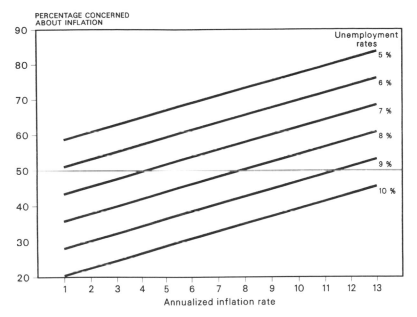

Figure 4.4 Percentages of the public more concerned about inflation than about unemployment at various stable combinations of unemployment and inflation (based on equation 4.2, assuming $U^N = 6\%$).

command more concern than unemployment from a pronounced majority of the mass public. And during major contractions, when unemployment rises above 8 percent and approaches double-digit levels (as during Ford's first year and Reagan's second and third years in office), the large majority of the public worries less about rising prices than about unemployment unless inflation is at runaway, double-digit-plus rates. But unemployment rates this high inevitably produce massive disinflation, and so it is not plausible, at least in the absence of a continuous series of exogenous price shocks, to entertain a macroeconomic configuration of persistent double-digit unemployment and inflation.

All things considered, these patterns must be discouraging for those who believe that the nation's welfare is best served by unrelenting, vigorous assaults on unemployment, designed to push the joblessness rate well below 6 percent. Yet the opinion data do help explain why policy-induced recessions have so often been used to fight inflations in the postwar American political economy. In many circumstances the existence of a broad-based political foundation for disinflationary macroeconomic policies producing extra unemployment is simply a fact of political life.

4.3 The Distribution of Concern about Inflation and Unemployment among Income, Occupational, and Partisan Groups

In view of the distributional consequences of inflation and unemployment reviewed in Chapters 2 and 3, it would be surprising if the public's relative concern about inflation and unemployment did not vary systematically across the classes. As E. J. Dionne, Jr., aptly put it, "The politics of jobs and the politics of inflation translate into the same thing: the politics of class."[16] But the class cleavages over the problems of unemployment and inflation are relative, not absolute. Many high-status, high-income people worry about unemployment, and many low-status, low-income people worry about inflation. Nonetheless, class differences are systematic and persist under a wide range of macroeconomic situations.

Figure 4.5 shows annual University of Michigan data on concern about inflation as opposed to unemployment among broad income

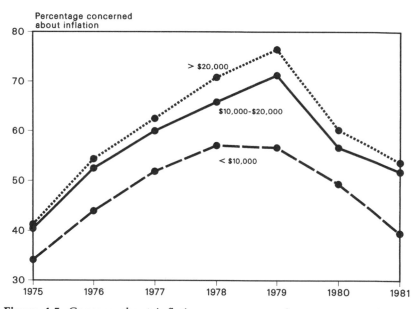

Figure 4.5 Concern about inflation versus unemployment among income classes. *Source:* Surveys of Consumer Sentiment, University of Michigan.

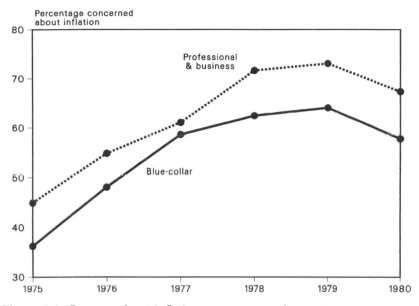

Figure 4.6 Concern about inflation versus unemployment among occupational classes. *Source:* Surveys of Consumer Sentiment, University of Michigan.

classes over time, and Figure 4.6 shows comparable data for broad occupational classes over time. Like the aggregate "more concerned about inflation" series graphed in Figure 4.2, concern about inflation in each income and occupational class is sensitive to macroeconomic trends. The percentage of each group more worried about inflation than about unemployment rises between 1975 and 1979 with the enormous increase in inflation rates following the OPEC energy price hikes. Concern about inflation then falls from the 1979 peak with the onset of high unemployment in 1980 and beyond. Yet in all years significant intergroup differences are apparent.

Across the highest and lowest income classes reported in the data (households with under $10,000 in income versus those with $20,000 or above), differences in relative concern about inflation typically run between 10 and 12 percentage points, although the cleavage falls to as low as 7 points in 1975 and rises to as high as 20 points in 1979.[17] The interoccupational group differences in concern about inflation are smaller, typically running between 5 and 10 percentage points. No doubt this is because occupation is a better indicator of "sociological" class than of "economic" class, whereas the reverse is true of household income. Yet, as noted above, both the income and occupational class differences are systematic and persist over time.

Blue-collar workers and low-income voters are more likely to be Democrats than Republicans; the reverse is true of upper-echelon white-collar groups and voters with higher incomes. So the opinion patterns observed across the income and occupational classes also show up across partisan groups.[18] Although data on concern about inflation and unemployment by party affiliation are not available for all years, what data we do have consistently indicate that Democrats are less inflation averse (more unemployment averse) than are Republicans, with the Independents typically falling in between (Figure 4.7). Moreover, cross-class and cross-partisan group patterns in "concern" about inflation and unemployment are translated into preferences about federal government *policy priorities*. Some relevant data from a couple of Gallup polls are reported in Table 4.1. Here again, Democrats, low-income voters, and blue-collar workers invariably are more likely than Republicans, white-collar workers, and high-income voters to think that the federal government should give more attention to curbing unemployment than to fighting inflation. All groups show sensitivity to the problem of inflation and acknowledge the

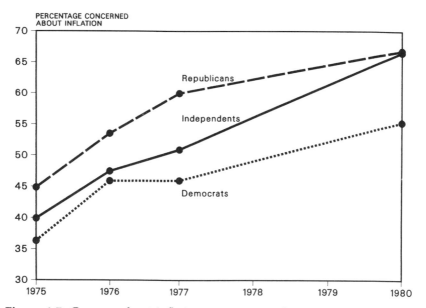

Figure 4.7 Concern about inflation versus unemployment among partisan groups.

Table 4.1   Policy priority of inflation and unemployment among income, occupational, and partisan groups (percent)

"Which do you think the federal government should give greater attention to—trying to curb inflation or trying to reduce unemployment?"

Variable	1975		1982	
	Curb inflation	Curb unemployment	Curb inflation	Curb unemployment
Income				
≥$25,000	NA	NA	54	41
$10,000–$25,000	NA	NA	42	51
0–$10,000	NA	NA	33	53
Occupation				
Professional and business	58	35	48	47
Clerical and sales	52	39	44	47
Blue collar	43	48	42	51
Political affiliation				
Democrat	41	48	37	57
Independent	43	45	44	50
Republican	58	32	56	36

Source: Gallup polls, January 1975, January 1982.
Note: NA signifies not available.

need to bring it under control, but the relative concern about and policy priority attached to inflation vary significantly across the classes.

If one believes, as I do, that economic policy is responsive to and constrained by the public's relative concern about economic problems, then the opinion data analyzed in this chapter help illuminate the political environment facing policy officials. More direct evidence on the political implications of macroeconomic performance, however, may be obtained from analyses of the response of mass support for the president to economic conditions, which is the focus of the next chapter.

5 Macroeconomic Performance and Mass Political Support for the President

> All political history shows that the standing of the government and its ability to hold the confidence of the electorate at a general election depend on the success of its economic policy.
>
> —Harold Wilson, former prime minister of Great Britain

> I think Dick's going to be elected President but I think he's going to be a one-term President. I think he's really going to fight inflation, and that will kill him politically.
>
> —Dwight D. Eisenhower

Although Prime Minister Wilson's declaration is perhaps somewhat exaggerated and President Eisenhower's forecast turned out to be wrong (Nixon was defeated in 1960), empirical studies have firmly established that macroeconomic performance has an important, and frequently decisive, impact on mass political support for elected officials in the United States and other developed electoral democracies.[1] And, as I noted in the Introduction, the response of political support to economic conditions yields electorally relevant information about the public's relative economic priorities and preferences, which comprise the voters' demand for economic outcomes.

The analyses in this chapter are based on quarterly time series of the proportions of those surveyed responding "approve" to the well-known Gallup poll question "Do you approve or disapprove of the way [name of the incumbent] is handling his job as president?"[2] Of course Gallup approval ratings are not election outcomes, but they do have a strong correlation with the vote share received by incumbent presidents running for reelection as well as with the vote shares received by nonincumbent nominees of the president's party.[3] The Gallup ratings also have proven to be good predictors of the success of the president's party in midterm congressional elections.[4] But, more important, the Gallup approval data provide the best available time-series index of presidents' mass political support between elections, when the policies are formulated and implemented and the real winners of elections are established.

Richard Neustadt observed twenty-five years ago that a president's standing in the approval polls greatly contributes to his public prestige, which in turn "is strategically important to his power."[5] This insight has been supported by events on many occasions before and since. To take a recent example, in the early summer of 1981 when President Reagan's approval rating was about 60 percent, his advisers, flush with the success of congressional passage of the Economic Recovery and Taxation Act, boasted that "some Democrats are getting the picture that by going with Reagan they are doing the popular thing." But what leverage with Congress the public may give to executives it also may take away. By the autumn of 1982, after the economy had undergone the worst contraction since the Great Depression and the president's Gallup approval rating had plummeted to 40 percent, Reagan's advisers were meekly conceding that "Congress is no longer dictated by a fear that Ronald Reagan can go to the country."[6]

Such anecdotal evidence is consistent with systematic, quantitative work showing that variations over time in congressional support for a president's legislative initiatives are systematically influenced by his Gallup poll approval ratings.[7] For these reasons the approval polls are widely viewed as the best regularly available index of the president's political stock with the mass public; consequently, they are watched closely by the administration, the opposition party, the bureaucracy, political journalists, and other political actors. Writing long after Neustadt, Donald Kinder summed up the importance of the president's approval rating this way: "Widespread support in the public augments a president's ability to bargain and to persuade. Confronted with a popular president, Congress, the private sector, the bureaucracy, the executive branch itself, all become more accommodating to presidential initiative."[8]

5.1 The Political Support Model

Most published time-series analyses of electoral outcomes and popular support for governing parties and chief executives registered by the polls have assumed, usually implicitly, that voters respond more or less homogeneously to economic and noneconomic events.[9] Voters' reactions to economic conditions and to other salient social and political issues are likely to vary significantly, however, because of differences in the objective, concrete interests at stake, and perhaps also because partisan attachments influence voters' perceptions and interpretations of politically relevant information. Hence, changes in political support generated, for example, by movements in unemployment or by the escalation of the Vietnam War and the unfolding of the Watergate scandal are unlikely to have been uniform within the electorate. Political elites of course realize that they do not face an undifferentiated mass public; they know that conscious policy shifts, as well as unanticipated events, yield political rewards and penalties that often vary sharply across electoral groups.

Inasmuch as time-series observations of individuals are not available and we are particularly interested in party-related cleavages in the electorate, the empirical analyses that will be presented here are for partisan groups identified in the Gallup surveys—Democrats, Republicans, and Independents. Partisanship divides the electorate into as homogeneous a set of political groups as we are likely to obtain in the American setting with a single variable. If economic performance is as important to the electorate as the survey data on the relative salience of various issues indicate, cleavages among voters concerning economic priorities should be clearly revealed by analysis of data on partisan groups. (See the data graphed in Chapter 4.) Moreover, dividing the electorate along party identification lines is probably the dimension of disaggregation most relevant to the thinking of elected political officials, and political officials determine macroeconomic policy.

The empirical equations developed below for movements over time in partisan groups' political support for incumbent presidents are based on the theory of utility maximization and on standard approaches to modeling binary choices in a dynamic context. I begin with a discussion of utility maximization and qualitative choice, and then consider the dynamics of the electorate's performance evaluations.

BINARY POLITICAL CHOICES UNDER UTILITY MAXIMIZATION

At each time t, voters (or, more precisely, respondents in the Gallup surveys) must decide whether or not to support (express "approval" of) the incumbent president. Utility maximization implies that voters will support the president if the utility (satisfaction) associated with the president's administration exceeds the utility (satisfaction) associated with the opposition. If the reverse is true—that is, if the utility anticipated under the opposition is perceived to be greater than that associated with the incumbent—voters will withdraw support from (express "disapproval" of) the president, which for theoretical purposes is taken to be a (relative and constrained) choice favoring the opposition.[10] In the simple case in which utilities are based solely on current performance, utility maximization means that voters will support the incumbent if observed (actual) contemporaneous outcomes are viewed as more favorable than hypothetical assessments of what the opposition's unobserved (shadow) performance would likely have been in current circumstances *if* the "out-party" held the presidency.

To formalize matters, let U^i denote the utility associated with the *i*th presidential administration, and let U^o be the utility associated with the opposition during the *i*th administration. If $Y = 1$ denotes supporting (approval) responses in the Gallup polls and $Y = 0$ denotes nonsupporting (disapproval, indifferent) responses, we have

$$Y = 1 \text{ if } U^i > U^o \text{ [that is, if } (U^i - U^o) > 0]; \tag{5.1}$$
$$Y = 0 \text{ otherwise}^{11}$$

Further, we can write the utility that voters associate with the incumbent president, U^i, and the utility that voters associate with the current opposition, U^o, as stochastic functions of observed (x) and shadow ($\hat{x}$) performance with respect to a matrix of variables, x^*, relevant to political choices:

$$U^i = \beta'x^{*i} + \varepsilon^i, \qquad U^o = \beta'x^{*o} + \varepsilon^o \tag{5.2}$$

where ε^i and ε^o denote errors stemming from imperfect perceptions of performance, omitted variables, and measurement error; β' denotes a vector of coefficients associated with the performance matrix x^*; and $x^* \equiv x, \hat{x}$ (actual and shadow performance outcomes).

It follows that the probability (P) of support for the incumbent, $P(Y - 1)$, is

$$
\begin{aligned}
P(Y = 1) = P &= P(U^i > U^o) \\
&= P[\beta'(x^{*i} + \varepsilon^i) > (\beta'x^{*o} + \varepsilon^o)] \\
&= P[\beta'(x^{*i} - x^{*o}) + (\varepsilon^i - \varepsilon^o) > 0] \\
&= P[\beta'x^*\text{diff} + \varepsilon > 0] \\
&= F[\beta'(x^*\text{diff})]
\end{aligned}
\tag{5.3}
$$

where F is the cumulative distribution function for ε, $\varepsilon = (\varepsilon^i - \varepsilon^o)$, and $\beta'x^*$diff denotes the difference between the incumbent and opposition performance; that is, $\beta'x^*$diff $\equiv \beta'(x^{*i} - x^{*o})$. The probability of nonsupport, $P(Y = 0)$, is simply $(1 - P)$.

At any given difference between the performance of the incumbent and that of the opposition, $\beta'x^*$diff, the choice probabilities, $P(Y = 1, Y = 0)$, hinge on the distribution of the random error term, $\varepsilon = (\varepsilon^i - \varepsilon^o)$. Therefore, the probabilities, P, are defined by a cumulative distribution function, F. Figure 5.1, in which the β-weighted sum $\beta'x^*$diff is graphed on the plane, illustrates the point. The greater the gap between voters' valuations of incumbent and opposition (actual and shadow) performances, which are scaled along the horizontal axis of the figure, the more certain the choice $Y = 1$ or $Y = 0$. For example, at $\beta'x^*$diff$_3$ in Figure 5.1, the incumbent's performance is viewed as superior to the opposition's by a large margin; that is, $\beta'x^*$diff is large and positive. In this case it would take a very big

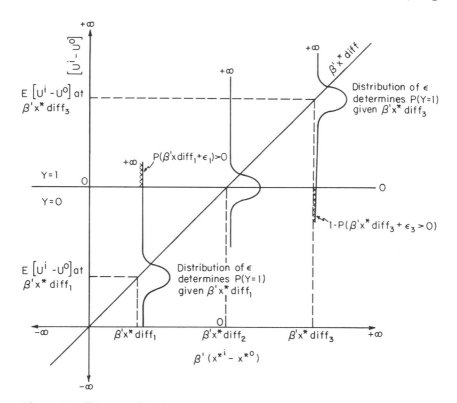

Figure 5.1   Binary political choices ($Y = 1$, $Y = 0$) under utility maximization.

random shock (ε)—more specifically, an idiosyncratic event of extraordinary and, therefore, unlikely dimensions, unfavorable to the incumbent—to produce the choice $Y = 0$ (a nonsupport or "disapproval" response in the Gallup poll). The probability of such an event is represented by the shaded region in the negative tail of the error distribution associated with $\beta'x^*\text{diff}_3$. Assuming a standard distribution, the area in the shaded tail therefore defines $P(Y = 0)$, and 1 minus the shaded area gives $P(Y = 1)$. By contrast, at $\beta'x^*\text{diff}_1$, the opposition's (shadow) performance is rated much more highly than the incumbent's (actual) performance, and it would take an equally large and improbable idiosyncratic event favoring the incumbent president to produce the choice $Y = 1$ (a supporting response in the poll). The probability of such an event is represented by the shaded area in the positive tail of the error distribution associated with $\beta'x^*\text{diff}_1$. At locations on the horizontal axis in the vicinity of $\beta'x^*\text{diff}_2$, on the other hand, voters perceive little or no systematic difference between the performance of the incumbent and that of the opposition ($\beta'x^*\text{diff}$ approaches 0), and so political choices depend critically on the direction (sign) of idiosyncratic factors (ε).

As Figure 5.1 suggests, it is sensible to assume that the random error terms have a bell-shaped distribution. The logistic and normal distributions are the obvious leading candidates. These differ only trivially, but for empirical analysis it is somewhat more convenient to assume that ε is distributed as the standard logistic. Substitution of the cumulative logistic function for F on the right side of the last line of equation (5.3) gives

$$P(Y = 1) = P = \frac{\exp(\beta'x^*\text{diff})}{1 + \exp(\beta'x^*\text{diff})} \tag{5.4}$$

It should be clear from equation (5.4) that the response probabilities (P) monotonically approach 1 as $\beta'x^*\text{diff}$ (the difference between the performance of the incumbent and that of the opposition, as weighted by voters) gets large, and monotonically approach 0 as $\beta'x^*\text{diff}$ gets small. But the response of P to movements in $\beta'x^*\text{diff}$ is not linear: the derivative (slope) of P with respect to $\beta'x^*\text{diff}$ is

$$dP/d(\beta'x^*\text{diff}) = P(1 - P) \tag{5.5}$$

The choice probabilities implied by equation (5.4) for values of the (multivariate, weighted) performance difference, $\beta'x^*\text{diff}$, are shown in Figure 5.2. This figure illustrates from another point of view the same basic story depicted in Figure 5.1. The slopes or tangents to the probability function graphed in Figure 5.2, which are defined by the derivative in equation (5.5), show the marginal increases (decreases) in political support brought about by marginal increases (decreases) in $\beta'x^*$diff. At the extremes of $\beta'x^*$diff the slopes are relatively flat, which means it is difficult for the incumbent to win or to lose additional political support by marginally changing performance. Among the incumbent's intense supporters, for whom $\beta'x^*$diff is large and positive, a sort of satiation point has been reached; efforts to improve relative performance will yield little in the form of increased support. The same is true of intense opponents, for whom $\beta'x^*$diff is large and negative. Only heroic efforts producing a very large improvement in $\beta'x^*$diff are likely to yield much of an increase in political support among those voters who are already alienated from the incumbent and strongly attached to the opposition. As $\beta'x^*$diff approaches 0, however, the slope of the probability response function becomes greater, reaching its maximum value at $\beta'x^*$diff $= 0$, which corre-

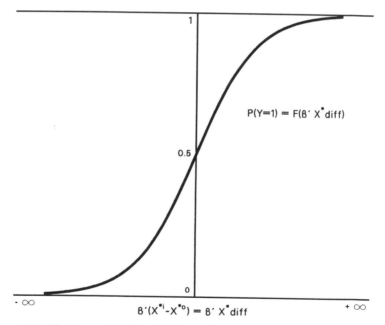

Figure 5.2 Choice probabilities $P(Y = 1)$ from the cumulative logistic function.

sponds to $P = 0.5$. The point at which $\beta'x^*\text{diff} = 0$, $P = 0.5$, is the "threshold of opinion change," and here the incumbent has the best prospects for increasing support with relatively small improvements in performance.[12] This implies that support-maximizing incumbents have more to gain, at least in the short run, from gearing policies to Independents, "floating voters," marginal supporters, and marginal opponents than from attempting to appeal to strong sympathizers or committed opponents.[13] And it is the reason that many theories of political competition predict that the policies advocated and pursued by competing parties and candidates tend to converge to the preferences of the median voter. (See Chapter 7 for more discussion of this point.)

Empirically, we do not observe time series of the binary responses of individuals n, $Y_{nt} = 1$, $Y_{nt} = 0$; instead, we have time-series data on the proportions of survey respondents in j partisan groups (Democrats, Independents, and Republicans) supporting the incumbent, P'_{jt}:

$$P'_{jt} = \sum_{n=1}^{N_j} Y_{njt}/N_{jt}$$

where P' denotes survey estimates of the true (population) proportions P.

It is therefore possible to take the inverse of the cumulative logistic operator, F, and write equation (5.4) (and the last line of equation 5.3) as

$$F^{-1}P'_{jt} = \beta'_j x^*\text{diff}_t + e_{jt} \tag{5.6}$$
$$\ln[P'_{jt}/(1 - P'_{jt})] = \beta'_j x^*\text{diff}_t + e_{jt}$$

where $e_t = (F^{-1}P'_{jt} - F^{-1}P_{jt})$.

Equation (5.6) expresses the natural logarithm of the observed group sample proportions, P'_{jt}, divided by $1 - P'_{jt}$ (the so-called logits) as a linear function of $\beta'_j x^*\text{diff}_t$.[14] The error term e_{jt} in the equation arises because we have substituted the survey proportions observed empirically for the true proportions (group probabilities) in the theoretical model (equations 5.3 through 5.5). Assuming independent samples from a binomial population, it can be shown that the error has mean zero and (heteroscedastic) variance approximated by $1/N_{jt} \cdot P'_{jt}(1 - P'_{jt})$, where N_{jt} is the number of respondents used to calculate P'_{jt}.[15] The appropriate estimating equation is therefore a weighted least-squares model with weights equal to the square root of the inverse of the variance of the error:

$$WT_{jt} \cdot \ln[P'_{jt}/(1 - P'_{jt})] = WT \cdot [\beta'_j x^* \text{diff}_t + e_{jt}] \tag{5.7}$$

where $WT_{jt} = [N_{jt} \cdot P'_{jt}(1 - P'_{jt})]^{1/2}$.

DYNAMIC PERFORMANCE EVALUATIONS

Equations (5.1) through (5.7) showed how the latent probabilities underlying the observed binary choices ($Y = 1$, $Y = 0$) can be modeled from time-series data on partisan groups using a utility maximization theory of political support. The equations presented thus far to lay out the modeling strategy are static, however, in the sense that time plays no essential role in the way voters evaluate performance. Yet past, current, and, perhaps, anticipated future performance is likely to influence voters' current political choices, so it is important to introduce dynamics into the system. For ease of presentation, I drop the group subscript j in most of the equations that follow, but it should be understood that left-side variables and all right-side parameters and disturbances are implicitly indexed for j partisan groups.

In American electoral politics individual politicians matter more and political parties matter less than in most Western democracies. The performance and personalities of particular presidents and presidential contenders weigh heavily on political behavior in the United States. The political support model accommodates this feature of American political life by writing the utility functions associated with the incumbent president and current opposition, which appeared in simplified form in equations (5.1) and (5.2), as the weighted sum of a president-specific or administration-specific component, Admin, and a party component, Party:

$$U^i_t = w \cdot \text{Party}^i_t + (1 - w) \cdot \text{Admin}^i_t + \varepsilon^i_t \tag{5.8}$$
$$U^o_t = w \cdot \text{Party}^o_t + (1 - w) \cdot \text{Admin}^o_t + \varepsilon^o_t$$

where $0 \leq w \leq 1$ and, therefore, $w + (1 - w) = 1$. Hence, the difference in the utilities associated with the incumbent and the opposition during the ith presidential administration is

$$(U^i_t - U^o_t) = w \cdot (\text{Party}^i_t - \text{Party}^o_t) \tag{5.9}$$
$$+ (1 - w) \cdot (\text{Admin}^i_t - \text{Admin}^o_t) + \varepsilon_t$$

where $\varepsilon_t = (\varepsilon^i_t - \varepsilon^o_t)$.

The Party components of the utility functions represent the stock of mass support of the parties. The concept bears some similarity to that of "party identification" in the political science voting literature, especially if party identification (ID) is viewed as a "running balance sheet of the two parties"[16] rather than as a "durable attachment, not readily disturbed by passing events and personalities."[17] In other words, my notion of a party's political stock gives less emphasis to affective content and more weight to objective performance than one usually associates with the traditional meaning of party identification. Party stocks are based on cumulative, discounted performance records with respect to actual outcomes (x) during periods when a party controlled the presidency and shadow outcomes ($\hat{x}$) during periods when the party did not hold the presidency. The difference between incumbent[18] and opposition party political stocks is therefore written

$$(\text{Party}_t^i - \text{Party}_t^o) = D_t \cdot \sum_{k=0}^{\infty} g^k \beta'(x_{t-k} - \hat{x}_{t-k}) \cdot D_{t-k} \qquad (5.10)$$

where g is a lag-weight decay rate, or discount rate parameter, lying between 0 and 1, $g = 1/(1 + \rho)$; x denotes actual performance and $\hat{x}$ denotes shadow performance; and $D_{t(t-k)} = +1$ during Democratic administrations and -1 during Republican administrations.

Notice that the product of the switching terms D_t and D_{t-k} equals $+1$ during all (current and past) periods when the present incumbent party held the White House and -1 during (past) periods when the current opposition party held the White House. This ensures that at each time t the right side of equation (5.10) generates a cumulative, discounted interparty contrast between current and past performance outcomes.

The administration-specific components of voters' utility functions resemble the Party components except that evaluations contributing to Admin are formed with respect to individual presidential administrations. Hence, only actual outcomes (x) during the ith administration contribute to Admin_t^i. Events prior to the ith president's tenure in office influence Admin_t^i only to the extent that voters form shadow assessments of how the current president might have performed during periods before he entered the White House. Conversely, the administration-specific component of the opposition's utility, Admin_t^o, is based on shadow performance assessments during the ith administration and on actual performance outcomes in prior periods. The difference between Admin_t^i and Admin_t^o is therefore

$$(\text{Admin}_t^i - \text{Admin}_t^o) = \sum_{k=0}^{\infty} g^k \beta'(x_{t-k} - \hat{x}_{t-k}) \cdot I_{t-k} \qquad (5.11)$$

where $I_t = +1$ during the ith presidential administration and -1 during previous administrations. In equation (5.11) the switching term I_{t-k} ensures that the right side of the equation gives the intended cumulative, discounted interadministration performance comparisons.

Neither the Party nor the Admin components of voters' utility functions can be tied to data without specification of the unobserved shadow performances. In the absence of time-series survey data on the performance voters imagine the opposition might have achieved each period had the out-party controlled the White House, the only feasible alternative is to set the weighted sums of unobserved shadow performances in equations (5.10) and (5.11) equal to a sequence of time-varying constants. For empirical purposes, these shadow constants will be updated for each presidential administration. Inasmuch as Party and Admin are weighted w and $(1 - w)$, respectively, in equation (5.9), the shadow performance constants, denoted $S(t)$, are proxies for the $\hat{x}_{t-k}$ sums:

$$S_{(t)} = -\beta' \sum_{k=0}^{\infty} g^k \left[w(D_t \cdot D_{t-k}) + (1 - w) \cdot I_{t-k} \right] \cdot \hat{x}_{t-k} \qquad (5.12)$$

where the (t) notation signifies the fact that S varies over administrations.

After indexing relevant terms for j partisan subgroups, we find that the difference between the utilities associated with the incumbent and those associated with the opposition during the ith administration may now, following equation (5.9), be written

$$(U_{jt}^i - U_{jt}^o) = \beta_j' \sum_{k=0}^{\infty} g_j^k [w_j \cdot (D_t \cdot D_{t-k}) \qquad (5.13)$$
$$+ (1 - w_j) \cdot I_{t-k}] \cdot x_{t-k} + S_{j(t)} + \varepsilon_{jt}$$

According to equation (5.3), the probability of political support for the incumbent in the jth partisan group, P_{jt}, is

$$P_{jt} = \text{Prob}(U_{jt}^i - U_{jt}^o) > 0$$

Remember, however, that we observe group proportions, P'_{jt}, rather than true probabilities, P_{jt}, in the survey data. Hence, given equations (5.6) and (5.7), the estimating equations take the form

$$WT_{jt} \cdot F^{-1}P'_{jt} = WT_{jt} \cdot \ln[P'_{jt}/(1 - P'_{jt})] \tag{5.14}$$

$$= WT_{jt} \cdot \left(\sum_{k=0}^{\infty} g_j^k \, \beta_j' \, [w_j \cdot (D_t \cdot D_{t-k}) \right.$$

$$\left. + (1 - w_j) \cdot I_{t-k}] \cdot x_{t-k} + S_{j(t)} + e_t \right) + \alpha_j$$

where α is a constant that "centers" the weighted regression and other terms are as defined earlier.

Although the lag functions in equations (5.10)–(5.14) run from 0 to infinity, the upper bound of the lag is merely a convenient fiction which should be taken to mean that performance may be evaluated back to the beginning of the relevant political era. It is assumed implicitly that knowledge of past performance is transmitted from generation to generation via political socialization.

IMPORTANT ANALYTICAL FEATURES OF THE MODEL
Several analytical features of the political support model should be fully understood and therefore are worth discussing at greater length. First, voters are assumed to evaluate an administration's performance *relatively* rather than *absolutely*. Ignoring for the moment shadow performances, which are approximated by the time-varying $S_{(t)}$ constants, voter approval of the president is modeled as a weighted average of two relative performance comparisons: (1) the cumulative performance of the current incumbent party in relation to the cumulative past performance of the present opposition party, and (2) the cumulative performance of the current administration in relation to the cumulative performance of *all* previous administrations of either partisan stripe.

The contributions of interparty and interadministration performance comparisons to a president's political support are weighted w and $(1 - w)$, respectively. So for $0 < w < 1$, the weights sum to 1. Insofar as observed performance outcomes are concerned, $w = 0$ implies that presidents are judged only by how they are doing in comparison to previous administrations, including previous administrations of their own party. On the other hand, $0 < w < 1$ means that there is a significant Party component to the electorate's current polit-

ical choices. For this reason poor (good) performance by prior administrations of the incumbent president's party will to some degree
adversely (favorably) affect voters' estimation of the incumbent's cumulative performance. Finally, $w = 1$ defines a purely party-based
political evaluation process in which only interparty performance
comparisons matter. In this case the performance of previous administrations is either added to or contrasted with the incumbent's record, depending on whether the White House was held by the president's party or by the current opposition party during earlier periods.

The parameter w has meaning only if past performance outcomes
significantly affect current political support. Because the present relevance of the information conveyed by past performance (x_{t-k}) decays
over time, the (lag) weights voters give to past outcomes are assumed
to decline at rate g^k, where g is a backward-looking discount rate
parameter $[1/(1 + \rho)]$ taking a value between 0 and 1. Hence, if x_{t-k} is
a matrix of performance outcomes experienced k periods ago ($k = 0$,
1, 2, 3, . . .), the outcomes are weighted

$$g^0 x_t = x_t, \ g x_{t-1}, \ g^2 x_{t-2}, \ g^3 x_{t-3}, \ \ldots$$

Voters need not weight current and past performance outcomes in
exactly this way. As long as recent outcomes are weighted more
heavily than past outcomes when voters make current political
choices, the geometrically decaying weight (discount rate) sequence
$g^k [1/(1 + \rho)^k]$ will yield a good approximation of the electorate's actual evaluation process.

Moreover, this feature of the model is testable. If, on average,
voters in a particular partisan group discount the past entirely and
consider only the current situation when evaluating performance,
then the estimated value of g should be about 0. (If $g = 0$, w is of
course irrelevant; w has no meaning independent of g.) Small pos-
itive(nonzero) values of g mean that voters discount past outcomes
heavily, but not completely. The best guide to future performance is
likely to be performance during the recent past, so a small value of g
would be consistent with an electorate that is forward looking rather
than retrospective in its political behavior.[19] Large values of g (approaching 1) imply that past performance outcomes play a very important role in explaining the president's current political support.
Clearly, then, g is an interesting parameter from a political point of
view; it summarizes how much the past performance record contributes to current political choices, which in turn has important implica-

tions for the timing of electorally motivated policy plans. (See Chapter 8, Political Business Cycles.)

Understanding of the g and w parameters and related features of the model can be deepened by considering a couple of stylized, hypothetical situations. First, consider a case in which a new president assumed office in the current period and administrations of the out-party held the presidency during all relevant prior periods. ("All relevant prior periods" may be taken to mean that the out-party was in the White House far enough back in time so that g^k is essentially 0.) The transition from Nixon-Ford to Carter would be an example of this case if g^{32} were approximately 0 (where $k = 32$ denotes quarters). The transition from Carter to Reagan would be another example if g^{16} were approximately 0. In these cases equation (5.14) implies that, prior to the current period (lag $k > 0$), $D_t D_{t-k}$ and I_{t-k} were both -1, and so we have lag sums of the form

$$- w \cdot \sum_k g^k x_{t-k} - (1 - w) \cdot \sum_k g^k x_{t-k} = - \sum_k g^k x_{t-k}$$

Hence, in the new president's first period, the logit of political support, $\ln[P'/(1 - P')]$, would depend on

$$\ln[P'_t/(1 - P'_t)] = \beta(x_t - g x_{t-1} - g^2 x_{t-2} \qquad (5.15)$$
$$- g^3 x_{t-3} - g^4 x_{t-4} - \ldots)$$

where for expositional purposes I have dropped the subscript j and the heteroscedasticity weight WT and have set $S_{(t)}$ and α to 0.

Equation (5.15) makes apparent the precise way in which a president's political support depends on cumulated, discounted relative performance. Other things being equal, the worse (better) the performance of the prior administration(s), the higher (lower) the initial approval rating of the new president tends to be. For example, suppose that the matrix of performance variables, x, includes only the rate of unemployment, which has been constant at 10 percent under the new and old administrations. If we assume further[20] that the coefficient of unemployment (β) is -0.02 and that $g = 0.8$, then by equation (5.15) $\ln[P'_t/(1 - P'_t)]$ will equal $+0.60$. In terms of percentage points in the polls, a logit of 0.60 corresponds to a 65 percent approval rating.[21] By contrast, had the new president inherited a more favorable 5 percent unemployment rate record from the preceding out-party administrations, his initial support would have been lower—on the order of $[P_t'/(1 - P_t')] = 0.30$, which corresponds to a 57 percent approval rating:

$$- 0.02 \cdot 5[(1 - 0.8)/(1 - 0.8) - 0.8/(1 - 0.8)] = 0.30$$
$$\exp 0.30/(1 + \exp 0.30) = 0.57, \text{ or } 57 \text{ percent}$$

A new president's support then, is proportional to the (mal) performance of the prior (out-party) administrations. In other words, new-party presidents following "bad acts" are likely to enjoy greater initial support than new-party presidents following "good acts."

As time passes, however, the incumbent's political support will gradually be determined more and more heavily by his own performance record. Just how quickly, as noted earlier, depends on the rate at which voters discount prior performance—that is, on voters' effective political memory represented by the decay rate parameter g. If the new administration in this hypothetical example had been in office for $k^* + 1$ periods, from lag $k = 0$ back to lag $k = k^*$, then the logit of political support would be

$$\ln[P_t/(1 - P_t)] = \beta(x_t + gx_{t-1} + \ldots + g^{k^*}x_{t-k^*} \tag{5.16}$$
$$- g^{k^*+1}x_{t-k^*-1} - g^{k^*+2}x_{t-k^*-2} - \ldots)$$

For performance held fixed at $\bar{x}$ during the old and the new administrations, equation (5.16) is equivalent to

$$\ln[P_t'/(1 - P_t)] = \beta\bar{x}(1 + g + g^2 + \ldots + g^{k^*} - g^{k^*+1} \tag{5.17}$$
$$- g^{k^*+2} - g^{k^*+3} - \ldots)$$

Summing up the geometric progressions in equation (5.17) gives

$$\ln[P_t'/(1 - P_t'] = \beta\bar{x}[(1 - g^{k^*+1})/(1 - g) - g^{k^*+1}/(1 - g)] \tag{5.18}$$
$$= \beta\bar{x}[(1 - 2g^{k^*+1})/(1 - g)]$$

Hence, the time path of political support for our hypothetical president, who has been in the White House for $k^* + 1$ periods (lag $k = 0$, 1, 2, . . . , k^*) and was preceded in office by administrations of the current out-party, is

$k^* = 0$: $\beta\bar{x}[(1 - 2g)/(1 - g)]$
$k^* = 1$: $\beta\bar{x}[(1 - 2g^2)/(1 - g)]$
$k^* = 2$: $\beta\bar{x}[(1 - 2g^3)/(1 - g)]$

.

.

.

$k^* = \infty$: $\beta\bar{x}[1/(1 - g)]$

It is now clear that if performance is held constant at $\bar{x}$ and $\beta\bar{x}$ is negative (which, in the more realistic multivariate case, may be taken to mean that negatively valued performance variables prevail over positively valued ones, and so the vector product $\beta'\bar{x}$ is negative), political support for new presidents will trend downward from initial level $\beta\bar{x}[(1 - 2g)/(1 - g)]$ toward the steady-state level $\beta\bar{x}[1/(1 - g)]$. The initial, first-period support levels are determined by the magnitudes of β, $\bar{x}$ and g, and the rate of decline toward steady-state values is determined by g (assuming, again, for illustrative purposes that performance is constant at $\bar{x}$). In our stylized example, if the new president who inherited a 10-percent unemployment rate from prior out-party administrations stays in office long enough for g^k to reach 0, and if the unemployment situation remains unchanged, his support will eventually decline from

$$\ln[P_t'/(1 - P_t')] = 0.60, \text{ or } 65 \text{ percent}$$

to

$$\ln[P_t'/(1 - P_t')] = -0.02 \cdot 10 \cdot \left(\sum_{k=0}^{\infty} 0.8^k\right)$$

$$= -\frac{0.02 \cdot 10}{1 - 0.8}$$

$$= -1.0$$

which implies a poll rating of 27 percent.

Of course if the incumbent president's performance is more favorable than that of earlier administrations, this trend will be offset. Conversely, the trend of declining support will be accelerated if the new administration's performance is less favorable than the situation inherited from the opposition. Eventually, support will converge [at rate g^k or $1/(1 + \rho)^k$] to the equilibrium level $[\beta\bar{x}/(1 - g)]$ implied by any sustained performance record.[22]

Next consider a hypothetical case in which the incumbent president was preceded by administrations of his *own* party, back in time through all relevant prior periods. In other words, as in the transitions from Kennedy to Johnson and from Nixon to Ford, the transition to the current president represents a shift of administration, but not a change in the party controlling the White House. In this situation the logit of political support for an incumbent who had been in office for $k^* + 1$ periods (from lag $k = 0$ back to lag $k = k^*$) would be given by the lag function

$$
\begin{aligned}
\ln[P_t'/(1 - P_t')] &= \beta[w \cdot (x_t + gx_{t-1} + \cdots + g^{k^*}x_{t-k^*} \\
&\quad + g^{k^*+1}x_{t-k^*-1} + g^{k^*+2}x_{t-k^*-2} + \cdots) \\
&\quad + (1 - w) \cdot (x_t + gx_{t-1} + \cdots + g^{k^*}x_{t-k^*} \\
&\quad - g^{k^*+1}x_{t-k^*-1} - g^{k^*+2}x_{t-k^*-2} - \cdots)] \\
&= \beta[x_t + gx_{t-1} + \cdots + g^{k^*}x_{t-k^*} \\
&\quad + (2w - 1)g^{k^*+1}x_{t-k^*-1} \\
&\quad + (2w - 1)g^{k^*+2}x_{t-k^*-2} + \cdots]
\end{aligned}
\tag{5.19}
$$

Despite appearances, equation (5.19) has implications very similar to those of equation (5.16). In fact, the magnitude of w only affects the initial support levels from which the dynamics may be evaluated. This will become clearer if we assume, as in the first example, that only the unemployment rate appears in the model, that it has a negative coefficient, and that unemployment performance has been constant over time at value $\bar{x}$. For fixed performance $\bar{x}$, equation (5.19) can be written

$$
\begin{aligned}
\ln[P_t'/(1 - P_t')] &= \beta\bar{x}[1 + g + g^2 + \cdots + g^{k^*} \\
&\quad + (2w - 1)g^{k^*+1} + (2w - 1)g^{k^*+2} \\
&\quad + (2w - 1)g^{k^*+3} + \cdots] \\
&= \beta\bar{x}\left(\frac{1 - g^{k^*+1}}{1 - g} + \frac{(2w - 1)g^{k^*+1}}{1 - g}\right) \\
&= \beta\bar{x}\left(\frac{1 + (2w - 2)g^{k^*+1}}{1 - g}\right)
\end{aligned}
\tag{5.20}
$$

Evaluating equation (5.20) shows that the time path of political support for a president who followed administrations of his own party and has occupied the White House for $k^* + 1$ periods (lag $k = 0$, 1, 2, . . . , k^*) is

$$
\begin{aligned}
k^* = 0: &\quad \beta\bar{x}\,[(1 + (2w - 2)g)/(1 - g)] \\
k^* = 1: &\quad \beta\bar{x}\,[(1 + (2w - 2)g^2)/(1 - g)]
\end{aligned}
$$

$$k^* = 2: \qquad \beta\bar{x}\,[(1 + (2w - 2)g^3)/(1 - g)]$$

.

.

.

$$k^* = \infty: \qquad \beta\bar{x}\,[1/(1 - g)]$$

It is apparent that for all values of w between 0 and 1, political support for the new president will again tend to decline over time. As w approaches 1 (and, hence as $2w - 2$ approaches 0)—that is, as the way in which voters evaluate performance approaches a pure Party process—the decline becomes less dramatic. This is so because for w close to 1 the electorate does not make a great distinction between the new president and prior presidents of the same party. As a result, the president's initial support level, $\beta\bar{x}[(1 + (2w - 2)g/(1 - g)]$, is close to the steady-state level, $\beta\bar{x}/(1 - g)$, which leaves little room for erosion of support, given a fixed stream of performance under the current and previous administrations of the same party. If w is exactly equal to 1, the process the electorate uses to evaluate performance makes no distinction at all between the new president and the sequence of prior presidents of the same party. Consequently, there is not any tendency for political support to decline with time after the new president assumes office.

The downward trend of political support becomes more pronounced as w approaches 0 (and, hence, as $2w - 2$ approaches -2), because voters make little distinction between prior administrations of the president's party and earlier administrations of the out-party. At $w = 0$, a pure Admin, or president-specific, process of performance evaluation prevails in the electorate. Here, the president's performance is judged relative to that of all previous administrations, with no distinction made between previous administrations of his own party and the out-party. Therefore, if $w = 0$, the present example collapses to the first one, in which the incumbent's initial support is proportional to the discounted (mal)performance of previous administrations. Hence, for the performance fixed at $\bar{x}$ and $\beta\bar{x} < 0$, support trends downward as in the first case from $\beta\bar{x}[(1 - 2g)/(1 - g)]$ toward $\beta\bar{x}/(1 - g)$.

If the parameter β were positive or, in the more realistic multivariate case, if positively valued outcomes prevailed empirically among the performance variables evaluated by voters, the trends discussed above would be inverted. In other words, there would be a tendency for a new president's support to trend *upward* over time until it reached the equilibrium level consistent with a particular sustained performance record. Yet negatively valued outcomes (such as unemployment and inflation) frequently weigh more heavily on political choices than do positively valued events (such as robust real income growth rates). The tendency of a new president's support rating to decline from early "honeymoon" levels, which many previous studies have picked up with ad hoc, exogenous time-trend and time-cycle terms,[23] is therefore an endogenous feature of the model. And, as a comparison of the time paths of political support in the two hypothetical examples shows, other things being equal, the endogenous trend is sharper when the transition to a new president also involves a change in the party holding the White House.

5.2   Empirical Results

THE VARIABLES: MEASURING POLITICAL SUPPORT AND ECONOMIC AND
POLITICAL PERFORMANCE

For the reasons reviewed in the last section, the dependent variables are weighted logits—WT $\cdot \ln[P'_{jt}/(1 - P'_{jt})]$—where P'_{jt} is the proportion of the jth group in quarter t responding "approve" to the Gallup approval question[24] and WT is the heteroscedasticity weight. The regression experiments are based on quarterly observations spanning the period from Kennedy to Reagan,[25] 1961:1 to 1984:1. The approval rating data used to form the logits are graphed by partisan group in Figure 5.3.

The economic performance variables on the right side of the regression equations include the unemployment gap, Ugap, which is the deviation of the official (civilian) unemployment rate from Gordon's calculation of the so-called natural rate (see the discussion of Ugap in Chapters 2 and 4), the consumer price index inflation rate, p, and the percentage rate of change of per capita real personal disposable income, r.[26] Clearly Ugap and p should enter the equations with negative signs and r should have a positive sign, although, as the previous discussion indicated, we can anticipate significant intergroup variations in the magnitude of the coefficients, especially the unemployment coefficients. The equations also include the rate of change of energy prices, p-oil, during the quarters when the two OPEC oil price shocks were absorbed: 1973:4–1975:4 and 1979:2–1981:2. Entering p-oil in the models allows to evaluate the idea that the public did not hold presidents fully responsible for the acceleration of prices, the decline in real income growth, and the rise in unemployment associated with the OPEC shocks, because these price hikes were imposed

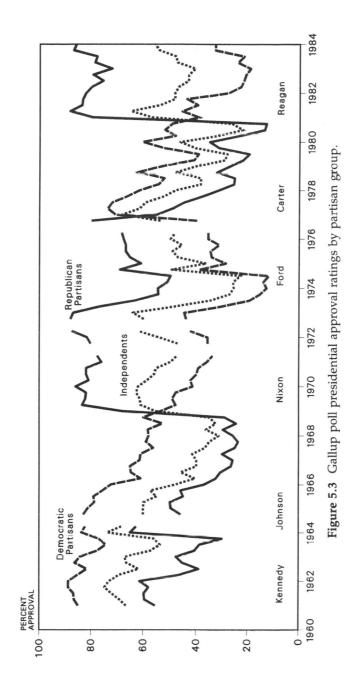

Figure 5.3 Gallup poll presidential approval ratings by partisan group.

externally and therefore were to a large extent beyond the control of domestic political authorities.

The reasoning behind the inclusion of p-oil may be clarified as follows. The deterioration of macroeconomic conditions caused by the OPEC shocks was proportional to the inflation of energy prices (p-oil). Let λ_p, λUgap, and λ_r denote, respectively, the parameters for the extra inflation, unemployment, and decline in real income growth rates viewed by the public as attributable to the oil shocks and hence outside the control of U.S. authorities.

$$\beta_p(p - \lambda_p \cdot p\text{-oil})$$
$$\beta_{Ugap}(Ugap - \lambda_{Ugap} \cdot p\text{-oil})$$
$$\beta_r(r + \lambda_r p\text{-oil})$$

should appear in the political support model in place of terms such as $\beta_p p$, $\beta_{Ugap}Ugap$, and $\beta_r r$. Inasmuch as λ_p, λ_{Ugap}, and λ_r cannot be estimated individually (they are not identified), however, including the term $\beta_{p\text{-oil}} \cdot p\text{-oil}$ additively in the estimation equations along with p, Ugap, and r represents the joint effect:

$$\beta_{p\text{-oil}} \cdot p\text{-oil} = (-\beta_p\lambda_p - \beta_{Ugap}\lambda_{Ugap} + \beta_r\lambda_r) \cdot p\text{-oil}$$

Given that β_p and β_{Ugap} are negative and β_r is positive, $\beta_{p\text{-oil}}$ clearly should be positive in the regressions if the public in fact did not hold incumbents fully accountable for the deterioration of the economy brought on by the OPEC shocks.

Three noneconomic variables important to American electoral politics are also included in the models. First, the regressions include the number (in thousands) of Americans killed in action in Vietnam, which is designed to pick up the war-induced deterioration of presidential approval ratings. Opposition to the Vietnam War made it impossible for Lyndon Johnson to seek renomination and reelection in 1968, and the deep divisions it created in the Democratic party helped elect Richard Nixon (who narrowly defeated Hubert Humphrey) to the presidency. Research suggests that the gruesome flow of body-bags, rather than autonomous moral misgivings or even impatience with the protracted duration of the conflict, is what best explains growth of the war's unpopularity among the general electorate.[27] The killed-in-action rate, therefore, is the most appropriate variable for capturing the erosion of domestic mass political support generated by intensification of the war.

Second, the equations include a Watergate variable to take account of the extraordinary decline in Nixon's political support generated by the greatest American political scandal of the postwar era. This variable was formed by summing discrete Watergate events in each quarter, weighted on a scale of 1 to 3 according to how strongly the president was incriminated personally by each event in national press reports. Because the Watergate variable is based on events that were identified and scored independently of the time path of Nixon's approval ratings, it is a genuine exogenous variable and not merely a term tailored to track the collapse of the president's mass political support in 1973 and 1974.

Finally, in view of the unique visibility of the president when public attention is focused on international affairs, the regressions include a "rally 'round the president" variable taken from John Mueller's work and extended through administrations subsequent to those in Mueller's studies.[28] Rally points are dramatic, sharply focused international events, normally of crisis proportions, that involve U.S. interests and, hence, the president as chief executive. A bipartisan spirit generally prevails during such events, and media criticism is muted. Consequently, presidents ordinarily enjoy a brief boost in their approval ratings. As Nelson Polsby put it: "Invariably, the popular response to a president during international crisis is favorable, regardless of the wisdom of the policies [the president] pursues."[29] Similarly, J. R. Lee observed: "[The president] becomes the focus of attention in times of crisis . . . symbolizing national unity and power . . . The public's reaction will include a feeling of patriotism in supporting presidential action, a desire not to hurt a president's chance of success."[30] The Rally variable is simply the number of rally events in each quarter.

The noneconomic variables were not included in the models simply to improve the regression fits. Although in this chapter we are mainly interested in the response of mass political support for presidents to macroeconomic performance, it is not possible to obtain accurate (unbiased and consistent) estimates of the relationship between macroeconomics and electoral politics if variables correlated with the economy that affect political support are omitted from the equations. Over the entire sample period, Rally events are distributed more or less independently of fluctuations in the economy, but this is not true of Watergate and Vietnam. When the first OPEC energy shock hit in late 1973, for example, the Watergate scandal was still running strong. Consequently, if no attempt were made to take account of Watergate events, some of the decline in Nixon's support caused by the scandal would be incorrectly attributed to the post-OPEC bulge in inflation, and the quantitative results would tend to exaggerate inflation's electoral importance.

Matters become more serious when we consider the correlation of unemployment and the intensity of the Vietnam War. The absorbtion of manpower by the military and the strong fiscal stimuli associated with our intervention in Vietnam produced a fully utilized economy and unusually low rates of unemployment. (Over the regression sample range, the correlation of the unemployment gap and the Vietnam killed-in-action variables is -0.60.) Indeed, the troughs of postwar unemployment occurred at the peaks of the Korean and Vietnam wars. Low unemployment enhances presidents' mass political support, whereas the Vietnam War obviously was a political liability for Presidents Johnson and Nixon. (Korea was also a major liability for Truman, but the quantitative analyses in this book begin with the Kennedy administration.) Hence, models that omitted consideration of Vietnam would tend to underestimate the political benefits of favorable unemployment performance. In fact, in the limiting case, failure to take account of the war might even lead to the conclusion that low or falling unemployment yields declines in political support.[31]

Estimates of the political support model for partisan subgroups—Democrats, Republicans, and Independents—based on equation (5.14) are reported in Table 5.1. As equation (5.14) indicates, the model is nonlinear by virtue of the parameters w and g, and so the regressions were undertaken using a standard nonlinear algorithm. Although the lag sums in the model extend to the distant ("infinite") past, observations on the right-side performance variables were generally available for 52 periods (quarters) prior to the first Gallup approval rating in the estimation range (1961:1). Therefore, the equations are estimated with finite lags without affecting the consistency of the estimates.

PARTISANSHIP, PRESIDENTIAL PERSONALITIES, AND HYPOTHETICAL
PERFORMANCE ASSESSMENTS: THE SHADOW PERFORMANCE CONSTANTS
Consider first the president-specific, shadow performance constants, $S_{(t)}$, in Table 5.1. Recall that the $S_{(t)}$ terms are designed to pick up voters' unobserved assessments of how those out of power might have performed had they controlled the White House. President-specific constants are very crude proxies indeed for such hypothetical

Table 5.1 Nonlinear, weighted least-squares estimates of the political support model, quarterly, 1961:1–1984:1

Independent variable	Partisan group (average sample fractions)		
	Democrats (0.46)	Republicans (0.26)	Independents (0.28)
Regression inter-cept, α	3.58	4.30	2.19
	(0.582)	(0.056)	(0.467)
Shadow constant, $S_{(t)}$			
Kennedy	0.985	−0.818	−0.038
	(0.042)	(0.045)	(0.049)
Johnson	0.652	−0.852	−0.321
	(0.040)	(0.045)	(0.052)
Nixon	−0.165	1.43	0.476
	(0.034)	(0.047)	(0.040)
Ford	0.154	1.45	0.891
	(0.057)	(0.070)	(0.072)
Carter	0.408	−0.554	−0.089
	(0.037)	(0.045)	(0.047)
Reagan	−0.765	1.44	−0.019
	(0.033)	(0.055)	(0.038)
Lag weight decay rate, g	0.834	0.771	0.842
	(0.005)	(0.012)	(0.007)
Party/Admin weight, w	0.697	0.748	0.783
	(0.021)	(0.033)	(0.028)
Noneconomic terms			
Vietnam			
β	−0.084	−0.069	−0.062
$\beta/(1-g)$	−0.506	−0.301	−0.392
	(0.003)	(0.005)	(0.003)
Rally events			
β	0.223	0.290	0.246
	(0.007)	(0.01)	(0.001)
Watergate			
β	−0.026	−0.017	−0.020
	(0.001)	(0.001)	(0.001)

Table 5.1   (*continued*)

Independent variable	Partisan group (average sample fractions)		
	Democrats (0.46)	Republicans (0.26)	Independents (0.28)
Economic terms			
Inflation rate (*p*)			
β	−0.028	−0.039	−0.031
$\beta/(1 - g)$	−0.166	−0.169	−0.195
	(0.001)	(0.002)	(0.002)
Per capita real disposable income growth rate (*r*)			
β	0.011	0.018	0.015
$\beta/(1 - g)$	0.068	0.081	0.095
	(0.001)	(0.002)	(0.001)
Unemployment gap (Ugap)			
β	−0.030	−0.025	−0.015
$\beta/(1 - g)$	−0.182	−0.109	−0.095
	(0.002)	(0.004)	(0.002)
Energy price inflation rate (*p*-oil)			
β	0.002	0.0011	0.0017
	(0.0004)	(0.0006)	(0.0005)
Fit			
Correlations of actual proportions and fitted proportions implied by the fitted logits	0.98	0.96	0.92

Notes: This table is based on 89 periods ($T = 89$). Asymptotic standard errors, based on the model assumption of unit variances, appear in parentheses.

assessments of shadow performance. As a practical matter, they necessarily absorb all president-to-president variation in approval ratings stemming from the unique appeal ("personality") of particular chief executives, as well as from unobserved factors favoring one party or the other that are unrelated to interparty and interadministration comparisons of explicitly measured performance. Nonetheless, these constants yield some useful information.

Since the equations are estimated for partisan groups in the electorate, it comes as no news whatsoever to learn that the shadow constants reflect the perceptual filter of party identification. Respondents in the surveys who generally consider themselves to be Democrats uniformly exhibit larger shadow constants during Democratic presidencies than during Republican presidencies. In other words, they normally see Democratic presidents as having greater personal appeal than Republican ones, and attribute less-favorable shadow performance to the Republicans when they are in opposition than to the Democrats when they are out of power. Just the reverse is true of respondents who report a general attachment to the Republican party. Among the Republican partisans, such factors as hypothetical assessments of out-party shadow performance and the idiosyncratic appeal of individual presidents in every case enhance support for Republican presidents and diminish support for Democratic presidents. Not surprisingly, the magnitudes of the constants for Independents (survey respondents who reported no party attachment) fall between those of the other two groups. Among Independents, assessments of unobserved shadow performance and of the appeal of particular presidents are not colored so obviously by partisan biases.

Intergroup patterns in the $S_{(t)}$ parameters are summarized in Table 5.2, which gives the time-weighted averages of the logit equation constants, along with the corresponding magnitudes in terms of approval percentage points actually registered by the Gallup polls. The entries in the table should be interpreted as follows. Among Democratic partisans, the weighted mean of the shadow constants for Democratic presidents is +0.65. Translated into percentage points in the Gallup polls, this implies that, on average, unobserved systematic and idiosyncratic factors added about 15 points to the approval ratings of Democratic presidents. For Republican presidents, the mean shadow constant in the equation for Democratic partisans is approximately −0.28. This translates to −6 percentage points in the approval polls. Among Republican respondents, the shadow constant means go in the opposite direction and the magnitudes are much larger.

Table 5.2   Weighted averages of shadow performance constants by party of the president

Partisan group	Impact on logit[a]|impact on percent approval[b]		
	Democratic presidents (1)	Republican presidents (2)	Bias toward Republican presidents [(2) − (1)] (3)
Democrats	+0.654 | +15.2%	−0.275 | −6.2%	−0.928 | −21.4%
Independents	−0.173 | −7.2%	+0.416 | +10.2%	+0.589 | +17.4%
Republicans	−0.744 | −18.3%	+1.44 | +32.8%	+2.18 | +51.1%
Weighted average of group biases:[c]			+0.31 | +9.0%

a. Impacts on logits are averages of the shadow constants for partisan groups and are calculated by weighting each president-specific constant by the fraction of the total number of periods each president was in office. In this case $T = 89$.

b. Impacts on approval percentages are calculated from expressions of the form $[F(\bar{y}_j) - F(\bar{y}_j - \bar{s}_j)]$ · 100, where the $\bar{y}_j$ are the average logits for each partisan group for Democratic and for Republican presidents; the $\bar{s}_j$ are the corresponding average shadow constants shown in the table; and F is the logistic distribution operator, $F(x) = \exp(x)/[1 + \exp(x)]$.

c. Averages of group biases are calculated by weighting the bias for each group by its fraction of the total survey samples, which are shown at the top of Table 5.1.

Support for Democratic presidents in the polls is diminished an average of 18 percentage points, and the approval ratings of Republican presidents are raised by a whopping 33 points.

The shadow constants of Independents also appear to be more favorable for Republican presidents than for Democratic presidents. Apparently, Independents typically find Republican presidents more appealing on personal grounds than Democratic presidents, and/or generally imagine the shadow performance of Republican oppositions to be more favorable than that of Democratic oppositions. This may mean that a significant number of the self-identified Independents in the surveys are "closet" Republicans. In any case, the constants in the equations for Independents indicate that, on average, the approval ratings of Democratic presidents are depressed by about 7 percentage points and the approval ratings of Republican presidents are raised by around 17 points. Clearly, much of the intergroup variation (as well as the variation over time) in popular support for presidents is unexplained by movements in the measured macroeconomic and political variables included in the model.

The weighted averages of the shadow constants indicate that, net of the impact of the substantive performance variables in the model, Republican presidents during the sample period have enjoyed a sizable advantage over their Democratic counterparts. The magnitudes of these "biases" in favor of Republican presidents, which are estimated by subtracting the relevant average for Democratic presidents from the relevant average for Republican presidents, are shown on the far right side of Table 5.2. For Independents, these computations show that, in terms of shadow constants, the bias toward Republican chief executives averaged about +0.59. This translates to 17 percentage points in the Gallup approval polls. Among Republican partisans, the bias was enormous, amounting to about +2.2, or 51 percentage points in the Gallup approval ratings. Naturally, the bias runs the other way among Democrats in the surveys. The difference of the average constants is −0.9, or −21 percentage points in the polls. But this pro-Democratic bias among Democrats is much smaller than the corresponding pro-Republican bias among Republican partisans. Other things being equal, Republican partisans were much more likely to support Republican presidents than Democratic partisans were to support Democratic presidents. Inasmuch as Democratic partisans made up about 46 percent of the electorate during the sample period whereas Republicans comprised only about 26 percent, such a differential was necessary for Republican presidents to achieve much support in the polls or, in fact, to be elected in the first place.

The combined pro-Republican biases of Republican partisans and Independents more than offset the pro-Democratic bias of Democratic partisans, however. Summing of the group biases, weighted by the relative sizes of groups in the electorate, shows that across the entire electorate Republican chief executives enjoyed a net political support advantage of about 9 percentage points in the polls (see the bottom of Table 5.2). Put another way, the macroeconomic performance of Democratic presidents had to be superior to that of Republican presidents in order for Democratic chief executives to achieve equivalent aggregate approval ratings.[32] The fact that Democratic presidents have had a much larger nominal partisan base in the electorate than have Republican presidents has not translated into an automatic support advantage—quite the contrary. Although the reasons for pro-Republican bias in political choices are unclear,[33] a similar phenomenon was noted by Donald Stokes, by Michael Kagay and Greg Caldeira in their analyses of the election survey data, and by Ray Fair in his study of aggregate presidential voting outcomes during the twentieth century.[34]

POLITICAL DISCOUNT RATES AND PARTY AND ADMINISTRATION
COMPARISONS: THE g AND w PARAMETERS

The g parameters in the equations define the rate of decay of the distributed lag coefficients for the performance variables—that is, the rate at which past outcomes are discounted when the electorate makes current political evaluations of the president. When g is equal to or near 0, the models collapse to the static specification used in many studies, in which only the most recent performance outcomes affect political support. On the other hand, a value of g close to 1 means, as noted earlier, that effective political memories extend far back in time and past outcomes are not discounted steeply when voters make contemporaneous political choices. The nonlinear least-squares estimates of g vary between 0.77 and 0.84, indicating that politically relevant memories of past performance are roughly homogeneous across partisan groups and extend many quarters back in time. The idea that political support is based on cumulative, relative performance is, therefore, not merely an appealing theoretical fiction. Assuming g to be less than 0.77 to 0.84 would yield inferior predictions of fluctuations in the logits of the Gallup approval rating data.

   Recall that if a performance variable x is held at some constant value $\bar{x}$ indefinitely, the ultimate impact on the political support index is $\beta\bar{x}/(1 - g)$, where β is the contemporaneous impact of $\bar{x}$ estimated by the relevant regression coefficient in Table 5.1. Given that $\beta\bar{x} \cdot (1 - g^{k+1})/(1 - g)$ is the impact after k lags, the proportion of the ultimate impact of sustained performance $\bar{x}$ felt by the kth lag[35] is $1 - g^{k+1}$. Hence, for a typical g equal to, say, 0.82, 18 percent of the ultimate impact of a sustained movement in x is felt contemporaneously, 55 percent is felt after one year (4 quarters), 80 percent after two years (8 quarters), and about 96 percent after four years (16 quarters).[36] The electorate is not quite as myopic, therefore, as some analyses of the American political economy have implied. Yet economic (as well as noneconomic) outcomes during the last half of the four-year presidential term clearly have decisive influence on political support on election days, and this leaves plenty of room for incumbents to pursue election-oriented macroeconomic policy plans. Certainly the heavy weight that voters seem to assign to recent outcomes—and the steep discounting of more distant outcomes—does not undermine the logic of political business cycle strategies.

   The w coefficients define the relative contribution of interadministration and interparty performance comparisons to a president's political support. The estimates of w in Table 5.1 vary between 0.7 and 0.8. This means that interparty performance comparisons are an important component of the process by which the electorate makes contemporaneous political choices. (Remember, however, that the shadow performance constants, $S_{(t)}$, undoubtedly embody important, unobserved, president-specific sources of political support.) A pattern illustrated theoretically by the hypothetical cases analyzed earlier is, then, empirically relevant. If we hold performance constant and negatively valued outcomes prevail, there is a tendency for a new president's political support to begin at a higher level and to trend downward more sharply when there has been a change in the party holding the White House as opposed to a simple shift in administration. Conversely, if we hold performance constant across comparisons and negatively valued outcomes outweigh positively valued ones, a president following administrations of his own party is likely to enjoy less of an elevated, "honeymoon" level of political support early in his term, but he is also likely to experience a less dramatic decline in political support over time.

Notice, however, that after 24 periods (six years) or so have elapsed, the lag function weights g^k become negligible in magnitude. Consequently, at this point the Party and Admin components of political choices are not distinguishable. (For example, 0.82^{24} is 0.0085, a quantity that for practical purposes may be treated as 0.) A president who makes it well into a second term, therefore, is typically not helped or hurt significantly by the record of his predecessors, whether they belonged to his own party or to the opposition party. Aside from unmeasured factors embedded in the $S_{(t)}$ constants, which include the unique appeal of individual presidents, as well as components of the parties' political stock not picked up by the substantive variables in the model, during a second term a president's approval ratings are based almost entirely on a distributed lag of his own current and prior performance. At the time of this writing, though, no president since Eisenhower has served two full terms.

POLITICAL SUPPORT AND NONECONOMIC EVENTS

The noneconomic terms in the model—Americans killed in action in Vietnam, international Rally events, and the Watergate scandal events—all enter the regressions in Table 5.1 with properly signed and statistically significant coefficients. Escalation of American losses in Vietnam and the unfolding of the Watergate scandal obviously contributed to the deterioration of Johnson's and Nixon's approval ratings, and Rally events were sources of upward movement in public support for all presidents.

Where it is sensible, two coefficients are reported for the performance variables in Table 5.1: the ordinary regression (β), which gives the contemporaneous response of the (logit) dependent variable to a unit increase in an independent variable, and the steady-state or long-run coefficient, $\beta/(1 - g)$, which gives the ultimate response of the dependent variable to a sustained unit increase in an independent variable. Because the lag rate of decay parameter g varies a bit across partisan groups, the $\beta/(1 - g)$ estimates render a slightly different impression of intergroup differences than do the β coefficients.

The estimates in Table 5.1 pertain to the impact of the performance variables on the logits of approval rates $\ln(P'_{jt}/(1 - P'_{jt}))$. Practical political interest, however, centers on sources of variation in the actual approval proportions in the polls, P'_{jt}. Because P' is a nonlinear function of $\ln(P'/(1 - P'))$, the response of the approval proportions to changes in performance is not obvious from the results in Table 5.1.[37] Therefore, to give an idea of the practical political consequences of fluctuations in the noneconomic variables, I computed the implied changes in the percentage of each group expressing approval of the president (100 P'_{jt}) following reasonable movements in the Vietnam, Rally, and Watergate variables.[38] The computations, which were done separately for Democratic and Republican presidents, are reported in Table 5.3.

The entries at the top of Table 5.3 indicate that a Vietnam killed-in-action rate of 1000 per quarter, sustained one full year, depresses approval rates between 4 and 6 percentage points. The magnitudes of these decreases in political support are modest, and Presidents Johnson and Nixon could have easily absorbed them and maintained their effectiveness in the White House. But the war dragged on much longer than a year, and the casualty rate rose much higher than 1000 per quarter. Continued "indefinitely," which given the values of the lag rate of decay coefficients (g) means 5 to 6 years (essentially the duration of the conflict in its shooting phase), the same killed-in-action rate of 1000 per quarter yields declines of between 6 and 12 points in approval ratings. American losses, however, climbed well above 1000 per quarter, or 4000 per year. In 1966 battle fatalities averaged 1200 per quarter, and they increased steadily thereafter, peaking at nearly 5000 per quarter during the first half of 1968, following the Tet offensive. As a result of this escalation of the war, nearly

Table 5.3 Gallup poll approval ratings: responses to Vietnam losses, Rally crisis events, and Watergate scandal events (percent)

Event	Democrats	Republicans	Independents
Vietnam killed-in-action			
1000 per quarter sustained 1 year—			
During Johnson	−5.9	−4.4	−4.9
During Nixon	−5.5	−3.8	−4.9
1000 per quarter sustained indefinitely—			
During Johnson	−11.7	−6.7	−9.6
During Nixon	−10.1	−5.8	−9.7
Battle fatalities 1967:1–1968:3 (during Johnson)	−27	−19	−22
Rally crisis events			
1 event in 1 quarter			
Democratic presidents	+4.5	+6.9	+6.2
Republican presidents	+5.1	+4.8	+6.2
3 events in 1979:4, 2 events in 1980:1 (during Carter)	+24	+17	+22
Watergate scandal events			
1 event tied directly to Nixon (+3)	−0.6	−0.3	−0.5
Change in Nixon's approval rating from 1972:2 to 1974:3 due to Watergate	−21	−17	−20

10,000 American troops were killed in 1967, and almost 15,000 were killed in 1968. President Johnson had paid a high price for the carnage in terms of lost political support even before he paid the ultimate political price in March 1968, when he found it necessary to announce that he would not seek renomination and reelection.

Simulation experiments with the political support equations indicate that by the third quarter of 1968, as a result of the high American killed-in-action rate after 1966, President Johnson's approval ratings in the Gallup polls were down 27 percentage points among Democratic partisans and 22 points among Independents, as compared to 19 points among Republicans in the electorate.[39] The simulation results yield the same intergroup pattern as do the other estimates (in Table 5.1 as well as in Table 5.3) of mass political reactions to the war. Even though battle fatalities generally ran higher during Johnson's tenure as commander in chief than during Nixon's, the political support of Democratic partisans (and Independents) was apparently much more sensitive to the Vietnam catastrophe than was that of Republican partisans.

These model-based results are consistent with public opinion data showing that opponents of the war and those advocating "dovish" policies were more likely to be black, less educated, of lower income, and Democratic by political affiliation.[40] Moreover, we know that the children of lower-status Americans suffered a disproportionate share of the Vietnam casualties.[41] So the comparatively large erosion of political support among Democrats caused by the escalation of the war probably stemmed at least partly from the fact that the social composition of the Democratic party's mass base included more of those segments of American society that bore the brunt of the war's human toll than did the Republican party's core constituency.

It makes little sense to think of indefinite repetition of Rally crisis events, and so Table 5.1 only shows estimates of the initial contemporaneous boost to the logit of presidential approval ratings associated with the Rally term. The logit model parameters in this table suggest that the impulse to rally 'round the president during international crises may be somewhat more prevalent among Republican partisans than among others. But intergroup differences are not large. The impact of Rally events on actual ratings, shown in Table 5.3, indicates that international crises typically raise support for presidents by 5 to 6 points in the polls.

Rally events are not very frequent; about 1.5 per year is the long-run average. On only five occasions between 1961 and 1984 has more than one event occurred in a quarter. President Carter, however, experienced a unique sequence of five distinct events from 1979:4 to 1980:1, related to the seizure of American hostages in Tehran and the Soviet invasion of Afghanistan. This unprecedented string of Rally events produced a dramatic recovery in Carter's approval ratings which, in the wake of accelerating prices and falling real incomes, had fallen by the third quarter of 1979 to a level not seen since the Watergate scandal (Figure 5.3). The estimates in Table 5.3, based on simulation experiments with the fitted political support equations, suggest that by 1980 : 1 the crisis events had raised Carter's quarterly average approval ratings by 17 or more percentage points in all groups. Although such a sequence is unlikely to be repeated in the future, the Carter episode illustrates the upper bounds of the impact of international crisis events on political support for the president. And even though the political benefits of Rally events are transitory, they were large enough in this case to help a severely weakened and vulnerable president to survive (more easily than many had anticipated) a vigorous challenge to his renomination by Senator Edward Kennedy.[42] By election day, however, the boost to Carter's standing with the electorate had worn off, and he was easily defeated by Ronald Reagan.[43]

The last noneconomic term in the model represents the Watergate scandal, which ultimately drove President Nixon from office. The logit model estimates in Table 5.1 reinforce the view that partisanship colored the electorate's response to the Watergate events. Nixon's support among Republican partisans was less adversely affected by the scandal than were his approval ratings among Independents and, especially, Democrats. Yet the computations in Table 5.3 show that a single Watergate revelation incriminating Nixon personally and scored +3 on the +1 to +3 Watergate-events importance scale had negligible impact on the President's approval rating. Nixon's problem was that the scandal escalated far beyond this level, as one revelation followed another. The press-weighted Watergate variable averaged about 15 in 1973 and peaked at 24 in 1973 : 2 during the Senate hearings. Simulating the equations to obtain the hypothetical time path of the president's political support had there been no Watergate scandal, indicates that between 1972 : 2 and 1974 : 3 Nixon's approval ratings were depressed 21 points among Democrats, 17 points among Republicans, and about 20 points among Independents. In the aggregate, then, Nixon appears to have suffered a loss of nearly 20 percentage points in the Gallup polls as a result of the Watergate events.[44]

MACROECONOMIC PERFORMANCE AND MASS POLITICAL SUPPORT

It is natural to expect political responses to macroeconomic performance to vary across electoral groups because, as shown in Chapters 2 and 3, the consequences of macroeconomic outcomes (particularly unemployment outcomes) are unevenly distributed within the electorate. The regression parameter estimates in Table 5.1 are broadly consistent with what we know about the distributional consequences of economic configurations. The contemporaneous or first-period impact of inflation (β) is largest for Republicans and smallest for Democrats, with Independents falling in between. But, as noted earlier, given the variation in the lag weight decay rates (g) across groups, the long-run or steady-state estimates $\beta/(1 - g)$ convey more useful information about intergroup patterns in the impact of the macroeconomy on political support. The long-run estimates in Table 5.1 indicate that cross-partisan group differences in sensitivity to inflation are not substantial, although again Democrats appear to be somewhat less averse to rising prices than are Republicans or, especially, Independents.[45] Inasmuch as lower-income and lower-occupational-status individuals are more likely to be Democrats than Republicans or Independents, these results square with the basic conclusion in Chapter 3 that inflations have not imposed disproportionately heavy burdens on less-advantaged groups in the electorate. For if the lower-income and lower-occupational-status classes were the main victims of inflations, we would expect a much larger negative inflation coefficient in the equation for Democrats than in the equations for Republicans or Independents.

Nonetheless, in the electorate generally, political support for presidents is adversely affected by high inflation rates. And because the inflation regression coefficients are estimated in the presence of the real income growth rate, the results mean that even when money incomes fully keep pace with rising prices, inflation still erodes presidential approval ratings. In other words, voters have a "pure" aversion to inflation that does not seem to hinge on whether inflation actually chips away at real income growth rates.

The parameter estimates for the growth rate of per capita real personal disposable income are smaller than the inflation estimates in all groups. And, as in the case of inflation, cross-partisan group differences in the response of political support to real income growth rates are not dramatic. In fact, insofar as the macroeconomy is concerned, only the unemployment gap coefficients reveal intergroup differences of real political importance. In view of the evidence presented in Chapters 2 and 3 showing that unemployment has much larger effects on the distribution of economic well-being than does inflation, this pattern is not surprising.

The long-run, steady-state estimates for Ugap, $\beta/(1 - g)$, indicate that the political support of Democratic partisans is 1.7 to 1.9 times more sensitive to unemployment fluctuations than is the political support of Republicans and Independents. Most political conflicts surrounding macroeconomic policies center, however, on the relative priority that should be given to inflation and unemployment. So, from a political point of view, it is probably more informative to examine the relative magnitudes of the associated coefficients across partisan groups. Multiplying the ratio of the unemployment gap and inflation parameters by −1 yields what is known as the marginal rate of substitution (MRS)—that is, the implicit rate at which voters are willing to substitute extra unemployment for inflation:[46]

| | Partisan Group | | |
Marginal rate of substitution	Democrats	Republicans	Independents
$\left(\dfrac{\text{Unemployment gap}}{\text{Inflation}}\right)$	1.1	−0.65	−0.49

The coefficient ratios, or marginal rates of substitution, suggest that in order for a given level of the political support index (the logit of the approval rate) to be maintained among Democratic partisans, an increase of 1 percentage point in the unemployment gap would have to be accompanied by a drop in the inflation rate of about 1.1 points. This suggests that Democrats in the electorate are just about indifferent to equivalent, compensating movements in unemployment and inflation. The marginal rates of substitution of unemployment for inflation for Republicans and Independents are much smaller. This implies that these groups have flatter, more inflation-averse preference (indifference) curves. Among Republicans and Independents, a politically innocuous increase of 1 percentage point in unemployment requires that inflation decline by approximately 0.65 and 0.48 point, respectively.

Alternatively, if the inflation rate rose by 1 point, the political support index for Democrats would remain unchanged if the unemployment gap fell by 0.9 point (1/−1.1). By contrast, it would take an unemployment decline of 1.5 (1/−0.65) to 2.0 (1/−0.49) percentage points per point of increased inflation to keep the political support of Republicans and Independents unchanged. It is clear, then, that what constitutes a politically acceptable short-run inflation-unemployment trade-off in the United States differs considerably across the parties' core constituencies. Yet, despite the partisan differences, these results also underscore the observations in Chapter 4 about how heavily the general electorate in the United States appears to weight inflation relative to unemployment. Even Democrats, who are significantly more unemployment averse than other electoral groups, seem to be willing to trade higher unemployment for lower inflation on an almost point-for-point basis. The objective, measurable economic costs of inflation and unemployment reviewed in Chapters 2 and 3 simply do not account for implicit preference schedules that are so inflation averse. Less tangible perceptual and psychological factors obviously play a large role in the American public's reaction to inflations.

Politicians watch actual approval ratings in the polls rather than logits. Therefore, I have computed the changes in the percentage of each partisan group supporting the incumbent president induced by increases of 2 percentage points in the unemployment gap, the real income growth rate, and the inflation rate. The computations are reported in Table 5.4.[47] Because the effects of transitory movements in the macroeconomy lasting only a quarter or so are small, the induced changes in approval ratings implied by the logit model coefficient estimates are computed for increases in the economic variables sustained 4 quarters, 8 quarters, and indefinitely.[48] Finally, because the responses of political support to changes in the macroeconomy depend on initial support levels (see the discussion of Figure 5.2 and equation 5.5 above), the computations for each partisan group are made from benchmarks equal to the group's mean approval rating for Democratic and Republican presidents. (The means are shown in the first column of Table 5.4.)

The intergroup patterns in the responses to increases in the economic variables mimic the patterns revealed by the logit model regression coefficients just discussed, except now the responses are expressed in terms of percentage-point changes in the approval polls. If sustained for 4 quarters (one year), a 2-percentage-point increase in the unemployment gap yields declines in presidential approval ratings ranging between about 2.4 and 4.2 percentage points, with the maximum response occurring, as expected, in the Democratic partisan group. The adverse political effects of the 2-point increase in unemployment accumulate with time. After 8 quarters, approval ratings are depressed from 3.6 points to over 6 points, with the response again largest for Democratic partisans. In the case of a severe contrac-

Table 5.4 Percentage changes in Gallup approval ratings induced by changes in macroeconomic performance

Average approval rating (percent)	Partisan group	Change of +2 in unemployment gap (Ugap) sustained—			Change of +2 in per capita real personal disposable income growth rate (r) sustained—			Change of +2 in inflation rate (p) sustained—		
		Four qtrs	Eight qtrs	Indefinitely	Four qtrs	Eight qtrs	Indefinitely	Four qtrs	Eight qtrs	Indefinitely
	Democrats:									
68.2	Democratic Presidents	−4.2	−6.3	−8.4	+1.5	+2.2	+2.9	−3.8	−5.7	−7.6
33.6	Republican Presidents	−4.1	−5.9	−7.6	−1.6	+2.4	+3.1	−3.7	−5.4	−7.0
	Republicans:									
37.7	Democratic Presidents	−3.3	−4.4	−5.0	+2.5	+3.4	+3.9	−5.0	−6.6	−7.5
75.6	Republican Presidents	−2.7	−3.7	−4.3	+1.9	+2.5	+2.9	−4.2	−5.8	−6.7
	Independents:									
50.3	Democratic Presidents	−2.4	−3.6	−4.8	+2.4	+3.5	+4.7	−4.8	−7.2	−9.6
49.5	Republican Presidents	−2.4	−3.6	−4.8	+2.4	+3.5	+4.7	−4.8	−7.2	−9.6

tion lasting two years, which created, say, an extra 4 points of unemployment, the political effects would be nearly twice as large,[49] ranging from 6 to almost 12 percentage points in the approval ratings. The remaining unemployment estimates in Table 5.4 show the impact on political support of a 2-point rise in unemployment that is sustained indefinitely—which, practically speaking, means 5 to 6 years. In this case approval falls by 7.4 to 8.4 percentage points among Democrats, as opposed to only 4 to 5 points among Republicans and Independents. These are large, politically important responses, and they clearly differentiate Democrats from Republicans and Independents.

The response of approval ratings to a 2-percentage-point increase in the growth rate of per capita real personal disposable income is more modest. (The mean growth rate during the regression sample period was 2 percent, and so this experiment represents a doubling of the average real income growth stream.) Table 5.4 indicates that the responses are generally largest for the Independents. In this group the rise in presidential approval ratings induced by a 2-point increase in the real income growth rate lasting indefinitely is a little less than 5 percentage points. An increase of the same magnitude in the inflation rate produces bigger political responses in all groups, comparable in magnitude to the responses to increased unemployment. Unlike the results for unemployment, however, the effects of inflation peak among Independents rather than among Democrats.

Inflation clearly took on special importance after the two OPEC oil price hikes. From the fourth quarter of 1973 to the third quarter of 1974, in the wake of the first OPEC oil price shock, energy prices in the United States rose 115 percent. From the second quarter of 1979 to the third quarter of 1982, during the second oil shock, U.S. energy prices increased about 170 percent.[50] Energy purchases amount to about 10 percent of total consumption, so the 1973–1974 rise in energy prices directly added more than 11 points to cumulative inflation, and the 1979–1980 rise added 17 points. Therefore, had voters held Presidents Nixon and Carter fully responsible for these accelerations of the general price level, presidential approval ratings probably would have declined by magnitudes significantly larger than those shown in Table 5.4 for an increase of 2 points in the inflation rate sustained 4 periods (8 points of cumulative inflation). In addition, the extra unemployment and lost real income associated with the shocks would have further depressed political support for the incumbents had the public held them solely accountable for the economic problems.

Yet the coefficient estimates for p-oil in Table 5.1 indicate that Nixon and Carter were not punished by the electorate for the full acceleration of prices (and rise in unemployment and decline in real income growth rates) following the two OPEC energy price shocks. The reason, no doubt, is that voters realized that to a great extent the shifts in the terms of trade imposed by the OPEC cartel were beyond the control of American authorities. Just how big a break voters gave incumbents during these crises is estimated by the simulation results reported in Table 5.5.[51]

During the first OPEC crisis the simulation estimates indicate that approval ratings were compensated by between 2 and 3 percentage points. The magnitudes are not trivial, but they are hardly large enough to have made much difference to President Nixon, whose political support in the polls fell about 20 points because of Watergate alone (see Table 5.3). Carter's approval ratings appear to have been compensated by larger margins—from 2 to 6 percentage points in various partisan groups. Relative to the severity of OPEC II and the adverse effects of the 1979–1980 recession created by the administration to offset the enormous rise in inflation, however, the magnitudes are quite modest. As we saw in Table 5.3, Carter benefited much more in late 1979 and early 1980 from the rally 'round the president effect associated with the foreign policy crises in Iran and Afghanistan.

In the discussion of Figure 5.2 and equation (5.5), I pointed out that responses of approval proportions to marginal changes in the economy and other variables are influenced by the proximity of each group's baseline approval proportion to 0.5—the so-called threshold of opinion change. Within partisan groups this does not seem to be of great importance empirically, as the responses to the near-marginal 4-quarter changes in the economic variables shown in Table 5.4 suggest. In each partisan group Democratic and Republican presidents

Table 5.5 Compensation of approval ratings (percent) during OPEC oil shocks (p-oil)

Partisan group	1973:4–1974:3 (during Nixon)	1979:2–1980:2 (during Carter)
Democrats	+2	+6
Republicans	ǀ 2	+2
Independents	+2.6	+4.5

generally suffer about the same loss of support from adverse marginal changes in the economy and gain about the same degree of support from favorable marginal changes.

Looking across partisan groups, however, the story is different. For both Democratic and Republican presidents, the baseline presidential approval ratings of Independents are more likely to lie in the vicinity of 50 percent (0.5) than are those of Democratic and Republican partisans. In other words, Independents typically are closer to the threshold of opinion change. The reason surely is that Independents are anchored less to any particular Democratic or Republican president by exogenous political loyalties (which are picked up by the president-specific shadow performance constants in the equations) than are voters who normally think of themselves as Democrats or Republicans. Consequently, in comparison to those of the other groups, movements in the Independents' approval ratings induced by changes in the economy and other performance variables are magnified by a factor that often runs as high as 1.4.[52] Insofar as systematic sources of approval change are concerned, it follows that Independents (who, on average, made up about 28 percent of the electorate during the sample period) have a greater tendency than other groups to drift into and out of a president's base of support in the mass public. Relative to their share in the electorate and to the weight they give performance variables, Independents ordinarily contribute more than either Democratic or Republican partisans to fluctuations in aggregate presidential approval ratings stemming from marginal changes in performance. Because Independents constitute something of a swing group, support-maximizing presidents have an incentive to pay special attention to their preferences and priorities.

5.3 A Concluding Word on the Economy and Political Support for Presidents

At the beginning of this chapter I introduced a dynamic model of political choice in which voters forced to make discrete judgments applied relative rather than absolute evaluation standards. The estimation results showed that past as well as current economic (and noneconomic) events influence voters' contemporaneous political judgments. However, past outcomes are discounted backward in time, undoubtedly because the present relevance of prior performance decays over time. The rate at which the past appears to be discounted by the electorate leaves plenty of leeway for incumbents, if they are so inclined, to pursue election-oriented, "political business cycle" economic strategies. For example, the estimates of lag weight decay rates indicate that outcomes in the quarter nearest the presidential election are weighted about 24 times more heavily than are outcomes in the first period of a 16-quarter presidential administration.[53] Viewed in terms of years rather than quarters, the same lag parameter estimates suggest that outcomes over the entire election year are weighted approximately 11 times more than outcomes over the first year of a four-year administration.[54]

Although I was mainly interested in the political implications of macroeconomic performance, in order to secure meaningful estimates of the impact of the economic conditions on political support for presidents it was necessary to take account of important noneconomic events correlated with inflation, unemployment, or real income growth rates. By and large the estimation results were consistent with the conclusions of earlier chapters. Chapter 4, which analyzed the Michigan data on public concern about inflation and unemployment, showed that the electorate has a substantial aversion to rising prices. This chapter connected such abstract concern about inflation more directly to political behavior. Estimates of the political support equations indicated clearly that movements in the inflation rate are an important source of fluctuations in presidential approval ratings in all partisan groups.

The review of the incidence and distributional costs of inflation and unemployment in Chapters 2 and 3 established that, aside from energy price shocks, unemployment was the major economic cause of redistributions away from lower income classes toward the higher income classes. The redistributive effects of inflations appeared to be small and not particularly disadvantageous to less affluent groups. Therefore, it was not surprising to see in this chapter that the political support of Democrats was much more sensitive to unemployment than was the political support of Republicans or Independents. Looking at the impact of unemployment on political support relative to that of inflation, we see the same alignment of partisan cleavages: Democrats versus Republicans and Independents. Although the "demand" for low inflation is pronounced among all groups, the estimation results imply that the relative priority given inflation as opposed to unemployment is markedly lower among Democratic partisans than among others. Voters who express a general attachment to the Democratic party made up just under half of the total electorate in the 1960s, 1970s, and early 1980s; this helps explain the tendency of presidents—particularly Republican presidents—to pursue policies aimed at trading extra unemployment for reduced inflation. I will return to this important point in Chapter 7, after considering in Chapter 6 the contribution of economic performance to recent presidential election outcomes.

6 Economic Performance and the 1980 and 1984 National Elections

> This campaign was about the failure of Jimmy Carter—about the way he messed up our economy and our standing in the world.
>
> —William Casey, former campaign manager, Reagan-Bush Committee

> 1980 was not a watershed election. According to all the post-election surveys we've done, the people wanted change in this election. They haven't necessarily ratified what we stand for. We have this great opportunity in the next years to show what we stand for works.
>
> —Paul Weyrich, head of the New Right's Committee for the Survival of a Free Congress

The 1980 and 1984 elections obviously represented a substantial victory for Ronald Reagan and, to a lesser degree, the Republican party. In 1980 Reagan received 55.3 percent of the two-party vote (50.7 percent of all votes cast) and became the first challenger to defeat an elected, incumbent president since Roosevelt beat Hoover in 1932. The Democrats' two-party share of the popular vote for the House of Representatives fell 3 percentage points (from 54.3 percent in 1978 to 51.4 percent in 1980), and they lost 33 seats,[1] going from 276 to 243. Democratic losses (Republican gains) in 1980 were even bigger in the Senate. The Democrats lost 12 seats, going from 58 to 46, and as a result the Republicans enjoyed their first Senate majority since 1954.[2] Among the victims of the debacle were more than half a dozen well-known liberal Democratic senators: McGovern (South Dakota), Bayh (Indiana), Culver (Iowa), Magnuson (Washington), Durkin (New Hampshire), Nelson (Wisconsin), and Church (Idaho).

After absorbing a 26-seat loss in the 1982 mid-term elections[3] (there was a standoff in the 1982 Senate contests, with no change in the preelection distribution of party strength), which occurred amid the highest unemployment rates since the Great Depression, the Republicans bounced back a bit in 1984. They gained 14 seats in the House,[4] too few to offset the losses of 1982 and reestablish a working House majority for the president on critical budget issues.[5] The Democrats picked up 2 seats in the Senate, which left them with the same 47-to-53 disadvantage they had right after the 1980 election. But the election of John Kerry (Massachusetts), Paul Simon (Illinois), Albert Gore (Tennessee), and Tom Harkin (Iowa) helped replenish the liberal, progressive wing of the Senate Democrats, which was so severely weakened in 1980.[6] As a result, President Reagan faced a more liberal and less compliant Senate and House, in 1985–1986 than he had in 1981–1982, when he achieved his greatest legislative successes.

By far the most decisive outcome in the 1984 elections was Reagan's showing in the presidential contest. He achieved a victory of landslide proportions, winning 59 percent of the popular vote and carrying 49 states. Reagan's Democratic opponent, Walter Mondale, carried only his home state, Minnesota, and the District of Columbia.

Put simply, there are two ways to interpret the 1980 and 1984 election outcomes. One interpretation, more popular among journalists and Republicans in or close to the administration than among academic specialists, is that these elections reflected a fundamental shift to the right of the electorate's preferences concerning the federal government's role in domestic social and economic affairs.[7] According to this view, the elections represented a dramatic erosion of political support for the federal economic intervention and social welfare efforts that began with Franklin Roosevelt's New Deal legislation in the 1930s and reached maturity with Lyndon Johnson's Great Society programs in the 1960s. By this interpretation, the 1980 election was a watershed election in which a majority of voters soundly rejected federal activism and welfare-state policies sustained under Carter and the Democrats. And 1984 reinforced 1980, signaling the development of a durable electoral majority favoring conservative Republicanism.

An alternative interpretation is that the 1980 election outcomes represented the predictable consequences of poor performance—particularly poor macroeconomic performance—under Carter and the Democrats. Similarly, given the favorable course of the economy during the last half of Reagan's first term and, in particular, the impressive economic performance of the election year, the 1984 results also were entirely consistent with the historical connection between the economy and voting outcomes. Although Reagan's edge over his opponents in terms of personal appeal and perceived leadership qualities surely influenced the outcomes of the 1980 and 1984 presidential contests, these elections basically should be seen as referenda on the incumbents' handling of the economy and, to a lesser degree, other problems.[8] According to this view, then, any president and incumbent party going before the electorate with the record of Carter and the Democrats in 1980 would have been in deep political trouble, and virtually any credible challenge to the president and the in-party—from the left or from the right—probably would have been successful. Analogously, an incumbent as personable as Reagan presiding over an extremely robust election-year recovery, no matter what his ideological coloration, would have been exceptionally difficult to turn out of office. Hence the 1980 and 1984 election results do not reflect a fundamental realignment toward conservative Republicanism; rather, they represent the usual political consequences of one administration's quite poor and another's remarkably good late-term economic performance.

These alternative interpretations, though oversimplified, hold great implications for the support that President Reagan's social and economic program will command in the years ahead. If Reagan's back-to-back defeats of Carter and Mondale were based largely on a realigning ideological shift in the electorate away from welfare-state liberalism, then Reagan's program of increased military spending, reduced social spending, and redistributions of the tax burden away from corporations and the rich is consistent with a new distribution of voter preferences and consequently should enjoy sustained, widespread support among voters and vote-sensitive politicians. On the other hand, if the Democrats' defeats in 1980 and 1984 stemmed primarily from poor economic performance during the latter part of the Carter administration and good performance during the latter part of Reagan's first term, then the program put in place in 1981–1982 (discussed in detail in Chapter 9) will have to yield a significant long-run improvement in America's macroeconomic performance in order to remain politically viable. As we shall see below, most of the evidence concerning the sources of the Republican victories in 1980 and 1984 supports the poor performance/good performance interpretation.[9]

6.1 Landslide Elections in Recent History

Nearly all party and election specialists agree that the last major realignment of the American party system occurred during the Great Depression of the 1930s and was initiated by Franklin Roosevelt's defeat of Herbert Hoover in 1932.[10] James Sundquist, a leading scholar of American party systems, described the Roosevelt-led re-alignment toward the Democrats this way: "The then-majority Republican party was overwhelmingly repudiated when Franklin Roosevelt defeated Herbert Hoover. Within four years—probably mainly within two years—Roosevelt succeeded in converting the anti-Hoover, anti-Republican protest vote of 1932 into a pro-Roosevelt, committed Democratic majority, and a new political alignment was in place."[11] One way to evaluate whether President Reagan's successes signaled a genuine realignment toward conservative Republicanism, then, is to compare changes in the balance of partisan forces over 1980–1984 and 1932–1936. Some relevant data appear in Table 6.1.

What distinguishes 1932–1936 from 1980–1984 is not Franklin Roosevelt's presidential election victories, although he won by landslides in both 1932 and 1936, but the fact that the Democratic party made enormous gains in the House and Senate that established the Democrats as the normal majority party in the Congress down to the present day. As the seat shifts reported in Table 6.1 show, not only did the Democrats gain 97 seats in the House and a dozen in the Senate with Roosevelt's initial victory in 1932, but they continued to increase their congressional strength over the next two elections. After the 1936 elections their net gain in the House amounted to 117 seats, they were 31 seats stronger in the Senate, and they dominated both branches of Congress. The pro-Republican shift in the Congress accompanying Reagan's 1980 victory was much smaller than the pro-Democratic shift of 1932; more important, the Republicans did not increase their 1980 House and Senate margins as a result of the next two elections. During Reagan's first term the Republicans never achieved a numerical majority in the House, and, with the help of conservative Democratic representatives, they enjoyed a working or programmatic majority only during the 1981–1982 session. Although the Republicans obtained a narrow majority in the Senate as a result of the 1980 shift, their Senate margin, in sharp contrast to that of the Democrats in the early 1930s, was no greater after the next presidential election than it had been four years earlier. And with 22 of the 34 seats up for election in 1986 held by Republicans, including many of the party's weakest incumbents,[12] the Republicans were likely to lose rather than gain Senate strength in the 1986 election. (In fact, the Democrats regained a Senate majority—by a 55 to 45 margin—in 1986.)

Table 6.1 Presidential voting outcomes and congressional seat shifts and landslide elections

President	Year	Percentage of popular vote	Percentage of electoral vote	No. of states won	House seat shift in favor of winner's party	Senate seat shift in favor of winner's party
Franklin Roosevelt	1932	57.4	88.9	42[a]	+97	+12
Roosevelt midterm	1934	—	—	—	+9	+10
Franklin Roosevelt	1936	60.8	98.5	46[a]	+11	+9
				Net gain:	+117	+31
			Postelection partisan balance:		333 D/89 R	75 D/17 R
Ronald Reagan	1980	50.7	90.9	44	+33	+12
Reagan midterm	1982	—	—	—	−26	+1
Ronald Reagan	1984	58.9	97.6	49	+16	−1
				Net gain:	+23	+12
			Postelection partisan balance:		253 D/182 R	47 D/53 R
Dwight Eisenhower	1956	57.4	86.1	41[a]	−2	0
			Postelection partisan balance:		234 D/201 R	49 D/47 R
Lyndon Johnson	1964	61.1	90.3	44	+37	+1
			Postelection partisan balance:		295 D/140 R	68 D/32 R
Richard Nixon	1972	60.7	96.7	49	+12	−2
			Postelection partisan balance:		242 D/192 R	56 D/42 R

Note: Seat shifts are computed from election to election for the party winning the presidential election.

a. Of 48 states

Landslides are not rare events in presidential races. Since 1824, when national popular vote tallies became routine, the winner has achieved at least 55 percent of the vote in nearly one out of three presidential elections. Like President Reagan, most of the big winners were incumbents seeking another term. Of the ten postwar presidential contests, four were won by clear landslides, which is consistent with the prewar pattern. Data pertaining to the postwar landslides are shown at the bottom of Table 6.1.

Ronald Reagan's 1984 vote share, 58.9 percent, falls between the 57.4 percent Dwight Eisenhower received in his 1956 reelection bid and the approximately 61 percent apiece received by Lyndon Johnson in 1964 and Richard Nixon in 1972. The 16-seat shift in the House accompanying Reagan's 1984 landslide was better than the 2-seat loss the Republicans suffered in 1956 with Eisenhower or even the 12-seat gain they achieved with Nixon in 1972. It was substantially less, however, than the 37-seat gain the Democrats enjoyed when Lyndon Johnson trounced Barry Goldwater in 1964. The 1984 House outcomes came as a bitter disappointment to the Republican national election apparatus, which had invested heavily in House races in hopes of giving President Reagan much more help on Capitol Hill.[13] Insofar as the House is concerned, then, the 1984 seat shift was not unusual. In fact, it was exactly equal to the mean shift (of 16 House seats) associated with postwar presidential landslides. The same is true of the 1984 shift in the Senate partisan balance. The Republicans' loss of 1 seat (computed on an election-to-election basis) falls just about in the middle of the range, which runs from −2 to +1, of Senate outcomes accompanying other big postwar presidential victories.

Casual analysis of presidential voting outcomes and congressional seat shifts in landslide elections indicates that President Reagan's successes in 1980 and 1984 have little in common with the great realignment toward the Democrats in the early 1930s. Instead, the 1984 election outcomes are most reminiscent of 1972. In that election year Republican incumbent Richard Nixon shellacked his Democratic opponent, George McGovern, but carried only 12 additional Republican Representatives and two fewer Republican Senators with him to Washington. As in 1972 and other postwar landslides, there is no obvious sign from the election statistics that the president has created a durable new majority in favor of conservative Republicanism. Yet Reagan clearly established himself as a powerful force in electoral politics. What accounts for his back-to-back wins?

6.2   Election Cycle Economics in 1980 and 1984

The macroeconomic history of the Carter administration is a textbook example of how *not* to run an economy to win reelection. When Carter entered the White House, unemployment stood at 7.7 percent—a hangover from the terrible 1974–1975 recession under Ford. Carter tackled the unemployment issue head on, and the administration pursued stimulative macroeconomic policies throughout 1977 and into 1978. The policies succeeded, helping to lower unemployment by almost 2 percentage points between the end of 1976 and the beginning of 1979. As described in Chapter 3, however, inflation accelerated steadily in 1977 and 1978 and ratcheted upward even more in 1979 following the second big round of OPEC petroleum price increases. This prompted the Carter administration in late 1978 to abandon the traditional Democratic goal of moving the economy toward full employment and to implement restrictive monetary and fiscal policies designed to put downward pressure on the inflation rate. The policy shift succeeded in creating an election-year recession, but because of the sluggish response of wages and prices to economic slack, the inflation rate declined only slightly during the last two quarters of 1980 from its mid-year peak. Consequently, President Carter and the Democrats went before the electorate in 1980 with the worst of all possible situations—high inflation, increased unemployment, and falling real income and output. Given the rate at which voters discount past outcomes (see Chapter 5), Carter gained less credit for the favorable economic performance of 1977, 1978, and early 1979 than he lost as a result of miserable performance during periods just prior to the 1980 election. Indeed, the time paths of unemployment and real income growth rates over Carter's term, shown in Figure 6.1, are just the reverse of what an election-oriented, vote-maximizing macroeconomic strategy would call for. (Electorally motivated economic cycles are analyzed in Chapter 8.)

In contrast to those of the Carter years, the time paths of unemployment and real income growth rates during Reagan's first term conform perfectly to the so-called political business cycle pattern, as the data in Figure 6.2 show. Reagan came into office committed to achieving substantial disinflation, and the requisite restrictive monetary policies were imposed without delay. The recovery that had begun during the last quarter of 1980 was aborted, and real incomes declined and unemployment rose sharply. Joblessness peaked at

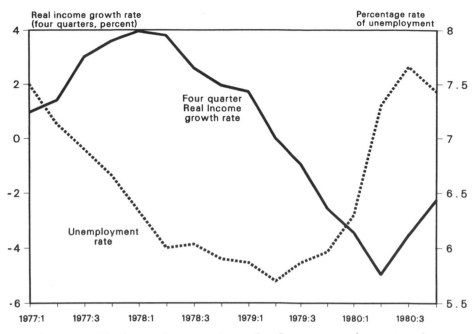

Figure 6.1 Election-cycle economics under Carter: unemployment and per capita real personal disposable income growth rates, 1977:1–1980:4.

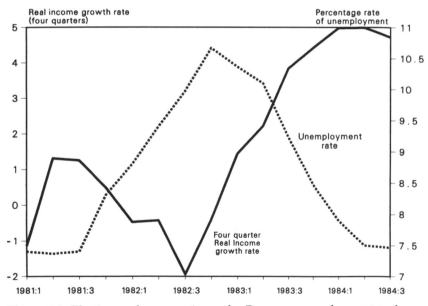

Figure 6.2 Election-cycle economics under Reagan: unemployment and per capita real personal disposable income growth rates, 1981:1–1984:3.

nearly 11 percent of the civilian labor force in the fourth quarter of 1982. Predictably, the collapse of output, incomes, and employment dealt a crushing blow to inflation. By 1983 the consumer price inflation rate was running at about 3 to 4 percent, compared to the double-digit rates of Carter's last two years.

After absorbing large losses in the 1982 House mid-term elections, however, the Reagan administration pushed hard (and successfully) for a shift in monetary policy. With monetary policy and fiscal policy coordinated in an expansive direction, a brisk recovery got under way. The unemployment rate fell continuously throughout 1983 and into 1984, though at the time of the presidential election it still was not lower than the rate Reagan had inherited from Carter. But the economy had been moving by leaps and bounds in the right direction for two years prior to Reagan's bid for reelection. The preelection growth rates of real incomes were especially impressive. In every preelection quarter after 1983:3, per capita real personal disposable income grew by more than 4 percent.[14] In the first three quarters of 1984, the growth rates were close to 5 percent. From an electoral point of view, it is hard to imagine a recovery timed more favorably. Unlike Carter and the Democrats in 1980, then, Reagan and the Republicans went into the 1984 election year with the best of all possible situations—low inflation (thanks to the sharp 1981–1982 contraction), falling unemployment, and rapidly rising real incomes.

The economic performance records of Carter and Reagan, along with those of other postwar administrations, may be compared more systematically through use of the data in Table 6.2. The evidence in Chapter 5 showed that mass political support for the president (as registered in the Gallup polls) is influenced by the unemployment rate, the Consumer Price Index inflation rate, and the per capita real personal disposable income growth rate, so these variables are shown in the table. The left side of the first column in Table 6.2 shows election-year records. It is obvious that Carter's economic record was an especially poor one. Carter's inflation and real income growth rate records are by far the worst ones listed. Carter's election-year unemployment gap (the deviation of the unemployment rate from the so-called natural rate), though better than Ford's in 1976 or Reagan's in 1984, was not favorable by historical standards either. Viewing the variables together, we see that macroeconomic conditions in 1980 were by a wide margin less favorable than those prevailing in all other postwar presidential election years.

Unlike Carter in 1980, Reagan presided over a very robust economy

Table 6.2 Election-year and cumulative economic performance records of postwar presidential administrations

Administration (election year)	Unemployment rate, Ugap (1)		CPI inflation rate, P (2)		Per capita real personal disposable income growth rate,[a] R (3)	
	Election year	Cumulative[b] weighted avg.	Election year	Cumulative weighted avg.	Election year	Cumulative weighted avg.
Truman (1952)	-2.07	-1.48	2.26	3.22	1.07	1.80
Eisenhower I (1956)	-1.03	-0.796	1.46	1.36	3.12	2.63
Eisenhower II (1960)	0.39	0.389	1.50	1.36	0.82	1.03
Kennedy–Johnson I (1964)	-0.40	-0.008	1.31	1.14	5.51	4.72
Johnson II (1968)	-2.04	-1.86	4.12	3.75	2.85	2.60
Nixon I (1972)	-0.23	-0.206	3.27	3.67	3.38	3.14
Nixon II–Ford (1976)	1.79	1.60	5.56	6.36	2.27	1.37
Carter (1980)	1.25	0.706	12.67	10.33	-3.25	-0.78
Reagan (1984)[c]	1.62	2.44	4.0	4.29	4.79	3.51

a. Nominal per capita personal disposable income deflated by the Consumer Price Index. All growth rates are formed by taking first (quarterly) differences of the natural logarithms and are expressed at annual rates.

b. The weighted average records are defined over the fifteen preelection quarters of each administration, from the last performance outcome backward to the first, using a decay rate–discount parameter of 0.8:

$$\left(1 \Big/ \sum_i g^i\right) \sum_i g^i X_{t-i-1}, \quad i = 0, 1, 2, \ldots 14$$

The value $g = 0.8$ is based on the empirical estimates for presidential election outcomes and presidential approval ratings. In the cumulative performance calculations for P and R, the CPI inflation rate was adjusted downward to take into account the (small) direct effects of the OPEC shocks.

c. Based on the first three quarters of 1984

in 1984. The administration's weak spot, as noted earlier, was unemployment, but the unemployment rate had declined quite steadily from the terrible levels of the 1981–1982 contraction. The real income growth rate picture was exceptionally good in 1984. In fact, 1984 was the best year for real incomes before or since the Johnson landslide election of 1964. The inflation situation was also favorable in 1984, especially in comparison to the double-digit rates prevailing when Reagan first entered the White House.

Because political support is based on an administration's cumulative performance and not just on its election-year record, the right side of column 1 in Table 6.2 gives a weighted average of the economic performance outcomes for the fifteen preelection quarters of each presidential term, starting with the quarter nearest the election (the July-August-September quarter) and going backward to the first quarter. The message conveyed by the cumulative weighted average performance records does not differ substantially from that of the election-year records, however.[15] Looking backward from the preelection quarter over the time range 1980:3 to 1977:1, we see that Carter's cumulative real income and inflation records were by far the worst of any postwar administration's. In addition, his administration had created a sizable unemployment gap in response to the OPEC II burst of inflation. It is not difficult to understand, therefore, why Jimmy Carter was the first elected incumbent to be defeated in a reelection bid since Herbert Hoover in 1932: Carter had the worst preelection economic record since Hoover. In fact, 1980 was the first election year since 1932 in which the year-on-year growth rate of real output and income was actually *negative*. This is one important reason why President Carter's Gallup poll approval rating plummeted in July 1980 (the trough of the 1980 recession) to 21 percent—the lowest level recorded since the Gallup organization began polling in the 1930s during the Roosevelt administration. In retrospect, it would have been surprising had Carter *not* lost the 1980 election.[16] On the other hand, given the cumulative inflation and real income growth rate records under Reagan, it comes as no surprise that he easily won the 1984 election.

6.3   Rule-of-Thumb Statistical Models for Presidential Voting Outcomes

The impression left by the statistical data in Table 6.2—that the economic record suffices to explain the Democrats' losses in 1980 and

1984—is reinforced by predictions of several rule-of-thumb statistical models for presidential-election-year outcomes. Evidence presented in Chapter 5 indicates that it was the collapse of the economy during the last year and a half of the Carter administration, rather than an ideological shift to the right, that accounted for the deterioration of Carter's Gallup approval ratings. Similarly, the great decline and subsequent dramatic recovery of President Reagan's approval ratings are also well accounted for by the course of economic performance during his first term. Gallup approval ratings are not electoral outcomes, but, as pointed out in Chapter 5, these ratings correlate quite highly with the vote shares received by incumbents running for reelection, as well as with the vote shares of nonincumbent nominees of the president's party. For all presidential elections from 1952 to 1976, the linear equation describing the relationship between the percentage of the two-party vote received by the incumbent party's nominee (Vote) and the preelection Gallup percentage approval rating of the president (Approve) is[17]

$$\text{Vote}_t = 33.3 + 0.373 \text{ Approve}_t \qquad (6.1)$$
$$\phantom{\text{Vote}_t = }(6.33)\ (0.11)$$

where $R^2 = 0.68$, the standard error of regression $= 4.2$, and the coefficient standard errors appear in parentheses.

President Carter's 1980 preelection approval rating was 32.5 percent. By equation (6.1),the forecast of Carter's two-party vote share in the 1980 election is, therefore, 45.4 percent $[33.3 + (0.373 \cdot 32.5)]$—only 0.8 percentage point above his actual two-party share of 44.6 percent and nearly 2 full standard errors lower than the 1952–1976 mean presidential vote share of 53.3 percent received by nominees of the incumbent party. President Reagan's 1984 preelection approval rating came in at a much healthier 60 percent.[18] Using the same equation to forecast Reagan's 1984 vote share yields a prediction of 55.7 percent. This is 3.2 points short of the 58.9 percent that the president actually received in the 1984 race, well within 1 forecast standard error. The main point, however, is that simple rule-of-thumb statistical models based on preelection approval ratings—models that in no way depend on the idea of realigning ideological shifts—predict Reagan to be a big winner in 1984 and Carter to be a clear loser in 1980.

A second and perhaps more convincing way of laying the 1980 and 1984 outcomes at the door of the economy is to examine the election results in light of the historical association between macroeconomic performance and the vote share received by the incumbent party's candidate. As the discussion in Chapter 1 made clear, the structure of the American political economy has changed profoundly from the prewar to the postwar period, and therefore it is sensible to confine the analysis to elections from 1952 onward. Because the political effects of unemployment, inflation, and the real personal disposable income growth rate cannot be estimated reliably from the rather small number of postwar presidential election observations, the estimation equation includes only real income growth rate performance.[19]

The following equation[20] best describes the association of the two-party vote share (in percentage points) of the incumbent party's candidate for president (Vote) and the weighted average of the (OPEC-adjusted) annualized quarter-on-quarter percentage rate of growth of real personal disposable income per capita (R), during the fifteen preelection quarters for each administration, for all elections from 1952 to 1980:

$$\text{Vote}_t = 45.7 + 3.30 \left[\sum_{i=0}^{14} 0.8^i R_{t-i-1} \left(1 \Big/ \sum_{i=0}^{14} 0.8^i \right) \right] \qquad (6.2)$$

$$(3.27)\ (1.49) \qquad (0.09)$$

where $R^2 = 0.63$, the standard error of regression $= 5.09$, and the coefficient standard errors appear in parentheses.

Figure 6.3 shows the scatterplot of vote shares and cumulative real income growth rates, along with the regression line implied by equation (6.2). Because so few observations were available, 1980 was included in the estimation range, and Carter's vote share prediction is based on the fitted value from the equation and is not an actual forecast. The year 1984 was excluded from the estimation sample, however, and so the prediction for Reagan (indicated by the asterisk) is a true forecast.

The regression-line prediction for Jimmy Carter's two-party vote share, based on a cumulative discounted real income growth rate record that was actually negative by the third quarter of 1983, is 42.5 percent. This is 2.1 points below the 44.6 percent vote share that Carter actually received in 1980. Reagan's cumulative real income growth rate record (which like the others, was computed by summing real growth rates back from the preelection quarter and applying lag-discount weights 0.8^i) by the third quarter of 1984 was a remarkably

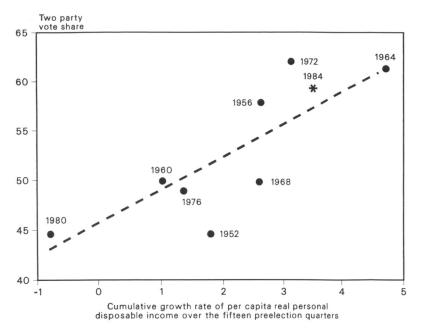

Figure 6.3 Cumulative real income growth performance and the vote for the incumbent party's presidential candidate.

good 3.5 percent. The forecast of Reagan's 1984 vote share from equation (6.2) is therefore 57.3 percent, which is only 1.6 points short of the 58.9 percent he in fact obtained in the 1984 presidential race.

These regression predictions reinforce the conclusion that Ronald Reagan's successes in 1980 and 1984 are readily explained by the traditional association between presidential election outcomes and real income growth rate performance under the incumbent. Any incumbent with a cumulative preelection real income growth rate record as poor as Carter's in 1980 would be expected to lose badly. Likewise, barring offsetting events outside the economy, the historical evidence shows that any incumbent presiding over preelection real income growth rates as favorable as Reagan's almost surely would be a big winner.

Although the economy has been the most important issue in recent presidential contests, noneconomic events have on several occasions exerted decisive influence on electoral outcomes. Two such occasions can be identified in Figure 6.3. The regression line projected in the figure yields large overpredictions (negative residuals) for the Democratic (incumbent party) candidates in 1968 and especially in 1952. Clearly, American involvement in Vietnam and Korea—interventions that ultimately became extremely unpopular and that play no role in the simple economic performance model of equation (6.2)—helped make the vote for the incumbent party's presidential candidate lower than that estimated from the real income growth rate records alone. Indeed, the regression line shown in Figure 6.3 suggests that had the United States not become involved in the Korean and Vietnamese conflicts during the Truman and Kennedy-Johnson administrations, respectively, the Democrats most likely would have won the 1968 presidential election and might well have won in 1952 also. (Recall that prominent Republican campaign appeals in 1952 and 1968 were Eisenhower's pledge to "go to Korea" and Nixon's "secret plan" to end the Vietnam War.) In other words, given the economic record prior to the 1952 and 1968 contests, both Adlai Stevenson and Hubert Humphrey might well have been winners had the Democrats, as the incumbent party, not been saddled with Korea and Vietnam.

But the main lesson to be drawn from equation (6.2) and Figure 6.3 is that, barring major noneconomic developments salient to the electorate (such as our military involvements in Korea and Vietnam), candidates of the incumbent party typically have received a comfortable majority of the two-party presidential vote whenever the cumulative annualized growth rate of real income over the fifteenth preelection quarters approached the postwar mean of 2.2 percent.[21] In fact, not one postwar candidate of the incumbent party was successful when the cumulative, geometrically weighted, average real income growth rate record was under 2 percent. Moreover, statistical analyses of congressional voting outcomes parallel to those shown here for presidential contests indicate that recent shifts in House and Senate seats are also well explained by the White House party's economic record.[22]

Because voters weight performance outcomes close to the election date much more heavily than outcomes earlier in the term (for $g = 0.8$, the weight given to the outcome in the preelection quarter is more than twenty times larger than the weight given to the outcome in the first quarter of a presidential term), a strong election-year economic record will compensate for truly miserable performance during the first couple of years of an administration. Conversely, miserable performance near the election will neutralize a very favorable record earlier in the term. President Carter's problem was that the disastrous economic performance of 1979–1980 swamped the quite favorable growth record of 1977–1978. President Reagan's advantage was that the extraordinary growth rates of late 1983 and 1984 more than compensated for the near-catastrophe of 1981–1982. Nixon's first election bid in 1960 was unsuccessful because the strong performance of 1959 was insufficient to neutralize the political consequences of the 1958 recession and especially the 1960 recession during the Eisenhower administration. In President Ford's case, even though election-year outcomes are weighted more heavily than the earlier record, the reasonably good 1976 growth rate was simply not favorable enough to overcome the political fallout from the deep recession of 1974–1975.

6.4 Evidence from the Surveys

Evidence from survey interviews of large numbers of individual voters is fully consistent with the conclusions drawn from statistical analysis of aggregate electoral and economic data. In 1980 and 1984 (as well as in 1976), the economy clearly loomed larger in voters' minds than did other issues. Indeed, data over time on responses to the Gallup poll question "What is the most important problem facing the country today?" (graphed in Chapter 4) show that economic concerns have dominated the public agenda since the early 1970s. A similar story is told by interviews conducted by the *New York Times*/CBS News and *Los Angeles Times* survey organizations with thousands of actual voters in selected precincts as they left the polls in 1980 and 1984.

Table 6.3 reports data from the exit poll interviews on issues identified/mentioned by Reagan supporters as affecting their vote. Neither of the highly charged social and moral issues—the Equal Rights Amendment or abortion—seems to have weighed heavily on the minds of more than a tiny fraction of Reagan voters in 1980 or 1984. This implies that the influence on the general election outcomes of anti-feminist groups and the "right-to-life" and "moral majority" movements was probably quite small,[23] notwithstanding all the publicity their activities received and all the money such groups raised.[24] Likewise, the highly publicized crisis in Iran, widely believed to have hurt Carter in the 1980 election, does not appear to have been especially important to very many of Reagan's supporters. Foreign policy and U.S. international prestige generally were more important to the Reagan constituency, especially in 1984. But these questions were overshadowed in both elections by the great economic issues of inflation and unemployment and by the related fiscal issues of federal

Table 6.3 Issues underlying support for Reagan in the 1980 and 1984 elections

Issues most important in affecting the vote for Reagan	Percentage of voters who cited in—	
	1980	1984
The economy (inflation, jobs, unemployment)	60	44
Federal taxes, spending	13	32
Federal budget deficit	26	20
Foreign relations and U.S. prestige	19	28
Crisis in Iran	9	—
Arms control	—	6
ERA and abortion	5	5

Sources: For 1980, *New York Times*/CBS News Election Day Poll, reported in the *National Journal*, November 8, 1980, p. 1877. For 1984, *Los Angeles Times* exit polls, reported in the *National Journal*, November 10, 1984, p. 2131.

Notes: The 1980 poll permitted two responses, whereas the 1984 poll allowed only one. Responses of the 1984 poll were therefore weighted by a factor of 2 to make the results more comparable with those of 1980. A couple of response categories for 1984 were available from the 1984 *New York Times*/CBS poll.

spending, taxing, and deficits.[25] To be sure, many of the concrete opinions underlying concern about federal taxation and expenditure reflect a genuine right-wing ideological chord. Although many voters endorsed a reduction in the scope of government in the abstract, the big federal social programs enjoyed overwhelming public support.

The 1980 General Social Survey, for example, found that only 33 percent of the public thought that "the government should provide fewer services . . . in order to reduce spending." Enormous majorities held the view that we were spending either "too little" or "about the right amount" on such major social program areas as health (92 percent), education (90 percent), solving the problems of large cities (76 percent), drug addiction (92 percent), improving the conditions of blacks (74 percent), and crime (94 percent).[26] Similarly, the postelection January 1981 *New York Times*/CBS News poll found that 72 percent of the public wanted to see federal spending "increased or kept about the same" for benefits to college students, 72 percent held the same view regarding unemployment compensation, 77 percent regarding pollution control, 75 percent regarding mass transit, 81 percent regarding highways, and 89 percent regarding Social Security cost-of-living benefits.[27] Only the food-stamp program in the *New York Times*/CBS News poll and a residual "welfare" category in the General Social Survey did not attract strong majority support. A total of 47 percent of the public thought spending on food stamps should remain the same or be increased, and 41 percent thought we were spending "too little" or "about the right amount" on "welfare." Nevertheless, divisions within the electorate over narrowly focused "welfare" programs, as opposed to more universalistic social programs, predate the Reagan victories by many years.[28]

Two years into President Reagan's first term, public support for social spending programs had not changed much. In the December 1982 Roper poll, 90 percent of the public thought we were spending too little or about the right amount for education, 84 percent believed the same was true for the environment, 91 percent for crime prevention, and 82 percent for energy efforts. Again, only spending for the residual "welfare" category did not receive overwhelming support: 48 percent thought spending was too little or about right, and 45 percent thought we were spending too much in this area.[29] Yet the September 1982 Gallup poll found 66 percent of the public opposing "a decrease in government spending for social programs, such as health, education and welfare," and in the January 1983 Gallup poll an overwhelming 83 percent registered opposition to cuts in "entitlement programs such as Social Security" in order to reduce the federal deficit.[30] Subsequent polls tell the same story. As William Schneider concluded after reviewing the 1983–1984 survey data, "The evidence is clear: there has been no Reagan revolution in public attitudes toward government," and "support for domestic social spending . . . has gradually increased during the Reagan presidency."[31]

The personal qualities selected by Reagan voters as reasons for their choice also reveal little evidence of ideological voting in 1980 and 1984. Table 6.4 shows the relevant data from the *New York Times*/CBS News and *Los Angeles Times* election-day surveys. The most striking feature of these data is that in both 1980 and 1984 only a very small proportion of Reagan supporters listed his conservatism as a reason for their choice. Instead, voters' sense that it was "time for a change" in 1980 and their perception that Reagan was a "strong" and, by 1984, "capable" and "experienced" leader were identified as the decisive factors. In light of the economic mismanagement of 1979–1980 and Jimmy Carter's well-developed capacity to appear vacillating and ineffective, it is hard to argue that such judgments were inaccurate or

Table 6.4   Personal qualities underlying support for Reagan in the 1980 and 1984 elections

Personal qualities affecting the vote for Reagan	Percentage of voters who cited in—	
	1980	1984
He's a strong leader	21	82
He's more capable	—	44
Time for a change	38	—
Vision for the future	—	24
His experience in government	6	34
He's my party's candidate	12	6
He's a real conservative	11	6
Better vice president	9	8

Sources: For 1980, *New York Times*/CBS News Election Day Poll, reported in the *National Journal*, November 8, 1980, p. 1877. For 1984, *Los Angeles Times* exit polls, reported in the *National Journal*, November 10, 1984, p. 2131.

Notes: The 1980 poll permitted two responses, whereas the 1984 poll allowed only one. Responses of the 1984 poll were therefore weighted by a factor of 2 to make the results more comparable with those of 1980. A couple of response categories for 1984 were available from the 1984 *New York Times*/CBS poll.

unreasonable, at least during the 1980 contest. Small wonder, then, that when the public was asked to evaluate comparatively the performance of the last eight presidents (Roosevelt to Carter) in the January 1981 Harris poll, only 2 percent thought Carter was "best on domestic affairs" and fully 44 percent thought he was "least able to get things done."[32] In any case, there is no sign from the survey data in Tables 6.3 and 6.4 that support for Reagan in the last two presidential elections reflected a significant surge in conservative political orientations among voters.

Recent trends in the ideological distribution of the electorate identified by various national surveys support this interpretation. Table 6.5 reports the relevant data. The various surveys used different questions and scales to assess the electorate's ideological orientation, but every one of them indicates that there was no great shift toward conservatism prior to or beyond the 1980 election. The University of Michigan's Survey Research Center (SRC) National Election Studies

Table 6.5 Recent trends in the ideological distribution of the electorate (percent)

Survey	1972	1974	1976	1978	1980	1982	1984
SRC National Election Studies							
Liberal	19	21	16	20	17	15	23
Moderate	27	26	25	27	20	23	35
Conservative	27	24	25	28	29	28	36
Gallup Polls							
Liberal (left)	27	—	20	—	19	21	
Middle-of-the-road	34	—	47	—	49	43	NA
Conservative (right)	39	—	33	—	31	36	
General Social Surveys							
Liberal	—	31	29	28	26	27	
Moderate	—	40	40	38	41	41	NA
Conservative	—	30	31	34	34	32	

Sources: For SRC surveys, Warren Miller et al., American National Election Studies Sourcebook (Cambridge, Mass.: Harvard University Press, 1980), p. 95; Interuniversity Consortium for Political and Social Research, Election Study Codebooks; and idem, 1984 Election Study Tape. For GSS surveys, The Roper Center, General Social Surveys, 1972–1980: Cumulative Codebook, July 1980, p. 70; and Public Opinion (October/November 1982). For Gallup surveys, Public Opinion (February/March 1981), 20; and Gallup Report, September 1982. Question wordings and ideological scales vary.

data in Table 6.5 show that the distribution of ideological orientations since 1972 has been quite stable. The percentage of Conservatives in the SRC samples is trendless. The percentages of Liberals and Moderates appear to be a few points lower in 1980 and 1982 than they were before, perhaps because a correspondingly small fraction of the electorate shifted into a residual a-ideological category (not shown in the table). The Gallup polls suggest there may have been a decline of 3 to 6 points from 1972 to 1980–1982 in the percentages of the electorate viewing themselves as Liberals or Conservatives, along with a parallel increase in the percentage of middle-of-the-roaders. The General Social Surveys indicate that the percentages of self-identified Conservatives and Moderates may have declined a point or two between the mid-1970s to the early 1980s, and the share of Liberals in the electorate may be down a couple of points. Although the ranks of the Liberals may have been trimmed by a few percentage points over the last decade, what we observe in the various surveys hardly suggests a major change in the political composition of the electorate. Survey evidence favoring the idea that the 1980 and 1984 election outcomes represented a realignment of ideological commitments toward conservatism is therefore almost nil.

The implications of equation (6.2) and Figure 6.1—that Reagan's victories are tied to poor real income performance under Carter in 1980 and to the remarkably good performance during his own administration in 1984—are supported by other survey data on individual financial experiences and voting in recent presidential elections. The data in Table 6.6 show the division of the vote among respondents in election-day exit polls who reported their family financial situation as having become "better," stayed "about the same," or become "worse" over the election year.[33] Because data are available for 1976 as well as 1980 and 1984, and because Jimmy Carter was a candidate in the first two elections and Ronald Reagan was a candidate in the last two, the survey results can be viewed as the outcomes of quasi-experiments: one candidate remains fixed, but his role varies from challenger to incumbent across each successive pair of elections.

In all three elections the economy was the dominant issue. In 1976 Carter was the challenger attacking Ford's economic record. He was of course successful; and in 1980, as the incumbent, Carter had to defend his record against the major challenge from Reagan and the nuisance factor posed by John Anderson's independent candidacy.[34] Analogously, Reagan, the challenger in 1980, had to defend his own record in 1984 in the contest with Walter Mondale. Table 6.6 shows considerable symmetry across the elections in the success of challengers and incumbents among voters with various perceptions of their economic experiences prior to the election. Among survey respondents reporting a stable family financial situation in periods prior to the election, the vote was split evenly between the challenger and the incumbent in 1976, 1980, and 1984. Reagan the incumbent was no more successful with the "about the same" group in 1984 than Reagan the challenger had been in 1980, or than Carter had been in 1976 as the challenger or in 1980 as the incumbent.

In 1976 Carter the challenger received more than three-quarters of the two-party vote of those perceiving a deterioration in their economic situation, but he won less than a third of the vote of those claiming an improvement in their economic situation. As the challenger in 1980, Reagan did about the same. He attracted more support than Carter had in the previous election among voters who considered themselves better off financially (40% versus 30%), but he did

Table 6.6 Family financial situation and the vote for the president, 1976, 1980, and 1984

"Compared to a year ago,[a] would you say that your family is financially better off today, about the same, worse off today, or not sure?"

Year and candidate	Better	Same	Worse
1976			
Carter	30%	51%	77%
Ford	70	49	23
N	3262	6924	3908
	(23%)	(49%)	(28%)
1980[b]			
Carter	55%/60%	46%/50%	25%/28%
Reagan	37/40	46/50	64/72
Anderson	8	8	11
N	1841	4602	3911
	(18%)	(44%)	(38%)
1984			
Reagan	81%	51%	27%
Mondale	19	49	73
N	NA	NA	NA
	(41%)	(40%)	(19%)

Sources: For 1976 and 1980, *New York Times*/CBS News election-day interviews with voters as they left the polls, reported in *New York Times*, November 9, 1980, and the *National Journal*, November 8, 1980, p. 1878. For 1984, *Los Angeles Times* exit polls, reported in the *National Journal*, November 10, 1984, p. 2132.

a. "Four years ago" in 1984.

b. The entries after the slash give the two-party vote shares excluding Anderson.

somewhat less well than Carter had among voters who considered themselves worse off (72% versus 77%). A similar pattern held in 1984, in that President Reagan was more successful, this time by quite a large margin (81% versus 60%), than President Carter had been in 1980 with voters who said they were better off financially. (Note, however, that the financial situation question asked in 1984 was not identical to the questions asked in 1980 and 1976.) Reagan and Carter, as the incumbents in 1984 and 1980, respectively, attracted essentially the same share of the vote (27% versus 28%) from those who felt worse off financially.

The principal lesson to be drawn from Table 6.6 is that Reagan's successes in 1980 and 1984 among voters reporting various economic experiences were on the whole quite predictable from the experiences of other challengers and incumbents, Democratic and Republican, in past elections in which the economy was the most salient issue. Inasmuch as the economic record, especially the real income record, of the Carter administration in 1980 was much less favorable than the Reagan record in 1984 (see Table 6.2), it is not surprising that at the time of the Carter-Reagan race the number of voters who felt better off was lower (18% versus 41%) and the number of voters who felt worse off was higher (38% versus 19%) than during the Reagan-Mondale race four years later. This is the main reason that President Carter got only about 45 percent of the two-party vote in 1980 whereas President Reagan got 59 percent in 1984.

6.5 Implications for the Future of Conservative Republicanism

Statistical models and survey data strongly indicate that the victories of Ronald Reagan and the Republican party in 1980 and 1984 were not based on conservative tides or ideological shifts to the right in the electorate. In 1980 dissatisfaction with Jimmy Carter's leadership and management of the economy and a concomitant desire for change were the main sources of the Democrats' defeat. Voters did not reject welfare-state liberalism; they punished Carter and the Democrats for economic mismanagement. President Carter was the first elected incumbent to be defeated since Herbert Hoover because Carter's economic record during periods just prior to the election was the worst since Hoover's. Indeed, there was more justice in the electorate's verdict in 1980 than there had been in its decision in 1932, because the macroeconomic knowledge and policy tools available to the Carter administration were much more developed than those at the disposal of political authorities fifty years earlier.

As Orren and Dionne noted,[35] there is considerable irony in the fact that Carter's defeat in 1980 was interpreted, at least initially, as a sign of the political collapse of welfare-state liberalism. For in the context of his time, Jimmy Carter was probably the least liberal Democratic president in this century, and he lost the election not because of his liberalism but because he pursued conservative anti-inflationary poli-

cies that produced an election-year recession on top of severe inflation. The victim of this irony was one of the most enduring public
perceptions in American political life: the idea that the Democratic
party was the party of prosperity and high employment. Thanks to
the legacy of the Great Depression, sustained by the 1953–1954, 1957–
1958, and 1960 recessions during the Eisenhower administration and
by the terrible 1974–1975 contraction during the Nixon-Ford administration, when Jimmy Carter was elected president in 1976 the Democratic party still enjoyed its traditional advantage of being the party
voters saw as best equipped to manage the economy.[36] The 1976 SRC
National Election Study, for example, showed that among voters who
saw a difference in the parties' effectiveness in managing the economy (not quite half the electorate) the Democrats were considered to
be better able to handle the unemployment problem by a factor of
nearly 4 to 1 (36.4 percent to 9.5 percent). The Democrats even led the
Republicans (by 28 to 19 percent) as the party seen as more likely to
better handle inflation. Four years and one Carter-induced recession
later, these Democratic advantages had vanished. In the 1980 preelection SRC survey, the Republicans were picked 2 to 1 over the Democrats as the party likely to better handle inflation (31 percent to 15
percent); the Republicans were also chosen over the Democrats as the
party likely to better handle unemployment (23 to 19 percent).[37]

After the first year of the Reagan administration the Democrats
regained the advantage of being seen as the party of prosperity, as
"Reaganomics" produced a near-catastrophe in the U.S. macroeconomy. In 1981–1982 Americans experienced higher unemployment and more idle capacity than they had at any time since the Great
Depression. But as the lag-weight parameter estimate for equation
(6.2) and the more extensive analyses of voter memories and discount
rates in Chapter 5, implied, the electorate is somewhat "myopic"
when it comes to making political choices based on economic performance. As a result of the extremely well timed and robust economic
recovery in the last half of Reagan's term, by the fall of 1984 Reagan
led Mondale by 20 percentage points or more as the candidate perceived as better able to keep the country prosperous.[38] A very good
leadership image (particularly in comparison to Mondale's) and,
more important, an economy that had improved dramatically led to
an equally dramatic recovery of Reagan's political fortunes and a
landslide win in 1984.

The outpouring of support for President Reagan in 1984 rested on a
foundation of substantial macroeconomic improvement-reduced in-

flation, falling unemployment, and high rates of real income growth. By featuring his economic and fiscal plan as a "program for economic recovery,"[39] Reagan had struck a responsive political chord. Indeed, the packaging and promotion of the president's program after the 1980 election exhibited political deftness not seen in Washington since Lyndon Johnson's successes with the Great Society legislation in the mid-1960s. As intended, the Reagan program reduced federal civilian expenditure, lowered taxation rates (especially those of the upper-income groups), and shifted the distribution of income away from low- and middle-income groups (especially the working poor) to the high-income classes. (See Chapter 9.) But Reagan had no mandate for such distributional changes after the 1980 election. In order to remain politically viable in the long run, his program must produce, as advertised, a durable economic recovery. If the Reagan program does sustain the macroeconomic conditions prevailing during the eighteen months prior to the 1984 election—or at least is correlated with long-lasting improvement in America's macroeconomic performance—the president probably will succeed in crystallizing a popular base for right-wing economic and social policies that might well last a generation or more. But enduring economic improvement there must be. Otherwise Reaganomics and the Reagan electoral successes will no doubt be interpreted in hindsight not as a reflection of a fundamental shift to the right but as a two-term political aberration.

The 1984 election results, then, yield little evidence that the anti-Carter vote of 1980 has been converted by President Reagan into a durable majority for conservative Republicanism. As Republican Senate leader Robert Dole put it after the 1984 election, "Republican ideas lag behind Reagan's popularity . . . Who are we without Ronald Reagan?"[40] Moreover, recent electoral trends seem to have reinforced rather than weakened the New Deal party system established during the last great party realignment of the 1930s. As conservatives who historically were anchored to the Democrats because of ethnicity, religion, or geography join the Republicans, and liberals who were affiliated with the Republicans for the same reasons embrace the Democrats, the left/right economic bases of party cleavages are becoming even more cleanly drawn than they were during the 1930s. As Sundquist has argued, the essential character of New Deal politics was never the politics of regional and ethnic-group coalitions ("the Democratic South and urban Catholics and Jews and blacks competing against a Republican rural and Protestant North"), but a politics based on contrasting ideas about the desirability of government activism, the conflicting economic interests of the "haves" and the "have nots," and associated economic policy conflicts.[41] Such cleavages are the main source of political influence on the economy and have important consequences for macroeconomic and distributional outcomes, a topic to which we turn in Chapter 7.

III   The Supply of Economic Outcomes

7 Political Parties and Macroeconomic Policies and Outcomes

When the chips were down, the Democrats have taken their chances on inflation and the Republicans on unemployment and recession. For a generation, every major mistake in economic policy under a Democratic president has taken the form of overstimulating the economy and every major mistake under a Republican president of overrestraining it.

—Arthur Okun

We tend to get our recessions during Republican administrations . . . The difference between the Democrats and the Republicans is the difference in their constituencies. It's a class difference . . . The Democrats constitute the people, by and large, who are around the median incomes or below. These are the ones whom the Republicans want to pay the price and burden of fighting inflation. The Democrats [are] willing to run some inflation [to increase employment]; the Republicans are not.

—Paul Samuelson

7.1 The Party Cleavage Model

In comparison to the major parties in most advanced industrial democracies, the Democratic and Republican parties have more heterogeneous social bases and are less distant ideologically. Nonetheless, in American national politics the Democratic party is indisputably the party of the "left," with strong ties to organized labor and differential appeal to lower income and lower occupational status groups, and the Republican party is just as clearly the party of the "right," with close connections to big business and comparatively great attractiveness to the upper levels of the income and class hierarchy. This is as true today as it was during the late New Deal era, at which time the displacement of traditional sectional politics by modern class politics was consolidated.[1]

These images of the parties—the Democrats as the party of lower income groups, the propertyless, and wage labor; the Republicans as the party of upper income classes, the propertied, and professionals—have endured for nearly a half century in the political perceptions as well as the voting behavior of the electorate. In Gallup surveys taken over the last four decades, for example, voters consistently have viewed the Democrats as best serving the interests of downscale groups and the Republicans as best accommodating the interests of upscale groups. Some illustrative data from the mid-1940s, 1950s, 1960s, and early 1980s are reported in Table 7.1. It is apparent from these surveys that once one moves outside the white-collar occupations and mid-range income groups—that is, outside the politically decisive lower-middle-to-middle-class zone of the social structure, which accounts for about a third of the active electorate, voters have little difficulty seeing where their interests are best served.

Table 7.1 Perceived Biases of the parties in favor of various socioeconomic groups

Entries are percentage responding Democratic minus percentage responding Republican to the question "As you feel today, which political party—the Republican or Democratic—do you think serves the interests of the following groups best?"

Socioeconomic group	1981	1965	1956	1947
Upper-income people	−58	NA	NA	NA
Below-average-income people	NA	NA	NA	+57
Corporate executives	−54	NA	NA	NA
Business owners and professionals	−39	−19	−44	−35
White-collar workers	−7	+11	−6	+1
Skilled workers	+36	+43	+23	+43
Unskilled workers	+52	+54	+33	+59
Labor union members	+53	NA	NA	NA
Unemployed people	+54	NA	NA	NA

Source: Computed from data published in Gallup Report, November 1981. Datum on below-average-income people from The Gallup Poll (New York: Random House, 1977), vol. 1, p. 559.

Notes: I have excluded "no opinion" respondents from the calculations. Data for the 1970s were not available.

Table 7.2 Income-related and occupation-related cleavages in voting in presidential elections

Entries are percentages reporting a Democratic vote in the lower income or lower occupational class minus percentages reporting a Democratic vote in the higher income or higher occupational class (voters only). Changing the signs of the entries gives the corresponding differences for Republican voting.

Group	1952	1956	1960	1964	1968	1972	1976	1980	1984
Income percentile 0–16 vs. percentile 95–100	+20	+18	+22	+20	+16	+26	+44	+43[a]	+43[b]
Income percentile 0–33 vs. percentile 68–100	+7	+3	−1	+13.7	+4	+10	+22	+20[a]	+27[b]
Unskilled workers vs. professionals	+35	+30	NA	+36	+40	+19	+25	+6[c]	NA
Other blue-collar vs. other white-collar workers[d]	+21	+12	+20	+14	+9	+2	+19		NA

Source: Data for 1952–1976 were computed from SRC data published in Warren E. Miller et al., American National Election Studies Data Source Book (Cambridge, Mass.: Harvard University Press, 1980), table 6.1.
a. Based on the SRC National Election Study.
b. Based on SRC data reported in Martin Wattenberg, The Decline of American Political Parties (Cambridge, Mass.: Harvard University Press, 1986), p. 144.
c. All blue-collar workers versus all white-collar workers, from New York Times/CBS News exit polls.
d. Unskilled workers are excluded from the blue-collar category, and professionals are excluded from the white-collar category.

Comparable patterns of class polarization have appeared to varying degrees in voting behavior in every election since the Great Depression.[2] Table 7.2 shows some relevant data for presidential elections beginning with 1952. Again, class cleavages in electoral support for the parties are greatest when the lower and upper tails of the income and occupational distributions are contrasted. Although the cleavages vary over time depending on the candidates and issues of the day, contrasting the voting behavior of the lowest income percentiles with that of the highest and comparing that of unskilled workers with that of professionals reveals sizable differences which show no sign of eroding with time.[3] The voting cleavages diminish toward the mid-ranges of the income and occupational hierarchies, indicating that the broad middle class is the main battleground of electoral competition between the parties.

Survey data on public concern about inflation and unemployment and statistical evidence on the response of political support for presidents to macroeconomic events, presented in Chapters 4 and 5, showed that the economic priorities of the parties' core constituencies diverge significantly. Democratic partisans are more sensitive to unemployment than are Republican partisans, and Republicans have a greater aversion to inflation than do Democrats. Moreover, the cleavages across partisan groups in relative preferences or "demands" for economic outcomes are broadly consistent with the intergroup variations in the objective distributional consequences of inflation and unemployment evaluated in Chapters 2 and 3. This is particularly true of partisan sensitivities to unemployment performance: the economic and broader social costs of extra unemployment fall much more heavily on the lower income and occupational status groups, who are more strongly attached to the Democrats than to the Republicans.

Big business and big labor are important centers of gravity for the Republican and Democratic parties. The views of trade union and corporate leaders on macroeconomic issues reveal conflicting interests and priorities much more sharply than does the distribution of opinions among broad groups in the mass public. The most candid account that we have of the thinking of business elites about inflations and recessions is recorded in a fascinating book by Leonard Silk and David Vogel. Silk and Vogel reported the following statements as representative of the views expressed by chairmen, presidents, and other high officers of the nation's largest corporations during a series of seminars sponsored by the Conference Board (a New York–based center for the promotion of enlightened, big-business-oriented ideas) in 1974–1975.[4]

On inflation:

> Recession is like a sore. Inflation is like cancer.
> Inflation decimates our ability to form capital and thus produce wealth.
> With high inflation, the only source of capital is government.

On recession:

> This recession [the deep 1975 contraction following the first OPEC shock] will bring about the healthy respect for economic values that the Depression did.

It would be better if the recession were allowed to weaken more than it will, so that we would have a sense of sobriety.

We need a sharp recession.

Contrast such corporate views with those of Nat Goldfinger, director of the AFL-CIO Department of Research, who in the early 1970s clearly articulated big labor's traditional position on unemployment and inflation:

> The national economic objective should be full employment . . . Somehow, recent studies of full employment in the United States have typically involved the twisted logic of defining it in terms of the price level . . .
>
> A careful examination of the American job market would show that under current conditions, full employment would probably involve an unemployment rate in the neighborhood of 2 or 2.5 percent . . .
>
> Business spokesmen, academic economists and political leaders should stop playing games with the economic and social objective of full employment.
>
> If trade-offs of different economic goals are thought to be necessary in establishing second-best objectives, whatever trade-off is involved in the employment goal should logically start from a well-defined full-employment base. In the view of the AFL-CIO, the full employment objective should be the top priority.[5]

Positions taken by party leaders (or ordinary voters) are usually not quite as graphic or ideological as those expressed by big business and big labor leaders. Nonetheless, cleavages in the basic economic priorities of party elites are consistent with those revealed by the opinions of trade union and corporate leaders and partisans in the general electorate. The best data we have on the priorities of party elites are the results of an April 1976 survey of county committee chairpeople, members of state committees, and members of the national committees, conducted by the Center for International Affairs at Harvard University and the *Washington Post*. The nation had just begun to recover from the first major bout of "stagflation." Inflation was running at an annual rate of about 5 percent; unemployment stood at just above 7.5 percent. Asked to rank, in order of importance, the solutions to ten national problems, the Democratic party elites on average ranked unemployment first and inflation second. Republican party officials placed curbing inflation in first place and ranked reducing unemployment sixth—behind reducing the role of government, maintaining a strong defense, developing energy resources, reducing crime.[6]

These contrasting economic priorities are reflected in the policy stances typically adopted by Democratic and Republican presidential administrations, which in turn generate a partisan dimension to macroeconomic outcomes.[7] Democratic administrations are more likely than Republican ones to run the risk of higher inflation rates in order to pursue expansive policies designed to yield lower unemployment and extra growth. Because Republican administrations weight the problem of inflation more heavily, they more readily and more vigorously pursue disinflationary policies and are more cautious about stimulating aggregate demand and employment. Republicans, then, generally worry more than Democrats about "arousing inflationary expectations," and their concern is translated into action by a tendency to run the economy at considerable "slack" in order to check inflation. As a result, six of the seven recessions experienced since the Treasury–Federal Reserve Accord of 1951, which made possible activist monetary policies coordinated with fiscal policies, occurred during Republican administrations.[8] Every one of these contractions was either intentionally created or passively accepted, at least for a while, in order to fight inflation.

Moreover, the parties have contrasting distributional goals that are consistent with the locations of their core constituencies in the hierarchy of income classes. Distributional outcomes are affected directly by tax and especially transfer policies, and the evolution of the tax-and-transfer system bears a clear connection to partisan control of the presidency. Consequently, as we shall see later, most of the modest progress that has been made in equalizing the distribution of after-tax, after-transfer incomes was achieved during Democratic administrations.

The broad outlines of this party cleavage, or "partisan," model of macroeconomic policies and outcomes are illustrated in Figure 7.1.[9] The macroeconomic priorities associated with the parties obviously are not absolute. Democratic governments are not completely insensitive to inflations; after all, the Carter administration intentionally moved the economy into a recession in response to the enormous OPEC-induced price bulge of 1979–1980. And Republican administrations are not oblivious to high unemployment; both President Ford and President Reagan eventually abandoned support of disinflationary monetary policies in the face of prolonged and deepening contractions. In the democratic, electorally competitive setting of American politics, neither party entertains or adheres to a fixed ideology or schedule of preferences, and any administration will ultimately re-

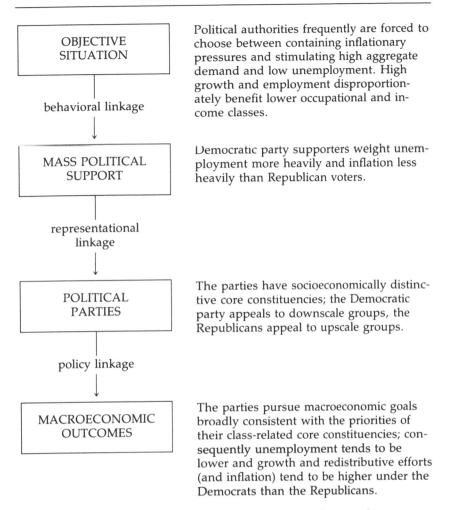

Figure 7.1 The partisan model of macroeconomic policies and outcomes.

spond to dominant macroeconomic problems that require distasteful actions inconsistent with its usual priorities and inclinations. Party-related policy cleavages are over the relative emphasis given to macroeconomic problems. Yet the pattern of policies and outcomes implied by the partisan model sketched in Figure 7.1 reflects important tendencies in the American political economy; and, as I will show, these tendencies have had significant consequences for trends in postwar macroeconomic performance.[10]

7.2   Unemployment and Real Output under the Parties

THE UNEMPLOYMENT MODEL

The following stylized framework may be used to evaluate empirically the central implications of the partisan model for the dynamics of unemployment outcomes. The Democratic and Republican parties have different target rates of unemployment, U^T, which are constrained by and therefore tend to vary about a "normal," or benchmark, unemployment rate, U^N. The unemployment target prevailing during Democratic presidential administrations is lower than the corresponding target during Republican administrations, which suggests the U^T equation

$$U_t^T = b_0 + U_t^N + b_1 \, \mathrm{Dem}_{t-1} \tag{7.1}$$

where Dem is a binary variable equal to +1 during Democratic administrations and 0 during Republican administrations and U^N is set equal to Robert J. Gordon's calculation of the natural rate of unemployment (introduced in Chapter 2).[11] The Dem term appears with a 1-period lag in equation (7.1) because the operative unemployment target in the current period (that is, the goal reflected in current policies) is based on the party in power in the previous period.[12]

Disregarding for the moment the 1-period lag in equation (7.1), we see that the unemployment target prevailing during Democratic administrations is given by $b_0 + U_t^N + b_1$, and the operative target during Republican administrations is given by $b_0 + U_t^N$. It follows that for $b_1 < 0$ (the result anticipated by the model), the Republican target will exceed the Democratic target by b_1. Conversely, $b_1 > 0$ (which is inconsistent with the partisan model) would mean that the Democratic target exceeded the Republican target by the same magnitude. The constant term b_0 accommodates the possibility that U^N systematically under- or overestimates the true normal rate anchoring partisan goals, and at the same time it permits asymmetrical party-induced deviations of actual from benchmark unemployment rates.[13]

Given behavioral lags in policy formulation, institutional lags in policy implementation, and structural lags in the working of the macroeconomy, administrations cannot achieve their economic objectives immediately. First, a new administration must work out the specifics of its macroeconomic "game plan," even though it probably assumed office with rather clear macroeconomic goals in mind. This ordinarily entails bargaining and negotiation among key actors on the new president's team, and although the process typically begins well before inauguration day, some delay inevitably is involved.[14] Second, whereas administrations are able to speed up (or slow down) the pace of government purchases of goods and services relatively quickly, securing sustained changes in the aggregate level of discretionary expenditures and bringing about changes in tax rates are different matters. Tax policy normally is very difficult to maneuver effectively for short-run, countercyclical purposes. An administration's fiscal policy initiatives—changes in taxation and expenditure—must await favorable congressional action before they are implemented, and sometimes this is a time-consuming process. As John Connolly, secretary of the treasury during the Nixon administration, complained, "By the time Congress understands what the facts are, and the time they see what's happening to the economy, and by the time they can act [to push tax legislation] through the rabbit's warren of Congressional procedures, it's at least six months too late."[15]

Finally, there are lags in the response of the economy to fiscal and monetary actions. Major monetary policy actions—notably changes in the money supply—are implemented almost immediately after the monthly meetings of the Federal Reserve Open Market Committee, but it takes several quarters before those changes have significant effects on the major macroeconomic variables. Fiscal actions may affect the economy more quickly, especially when accompanied by a supportive monetary policy, but, as noted above, they typically are slower to be implemented because of institutional arrangements in the American system of government.

For these reasons administrations are able to adjust the actual unemployment rate, U, to their preferred rate, U^T, only partially each period. A sensible unemployment adjustment mechanism, therefore, is

$$U_t - U_{t-1} = \phi_1(U_t^T - U_{t-1}) + \phi_2(U_{t-1} - U_{t-2}) \qquad (7.2)$$
$$+ b_2 \, \text{Shock}_{t-1} + e_t$$

where $0 < \phi_1, \phi_2 < 1$, and e is a well-behaved disturbance.

Hence policy-induced changes in unemployment from one quarter to the next are capable of closing only a fraction (ϕ_1) of the gap between the current target and the actual unemployment outcome in the previous period. Holding aside for the moment the other terms in equation (7.2), we see that a high value of ϕ_1 (close to 1) means that policy makers are able to adjust actual unemployment to their target quite rapidly. But in view of the structural rigidities in the economy and institutional rigidities in the polity mentioned earlier, high values of ϕ_1 are implausible. Governments simply cannot maneuver quantities such as the aggregate unemployment rate quickly. It is likely, then, that ϕ_1 lies closer to 0 than to 1 (particularly in quarterly time), which implies relatively long lags in the adjustment of actual to preferred rates of unemployment.

The remaining terms in equation (7.2) add a bit more realism to the adjustment model. Additional structural inertia in the time path of unemployment is accommodated by the lagged-rate-of-change term on the right side of the equation. In addition to the gradual policy-induced adjustments of actual outcomes to targets, the current change in unemployment is influenced by the momentum of change over the previous period. Fluctuations in unemployment due to major shocks exogenous to the domestic political economy, notably the great oil supply shocks of 1973–1974 and 1979–1980, which had adverse effects on aggregate demand and employment as well as on inflation, are represented by the variable Shock.

Substituting equation (7.1), the unemployment target function, into the adjustment mechanism in equation (7.2) and solving for U yields a nonlinear, second-order dynamic equation for the partisan model of unemployment outcomes:

$$U_t = \phi_1 \cdot b_0 + (1 - \phi_1 + \phi_2)U_{t-1} - \phi_2 U_{t-2} + \phi_1 U_t^N \tag{7.3}$$
$$+ \phi_1 \cdot b_1 \, \text{Dem}_{t-1} + b_2 \, \text{Shock}_{t-1} + e_t$$

THE REAL OUTPUT MODEL

Movements in unemployment and real income and output are intimately connected, and pursuing an unemployment goal necessarily involves pursuing a compatible real output goal. Indeed, the closely synchronized movement of unemployment and real output, described by Okun's Law (see Chapter 2), is one of the most fundamental empirical regularities in macroeconomics. A party cleavage model for the time path of real output suitable for empirical estimation follows straightforwardly, then, from the stylized framework presented above for unemployment. The real output targets prevailing under partisan regimes are given by

$$\ln Q_t^T = b_0 + \ln Q_t^N + b_1 \, \text{Dem}_{t-1} \tag{7.4}$$

The real output variables in equation (7.4) are in natural log form so as to represent output targets, Q^T, as proportional rather than absolute deviations from "normal" output levels, Q^N. The normal, or benchmark, real output levels, which anchor the partisan targets, are measured by Gordon's natural real output series and are compatible with the corresponding measure of normal unemployment in equation (7.1).

As before, the Dem variable is coded +1 for Democratic administrations and 0 for Republican administrations, and it is lagged 1 period because the current operative target is determined by the party in power during the previous period. Hence, this lag aside, proportional deviations of real output targets from normal levels (ln Q_t^T − ln Q_t^N being proportional differences) will be $b_0 + b_1$ under the Democrats and b_0 under the Republicans. According to the partisan model, the parameter b_1 should be negative, in which case the real output target of the Democrats exceeds that of the Republicans by a factor of b_1.

Politically driven changes in log real output (which, remember, are proportional changes) are modeled by the same partial adjustment scheme used for unemployment—namely,

$$\ln Q_t - \ln Q_{t-1} = \phi_1(\ln Q_t^T - \ln Q_{t-1}) + \phi_2(\ln Q_{t-1} \qquad (7.5)$$
$$- \ln Q_{t-2}) + b_2 \, \text{Shock}_{t-1} + e_t$$

where $0 < \phi_1, \phi_2 < 1$, and e_t is an error term with the usual desirable properties. The interpretation of the real output adjustment equation is identical to that of the corresponding unemployment equation. Institutional arrangements and the structure of the macroeconomy impede rapid, policy-induced real output adjustments; consequently, administrations are able to close only a fraction of the gap (ϕ_1) between target and actual output levels each period. Moreover, the lagged rate of change of output (ln Q_{t-1} − ln Q_{t-2}) influences the current growth rate through additional structural inertia. Finally, as in the case of unemployment, real output is affected after a 1-period lag by shocks exogenous to the domestic economy (Shock).

Substituting the output target equation (7.4) into the adjustment equation (7.5) and solving for ln Q yields the following nonlinear, second-order dynamic equation for real output outcomes:

$$\ln Q_t = \phi_1 \cdot b_0 + (1 - \phi_1 + \phi_2) \ln Q_{t-1} - \phi_2 \ln Q_{t-2} \qquad (7.6)$$
$$+ \phi_1 \ln Q_t^N + \phi_1 \cdot b_1 \, \text{Dem}_{t-1} + b_2 \, \text{Shock}_{t-1} + e_t$$

7.3   Empirical Results for the Models

The unemployment and real output models were estimated over the period 1953:1–1983:2 (quarterly). The starting date of the nonlinear regressions was chosen to correspond to the beginning of the first full presidential administration (Eisenhower) following the Treasury–Federal Reserve Accord of 1951. As mentioned earlier, the accord relieved the Federal Reserve of its wartime obligation to support the prices of Treasury securities, which made possible an activist monetary policy responsive to the objectives of presidential administrations. Political leverage on the macroeconomy, then, was less constrained by domestic institutional arrangements during the post-accord era than it had ben during the earlier postwar years. Therefore, the accord marks the starting point of the period most appropriate for evaluating the importance of political influences on economic policies and outcomes.

Estimation results for the partisan models of unemployment and real output, as summarized by equations (7.3) and (7.6) above, appear in columns 1 and 4 of Table 7.3. The coefficients of all variables in these two regressions have the anticipated sign and easily satisfy the usual standards of statistical significance. Looking first at forces exogenous to the domestic political economy, we see that the parameter estimates for b_2 register the immediate impacts of the 1973–1974 and 1979–1980 oil supply shocks, which, as was pointed out in earlier chapters, adversely affected output and employment as well as inflation. The estimates indicate that each unit rise in the Shock term— that is, each 1-percentage-point rise in the price of imported oil weighted by the net share of oil imports in GNP—initially depressed real output by about 0.9 percent and then increased the percentage rate of unemployment by 0.3 point after a 1-period lag.[16]

The actual effects of the OPEC oil shocks on unemployment and real output were more severe than the face values of the coefficients indicate for two reasons. First, the Shock variable used in the regressions takes values higher than unity. The first OPEC shock, which began in 1973:4, reached a peak value of 1.6 in 1974:3 before tailing off in early 1975. And the second OPEC shock, beginning in early 1979, peaked at about 1.5 in 1980:1 before winding down at the end of that year. Second, the full impact of the shocks was not felt immediately because of the dynamic structure of the economy. The economy was slow to respond to the adverse supply shocks when they first occurred, and it was slow to readjust to normal once they had

Table 7.3 Estimates for the partisan models of unemployment and real output outcomes, quarterly, 1953:1–1983:2

Models:

$$U_t = \phi_1 \cdot b_0 + (1 - \phi_1 + \phi_2)U_{t-1} - \phi_2 U_{t-2} + \phi_1 U_t^N + \phi_1 \cdot b_1 \text{Dem}_{t-1} + \phi_1 \cdot b_2 \text{Shock}_{t-1} (+ \phi_1 \cdot b_3 \text{Congress}_{t-1} + b_4 \text{War}_t)$$

$$\ln Q_t = \phi_1 \cdot b_0 + (1 - \phi_1 + \phi_2) \ln Q_{t-1} - \phi_2 \ln Q_{t-2} + \phi_1 \ln Q_t^N + \phi_1 \cdot b_1 \text{Dem}_{t-1} + \phi_1 \cdot b_2 \text{Shock}_{t-1} (+ \phi_1 \cdot b_3 \text{Congress}_{t-1} + b_4 \text{War}_t)$$

Variable	Unemployment (U)			log real output ($\ln Q$)		
	(1)	(2)	(3)	(4)	(5)	(6)
b_0	0.8431	-0.5451	0.9435	0.0321	0.0022	0.0226
	(0.5501)	(4.7298)	(0.4374)	(0.0202)	(0.1160)	(0.0195)
ϕ_1	0.0757**	0.0782**	0.0971**	0.0890**	0.0863**	0.1008**
	(0.0202)	(0.0221)	(0.0248)	(0.0261)	(0.0281)	(0.0305)
ϕ_2	0.5608**	0.5650**	0.5802**	0.3245**	0.3204**	0.3342**
	(0.0723)	(0.0740)	(0.0731)	(0.0860)	(0.0878)	(0.0871)
b_1 (Dem$_{t-1}$ = +1 for Democratic President, 0 otherwise)	-2.1140*	-2.1731*	-1.5105*	0.0614*	0.0603*	0.0529*
	(0.9400)	(0.9420)	(0.7496)	(0.0242)	(0.0253)	(0.0223)
b_2 (Shock$_{t-1}$)	0.3127**	0.3131**	0.2838**	-0.0093**	-0.0093**	-0.0090**
	(0.0904)	(0.0907)	(0.0921)	(0.0026)	(0.0026)	(0.0026)
b_3 (Congress$_{t-1}$, Democratic % in House)	—	0.0238	—	—	0.0005	—
		(0.0810)			(0.0022)	
b_4 (War = +1, 0)	—	—	-0.1277	—	—	0.0017
			(0.0871)			(0.0023)
Adjusted R^2	0.963	0.963	0.963	0.999	0.999	0.999
Standard error of regression	0.3224	0.3236	0.3208	0.0090	0.0090	0.0090

* Significant at 0.05 level, two-tail test.
** Significant at 0.01 level, two-tail test.

Notes: The Shock term measures the adverse impact on GNP of the OPEC-induced increases in world oil prices (shifts in the terms of trade). It is constructed along the lines proposed by Jeffrey Sachs in "The Oil Shocks and Macroeconomic Adjustment in the United States," *European Economic Review* 18 (1982), table 1, p. 244, namely,

$$\text{Shock}_t = [(\ln(\text{Poil}_t/\text{Poil}_{t-4}) - \ln(\text{Pgnp}_t/\text{Pgnp}_{t-4}) \cdot \tfrac{1}{4}(S_t + S_{t-4}] \cdot 100$$

where Poil is the dollar price of oil imports (Saudi Arabian crude), Pgnp is the GNP deflator, and S is the net share (imports minus exports) of oil in GNP. The Shock variable takes nonzero values over the periods 1973:4–1975:4 and 1979:1–1980:4. Standard errors appear in parentheses.

passed. Consequently, the energy price shocks ultimately raised unemployment by more than 2 percentage points above the normal rate
and depressed real output by as much as 6 percentage points below
normal in 1975 and again in 1980. These major macroeconomic events
clearly were beyond the control of domestic political authorities (in
particular, Presidents Ford and Carter), and therefore it is important
to take them into account by including the Shock term in the models
when the impact of partisan administrations on domestic macroeconomic performance is estimated.

The most important results for the purposes of this chapter are the
estimates for the Dem parameter, b_1, and the associated adjustment-
to-target parameter, ϕ_1. The b_1 coefficients in Table 7.3 estimate the
magnitudes of cross-party differences in macroeconomic targets
(equations 7.1 and 7.4) and therefore directly estimate the impacts of
changes in party control of the presidency on unemployment and real
output after all lags of adjustment.[17] The results clearly support the
basic partisan hypothesis. In the first unemployment regression
(column 1 of Table 7.3), the implied long-run effects of Dem are on
the order of −2.0, which means that after adjustment lags the unemployment rate tends to be about 2 percentage points lower under the
Democrats than under the Republicans. The results for the corresponding regression equation for log real output (column 4 of Table
7.3) indicate that alterations in partisan rule sustained long enough
for adjustment lags to work through the system yield a (proportional)
interparty difference of about 0.06. In other words, after lags for
adjustment, real output tends to be about 6 percent higher under the
Democrats than under the Republicans. What this boils down to in
the American political economy today, where normal unemployment
is in the vicinity of 6 percent, is that once we look beyond political
rhetoric to the pattern of actual postwar macroeconomic outcomes,
the evidence suggests that in current circumstances Democratic administrations will tend to pursue seriously an unemployment goal of
about 5 percent and Republican administrations are likely to pursue a
target closer to 7 percent. More precisely, if we let U^N equal 6 percent
(and take b_0 at face value), the first model of Table 7.3 implies a
Democratic unemployment rate target of $6.0 + 0.843 - 2.11 = 4.76$
percent and a Republican target of $6.0 + 0.843 = 6.87$ percent.

In principle, these estimates are sensitive to the choice of U^N, which
in the analyses above was set equal to Robert Gordon's "natural"
unemployment rate series. (For reasons discussed in Chapter 2, Gordon's U^N grows from 4.9 percent in 1947 to 6 percent in the mid-

1970s.) Estimates of interparty differences were not affected substantially by variations in U^N, however. For example, assuming U^N is constant (and hence is absorbed by b_0 in the regression equation) yields an estimate of b_1 of -2.29 with a standard error of 1.1. Assuming U^N grows from about 4 percent in the late 1940s to 6 percent in the early 1980s (which corresponds to Gordon's earlier computations of the natural unemployment rate) yields a b_1 estimate of -1.85 with a standard error of 0.83.[18]

Because estimates of the parameter ϕ_1 are substantially less than 1 (lying between 0.075 and 0.09) and also because the structural inertia parameter ϕ_2 is significantly different from 0, there are, however, important lags in the adjustment of actual macroeconomic outcomes to partisan targets. Consequently, the steady-state effects—that is, the net differences in unemployment and log real output implied by the equations if one and then the other party were to control the presidency for a prolonged period—are less interesting than the period-to-period dynamic effects for partisan regimes of finite, politically meaningful durations. In fact, if normal unemployment, U^N, were a true "natural" rate (in the sense that U held below U^N would yield ever-accelerating prices and U held above U^N would yield ever-decelerating prices), then it would not be meaningful to speak of steady-state effects at all. The partisan effects necessarily would be bounded in time.[19] They could not persist indefinitely without creating hyperinflation (under the Democrats) or hyperdeflation (under the Republicans).

Neither political party has held the presidency for more than two terms in succession during the postwar period, so Figures 7.2 and 7.3 show time paths of the net responses of unemployment and real output, respectively, to cycles of 32 quarters of Democratic party control of the presidency followed by 32 quarters of Republican control (eight-year partisan cycles). Because the figures display *net* responses—that is, systematic partisan effects stripped of stochastic and other sources of variation—and because the autoregressive coefficients of the equations do not generate endogenous cycles, the time paths are smooth,[20] unlike "real world" outcomes.

Despite the adjustment lags, the equilibrium interparty differences after the 32-quarter (eight-year) partisan cycles illustrated in the figures are nearly identical to the long-run differences discussed above: approximately 2 percentage points in the case of unemployment and 6 percentage points for real output.[21] The adjustment paths to the contrasting partisan targets for both unemployment and real output

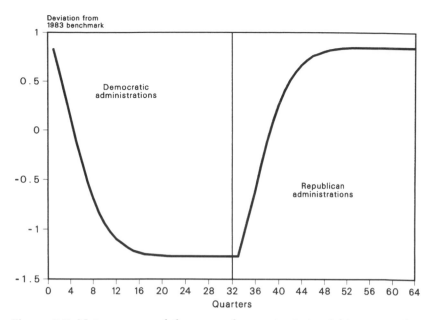

Figure 7.2 Net response of the unemployment rate to eight-year partisan cycles. *Source:* Based on Table 7.3, column 1.

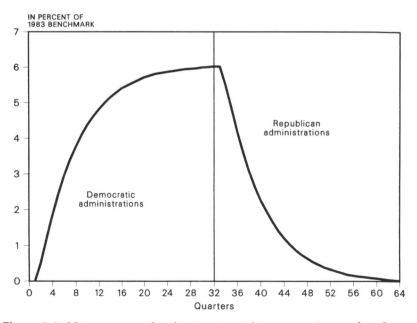

Figure 7.3 Net response of real output to eight-year partisan cycles. *Source:* Based on Table 7.3, column 4.

are almost completed after 16 quarters, or four years.[22] Therefore, in the absence of major adverse exogenous shocks to the economy that are beyond the control of domestic policy makers, the unemployment and real output goals of the typical administration characteristically are realized by the end of one full presidential term.[23] Indeed, the results reported in the figures indicate that about two-thirds of the total impact of an eight-year stretch of Republican or Democratic control of the presidency usually is observed during the first two years. The inclination of some first-term presidents to lay the blame for painful macroeconomic situations on the mistaken policies of their predecessors is not without some foundation, particularly when such attempts to off-load responsibility are made during the early periods of a first term.[24] By the time a president stands for reelection, however, macroeconomic ills (exogenous shocks aside) are squarely the responsibility of the incumbent administration.[25]

Naturally there have been variations across administrations in how closely outcomes (and, implicitly, targets) conform to the stylized estimates of the partisan models, which are based on the weighted average of outcomes during all administrations in the regression range.[26] Reestimation of the unemployment and real output equations after elimination of each four-year administration, one at a time, yields results that again clearly support the basic thrust of the partisan model, but in two cases the magnitudes of the interparty differences are diminished. Economic activity during the Johnson administration (1965–1968) was particularly vigorous, and when this period is omitted from the regression range the interparty unemployment difference falls to about 1.5 percentage points and the corresponding real output difference falls to about 4 percentage points. An equally extreme case (perhaps more extreme) on the Republican side is the Reagan administration, which pursued an especially vigorous disinflationary policy during 1981 and 1982. (President Reagan's economic and social program is analyzed in detail in Chapter 9.) Dropping the Reagan periods from the regression range reduces the estimated unemployment and real output interparty differences to 1.2 and 3.5 percentage points, respectively. Yet to some degree it is precisely these "extreme" cases that provide the most useful information about the core goals and policy tendencies of the parties. In any case, estimates of partisan influences on macroeconomic outcomes are not sensitive to the deletion of any other administration from the regression ranges.

The Democrats were unusually weak in Congress during the first half of the Reagan administration and unusually strong during the first half of the Johnson administration, so it is possible that the patterns just discussed partly reflect the influence of the partisan balance in Congress on the formation and implementation of macroeconomic goals. Democratic administrations may pursue especially ambitious unemployment and real output targets when the partisan balance in Congress is strongly in their favor. Similarly, Republican administrations may push their inclination to contain outbreaks of inflation more vigorously by pursuing very modest unemployment and real output goals when the balance of party forces in Congress is more advantageous than usual.[27]

This plausible elaboration of the partisan model is easily accommodated by adding to the unemployment and real output target equations variables measuring the strength of the parties in Congress and then making appropriate substitutions into the corresponding adjustment equations to obtain revised regression models. Columns 2 and 4 of Table 7.3 report the estimation results for revised models in which the percentage of Democratic party members in the House of Representatives is used to measure the partisan balance in Congress. The estimates for the Congress term, however, do not remotely approach statistical significance, and the magnitudes are inconsequential. Extension of the regression-estimating equations to include variables measuring the strength of the parties in the Senate and interactions between the party controlling presidency and the partisan balance in Congress also failed to reveal any evidence of important congressional influence on the pattern of postwar unemployment and real output outcomes already established.[28]

In the framework of a highly stylized partisan model, then, the principal systematic political influence on macroeconomic outcomes distinguishing one major party from the other is simply whether the president is a Democrat or a Republican. This may stem in part from the fact that the Democrats typically have enjoyed majorities in both the House and the Senate, and comfortable ones at that. Therefore, sizable variations in the partisan balance in Congress may not have been frequent enough or sustained long enough to permit statistical estimation of what in principle might be a source of significant political influence on macroeconomic targets and outcomes. The absence of easily detected congressional influence is undoubtedly also due to the fact that, as a practical matter, modern macroeconomic policy is largely an executive responsibility. The mechanics of macroeconomic policy necessarily relegates Congress to a rather peripheral role except, perhaps, when dramatic departures from customary practice are initiated by the president. Yet the experience of 1981, when President Reagan's Economic Recovery and Taxation Act sailed through Congress, shows that even major changes to the established structure of taxation and expenditure may in some situations encounter ineffective congressional resistance.

The unemployment and real output regression equations in columns 3 and 6 of Table 7.3 include an "exogenous" War term—a binary variable coded +1 during the periods of American involvement in the Korean and Vietnamese civil wars and 0 otherwise.[29] The American interventions in Korea and Vietnam were not exogenous events in a strict sense, as the OPEC oil shocks were, but they were external to the political-economic forces relevant to the party cleavage model. The sizable fiscal stimuli to the economy generated by American participation in these conflicts show up clearly in the steadily declining unemployment rates and high real output growth rates of the war years. Indeed, in no other time since World War II (when war production made a decisive contribution to bringing us out of the Great Depression) has the United States experienced such low rates of unemployment.[30] The War term was added to the equations to distinguish, albeit crudely, the partisan effects of interest from war-related boosts to domestic macroeconomic performance.

Although our military engagements in Korea and Vietnam surely contributed to the favorable unemployment and real output records of the early 1950s and late 1960s, the estimates of the War parameter, b_4, are not sharp enough to permit firm conclusions to be drawn about likely magnitudes. The main reason for undertaking the regression experiments reported in columns 3 and 6 of Table 7.3, however, was to obtain estimates of the macroeconomic consequences of oscillations in party rule that are not distorted by the special circumstances of a wartime political economy. The b_1 coefficients in these equations, then, yield what can be thought of as point estimates of the lower bound of interparty differences in unemployment and real output targets and outcomes.[31] The results indicate that the lower bound of the partisan-based effects on unemployment is approximately 1.5 percentage points, as opposed to the interparty difference of about 2 points discussed earlier. In the case of real output performance, the Dem coefficient is on the order of 0.053, which suggests that the typical cross-party difference in the deviation of actual output from normal output may be closer to 5 percent than to the 6 percent obtained earlier. Yet even these lower-bound estimates mean that which party controls the presidency characteristically has important consequences for the course of real output and unemployment. In fact, as we shall see in the next chapter, the partisan stripe of presidential administrations is the most predictable and important source of political influence on macroeconomic outcomes.

7.4 Distributional Outcomes under the Parties

Government policies affect the *distribution* of economic well-being as well as such aggregate economic quantities as real output and the unemployment rate. And given the distinctive, though by no means totally homogeneous, socioeconomic composition of the parties' core supporters, the Democrats and Republicans also have contrasting distributional goals. Indeed, in his critical and skeptical review of the evidence that macroeconomic performance influences voting behavior, Nobel Prize–winning economist George Stigler argued that there is little or no difference in the commitment of Republican and Democratic administrations to high employment and real income growth but that the "economic bases of party affiliation must be sought in [the] area of income redistribution.[32] Distributional outcomes and macro, or aggregate, economic outcomes are not disconnected, however, as Stigler suggested.[33] As we saw in Chapter 3, fluctuations in the rate of unemployment have important consequences for the distribution of (pretax) income among American families, with increases in unemployment being associated with income shifts from the bottom two-fifths of the distribution to the top fifth. (See Chapter 3, Table 3.3, and the associated discussion.) In view of the evidence presented in Chapter 2 on the incidence and net costs of unemployment to individuals, it comes as no surprise that the lower income classes are the relative, distributional losers from recessions. Therefore, by virtue of the connection of unemployment fluctuations to movements in income shares alone, the relative (as well as the absolute) income position of the lower income classes should improve under the Democrats, because, as we have seen, Democratic administrations tend to pursue (successfully) more ambitious output and unemployment targets than do Republican administrations.

FISCAL POLICIES AND THE INCOME DISTRIBUTION
The impact of interparty differences in macroeconomic performance on distributional outcomes is only part of the story. Government

fiscal operations—in particular, taxes and transfers—directly affect the distribution of income. Examined in isolation, the federal personal income tax is moderately progressive, though less so now than it was before the Reagan administration initiated changes in 1981. Just after the 1981 tax legislation was enacted, nominal personal tax rates began at 11 percent on incomes above the zero income bracket for joint returns of $3400 and rose to 50 percent on joint-return incomes above $162,400. But nobody pays the nominal or book rates. Much of the income flow to households either is not defined as income by the tax code; may be deducted, exempted, or excluded from taxable income; or is taxed at special low rates. A disproportionate share of such tax breaks go to the rich, and so the *effective* federal personal tax schedule is much less progressive and less clearly defined about lower rates than is the nominal schedule. Average effective tax rates now begin to bite at incomes above $5000, peak at an average effective rate of only about 26 percent for incomes in excess of three-quarters of a million dollars, and actually decline to about 23 percent for the very highest incomes of a million dollars and over.[34]

The progressivity of federal taxes on personal incomes is further eroded by payroll taxes that finance the Social Security (OASDI) and unemployment compensation programs.[35] Payroll taxes are levied as a flat percentage on wages and salaries up to a ceiling ($37,800 in 1984 for Social Security). Consequently, they tend to be progressive for incomes at the lower range of the scale, because taxable wages make up a small fraction of the income of the very poor; proportional at the middle-income range, because the flat rate applies uniformly where households receive little by way of property income and wages are below the ceiling; and are regressive thereafter, because wage incomes rise above the ceiling and property income becomes a significant factor. Overall, payroll taxes clearly diminish the progressive thrust of income taxes, and their impact has grown over time. In 1955 the federal government's payroll tax receipts amounted to less than a quarter of individual income tax revenues; by the early 1980s this ratio had risen to almost three-quarters. If we assume (as most economists do) that employers' payroll tax shares are shifted onto employees, Social Security taxes now exceed ordinary income tax liabilities for more than half of the taxpayers covered by the Social Security program. Nonetheless, the combined impact of all federal taxes on persons is progressive, with total effective federal tax rates ranging from just under 10 percent on the lower incomes to between 25 and 30 percent on very high incomes. Although much less egalitarian than is sometimes believed, the structure of federal taxation does, then, make a modest contribution to after-tax income equality.[36]

The major sources of government-induced income redistribution, are cash and in-kind transfers.[37] The important transfer programs initially were designed either to provide a "safety net," assuring a minimum level of income support to those without other means, or to make up for temporary income losses owing to events beyond an individual's control. The enactment dates listed in Table 7.4 show that the big programs were established during two great waves of social innovation under forceful Democratic presidents. In the 1930s Franklin Roosevelt's New Deal ushered in Social Security (OASDI), Unemployment Insurance (UI), Aid to Families with Dependent Chil-

Table 7.4 Major income transfer programs

Program	Date enacted	Percent spent on pretransfer poor in 1974	Expenditures as a percentage of total pretransfer personal income[a]	
			1965	1981
Cash benefits				
Social Security (OASDI)	1935	58.8	3.3	6.6
Unemployment Insurance (UI)	1935	20.8	0.50	0.89
Aid to Families with Dependent Children (AFDC)	1935	91.8	0.4	0.61
Supplemental Security Income (SSI)	1965 (1972)	77.8	0.54	0.41
In-kind benefits				
Housing assistance	1937	65.0	0.06	0.32
Food stamps	1964	83.0	0.01	0.46
Medicaid	1965	73.0	0.10	1.3
Medicare	1965	59.0	—	1.8
Total[b]	—	—	6.3	14.0
Total as percentage of GNP[b]	—	—	4.6	10.0

Sources: Computed from data in Sheldon Danziger et al., "How Income Transfer Programs Affect Work, Savings and the Income Distribution: A Critical Review," Journal of Economic Literature 14 (September 1981), 977.

a. Personal income in the national accounts less cash transfers to persons

b. Including expenditures on smaller programs not listed

dren (AFDC), and Housing Assistance. The New Deal programs had both countercyclical and redistributive objectives. As Roosevelt said in 1937, "What we are trying to do is build up national income [aggregate demand] with special reference to increasing the share of national income to [the bottom] one-third."[38] The second great buildup of the federal transfer system came during Lyndon Johnson's presidency. In the mid-1960s Johnson's Great Society and "national war on poverty" dramatically increased federal efforts to improve the economic well-being of the aged and low-income groups with the Supplemental Security Income (SSI),[39] Food Stamps, Medicaid, and Medicare programs.

To be sure, several of the important programs now in place— among them the two largest, Social Security and Medicare—are not targeted on low-income groups alone. Social Security payments and Medicare coverage are available to almost all households, rich and poor alike, upon retirement (well over 90 percent of all households are enrolled in the Social Security system), and the structure of benefits is only moderately redistributive. Nonetheless, with the escalation of real benefits during the 1960s and 1970s, Social Security essentially eliminated chronic economic hardship among the aged, once the demographic group with the highest incidence of poverty, and this was a remarkable accomplishment.

Unemployment Insurance benefits also are not targeted exclusively on the poor. Unemployment compensation goes to anyone in a covered occupation who becomes unemployed, and in the mid-1970s only about a fifth of total UI benefit payments went to people below the official poverty line established by the Social Security Administration (see Table 7.4). Considering, however, that only about 12 percent of the population was officially designated as poor in the mid-1970s and the fraction of "working poor" for whom UI benefits were relevant was much smaller, because a large proportion of the poor were in "dependent" poverty and outside the labor force, the benefits to the working poor were substantial.[40] Moreover, the incidence of unemployment is greater among those in lower status occupations than among the rest of the workforce, and the fraction of normal employment income replaced by UI benefits is of course highest for low-wage occupations (see Chapter 2), so the Unemployment Insurance program clearly does contribute directly to equalization of income. The program's indirect contribution to the economic well-being of low-income groups, however, may be even more important. By shoring up aggregate demand during recessions, unemployment insurance helps to prevent severe contractions that most affect the lower echelons of the income and occupational hierarchy.

The transfer programs that critically affect the well-being of low-income groups are AFDC, Food Stamps, Supplemental Security Income, and Medicaid. Upwards of three-quarters of the expenditures for these programs go to people who fall below the official poverty line—that is, to very poor people indeed.[41] Almost all the expenditures flow to people in the bottom quintile of the pretransfer income distribution. Expressed as percentages of pretransfer personal income (shown in Table 7.4), the amounts going to these programs might appear small. Despite substantial growth during the 1960s and 1970s, expenditures on AFDC, Food Stamps, SSI, and Medicaid added up to only 2.8 percent of gross personal income when Ronald Reagan assumed office in 1981. But remember that the bottom quintile of the income distribution commands only about 5 percent of pretransfer income.[42] So a transfer in the amount of 2.8 percent of total pretransfer personal income to the bottom quintile raises that group's share by more than 55 percent (2.8/5.0). If, as specialists suggest, the value to recipients of in-kind programs such as Medicaid should be put at 70 percent of cost,[43] then the "value" of AFDC, Food Stamps, SSI, and Medicaid was 2.4 percent of aggregate pretransfer income in 1981, enough to raise the posttransfer share of the bottom quintile by about 48 percent (2.4/5.0).[44] From the point of view of the top quintile of the distribution, which commands about 40 percent of personal income, a shift of between 2 and 3 percent is hardly noticeable; for the poor and near-poor it represents an enormous change in economic well-being.

Income transfer spending, then, increased from negligible proportions in the pre–New Deal era (see Chapter 1, Table 1.4) to about 14 percent of total pretransfer personal income (and 10 percent of GNP) by the end of the Carter administration. As the data at the bottom of Table 7.4 show, it more than doubled relative to personal income and GNP during the fifteen years following the Great Society. Such spending has had a strong influence on distributional outcomes over time in the American political economy. Relative to a hypothetical zero-public-transfers base, Danziger, Haveman, and Plotnick estimate that programs in force in the late 1970s reduced "official" income poverty (the fraction of the population falling below the Social Security Administration's poverty-line income) by 75 percent and reduced overall income inequality, as measured by the Gini coefficient, by about 20 percent.[45] If we could reliably calculate the value to various income classes of job training, public-works jobs, aid to depressed areas, employment services, and similar programs, the redistributive impact of government fiscal activity might well look bigger. What concerns us here, however, is the federal government's impact on distributional outcomes in relation to variation in party control.

TRENDS IN THE DISTRIBUTION OF NET INCOMES FROM TRUMAN
TO CARTER
Table 7.5 shows data on the distribution of "net," or "post-fisc," income shares—that is, income shares after cash transfers, the imputed value of in-kind transfers, and federal income and social insurance tax liabilities have been taken into account—over time, by end-

Table 7.5 Ratio of the net income share of the top 20 percent to the share of the bottom 40 percent of the distribution among families, end-of-administration intervals

1948–1949	1.97	
		Truman
1952–1953	1.72	
		Eisenhower I
1956–1957	1.66	
		Eisenhower II
1960–1961	1.76	
		Kennedy–Johnson I
1964–1965	1.67	
		Johnson II
1968–1969	1.49	
		Nixon I
1972–1973	1.54	
		Nixon II–Ford
1976–1977	1.5	

Source: Data computed by Christopher Dennis, California State University, Long Beach, from raw statistical sources.

Notes: Net income includes employment income; interest, dividends, rents, and royalties; cash transfers from government; private and government pension payments; regular cash receipts from other private sources (all of which yield "census" income); and the estimated value of in-kind government benefits (including federal, state, and local educational expenditures) less federal income tax and social insurance contributions. Families are households of two or more related people.

of-administration intervals, from Truman up to Carter.[46] The distributional measure used is the ratio of the share of the top quintile of the distribution, which receives little if any transfer income (apart from public pensions) and is hit hardest by progressive federal taxation, to the share of the bottom 40 percent of the distribution, which is most sensitive to unemployment fluctuations[47] and receives virtually all cash transfer income (again, public pensions excepted). The 20-to-40 ratio essentially contrasts the relative experience of the upper middle class and the rich (the top 20 percent) with that of the lower middle class and the poor (the bottom 40 percent). Although this ratio, like all distribution measures, has limitations, it captures most of the action in the underlying quintile share data. At the same time, it corresponds nicely to the parties' core constituencies insofar as they are income related. Though tilted heavily toward the Republicans at the upper range, the "omitted" quintiles—the middle 40 percent of the net income distribution, corresponding to the broad middle classes—are the critical battleground of party competition for marginal votes.

Table 7.5 shows that the 20-to-40 ratio declined from about 2 to 1.5 between the late 1940s and mid-1970s—a growth in equality of 24 percent by this inequality measure $[(1.97 - 1.5)/1.97 = 0.24]$. More important for our purposes, the data show a clear association with partisan control of the presidency. When Harry Truman began his first full presidential term in 1949, having defeated Thomas Dewey in the 1948 election, many of the foundations of the American welfare state were already in place as a result of Franklin Roosevelt's New Deal, and the 20-to-40 inequality ratio stood at about 2. The Truman administration successfully increased financing of the major programs but was blocked by congressional Republicans from establishing significant extensions, most notably the president's proposed national health insurance program. Nevertheless, by the time Truman left office the inequality ratio had been depressed to about 1.7.

During the Eisenhower administrations there was little serious attempt to roll back redistributive programs—just inaction. Amidst the mass poverty of the Great Depression, Herbert Hoover had declared: "I am opposed to any direct or indirect government dole. . . . Our people are providing against distress from unemployment [by individual action] in true American fashion."[48] Yet a generation later, and in far better times, President Eisenhower and the bulk of the Republican party for the most part accepted the "safety net" philosophy underlying New Deal transfer schemes. In his memoirs Eisenhower summed up mainstream Republican thinking of the period this way: "No great intelligence is required to discern the practical necessity of establishing some kind of security for individuals in a specialized and highly industrialized age . . . it [is] impossible for any durable government to ignore hordes of people who through no fault of their own suddenly find themselves poverty stricken."[49] Hence the system of federal income transfers launched by Roosevelt and nourished by Truman survived eight years of Republican control intact. By the end of Eisenhower's first term, net income inequality actually had declined a bit, though at the time of Kennedy's inauguration the 20-to-40 ratio stood just slightly higher than the level Eisenhower inherited from Truman.

During the Kennedy-Johnson era a flood of new programs were pushed through Congress, including community action, aid to depressed areas, job training, and aid for elementary and secondary education, in addition to the SSI, food stamps, Medicaid, and Medicare programs listed in Table 7.4 and discussed above. In view of the number, diversity, and overlapping functions of the new programs, the post-Johnson federal transfer system was characterized, with some justification, as "confused and tangled," as lacking "clear and overarching purpose,"[50] and as a great "social pork barrel."[51] Although the innovations of the 1960s did indeed reduce the coherence of the income transfer system, Johnson's Great Society and war-on-poverty programs still helped significantly to equalize net incomes; Richard Nixon inherited an inequality ratio of about 1.5 when he assumed office in 1969.

Although President Nixon had an imaginative proposal for rationalizing the somewhat baroque network of welfare programs built up during prior Democratic administrations—this Family Assistance Plan, which owed much to an innovative adviser, Daniel Moynihan—little of substance was done during the Nixon-Ford years to improve equality. Inequality in the distribution of net incomes was essentially the same in 1977 when Carter entered the White House as it had been eight years earlier at the beginning of Nixon's first term.

The course of redistributive policies and outcomes during the postwar period, then, is one of Democratic initiatives that successfully (though modestly) moved toward equality, followed by periods of Republican inaction, followed by new Democratic efforts to improve the relative position of low-income groups, and so on.[52]

ESTIMATING THE IMPACT OF PARTISAN FORCES ON THE TREND OF NET
INCOME DISTRIBUTION

The argument briefly sketched above about the impact of oscillations
in party control of the federal government on distributional outcomes
over time may be evaluated more formally against the data using the
following familiar framework. Letting I denote the 20-to-40 inequality
ratio for net income shares, we have the function for the parties'
(annual) targets:

$$I_t^T = b_0 + I_{t-1} + b_1 \, \text{Dem}_{t-1} + b_2 \, \text{Congress}_{t-1} \qquad (7.7)$$

where, as earlier, Dem equals $+1$ during Democratic presidential
administrations and 0 otherwise and Congress denotes the partisan
balance in Congress.

Partisan targets for the distribution of net income are anchored by
the situation prevailing in the previous year, I_{t-1}, as opposed to some
other benchmark (say, an idealized standard or the distribution of
pretax, pretransfer income ground out by the market economy), because once in place, income transfer and related policies underlying I_t
are difficult to dislodge. Prior to the Reagan period, Republican administrations made little serious attempt to roll back established
transfer programs (with established constituencies). Instead, Republican presidents typically sought to prevent the introduction of new
programs or the expansion of the scope of existing programs. Termi-
nation of major programs already in place was simply not politically
realistic, either in the United States or in more "developed" welfare
states with more ambitious transfer schemes (re)distributing a much
larger fraction of national income. In this regard, conservatism in the
United States and in other advanced industrial democracies has usually meant just that: conservation, not reaction. Hence, the existing
net distribution (I_{t-1}) constrains the formation of new distributional
goals (I_t^T), and we anticipate that b_0 will be approximately 0.

The formation, financing, and implementation of policies directly
affecting the income distribution involve much longer lags than those
associated with conventional macroeconomic policies affecting aggregate output and employment. So even though the I^T equation is
annual (because income distribution data are available only annually), the partisan terms Dem and Congress are lagged 1 period
(year). The operative target embodied in current policies and outcomes for the distribution of net incomes is therefore based on the
party in power in the previous year. Inasmuch as a downward move-

ment in I represents a decline in the inequality of the distribution of net incomes, by the partisan model the parameter b_1 should be less than 0; that is, Democratic administrations aim for (and, after adjustment lags, achieve) greater income equality than do the Republican administrations. Similarly, inasmuch as the Congress variable denotes the relative strength of the Democrats, b_2 should also be less than 0.[53]

Adjustment of actual distributional outcomes to the operative partisan target is expressed by the first-order partial adjustment equation

$$I_t - I_{t-1} = \phi(I_t^T - I_{t-1}) + e_t \qquad (7.8)$$

where, as before, in principle ϕ is less than 1 and represents the fraction of the adjustment achieved each period.[54] After deriving the estimating equation by substituting equation (7.7) into (7.8), however, we can see that in this case ϕ is not distinguishable from the other parameters (ϕ is not identified):

$$I_t = I_{t-1} + \phi \cdot b_0 + \phi \cdot b_1 \, \text{Dem}_{t-1} + \phi \cdot b_2 \, \text{Congress}_{t-1} \qquad (7.9)$$

Table 7.6 reports the estimation results for equation (7.9). The regression model in column 1 of Table 7.6 shows the impact of Dem (Democratic presidential administrations) alone. The models in columns 2 and 3 add the percentage of Democratic House members and then of Democratic Senate members to the basic specification, on the plausible assumption that Democratic strength in Congress (not only Democratic party control of the presidency) helps account for politically (tax-and-transfer policy) induced declines in the inequality of net income shares. The results indicate that only Democratic control of the presidency has a systematic connection to the postwar improvements in net income equality. Neither Democratic party strength in the House or in the Senate nor the conjunction of Democratic control of the presidency and a favorable partisan balance in the Congress[55] appears to have had strong influence on the course of inequality beyond that associated with oscillation of the parties in the White House.

The parameter estimate for $\phi \cdot b_1$ Dem in the regression model in column 1 implies that the inequality ratio declined (after a lag) by about 0.046 *per year* during Democratic administrations, or about 0.36 $(8 \cdot 0.046)$ over two terms (eight years).[56] If the highly insignificant intercept parameter $\phi \cdot b_0$ is taken at face value, the decline in inequal-

Table 7.6 Estimates for the partisan models of the distribution of net income, annual 1948–1978

Model:
$$I_t = I_{t-1} + \phi \cdot b_0 + \phi \cdot b_1 \, \mathrm{Dem}_{t-1} + \phi \cdot b_2 \, \mathrm{DemHR}_{t-1} + \phi \cdot b_3 \, \mathrm{DemSen}_{t-1}$$

	(1)	(2)	(3)
$\phi \cdot b_0$	0.00812	0.115	0.107
	(0.0172)	(0.110)	(0.110)
$\phi \cdot b_1$ (Dem_{t-1} = +1 for	−0.0455*	−0.0439*	−0.0549*
Democratic president,	(0.0247)	(0.0247)	(0.0271)
0 otherwise)			
$\phi \cdot b_2$ (DemHR_{t-1} =	—	−0.00187	−0.00452
Democratic % in House)	—	(0.0019)	(0.003)
$\phi \cdot b_3$ (DemSen_{t-1} =	—	—	0.00292
Democratic % in Senate)	—	—	(0.0029)
Adjusted R^2	0.78	0.78	0.78
Standard error of regression	0.137	0.132	0.127

* Significant at the 0.05 level, one-tail test.
Notes: The variable I equals the ratio of the share of net income received by the top 20 percent of the distribution to the share received by the bottom 40 percent of the distribution among families. See Table 7.5. Standard errors appear in parentheses.

ity over two successive Democratic presidential terms is on the order of 0.30, or 8 · (0.46 − 0.008). Evaluated around a benchmark of 2—the value of the inequality ratio at the beginning of the series in the late 1940s—this translates to a reduction in inequality of between 15 and 18 percent after an eight-year stretch of Democratic control of the White House (−0.30/2.0; −0.36/2.0). As noted earlier, over the entire range of the data (1947–1978), inequality declined by about 25 percent; as the data in Table 7.5 and the estimates in Table 7.6 show, this decline was concentrated during the fourteen years of Democratic administrations in the sample.

A DEMAND FOR MORE EQUALITY?

A 25-percent improvement in the equality of net incomes, though hardly trivial, is perhaps less than might be expected in a democracy in which electoral politics is organized partly around have/have-not issues. After all, by 1978 (the end of the data series) the inequality ratio stood at 1.5; the income share of the top 20 percent of the distribution (net of federal taxes, transfers, and the imputed value of other public expenditures) was one-and-a-half times larger than the share of the bottom 40 percent. To be sure, there is a limit to how much redistribution can be achieved by government through the tax-and-transfer system if a market-based economy is to be sustained. At some point one bumps squarely into Okun's "leaky bucket" dilemma: The administrative costs of large-scale tax collection and transfer programs and the adverse effects on incentives to work and to produce in the market begin to exceed redistributive gains by any sensible standard.[57] Yet experiences elsewhere—notably in the more egalitarian, highly efficient, and productive welfare states of northern Europe—suggest we are probably well short of that point in the United States.

Class-related differentials in political participation may underlie the failure of Democratic administrations to achieve more redistribution during the postwar era. Lower income (and lower occupational status) groups in the United States vote with much less regularity than do the higher income (and higher occupational status) classes. Wolfinger and Rosenstone's analysis showed that voting turnout rises more or less linearly with income, varying in 1972 from 46 percent in the bottom decile of the income distribution to 86 percent in the top decile—a gap of 40 percentage points.[58] This strong association between income (and status generally) and voting turnout, which distinguishes the United States from most advanced industrial democracies, biases electoral politics in this country in favor of the well-to-do and probably helps explain the Democratic party's comparatively cautious approach to redistribution. But Page's analysis of pertinent survey data (which, unfortunately, are rather thin) suggests that there has been no strong, unfulfilled demand for radical redistributive efforts in the United States. On the contrary, Page concluded that "Americans were getting about as much income tax progressivity as they wanted" and that the "overall shape of social welfare policy . . . is broadly consistent with the expressed preferences of the public for social insurance and some assistance to the needy but not much redistribution of income."[59] The prevalence of such views, even among the lower ranges of the income distribution, obviously serves the economic interests of the privileged well. An attempt to explain this phenomenon, however, would take us deep into the origins of American political culture and American "exceptionalism," a topic well beyond the scope of this book.[60]

7.5   Macroeconomic Policies

Thus far I have tried to show that the partisan stripe of presidential administrations has significantly affected macroeconomic and distributional outcomes in the postwar American political economy. Political officials do not directly control outcomes, however; they control policies. Table 7.4 and the associated discussion established that the major fiscal actions affecting the distribution of net income—the big transfer programs targeted for low-income groups—were the creatures of Democratic administrations. The association between Democratic presidencies and improvements in equality of net incomes, which was illustrated by the raw time-series data in Table 7.5 and nailed down more precisely by the estimates for dynamic models in Table 7.6, is clearly not coincidental. Conclusions about the impact of partisanship on macroeconomic outcomes can be deepened and rendered more convincing, however, by an explicit analysis of partisan-induced variations in macroeconomic policies.

Federal budgetary totals, along with aggregate federal taxes and monetary actions, form administrations' macroeconomic policies. Exogenous shocks aside, they determine the path of interest rates, unemployment, output, and inflation. The macroeconomic impact of the budget is difficult to assess with precision, and the measurement of "fiscal thrust" remains controversial. Other things being equal, deficits are expansionary and surpluses are contractional. But the numbers must be cyclically corrected, because income- and employment-contingent taxes and transfers automatically push the budget into deficit during recessions (as corporate and personal tax liabilities fall and transfer payments rise) and into surplus during booms (as the process goes into reverse, with tax receipts increasing and transfers declining; see Chapter 1). This has stimulated a great many proposals for measuring the "high employment" or "full employment" surplus/deficit, but none enjoys the complete confidence of the applied research community.[61]

Measurement of the macroeconomic thrust of monetary policy is less controversial than assessment of fiscal thrust.[62] What matters for the economy on the monetary policy side is the growth rate of the money supply relative to the ongoing inflation rate—that is, the rate of growth of the real money supply.[63] At negligible inflation rates, a 5-percent money supply growth rate is expansionary; at double-digit inflation rates, the same monetary policy cannot adequately finance the flow of nominal transactions and will inevitably produce a crushing disinflationary contraction. Moreover, as was pointed out earlier, in the short run monetary policy is easier to maneuver and more decisive than fiscal policy; the impact of fiscal initiatives is largely dissipated unless monetary policy is accommodating.

In the party cleavage model, unemployment is the outcome variable that most clearly reveals the macroeconomic priorities of the parties, with output (and inflation) playing a more derivative role. Thus a natural way to evaluate the partisan model is to analyze variations over time in money supply growth rates and fiscal thrusts, conditional on received inflation rates, in relation to shifts in party based unemployment targets.

THE MONEY SUPPLY MODEL

The empirical framework of the money supply model follows that used earlier. Beginning with monetary policy and letting m denote the (quarterly) growth rate of the M1 money supply,[64] we have the target equation

$$m_t^T = a_0 + \lambda(U_t^T - U_{t-1}) + c\bar{p}_t \tag{7.9}$$

where $\bar{p}$ denotes the ongoing inflation rate (of the GNP implicit price deflator) and, as before, U^T and U denote the target and actual rates of unemployment, respectively.[65] Hence the money supply growth rate target of an administration is proportional to the gap between its unemployment target and the actual unemployment rate observed in the previous quarter. When the partisan unemployment target lies below the observed unemployment rate, administrations seek to close the gap by pushing the Fed to raise the money supply growth rate (relative to the inflation rate). Conversely, when observed unemployment is below target, political pressure on monetary authority is relaxed—or actually goes the other way—and the money supply tends to decelerate. Clearly the model implies that λ should be less than 0.

The monetary growth target is also conditioned by the ongoing inflation rate, $\bar{p}$, because movements in the real money supply, $(m - p)$, are what move unemployment and real output.[66] If administrations (and, more directly, the Federal Reserve) are indifferent to the inflation rate when forming monetary growth rate targets, c (the coefficient of $\bar{p}$) should be in the vicinity of 1. A value for c of less than 1, which is more plausible, means that monetary policy goals do not fully accommodate inflationary trends. As we shall see later, $c < 1$

implies that insofar as monetary policy is concerned unemployment goals are relaxed in order to fight inflation.[67]

The adjustment-to-target equation for the money supply growth rate is

$$m_t - m_{t-1} = \phi_1(m_t^T - m_{t-1}) + e_t \qquad (7.10)$$

As in the previous models, ϕ_1 represents the fraction of the gap between the target money supply growth rate and the actual rate of the previous period that is closed each quarter. Hence ϕ_1 should lie in the interval $0 < \phi_1 < 1$. Unlike unemployment and real output (and most fiscal instruments), however, which exhibit considerable inertia and only can be adjusted slowly from one period to the next because of the institutional and structural factors discussed earlier, the money supply can be brought into line with partisan targets quickly as long as the Federal Reserve is responsive to an administration's preferences. The historical studies reviewed in the Introduction indicate that the Fed generally has been quite responsive to presidents' objectives, and therefore in the case of money supply growth equations ϕ_1 should lie closer to 1 than to 0.

Substituting equation (7.9) into (7.10) and solving the m_t yields

$$m_t = \phi_1 \cdot a_0 + (1 - \phi_1)m_{t-1} \qquad (7.11)$$
$$+ \phi_1 \cdot \lambda(U_t^T - U_{t-1}) + \phi_1 \cdot c\bar{p}_t + e_t$$

Recalling from equation (7.1) that the partisan-based unemployment targets are given by[68]

$$U_t^T = b_0 + U_t^N + b_1 \, \mathrm{Dem}_t \qquad (7.12)$$

we use substitution to get this dynamic, nonlinear estimating equation:

$$m_t = a + (1 - \phi_1)m_{t-1} + \phi_1 \cdot \lambda(U_t^N + b_1 \, \mathrm{Dem}_t - U_{t-1}) \qquad (7.13)$$
$$+ \phi_1 \cdot c\bar{p}_t + e_t$$

where $a = \phi_1 \cdot (\lambda \cdot b_0 + a_0)$, U^N is the benchmark or natural unemployment rate, U is the actual unemployment rate, and Dem is $+1$ during Democratic presidential administrations and 0 during Republican administrations.

THE FISCAL POLICY MODEL

Although monetary and fiscal policies have been known to head in opposite directions, by and large we expect the direction of monetary and fiscal thrusts to reflect the same underlying unemployment (and output and inflation) goals. The fiscal policy analyses are based on the Department of Commerce's "full employment" federal revenues and expenditures series, a widely used measure of the cyclically adjusted federal budget. Specifically, Fisc, the fiscal thrust indicator used in the experiments reported here, is the percentage deviation of high employment revenues from high employment expenditures. The magnitude of the cyclically adjusted federal surplus/deficit is therefore scaled to a base of current-period federal revenues and expenditures.[69] Other things being equal, negative values of Fisc (in other words, high employment deficits) represent expansive fiscal thrusts that tend to raise output and employment, where positive values (or high employment surpluses) have contractive effects that lower output and employment.

The fiscal policy target equation is

$$\text{Fisc}_t^T = a_0 + \lambda(U_t^T - U_{t-1}) + c_1 \bar{p}_t \tag{7.14}$$

where the terms are defined for equation (7.9). Clearly λ should be less than 0 in equation (7.14), because administrations are expected to shift fiscal policy in an expansive direction (Fisc < 0) when unemployment is above the target ($U > U^T$) and to move the adjusted budget toward surplus (Fisc > 0) when unemployment is below target ($U < U^T$). The equation also allows for the possibility that the priority that administrations give their unemployment goals and, hence, administrations' fiscal targets may be influenced by the ongoing inflation rate. In particular, if administrations tend to relax their unemployment targets with rising inflation rates, then c should be greater than 0.

The Fisco adjustment-to-target equation is

$$\text{Fisc}_t - \text{Fisc}_{t-1} = \phi_1(\text{Fisc}_t^T - \text{Fisc}_{t-1}) \tag{7.15}$$
$$+ b_2(U_t - U_{t-1}) + b_3 \text{War}_t + c_2 \bar{p}_t$$

where War is a binary variable that is equal to $+1$ during the Vietnam War years and 0 otherwise and other variables are as defined previously. The fiscal policy adjustment equation includes several terms in addition to the gap between fiscal goals and outcomes. The Department of Commerce full-employment budget data used to create Fisc are not completely free of cyclical influences, and so the rate of change of unemployment, $(U_t - U_{t-1})$, appears in the equation to net out responses of Fisc to the business cycle that do not stem from intentional actions to achieve unemployment targets. The binary variable War is included in the adjustment equation to purge the parameter estimates of the enormous fiscal expansions associated with the Vietnam War (particularly during the Johnson administration), which were not based on domestic macroeconomic goals of the parties. Finally, $\bar{p}$ appears here, as well as in the target equation, because federal revenues are automatically affected by inflation through the income tax system and expenditures are similarly affected by inflation via the indexing of transfer programs.

Substituting the unemployment target function in equation (7.12) for U^T in equation (7.14) and then substituting the fiscal policy target equation for Fisc^T in equation (7.15) yields the model used in the regression experiments:

$$\text{Fisc}_t = \alpha + (1 - \phi_1)\text{Fisc}_{t-1} + \phi_1 \cdot \lambda(U_t^N + b_1 \, \text{Dem}_t \tag{7.16}$$
$$- U_{t-1}) + b_2(U_t - U_{t-1}) + b_3 \, \text{War}_t + c\bar{p}_t$$

where $a = \phi_1 \cdot (\lambda \cdot b_0 + a_0)$, $c = (c_2 + \phi_1 \cdot c_1)$, and all other variables are as defined earlier.[70]

EMPIRICAL RESULTS FOR THE MONETARY AND FISCAL POLICY MODELS
Regression results for equations (7.13) and (7.16), in which the ongoing inflation rate, $\bar{p}$, is measured by the lagged rate of change of prices, p_{t-1} and p_{t-2}, are reported in Table 7.7. The estimates of λ in the table represent the influence of gaps between unemployment targets and actual unemployment rates on the formation of money supply growth rate targets and fiscal policy targets. In the money supply models, λ lies between -0.8 and -1, which means that nominal money growth targets tend to move nearly point for point with deviations of U from U^T. Hence, other things being equal, the money supply tends, after all adjustment lags, to increase 0.8 to 0.9 percentage point for each point that the unemployment rate lies above the unemployment target. The results for the Fisc models indicate that the same 1-point gap between actual and target rates of unemployment ultimately induces a change in the cyclically adjusted deficit equal to between 3 and 4 percent of the revenue/expenditure base.

The ϕ_1 parameter measures the speed of adjustment of money supply growth rates and cyclically adjusted surpluses/deficits to par-

Table 7.7   Estimates for the partisan models of monetary policy (M1 growth rate) and fiscal policy (the percentage gap between cyclically adjusted federal revenues and expenditures), quarterly

Models:
1953:1–1983:2
$$m_t = \alpha + (1 - \phi_1)m_{t-1} + \phi_1 \cdot \lambda(U_t^N + b_1 \text{ Dem}_t - U_{t-1}) + \phi_1 \cdot c\bar{p}$$

1955:2–1983:2
$$\text{Fisc}_t = \alpha + (1 - \phi_1) \text{Fisc}_{t-1} + \phi_1 \cdot \lambda(U_t^N + b_1 \text{ Dem}_t - U_{t-1})$$
$$+ b_2(U_t - U_{t-1}) + b_3 \text{ War}_t + c\bar{p}$$

Variable	Monetary policy (m)		Fiscal policy (Fisc)	
	(1)	(2)	(3)	(4)
α	+1.439**	+1.309**	+1.129*	+1.205*
	(0.531)	(0.546)	(0.645)	(0.671)
λ	−0.915**	−0.875**	+3.747**	+3.675**
	(0.272)	(0.270)	(0.748)	(0.752)
ϕ_1	+0.629**	+0.638**	+0.313**	+0.318**
	(0.084)	(0.085)	(0.064)	(0.066)
b_1 (Dem$_t$ = +1 for	−1.852*	−1.974*	−1.581**	−1.614**
Democratic president,	(0.987)	(1.043)	(0.542)	(0.554)
0 otherwise)				
$b_2(U_t - U_{t-1})$			−1.735**	−1.670*
			(0.728)	(0.735)
			−3.329**	−3.341**
b_3 (War = +1, 0)			(0.964)	(0.968)
$c\bar{p}$ (inflation)				
$c_1 p_{t-1}$	+0.379**		−0.257*	
	(0.141)		(0.119)	
$\sum_{j=1}^{2} c_j p_{t-j}$		+0.432**		−0.278*
		(0.148)		(0.127)
Adjusted R^2	0.360	0.361	0.802	0.800
Standard error of regression	+2.730	+2.729	+2.858	+2.869

* Significant at 0.05 level, one-tail test.
** Significant at 0.01 level, one-tail test.
Note: Standard errors appear in parentheses.

tisan-defined targets. As anticipated, the monetary policy adjustment lags are much shorter than the corresponding fiscal policy adjustment lags. In the money supply growth rate equations in Table 7.7, ϕ_1 is estimated to be about 0.63, which implies that 63 percent of the adjustment of m to m^T is completed within one quarter. Given that the rate at which m adjusts to m^T is

$$m_t = \phi_1 \sum_i (1 - \phi_1)^i m^T_{t-1-i}$$

more than 85 percent of the adjustment has been completed after two quarters have elapsed and almost 95 percent has been realized after three quarters.[71] Federal Reserve policy actions appear to respond relatively quickly to the unemployment-based money supply growth rate targets of the typical Democratic or Republican administration.

By contrast, in the fiscal thrust equations, ϕ_1 is estimated to be about 0.31. This indicates that only 30 percent or so of the gap between fiscal targets and actual fiscal outcomes is closed within one quarter, about 77 percent is closed after four quarters (a year) have elapsed, and approximately 95 percent is closed after eight quarters (two years). The finding that fiscal policy is generally slower than monetary policy to reflect fully an administration's unemployment goals is consistent with earlier observations about the institutional setting within which macroeconomic policies are implemented.

From the point of view of political analysis of the American political economy, the most important coefficient in the equations in Table 7.7 is the parameter of Dem, b_1, which distinguishes the monetary and fiscal targets and, hence the unemployment targets, of Democratic and Republican administrations. If the party cleavage model for unemployment outcomes is valid, the estimates of the b_1 parameter in the money supply model and the fiscal thrust model should be consistent with the estimates obtained in the unemployment equations reported previously in Table 7.3—that is, they should fall in the range −1.5 to −2. Therefore, estimates for b_1 in Table 7.7 simultaneously provide an external test of the validity of the partisan model of unemployment outcomes and of the conclusions reached in the Introduction about the responsiveness of the Federal Reserve to the goals of presidential administrations.

The estimates of b_1 range between −1.60 and −2, values that mirror almost perfectly the estimates of interparty differences in unemployment targets and outcomes obtained for the unemployment models in Table 7.3. In light of the fact that the b_1 parameter estimates for the money supply and fiscal thrust equations in Table 7.7 were obtained independently of the corresponding coefficient estimates for the earlier unemployment equations, the near-equivalence of the estimates across the respective nonlinear regressions yields strong evidence favoring the validity of the partisan model. An important qualification soon to be discussed aside, these results suggest that in determining rates of monetary expansion and contraction the Federal Open Market Committee "independently" pursues policies that bring the unemployment rate into line with the target of the party controlling the presidency. Similarly, notwithstanding the large cyclically adjusted deficits of the Reagan years (which were neutralized for much of the time by monetary contraction and were motivated by distributional rather than stimulative objectives), fiscal policy accommodates the same partisan goals, although the estimates of ϕ_1 in the Fisc regressions suggest that the rate of adjustment of fiscal policy is usually more sluggish than that of monetary policy. Nonetheless, relative to the prevailing unemployment and inflation rates, both monetary and fiscal policies generally are much "looser," or more expansive, during Democratic administrations than during Republican ones. The reason is that Democratic administrations typically pursue more ambitious unemployment goals—more ambitious by a factor approaching 2 percent.

Yet monetary policy also has responded to inflation. The parameter estimates for the $\bar{p}$ term in Table 7.7 show that money supply growth rates usually have fallen well short of completely accommodating the ongoing rate of inflation; in all regressions (those shown as well as equations specified with longer lag sums for inflation), the coefficient of $\bar{p}$, $\sum_j c_j$, is significantly less than 1. Consequently, real money supply growth rates, $(m - \bar{p})$—which, as emphasized earlier, are what affect real output and unemployment performance—have been constrained by inflation rates. Interpreted slightly differently, this means that as a practical matter the unemployment targets bearing on monetary policy tend to have been adjusted upward with increasing inflation rates.

To gain a clearer idea of this line of reasoning, consider the model in column 2 of Table 7.7. Rewriting the equation after solving out adjustment lags (which, as indicated earlier, are relatively brief) yields

$$m_t = a/\phi_1 + \lambda(U_t^N + b_1 \, \text{Dem}_t - U_{t\,1}) + c\bar{p}_t \tag{7.17}$$

where $c\bar{p}_t = c_1 p_{t-1} + c_2 p_{t-2}$ and designates the ongoing inflation rate.

Assuming for the purposes of stylized analysis that $p_t = p_{t-1} = p_{t-2} = \bar{p}$, we may form the real money supply growth rate equation:

$$(m - \bar{p})_t = a/\phi_1 + \lambda(U_t^N + b_1 \, \mathrm{Dem}_t - U_{t-1}) + (c - 1)\bar{p} \quad (7.18)$$

Current and especially future rates of unemployment and inflation are of course not exogenous to (independent of) current and future monetary growth rates. Moreover, unemployment and inflation are jointly endogenous (causally related). Indeed, as has been mentioned repeatedly, monetary expansions (contractions) relative to ongoing inflation raise (depress) employment and output. In turn, when output is pushed above capacity and unemployment is pushed below the "natural" rate (which U^N approximates), the core inflation rate begins to drift upward. The standard rule of thumb is that annual core inflation rises (falls) about one-half point for each percentage point that annual unemployment stands below (above) the natural rate. In view of these feedback relations, it is not sensible to evaluate quantitatively the longer run, or steady-state, implications of equation (7.18), because this requires holding U and p fixed indefinitely.

Nonetheless, it is clear from the estimates in Table 7.7 that high ongoing inflation rates often have not been fully accommodated by postwar monetary policy. In equation (7.17) the coefficient c is less than 1; consequently, in equation (7.18) $(c - 1)$ is less than 0. It follows that if inflation is high enough relative to the gap between the desired and actual unemployment rates, the Fed tends to hold the nominal money supply growth rate well short of the inflation rate. In other words, the real money supply growth rate becomes negative, $(m - \bar{p}) < 0$, even when U^T lies below U_{t-1}.[72] As noted above, such situations may be viewed as inflation-induced upward adjustments in the policy-relevant unemployment target, U^T. In other words, the unemployment targets implicitly pursued by the Federal Reserve are conditional on the ongoing inflation rate and therefore tend to be relaxed with sustained increases in inflation. There is no evidence that the inflation sensitivity of monetary policy interacts with the party controlling the White House, however,[73] so the upward drift of monetary policy–relevant unemployment targets with inflation (and the downward drift with disinflation) does not alter the interparty differences implied by the estimates of b_1 in the models in columns 1 and 2 of Table 7.7. At all observed inflation rates, monetary policy under the Democrats has been consistent with an unemployment goal that is about 2 percentage points lower than the goal associated with policy under Republican administrations facing a similar inflationary environment.

Whether the inflation sensitivity of money supply growth rates represents relaxation of unemployment targets by presidential administrations or whether it reflects "independent" anti-inflationary activity by the Federal Reserve is impossible to say from the quantitative evidence. It is clear from the estimates of $c\bar{p}$ in the Fisc models in Table 7.7, however, that in general inflation has not led to contractions of fiscal policy. Unlike the results for the monetary policy models, the fiscal policy regressions yield no evidence that cyclically adjusted federal budget surpluses are systematically associated with sustained high rates of inflation. If anything, adjusted federal expenditures appear to exceed adjusted revenues by one-quarter of a percentage point per extra point of inflation.

The partisan models for unemployment analyzed previously are essentially reduced-form equations in which policy variables have been solved out. Another way to gain information about the inflation sensitivity of the parties' unemployment goals is to enter lagged inflation terms directly into the earlier U^T function (equation 7.1) and reestimate the resulting unemployment equations. This amounts to estimating models in the form of equation (7.3) after adding the terms $\phi_1 \cdot \sum_j c_j p_{t-j}$ for $j = 1, 2, 3, \ldots$. This approach gets around much of the mutual endogeneity problem noted above. Depending on the precise lag specification, it produces uniformly positive estimates of $\sum_j c_j$ that range in magnitude between 0.08 and 0.15 but are always statistically insignificant. The strongest inference that might be drawn from such results (and it is a conclusion that is more conjectural than firmly supported by quantitative evidence) is that the parties' effective unemployment targets are raised on the order of one-tenth of a percentage point per point of sustained inflation.[74]

The idea that administrations of both parties relax unemployment goals with rising inflation is surely consistent with impressions of recent macroeconomic policy history, and not at all at variance with a party cleavage perspective on macroeconomic policies and outcomes. After all, even Democratic presidents' political support in the core Democratic constituency is adversely affected by inflation, although, as we saw in Chapter 5, Democratic partisans attach more weight to unemployment relative to inflation than do Republican partisans. Presidents Ford, Carter, and Reagan each supported policies that pushed unemployment well above the targets typically associated with Democratic and Republican administrations (currently about 5 and 7 percent, respectively) when inflation escalated to double-digit rates after the two great OPEC oil shocks.

Yet neither party cleavages over the importance of unemployment nor the adjustment of partisan goals to bursts of inflation account for the special political pressures on the economy that may build up during election years. So we turn in Chapter 8 to the question of electorally motivated economic policy and outcome cycles.

8 Political Business Cycles

The [inflationary] bias increases in election years. For those in or close to the seats of state power, the costs of paying the piper fall sharply after a successful election day. The myopia of voters, including those with Ph.D.'s in economics, makes the game possible. Are we destined to add to our list a new cycle with a periodicity of four years?

—David Meiselman

The argument that business cycles frequently are driven by electoral politics is simple, important, and immensely appealing to laypeople and scholars alike. For these reasons the so-called political business cycle has received more attention, particularly outside of professional circles, than any other idea appearing in recent academic work on political economy. Yet the thesis that economic cycles often are influenced by the election calendar rests on a rather fragile empirical foundation.[1]

8.1 The Theory of Election Cycles

The core proposition of all political business cycle arguments is that economic activity tends to cycle about election dates, with unemployment falling and real output and income rising at unsustainable rates just prior to elections in response to the efforts of incumbents to create favorable economic conditions during the voting season—especially during the presidential voting season. After a lag, this inevitably yields an accelerating price level, which is reversed (if at all) by painful disinflationary actions taken after elections are safely over. As Nordhaus put it in his seminal theoretical analysis, "Within an incumbent's term in office there is a predictable pattern of policy, starting with relative austerity in early years and ending with the potlatch right before elections."[2]

The stylized election cycle model rests on several assumptions about the working of the macroeconomy and the nature of competitive electoral politics:

1. The overriding goal of incumbents is to win elections, and so presidents manage the economy in order to maximize votes.[3]

2. Electoral outcomes are influenced significantly by macroeconomic performance, and voters weight election-day performance more heavily than performance earlier in the term. Therefore incumbents lose less from early poor performance than they gain from good performance nearer election day. Voters also discount sharply or are only dimly aware of the future consequences of election-period economic maneuvering.

3. Governments can boost employment, output, and growth to levels not sustainable in the long run by monetary and fiscal stimulation, although at the eventual cost of escalating inflation rates.

4. The full inflationary consequences of unrealistically low unemployment and excessive real income and output growth rates appear only after politically meaningful lags. The structure of the macroeconomy therefore allows incumbents to exploit a "window" of political-economic opportunity by engineering unusually favorable real activity at relatively low inflation rates around the time of elections.[4]

The failure of assumption 1 or 3 makes the economy exogenous to politically motivated policy action, whereas the failure of assumption 2 or 4 disconnects electoral politics from economic performance. None of the assumptions underlying the political business cycle model is implausible; indeed all but one are supported by substantial empirical evidence. As far as the macroeconomic assumptions (assumptions 3 and 4) are concerned, only strict adherents of new classical, rational-expectations economic theories would deny that systematic monetary and fiscal actions affect real output and employment or that the full inflationary effects of pushing the macroeconomy to a high level of activity are only gradually realized.[5] And experience has decisively repudiated the strong new classical rational-expectations view, which holds that anticipated fiscal thrusts and anticipated expansions of the money supply above the growth rate of potential real output pass entirely through to inflation, without having any impact on real output and unemployment, even in the short run. Consequently, strong forms of new classical rational-expectations theory are now almost universally seen as having negligible empirical relevance. Empirical evidence also strongly supports assumption 2—that economic conditions affect electoral outcomes and that voters discount performance backward in time (in other words, that voters weight current economic conditions more heavily than past conditions in making contemporaneous political choices).[6]

The weakest assumption of political business cycles theories is assumption 1. The idea that presidents attach overriding importance to maximizing aggregate political support (votes) on election day implies a questionable characterization of the typical administration's macroeconomic policy behavior. Democratic administrations, for example, may be reluctant to sacrifice the interests of their core constituency early in the term by pursuing contractive, disinflationary policies in preparation for a low-inflation, transitory, election-year boom. Analogously, Republican presidents may be loath to discount heavily the postelection surge of inflation that would inevitably follow excessive stimulation of the macroeconomy, even if such behavior clearly would yield a vote harvest.

Moreover, presidents of either partisan stripe presumably want to pass their legislative programs, and we know that their success in so doing depends to a significant extent on their mass political support over the entire electoral term, as legislative initiatives are fed by the administration to Congress.[7] The desired *stable* stock of public support across *interelection* periods is inconsistent with a cyclical macroeconomic policy plan designed to produce an election-period heaping of voter goodwill. Nonetheless, the electoral business cycle model is plausible, and whether it accurately identifies a systematic source of political influence on macroeconomic policies and outcomes in the American political economy can only be resolved empirically.

8.2   Empirical Analysis of Election Cycles

MODELS

The party cleavage model introduced in Chapter 7 is easily augmented to yield an appropriate framework for new empirical analyses of electorally motivated economic cycles. Focusing first on unemployment and real output outcomes, we see that the political business cycle hypothesis requires that the equations for partisan economic targets (equations 7.1 and 7.4) be modified to include a suitably specified election-cycle term (or terms):

$$Y_t^T = b_0 + Y_t^N + b_1 \text{ Dem}_{t-1} + a_1 \text{ Elect}_t \tag{8.1}$$

where Y^T denotes target unemployment (U^T) and log real output ($\ln Q^T$), Y^N denotes normal unemployment (U^N) and log real output ($\ln Q^N$), Dem is coded +1 during Democratic presidential administrations and 0 otherwise, and Elect denotes a suitable election-cycle variable.

The adjustment-to-target equations are, as in Chapter 7,

$$Y_t - Y_{t-1} = \phi_1 (Y_t^T - Y_{t-1}) + \phi_2(Y_{t-1} - Y_{t-2}) + b_2 \text{ Shock}_{t-1} + e_t \tag{8.2}$$

Substitution for Y^T in equation (8.2) gives dynamic estimating equations of the form

$$\begin{aligned}
Y_t = {}& \phi_1 \cdot b_0 + (1 - \phi_1 + \phi_2)Y_{t-1} \\
& - \phi_2 Y_{t-2} + \phi_1 Y_t^N \\
& + \phi_1 \cdot b_1 \text{ Dem}_{t-1} + b_2 \text{ Shock}_{t-1} \\
& + \phi_1 \cdot a_1 \text{ Elect}_t + e_t
\end{aligned} \tag{8.3}$$

The interpretation of the election cycle–augmented partisan model is essentially the same as that given earlier. The parties have contrasting macroeconomic targets which, depending on speeds of adjustment, eventually lead to interparty differences in economic outcomes equal to b_1. The empirical estimates reported previously indicate that, after adjustment lags, unemployment tends to be from 1.5 to 2 percentage points lower and real output from 5 to 6 percentage points higher under the Democrats than under the Republicans. According to the political business hypothesis, however, electoral considerations motivate administrations of *both* parties to attempt to lower unemployment and raise real income and output during the election season, no matter what partisan goals a president otherwise entertains. Excluding partisan forces and exogenous shocks from the augmented model and solving for the dynamic time path of Y in terms of election-period effects alone yields

$$\begin{aligned}
Y_t = {}& \frac{1}{1 - \theta_1 L - \theta_2 L^2} \phi_1 \cdot a_1 \text{ Elect}_t \\
= {}& \sum_{i=0}^{\infty} w_i \text{ Elect}_{t-i}
\end{aligned} \tag{8.4}$$

where θ_1 denotes $(1 - \phi_1 + \phi_2)$; θ_2 denotes $-\phi_2$; L is the lag operator such that $L^i X_t = X_{t-i}$; $w_0 = \phi_1 \cdot a_1$; $w_1 = \phi_1 \cdot a_1 \cdot \theta_1$; and $w_j = \theta_1 w_{j-1} + \theta_2 w_{j-2}$ for $j > 1$.

If we let t^* be the election quarter and code Elect $+1$ during the four election-year quarters and 0 otherwise, under the assumption that incumbents typically begin their election-oriented economic push in the first quarter of the election year, the macroeconomic consequences of the political business cycle are traced over the election year and thereafter by the sequence

$$
\begin{aligned}
t^* - 3: &\quad \theta_1 \cdot a_1 \\
t^* - 2: &\quad \theta_1 \cdot a_1(1 + \theta_1) \\
t^* - 1: &\quad \theta_1 \cdot a_1[1 + \theta_1 + (\theta_2 + \theta_1^2)] \\
t^*: &\quad \theta_1 \cdot a_1[1 + \theta_1 + (\theta_2 + \theta_1^2) + (\theta_1(\theta_2 + \theta_1^2) + \theta_1 \cdot \theta_2)] \\
t^* + 1: &\quad \theta_1 \cdot a_1[\theta_1 + (\theta_2 + \theta_1^2) + (\theta_1(\theta_2 + \theta_1^2) + \theta_1 \cdot \theta_2)] \\
t^* + 2: &\quad \theta_1 \cdot a_1 + [(\theta_2 + \theta_1^2) + (\theta_1(\theta_2 + \theta_1^2) + \theta_1 \cdot \theta_2)] \\
t^* + 3: &\quad \theta_1 \cdot a_1 + [(\theta_1(\theta_2 + \theta_1^2) + \theta_1 \cdot \theta_2)]
\end{aligned}
$$

and so on.[8]

According to the election cycle hypothesis, the parameter a_1 should be negative for unemployment (when Y in equations 8.1 through 8.4 designates U) and positive for log real output (when Y designates $\ln Q$). Given equation (8.3) and an Elect variable that is coded $+1$ during the four election-year quarters, estimates for ϕ_1 and ϕ_2 generating smooth dynamics such as those obtained earlier in Table 7.3 will produce exponential-like decay of unemployment over the election year and a corresponding election-year surge in real output approximating an inverted exponential growth path.[9] As the illustrative sequence shown above for periods $t^* - 3$ to $t^* + 3$ indicates, however, these election-year boosts to output and employment dissipate rather quickly over postelection periods, because the transitory stimulations of the macroeconomy are terminated at the election quarter, t^*.

ESTIMATION RESULTS

Results of the election-cycle–augmented partisan models appear in Table 8.1. Equations were estimated for log real output, the unemployment rate, the growth rate of the M1 money supply, the cyclically adjusted federal budget surplus/deficit (denoted "Fisc" in Chapter 7), and the growth rate of real personal disposable income per capita.[10] The growth rate of real per capita disposable personal income was added to the analysis because this variable repeatedly has been

Table 8.1 The impact of election cycles on macroeconomic outcomes and policies, quarterly, 1953:1–1984:3

	Unemployment, U (1)	Log real output, ln Q (2)	Growth rate of real personal disposable income per capita, r (3)	Growth rate of M1 money supply, m (4)	Percentage gap between cyclically adjusted federal revenues and expenditures, Fisc (5)
Model 1					
Presidential election years	−0.351	+0.004	+1.11	+1.06	−1.69
Dem (+1 for Democratic administrations; 0 for Republican administrations)	−1.97**	+0.063**	+1.22*	−2.05*	−1.25
Model 2					
Years of and years preceding presidential elections (last half of presidential terms)	−0.610	+0.012	+1.27*	+0.741	+0.284
Dem	−2.03**	+0.065**	+1.22*	−2.11*	−1.24

Model 3

Congressional and presidential election years (even years)	+0.105	−0.006	−0.423	+0.7?3	−2.04
Dem	−1.94**	+0.063**	+1.20*	−2.06*	−1.26

Model 4

Individual years of presidential elections (incumbent seeking election)

1956 (Eisenhower)	−1.07	+0.006	−0.154	−1.1?	+3.28
1960	−0.478	−0.019	−2.35	−2.06	+5.14
1964 (Johnson)	−0.155	−0.005	+3.28*	+0.398	−3.31
1968	−1.09	+0.006	+0.080	+3.65*	+0.559
1972 (Nixon)	−0.834	+0.042*	+3.04*	+5.22*	−8.57**
1976 (Ford)	−0.475	+0.005	+0.521	+0.551	−3.05
1980 (Carter)	−1.06	−0.007	+1.13	−0.375	+3.80
1984 (Reagan)	−0.682	+0.007	+3.62*	+0.488	−22.0**
Dem	−1.49*	+0.069**	+1.04*	−1.70*	−1.718**

* Significant at the 0.05 level, one-tail test.
** Significant at the 0.01 level, one-tail test.

Note: Significance levels (*, **) for the election variables are based on the a_1 estimates, but coefficient values shown are the implied effects at election quarters, given the estimates of a_1, λ, ϕ_1, and ϕ_2. See equation (8.4) in the text. In columns 1, 4, and 5, the coefficients of Dem represent the implied long-run effects (after all adjustment lags) of Democratic administrations on the unemployment rate. In columns 2 and 3, the Dem parameters represent the long-run effects of Democratic administrations on real output and real income growth rates, respectively. The Fisc equation time range, which was determined by the availability of the data, in 1955:2 to 1984:2.

shown to have a strong influence on the electoral success of the incumbent party's candidates. For this reason the real income growth rate is often prominently featured in discussions of the political business cycle.[11]

Estimates were obtained for several plausible specifications of the election-cycle variable (denoted "Elect" in the equations above). To conserve space, Table 8.1 reports parameter estimates only for the particular election-cycle variable appearing in each regression equation, along with the partisan term (Dem). Including the Dem term allows us to evaluate the robustness of the partisan effects discussed in Chapter 7 in the presence of variables providing for election-period stimulations of the macroeconomy.

In model 1 at the top of Table 8.1, the election-cycle variable is coded +1 during the four quarters of presidential election years and 0 otherwise. This is the same coding used earlier in this chapter to illustrate the general empirical implications of the political business cycle argument. The parameter estimates for model 1, then, indicate whether macroeconomic outcomes were consistently more favorable and policies consistently more expansive in presidential election years than in other years. The sign of the presidential-election-year parameter is consistent with the political business cycle hypothesis in all equations. The presidential-election-year coefficients are negative in the equations for unemployment and the cyclically adjusted federal surplus/deficit, and positive in the regressions for real output, the real personal income growth rate, and the money supply growth rate. None of the election-year parameters achieved statistical significance at the usual test levels, however.[12] Hence the results for model 1 yield no persuasive evidence that presidential election years, viewed together, generally have been occasions of unusual monetary and fiscal expansions or of short-run surges in output, real incomes, and employment.

The election-cycle variable used in the equations generating the estimates for model 2 of Table 8.1 is coded +1 for each presidential election year and the year preceding it. This specification of the political business cycle hypothesis is a bit more faithful than the others to the stylized cycle described in Nordhaus's seminal article.[13] It allows for relative austerity during the first half of presidential terms, followed by expansions during the entire second half—not just in election years as in model 1. In all equations except Fisc, the election-cycle parameter estimate has the sign anticipated by the political business cycle model. But only in the real income growth rate equation is the election-period coefficient statistically significant. Therefore the idea that electorally motivated economic performance and policy cycles have been a pronounced feature of the postwar American political economy is not strongly supported by these results. Real personal disposable income growth rates do appear to have been unusually high in the latter part of presidential administrations, however, just as most political business cycle arguments predict.

Research on economics and electoral politics has quite firmly established that macroeconomic performance affects the success of the president's party in midterm congressional elections as well as in presidential election years.[14] Accordingly, the party controlling the White House has electoral motivation to stimulate the economy in all even-numbered years, not just in years of presidential elections. But the successful implementation of such a finely tuned election strategy requires an exceptionally well developed capacity to maneuver the macroeconomy for short-run political purposes. Motivations aside, such political fine tuning of the macroeconomy seems rather implausible given institutional impediments in the political system and structural inertia in the economic system. Undoubtedly this is one important reason why the estimates for model 3 in Table 8.1 indicate so clearly that this variant of the election cycle argument is inconsistent with postwar experience. The election-cycle coefficients are uniformly insignificant and are correctly signed in only two of the five equations.

Incumbent presidents seeking reelection obviously have a special incentive to pursue an election-cycle macroeconomic strategy, and they are well situated to do so.[15] They need only play the game once, concentrating all efforts at short-run macroeconomic manipulation on a single presidential election, leaving the entire second term for the pursuit of "golden rule" policies or of policies that are more consistent with the enduring ideological preferences of their party. Democratic incumbents might be more likely than Republicans to play the election-cycle game, because throwing caution about inflation to the winds by inducing macroeconomic expansions during presidential election years is more in tune with the traditional Democratic emphasis on high growth and low unemployment. If the political business cycle hypothesis has any general validity, its consequences should be clearly apparent during years when sitting presidents, especially Democratic ones, sought election.

The estimates for model 4 of Table 8.1 are from equations with individual presidential-election-year terms. Use of these terms allows us to identify particular instances of election-related economic policy and outcome fluctuations. Several electorally well timed improvements in the macroeconomy are apparent from these estimates. The estimates for 1972 yield the most broadly based evidence of an election-year macroeconomic expansion. In 1972, real output and the growth rate of per capita real personal disposable income, as well as the money supply growth rate and the cyclically adjusted federal deficit, were much higher than could be expected as a result of the partisan forces described earlier and ordinary stochastic fluctuations. Indeed, without the 1972 experience to stimulate interest in the topic, it is doubtful that most of the subsequent writing about the political business cycle phenomenon ever would have appeared.

The economy's spurt in 1972 was fueled by both monetary and fiscal policy. The Nixon administration strongly signaled its desire for an expansive monetary policy to the Federal Reserve; the Fed, headed by Arthur Burns, seems to have accommodated the political pressure.[16] The results for the M1 money supply in model 4 indicate that monetary growth in 1972, given the pace of inflation, was way above the rates consistent with a policy plan aimed at achieving the Republicans' traditional unemployment and real output goals. The rate of growth of the real money supply (and remember, it is the real money supply growth rate, not the nominal growth rate, that affects aggregate output, incomes, and employment) was higher in 1972 than in any other year of the entire 1953 to 1984 period except 1983.[17] This big monetary expansion, which former Fed governor Sherman Maisel and others openly attributed to the Fed's responsiveness to President Nixon's electoral ambitions, surely contributed to the election-year fillip in real disposable personal income growth rates and real GNP. Expansive monetary policy in 1972 also favorably affected the unemployment rate. But employment responds more slowly than does output to stimulative policies, so much of the ensuing decline in unemployment did not occur until 1973. Consequently, a significant election-year response is not registered by the estimate for unemployment shown in Table 8.1.[18]

As the estimate of the large election-year federal deficit reported in Table 8.1 shows, fiscal policy also helps explain the favorable income performance of 1972. Edward Tufte has traced the 1972 fiscal expansion to the flow of transfer payments. In fact, presidential influence on the short-run flow of federal transfers is the cornerstone of his political business cycle argument. Tufte argues that engineering election cycles in real disposable income "does not require . . . any great skill at macroeconomic planning, management, or theory" because it involves nothing "much more subtle than getting a lot of checks in the mail before the first Tuesday in November."[19]

Yet the most dramatic change in transfers in 1972 was the permanent 20-percent increase in Social Security benefits—the result of legislation passed by the Democratic-controlled Congress and, despite vague threats of a presidential veto, signed into law by President Nixon in September 1972 in time for the mailing of checks to beneficiaries on October 1. This produced an impressive election-quarter spike in the cyclically adjusted federal deficit and, more important, in real personal disposable income (the increase in Social Security benefits accounted for over half of the 1972:4 rise in aggregate personal income), which was accentuated by the fact that the associated rise in Social Security payroll taxes did not take effect until the following January. Viewed year on year, however, the main impact of the Social Security benefits increase was felt in 1973, not in 1972. Along with the lagged impact of the 1972 expansion of the money supply, this explains why the economy performed so much better in 1973 than it had the year before.

If the 1972 expansion was the most broadly based preelection expansion, the 1984 expansion was the most sharply defined one. Even though unemployment and real output were moving in the correct direction for nearly two years prior to the election,[20] by the end of 1984 the unemployment level was still too high and the level of real output was still too far from its potential for these variables to be identified in the election-cycle regressions (or, for that matter, by a casual observer) as unusually favorable. After all, during the election quarter unemployment stood at about 7.5 percent (essentially the same rate Reagan inherited from Carter) and real GNP was more than 5 percent short of potential (also no better than the situation in Carter's last quarter). Therefore the estimates of the 1984 election-cycle variable are not significant (and in the case of unemployment, not even correctly signed) for these variables.

The striking feature of the course of macroeconomic developments during the first Reagan administration is the rate at which the economy moved in a favorable direction over the last half of the term. As was pointed out in Chapter 6, the flow of the economy over the Reagan years is a textbook illustration of a political business cycle. The well-timed directional or cyclical behavior of the economy under Reagan is registered by the election-year estimate for the growth rate of aggregate real disposable income. Following the miserable performance of 1981 and 1982, an explosion of real income growth rates began in late 1983 and continued into 1984. During the first three quarters of the election year, quarter-on-quarter growth rates of per capita real personal disposable income averaged 5.2 percent. Such robust growth rates were indeed out of the ordinary, and the election-cycle parameter for 1984 real income performance easily achieves statistical significance.

Although the relaxation of monetary policy in late 1982 made possible the economic recovery of 1983–1984, money supply growth rates, *given the dismal levels of real output and unemployment*, were not unusually high during preelection periods. Therefore the 1984 presidential-election parameter in the M1 growth rate regression equation is not significant. Fiscal policy was the driving force behind the brisk expansion of incomes over the last two years of Reagan's first term. The most important fiscal event under Reagan was enactment of the Economic Recovery and Taxation Act of 1981, which cut personal tax rates by 23 percent in three stages between 1981 and 1984. The full effect of the tax cut, which did not begin to be matched by cuts in federal expenditures, was first felt in the 1984 election year. Consequently, an enormous gap opened up between federal revenues and expenditures, and after-tax personal incomes rose dramatically. The unprecedented preelection fiscal stimulation shows up in the extraordinarily large, highly significant 1984 election-cycle coefficient in the Fisc equation, shown near the bottom of Table 8.1.

The only other evidence of unusually favorable election-year economic performance in model 4 of Table 8.1 is the behavior of the real personal disposable income growth rate in 1964. Monetary policy was expansionary over that year, but as the insignificant estimate for the 1964 election parameter indicates, the M1 growth rate was not exceptionally high for a Democratic administration committed to driving down the unemployment rate. The election-year coefficient for the cyclically adjusted budget deficit is not quite significant either. But we know that the main source of the special behavior of the real income growth rate in 1964 was a special fiscal event—the much analyzed 1964 personal income tax cut.

First proposed publicly by President Kennedy in June 1962, introduced in Congress in January 1963, and signed into law by President Johnson in February 1964, the Revenue Act of 1964 injected into the economy a 14-billion-dollar fiscal stimulus (43 billion in 1984 dollars). The tax cut represented a large fiscal stimulation (over 2 percent of 1964 GNP), and it helped fuel the unusually brisk growth rate of real income in 1964. It is quite plausible that Johnson's vigor in pushing the tax cut and Congress's favorable action on it after more than a year of resistance were influenced by electoral considerations.[21] Yet the initial impetus for what economic-policy specialist G. L. Bach later described as the "boldest fiscal move in a generation"[22] long predated the 1964 election. Further, unlike the amply documented 1972 case, the 1964 real income surge was not accompanied by anecdotal evidence favoring an election-cycle interpretation. What we do have from the written record is President Johnson's repeated insistence, as he built the case for fiscal stimulation, that "the number 1 priority . . . is more jobs. This is our dominant domestic problem and we have to face it head-on."[23] Johnson's rhetoric was consistent with his performance. The Kennedy-Johnson administrations presided over the longest expansion in postwar U.S. history, an expansion that began with the recovery from the Eisenhower recession of 1960–1961 and ended with the recession of 1970, which was induced by the Nixon administration to fight the upward drift of inflation that began in the late 1960s.

The estimates of the impact of variations in party control of the White House on economic policies and outcomes are given by the Dem parameters at the bottom of each row in Table 8.1. Unlike the election-cycle coefficients, they generally are quite robust in the presence of various specifications of the election cycle. Moreover, in most cases the partisan effects estimated in the political business cycle equations are virtually identical to those obtained in Chapter 7. In all election cycle models, the implied long-run interparty difference in real output performance is approximately 6 percent (column 2 of Table 8.1).[24] The direct estimates of the impact of partisan control of the presidency on the unemployment rate, which appear in the equations in the first column of Table 8.1, also conform to previous results. The Dem parameters in these regressions indicate, as in Chapter 7, that Democratic administrations typically aim for and achieve unemployment targets between 1.5 and 2 percentage points lower than do Republican administrations facing similar circumstances. These results are reinforced by indirect estimates of partisan effects on unemployment, given in Table 8.1 by the Dem coefficients in the money supply and fiscal policy equations in columns 4 and 5, respectively.

The importance of the partisan stripe of presidential administrations for annualized, quarter-over-quarter real disposable income growth rates, estimated by the coefficients reported in the third column of Table 8.1, is also compatible with the analogous results for the other economic variables. The Dem parameters in these equations suggest that Democratic administrations typically turned in a real income growth rate record that, after relatively brief adjustment-to-target lags, was about 1.2 points higher than the growth rates achieved by Republican administrations during the postwar period.

Sustained empirical analysis of appropriately specified statistical models indicates, then, that postwar political business cycles have been confined primarily to the preelection behavior of real income growth rates. Of the eight postwar presidential election years analyzed in this chapter, 1972 and 1984 are the most convincing examples of electorally well timed growth rate expansions with clearly identifiable monetary and fiscal policy origins. In comparison to the usual macroeconomic consequences of variations in party control of the presidency, election-based economic cycles are relatively infrequent, less broad based, and more short lived. Some readers may find conclusions based largely on estimates from nonlinear regression models less than completely persuasive—and perhaps justifiably. So at this point let us put aside the statistical models and review the directly observable connections between postwar elections and macroeconomic fluctuations. We shall focus on the two economic variables that have been most prominently featured in election-cycle research and writing: the unemployment rate and the real income growth rate.

8.3   Election Cycles and Partisan Cycles

UNEMPLOYMENT CYCLES

Annual unemployment rates are displayed in relation to postwar presidential elections in Figure 8.1. For the reasons discussed in Chapter 1, the so-called natural rate of unemployment trended upward by at least 1–2 percentage point between the early 1950s and late 1970s, and the unemployment rate time plot, stripped of cyclical fluctuations, reflects this trend. The figure also shows a pattern familiar to all specialists: Unemployment declined by varying (but usually small) margins from the preelection year to the election year in all postwar presidential election years except 1960 and 1980. (And on both of the latter occasions, the incumbent party lost the White House.) Although sometimes taken as evidence of a political business cycle, on closer inspection this pattern yields little support favoring the idea that electorally motivated manipulations of the macroeconomy are a systematic feature of postwar policy behavior.

Beginning with the election year 1952,[25] we see that unemployment did indeed fall, just as the political business cycle thesis would predict. But President Truman declined to take any action to stimulate the economy, which might have improved (though almost surely not decisively) Adlai Stevenson's showing against Eisenhower, an extremely popular war hero who would have been difficult to defeat under the best of circumstances.[26] In fact, in 1952 Truman resisted congressional attempts to eliminate the excess profits tax, which had been enacted after the outbreak of the Korean War, even though accepting such a tax-cut bill might have accelerated investment and economic activity generally, to the benefit of the Democrats' efforts to keep the White House.[27] The point to be emphasized, however, is that the decline of unemployment between 1951 and 1952 had nothing to do with the election. It was merely part of a continuous downward trend of unemployment from 1949 to 1953 that was propelled by the Korean War boom. Indeed, as a result of the production stimulated and manpower absorbed by the war effort, the unemployment rate actually declined in the first half of 1953 to 2.6 percent—the lowest rate achieved during the entire postwar period. Given the structure of U.S. labor markets, unemployment was bound to rise once an end to the war was successfully negotiated, no matter which

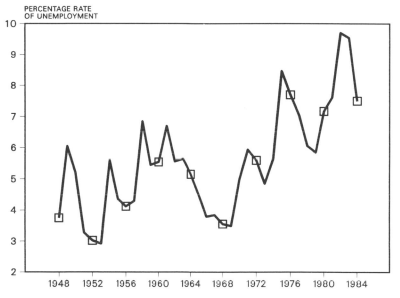

Figure 8.1 Postwar elections and annual unemployment rates, 1948–1984.

party controlled the White House. Hence the upturn in unemployment in the latter part of 1953, which has been viewed as characteristic of a four-year politically induced unemployment cycle, was inevitable once the economy was no longer on a war footing.

The Eisenhower administrations are sometimes excluded from consideration as candidates for election-oriented macroeconomic policy behavior[28] because of Ike's commitment to a balanced budget and his well-documented aversion to arousing inflationary forces via "excessive" economic stimulation. Here are some samples:

> Critics overlooked the inflationary psychology which prevailed during the mid-fifties and which I thought it necessary to defeat . . . The anti-inflation battle is never-ending, though I fear that . . . the public was apathetic, or at least ill-informed, regarding this issue.[29]

> We do not wish to realize this objective [economic growth] at the price of inflation, which not only creates inequities but is likely, sooner or later, to be followed by depression.[30]

> Appeasement is just as dangerous in dealing with inflation as in dealing with aggression.[31]

Economic policies and outcomes under Eisenhower were in tune with his anti-inflation rhetoric. Contractions were frequent—1953–1954, 1957–1958, and 1960–1961—and were either intentionally induced or passively accepted in order to keep downward pressure on the pace of wage and price increases. Indeed, the contrast of the Eisenhower administrations' priorities with those prevailing during the Kennedy-Johnson years dramatically illustrates the partisan view of politics and macroeconomics. Curiously, however, the two biggest "Eisenhower recessions," those of 1954 and 1958, nicely bracketed Ike's successful 1956 reelection bid. As the data in Figure 8.1 show, unemployment fell sharply from 1954 to 1956, and it rose even more sharply after the election with the 1957–1958 contraction. Viewed out of context, the 1956 experience might (erroneously) be seen as suggesting that, when it came to his own reelection, Ike skillfully played a four-year unemployment cycle game.

It is obvious in retrospect that the macroeconomic performance of the Kennedy-Johnson administrations was little short of extraordinary. Beginning with the recovery from the last Eisenhower recession of 1960–1961 and ending with the Nixon-induced 1969–1970 contraction, the United States enjoyed the longest expansion in its postwar history. The Revenue (tax-cut) Act of 1964, discussed above in conjunction with the "unusual" growth of real income in that election year, obviously helped prolong the expansion, breaking the traditional three-and-one-half-year periodicity of U.S. recessions. So did the fiscal and monetary stimuli of 1965–1968, associated with the (hidden) deficit financing of the Vietnam War. Consequently, unemployment fell steadily from 1961 until the incoming Nixon administration reversed the trend in 1969 by launching restrictive monetary and fiscal policies designed to check the escalation of inflation. (See the discussion of trends in core inflation in Chapter 3.) The fact that this continuous decline of unemployment spans the 1964 and 1968 elections is, then, no evidence of a four-year political cycle in the unemployment rate. But, the effects of war finance aside, it clearly does reflect the high priority attached to growth and employment during the last eight-year stretch of Democratic control of the presidency.

Few observers fail to acknowledge the ample evidence that economic policies and outcomes during President Nixon's first administration were significantly affected by the presidential election calendar. The first few years of the administration also fit the stylized pattern of Republican economic priorities well: An orthodox policy of fiscal and monetary restraint was pursued to raise the rate of unemployment and contain the inflationary pressures inherited from the Johnson administration. But as 1972 approached, Nixon jettisoned Republican orthodoxy in a successful effort to generate an election-year expansion. In August 1971 the administration launched the New Economic Policy (NEP), a comprehensive program that included fiscal stimulation, monetary expansion, a wage-price freeze, and a devaluation of the dollar. From the point of view of vote maximization, however, the timing was not optimal. Although the unemployment rate fell and the real income growth rate rose in 1972, the favorable effects of the NEP peaked in 1973, after the election (see Figures 8.1 and 8.2). But this is nitpicking. The economy is not a piece of machinery that can be closely calibrated or fine-tuned. The important point is that electoral motives were an important impetus behind Nixon's preelection New Economic Policy, and the NEP did improve economic performance during the election year.[32]

Gerald Ford, who became president after Nixon's forced resignation in August 1974, was a quintessential Republican chief executive whose economic priorities and policy actions conformed closely to the party cleavage model. A man of genuine Republican principle, more reminiscent of Eisenhower than of Nixon, President Ford did little by way of macroeconomic stimulation to enhance his election chances in

1976. As noted in Chapter 3, the Ford administration initially refused to respond to the OPEC oil supply shock with policies to restore aggregate demand. Instead it launched the "Whip Inflation Now" program of fiscal and monetary restraint, which helped prolong the deep post-OPEC slump in employment and output through 1974 and into 1975. The program was accompanied by considerable anti-inflation rhetoric, as when the president declared to a joint session of Congress in October 1974: "I say to you with all sincerity, that our inflation, our public enemy number one, will, unless whipped, destroy our country, our homes, our liberties, our property, and finally our national pride, as surely as any well-armed wartime enemy."[33] Only after a long and sharp decline in real output did President Ford finally propose a one-year tax rebate in January 1975. The Democratic-dominated Congress passed the bill two and a half months later, after increasing the amount of the rebate substantially and redistributing it in favor of low-income and middle-income individuals.

Although 1976 was a recovery year, with real income, output, and employment rising, other than proposing an additional tax cut of 10 billion dollars (tied to a 28-billion-dollar spending reduction scheduled for later in the year), the Ford team made little effort to speed the process along.[34] On the contrary, the administration vigorously resisted spending initiatives from the Democratic-controlled Congress. The battle between the president and the Democratic congressional leadership over fiscal policy raged throughout 1976. The Democrats argued that "stimulative economic policies at a time like this create jobs, productivity and income, not inflation," and accused the administration of purveying "ignorance and misinformation to the public on matters of economic policy."[35]

President Ford responded by denouncing the Democrats' attempts to stimulate the economy by increasing the budget deficit ("the added inflationary impact . . . defies rational calculation"), by deriding the Humphrey-Hawkins full-employment bill ("a vast election year boondoggle"), and by vetoing several Democratic-sponsored public works jobs bills ("empty promises and giveaway programs").[36] Moreover, the administration inexplicably underspent its own budget by about 3 percent in the second and third quarters of 1976, which helped slow the recovery and raise unemployment a few tenths of a point just before the election.[37] It was hardly that the administration failed to understand the importance of election-period economics. As L. William Seidman, an economic adviser and member of Ford's inner circle, commented at the time: "When things turn sluggish, we lose some [political] advantage." Nonetheless, Seidman went on to report: "As for the economic lull, we considered the use of stimulus to make sure we didn't have a low third quarter [in 1976], but the President didn't want anything to do with a short-term view."[38]

All in all, then, there is no sign of significant electorally motivated macroeconomic policy action during Gerald Ford's brief tenure in the White House. Indeed, in view of the narrow margin of Jimmy Carter's victory in 1976, Ford may well have been elected to a full presidential term had he cultivated the stimulative instincts of the congressional Democrats, or even gone along with their concrete stimulative proposals. Anti-inflation partisan principle, however, overrode electoral calculation.

The course of macroeconomic policies and outcomes during the Carter administration looks like a stylized political business cycle run backward. Having inherited a 7.7 percent unemployment rate from Ford, Carter acted just as a Democratic president should. (For more details see Section 3.2.) Monetary policy turned expansive as did fiscal policy, especially after Congress passed the administration's demand-oriented tax-cut proposals four months into the term. The stimulation worked, and, as Figure 8.1 indicates, unemployment fell continuously until the end of 1979. Inflation began to drift upward, however, and then skyrocketed to double-digit rates after the economy was hit by the second big OPEC oil price hike in 1979. In response, the Carter administration essentially abandoned its goal of moving the economy to full employment (defined earlier by the president to be 4.75 percent), and the thrust of macroeconomic policy was reversed completely. The cyclically adjusted deficit was reduced, and the real money supply declined sharply. The policy shift exacerbated the adverse effects of the second OPEC price hike on employment and output and helped push the economy into recession during the election year. As Chapter 6 showed, this election-year contraction was the main reason that Carter and the Democrats took such a trouncing at the polls in 1980. It is difficult to imagine a macroeconomic policy plan less suited to reaping a vote harvest on election day, at least insofar as unemployment and real incomes are concerned.

By contrast, the Reagan years are thoroughly consistent with both the political business cycle hypothesis and the party cleavage model of macroeconomic and distributional goals. Despite rhetoric about maintaining "safety nets" and reviving high growth, the Reagan team, unlike previous Republican administrations, attempted to roll back federal redistributive activity and displayed with a vengeance the traditional Republican aversion to inflation. (See Chapter 9 for a detailed account of the Reagan administration's economic and social program.) Fiscal policy was expansive, particularly in the latter half of the term, as the so-called supply-side tax cuts and the rise in military expenditures overwhelmed the social expenditure reductions that the administration was able to get through Congress. As noted earlier, this produced extraordinarily large cyclically adjusted deficits in 1983 and especially 1984. But the potentially stimulative effects of the modest fiscal expansion during Reagan's first two years in office were completely offset by a crushingly restrictive monetary policy which, on the whole, enjoyed the president's full support. Real income and output collapsed, and by the end of 1982 unemployment stood at 10.7 percent, the highest rate since the Great Depression. Predictably, inflation fell sharply as the contraction deepened. Although there was some wild-eyed talk in the early days of the Reagan presidency of simultaneously achieving high supply side–induced growth rates and rapid monetary policy–induced disinflation, this episode clearly revealed the administration's preference for lowered inflation, despite the enormous cost in lost output and higher unemployment.

The concern of many in the Reagan administration during late 1981 turned to near panic by late 1982, however, as the economy went deeper and deeper into recession. Many feared that a truly catastrophic collapse was a genuine possibility. Having been burned by the 1982 congressional election outcomes, Reagan—with an eye, no doubt, on the upcoming presidential election—totally abandoned support of hard-line monetarism and strongly signaled the Federal Reserve of the administration's desire for a more rapid rate of growth of the money supply.[39] Federal Reserve resistance melted away, and with monetary policy now coordinated with fiscal policy in an expansive direction, the long-promised recovery got under way. By late 1983 unemployment was falling rapidly, and real output and income were rising about a comparatively favorable base rate of inflation. Although on election day there was still a large "Okun gap" in real output, and unemployment was no lower than it had been in Carter's last year, the economy had been moving rapidly for two years in the right direction. Consequently, public confidence in "Reaganomics" recovered from the abysmal levels of 1982, and the president was reelected handily. Given the administration's commitment to disinflation, the president had the good political sense to impose the pain without delay, which made possible an electorally well timed growth strategy for the last half of the presidential term. The correspondence to Nordhaus's politically optimal economic cycle is striking.

REAL INCOME GROWTH RATE CYCLES

As was pointed out earlier, empirical studies have repeatedly shown that voting outcomes are affected significantly by election-year real income (or real output) growth rates. Presidential and congressional candidates of the party controlling the White House are helped by robust growth rates and hurt by sluggish ones. In comparison to unemployment rates, real income growth rates respond relatively quickly to policy stimulation. The personal disposable component of aggregate national income may be especially susceptible to short-run political control via presidential manipulation of the flow of transfer payments. For these reasons fluctuations of personal disposable income have been closely scrutinized in studies of election cycles in the economy.

Postwar movements in annual per capita real personal disposable income growth rates are shown in Figure 8.2. We must stare hard and exercise some imagination to detect a pervasive election-cycle pattern in these data. Over the entire period[40] the average annual growth rate in nonelection years is 2.2 percent, as compared to 2.6 percent in years in which an incumbent president was running for election, but only 1.4 percent in presidential election years without an incumbent in the race and 1.7 percent in midterm (congressional) election years. Only presidential elections contested by incumbents, then, show clear signs of satisfying the political business cycle theory. It is obvious from casual inspection of Figure 8.2, however, that this selective "election effect" on postwar real income growth streams depends heavily on the 1964 and 1984 experiences. In fact, without 1964—a year in which we would be hard pressed to find evidence of electorally inspired policy actions—the average real income growth rate for presidential years with incumbents running falls to 2.2 percent, which is identical to the mean for nonelection years.[41]

If the Eisenhower period is excluded on the grounds that Ike's fidelity to ideological principles immunized him from the temptations of the political business cycle, the picture does not change appreciably. Now the mean growth rates for nonelection years and presidential years without incumbents in the contest are indistinguishable at 2.1 percent, as opposed to 2.4 percent for midterm elections. And, as before, the mean growth rate for presidential years with incumbents in the contest is 2.6 percent. If 1964 is excluded, the average real

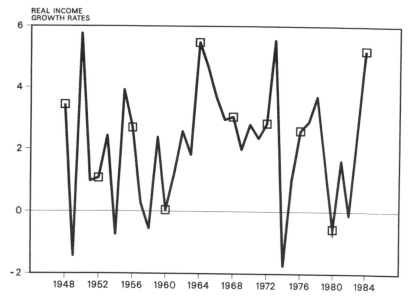

Figure 8.2 Postwar elections and annual growth rates of real personal disposable income per capita, 1948–1984.

	Average growth rates (percent)				
	No election	Presidential elections, no incumbent	Midterm elections	Presidential elections, incumbent running	All years
Entire period	2.2	1.4	1.7	2.6	2.2
Excluding Eisenhower period	2.1	2.1	2.4	2.6	2.4

income growth rate for presidential years with incumbents running is again the same as the mean for nonelection years—2.1 percent.

We must not lose sight, however, of the fact that real income growth rate cycles centered on presidential elections contested by incumbents have occasionally occurred. Again, President Reagan's first term is the most dramatic example. In fact, the behavior of real income growth rates over 1981–1984 in relation to Reagan's support

in the electorate, which is graphed in Figure 8.3, conforms perfectly
to the stylized political business cycle. It is difficult to imagine a more
telling illustration of the politically well timed real income growth rate
cycle.

8.4   Politics and the Economy

Directly observable fluctuations in macroeconomic outcomes, the
qualitative and anecdotal record, and parameter estimates from theoretically constrained statistical models designed to take into account
the impact of wartime fiscal thrusts, exogenous international shocks,
structural and policy inertia, and contrasting partisan priorities all
indicate that election cycles have not been a consistent feature of the
postwar American political economy. Yet the qualitative and quantitative records reveal several likely instances of electorally focused
economic expansions, although these appear idiosyncratically rather
than systematically, with those of 1972 and 1984 being the principal
illustrations. Of course, no incumbent president desires or plans to go
into an election year with the economy in recession. But if transitory,
politically motivated cycles had been a regular and pronounced fea-

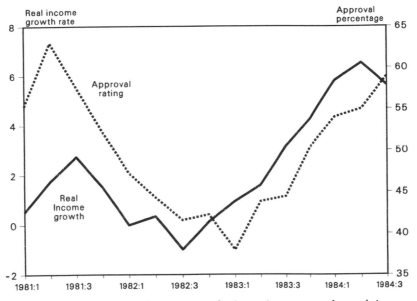

Figure 8.3 The political business cycle in action: quarterly real income
growth rates and Reagan's Gallup poll approval ratings, 1981:1–1984:3.

ture of postwar economic life, voters (aided by the media and the out-party) undoubtedly would have come to recognize, to discount steeply, and perhaps even to punish such contrived election-period fillips in economic performance. Ultimately such "learning" on the part of the electorate would undermine incumbents' incentives to pursue cyclical macroeconomic policy strategies in the first place.[42]

Macroeconomic and distributional outcomes are not disconnected from systematic political forces, however. As we saw in Chapter 7, most important low-income assistance programs were promoted and implemented by Democratic administrations, and almost all of the modest postwar improvement in the distribution of net incomes was achieved under the Democrats. Furthermore, analyses of macroeconomic trends and fluctuations under the parties show that Democratic administrations typically aim for more ambitious unemployment and real output targets than do Republican administrations. Consequently, unemployment and output (relative to natural, benchmark levels) tend to cycle across partisan regimes. To be sure, macroeconomic outcomes are constrained by the economy's endogenous capacities and are buffeted by uncontrollable and unanticipated exogenous shocks. But substantial interparty differences in performance—amounting to as much as 2 percentage points in the case of unemployment, 5 to 6 percent for real output, and 1 percent for real income growth rates—consistently show up in the statistical analyses. Such partisan-based differences in economic priorities and performance appear to be more durable and predictable than the occasional election-motivated cycles that have so excited journalists.

Yet lower unemployment and higher capacity utilization and growth have meant higher rates of core inflation than would have prevailed otherwise. As a result, Democratic administrations have been more likely than Republican administrations to get into difficulty with the electorate by pursuing overly ambitious unemployment goals that yield extra inflation. The Republicans, on the other hand, have more frequently suffered electoral setbacks because of their enthusiasm for disinflationary bouts of economic slack. Such "overshooting" is probably a major reason why neither party has managed to hold the presidency for more than two terms since the Second World War. Hence, a short- to medium-run trade-off between unemployment and inflation not only is a critical feature of the macroeconomy; in conjunction with the differing macroeconomic priorities of the parties, it also underlies an important source of partisan electoral change in an era in which elections increasingly have hinged on economic performance. Cycles in partisan control of the presidency and cycles in unemployment and inflation outcomes are therefore intimately connected. And although the inflation-unemployment configurations associated with the parties are at odds with what one would expect from median voter theories of (convergent) policy behavior, they are broadly in accordance with the objective interests and revealed preferences of the parties' class-related core constituencies.

Macroeconomic outcomes, then, are not altogether endogenous to the economy, but are significantly influenced by long- and short-term political choices—choices that can profoundly affect the level and distribution of economic well-being. I have tried to show in this chapter that economic priorities and outcomes are occasionally affected by the electoral calendar but more systematically depend on the partisan stripe of presidential administrations. The real winners of elections are revealed by examining the policy consequences of partisan electoral change rather than by simply tallying the votes. Never has this been clearer than after the transition from Carter to Reagan, and so I conclude this book with an examination of the Reagan administration's economic and social program in Chapter 9.

9 Macroeconomic and Distributional Outcomes during Reagan's First Four Years

> The hard part of the supply-side tax cut is dropping the top rate from 70 to 50 percent—the rest is a secondary matter . . . in order to make this palatable as a political matter you had to bring down all the brackets . . . Kemp-Roth was always a Trojan horse to bring down the top rate.
>
> —David Stockman, director of the Office of Management and Budget in the Reagan administration

> This election [1984] is an investment banker's dream world.
>
> —William Benedetto, head of corporate finance for Dean Witter, Reynolds

President Reagan inherited an economy plagued by high inflation and unemployment and low growth and productivity. Just as the Great Depression of the 1930s gave rise to a pervasive loss of confidence in the capacity of the market to sustain full employment, the persistent inflation of the post-OPEC years, all too frequently punctuated by contractions of output and employment, created the widespread impression that neither moderate Keynesian activism nor moderate conservative orthodoxy could cope satisfactorily with the nation's economic problems. Many voters believed, as we saw in Chapter 6, that it was "time for a change."

The Reagan administration brilliantly exploited this "window of opportunity." More important changes in economic and social policy were achieved during President Reagan's first term than at any time since Lyndon Johnson's Great Society. Among other things, Reagan's success in selling and implementing his economic program laid to rest the idea that the post-Watergate presidency was hopelessly immobilized by a fickle public, an unresponsive bureaucracy, and a resurgent Congress. As James David Barber, a leading analyst of the presidency, put it: "Reagan has ruined the argument that there's something endemic in our system that prevents innovative leadership."[1]

Monetary policy during the Reagan years leaned harder and longer against inflation than at any time since the Eisenhower administrations. The monetary restraint succeeded in breaking the inflationary legacy of the 1970s, but at the cost of the highest unemployment rates since the last years of the Great Depression. Unlike previous postwar Republican presidents, Reagan sought to roll back social spending rather than simply hold the line, and he succeeded in reversing the trend of increasing federal commitments to the poor and near-poor. Federal budget priorities were shifted significantly away from social spending to military spending. And, most important of all, Reagan achieved a dramatic redistribution of the federal tax burden from corporations and high-income classes to moderate- and low-income groups.

In most respects the Reagan administration represents an empirical upper limit of the economic and distributional policy tendencies identified in Chapter 7 as characteristic of the Republican party. There is, of course, much more to the story of social and economic policy during President Reagan's first term than can be summarized here; in this chapter I shall confine my attention to the domestic macroeconomic and distributional questions that occupied earlier chapters of this book. Let me begin with the great macroeconomic issues: growth, unemployment, and inflation.

9.1   Macroeconomic Goals, Policies, and Outcomes under Reagan

IMPLAUSIBLY OPTIMISTIC PROJECTIONS

All presidential administrations are inclined to be optimistic when outlining their macroeconomic goals,[2] but the Reagan administration's February-March 1981 projections represent something of a record. The main elements are summarized by the numbers (see Table 9.1 later in this section). The administration forecast a rise in real output of 25 percent between 1980 and 1986, with annual growth rates of 4 to 5 percent from 1982 to 1984 and beyond, as compared to growth rates that averaged about 3 percent per year during the 1970s.[3] Unemployment was projected to fall from the 7.4-percent rate inherited from the Carter administration (the consequence of the 1979–1980 OPEC oil price shock and the recession induced by Carter to fight the escalation of inflation) to about 6.4 percent during 1984, and then to 5.5 percent by 1986. Over the same period inflation would be halved, declining steadily from the near-double-digit rates prevailing when Reagan entered the White House to 6 percent per year by 1984, and to 5 percent per year by 1985–1986.

Most economists (including the majority of Reagan's orthodox conservative economic advisers) viewed these forecasts with profound skepticism, if not outright disbelief. Taken separately, the growth and unemployment projections on the one hand and the inflation projections on the other hand were credible. If inflation rate forecasts were not considered, then, the projected growth of output was plausible and fully consistent with the anticipated decrease in unemployment. During calendar year 1980 actual real output was more than 3 percent short of potential output and the actual unemployment rate stood more than a full percentage point above the so-called natural rate. Hence there was no reason that an expansive macroeconomic policy could not achieve real GNP growth rates of 4 to 5 percent for several years, which by Okun's Law (see Chapter 2) were bound to yield big declines in unemployment. What was implausible was the administration's claim that inflation would be dramatically reduced *at the same time* that output and employment were rapidly expanding.

Under the macroeconomic policy scenario announced by the administration in 1981, disinflation would be achieved through a gradual reduction in money supply growth rates of about 1 percentage point per year. Hence, the annual rate of growth of the money supply would be lowered from the 7-percent rate prevailing when Reagan was inaugurated to something like 4 percent per year by 1984. Inasmuch as inflation and nominal GNP growth were running at near-double-digit rates in 1980–1981, the administration's monetary targets implied that the growth rate of the real (price deflated) money supply would be negative, at least for a year or two. This was sure to throw the economy into contraction, putting heavy downward pressure on wages and prices. In other words, under the monetary policy proposed by the administration, there would be insufficient liquidity in the economy to finance the ongoing pace of nominal transactions, and until prices adapted fully to the new monetary regime, the growth of quantities as well as of prices would be slowed. Postwar experience had repeatedly showed that the process of wage and price adaptation to disinflationary monetary policies was sluggish; therefore, large sacrifices of output and employment were required to reduce inflation significantly.[4] James Tobin, a distinguished Keynesian, aptly summarized the cold facts this way: "[In the absence of an incomes policy] the only mechanism by which monetary deceleration produces disinflation is by creating sufficient economic distress that workers and employers, desperate to protect jobs and solvency, settle for lower wage and price increases than those currently prevailing."[5]

SUPPLY-SIDE THEORY TO THE RESCUE

How, then, did the administration hope to achieve simultaneously its output, unemployment, and inflation forecasts? Certainly there was little comfort to be found in the theoretical views of leading economists—Keynesian and traditional monetarists alike—or in the abundant empirical evidence on the high output costs of disinflation in the postwar U.S. macroeconomy. Here the theory—or, perhaps more accurately, the ideology—of the new "supply-side economics" proved useful.

In their contemporary, controversial form, supply-side ideas are most prominently associated with Arthur Laffer, a University of Southern California economist who built on some less outlandish ideas of Robert Mundell, a very distinguished economist now at Columbia University. The theories were popularized by Jude Wanniski, once an editorial writer for the *Wall Street Journal* and now a private consultant,[6] and by Irving Kristol, a New York City neo-Conservative intellectual and essayist. More than anyone else, Jack Kemp, an ambitious, personable Congressman from Buffalo, was responsible for bringing supply-side ideas into the political process. As a result of his dynamic salesmanship of supply-side policies, Kemp became a real force in the Republican party.

The supply-siders argued that tax rates on income from labor and capital were high enough in the United States to have large, adverse effects on the supply of work effort, saving, and investment. The disincentive effects at prevailing rates were believed to be great enough that tax reductions on the scale of the Kemp-Roth proposals[7] would sharply raise the incentive to work, save, and invest and therefore would stimulate dramatic increases in productive effort, employment, and real output. Labor productivity (output per worker) would be further enhanced as the increase in savings and investment induced by a supply-side tax cut built up the stock of capital per worker.

Most supply-siders claimed that tax-rate reductions would be self-financing. The supply side–fueled expansion of output would enlarge the federal tax base so much that government revenues would not fall, despite lower tax rates. Indeed, radical supply-siders, believ-

ing that the current tax system was well within the so-called prohibi-
tive range of the Laffer curve, went so far as to assert that revenues
would actually rise as the incentives created by higher after-tax returns on work effort and investment took hold and unleashed a great
surge of economic activity.[8] Consequently, the administration's forecast of a balanced federal budget by fiscal year (FY) 1984 would not be
endangered by an aggressive supply-side policy of tax reduction.

President Reagan never consistently adhered to the radical view.
Early in the 1980 primary season, he argued that no spending cuts at
all would be necessary to finance the Kemp-Roth proposal of a 27-
percent across-the-board cut in personal rates to be phased in over
three years. George Bush, then Reagan's chief rival for the Republican nomination, promptly labeled this notion "voodoo economics."
Under pressure from his more orthodox, conservative economic advisers, Reagan later agreed that spending cuts would be necessary to
keep the budget in balance, although he often talked of painless
reductions confined to areas of "waste, fraud and abuse." Nonetheless, Reagan made the Kemp-Roth tax cut the centerpiece of his fiscal
program. And after a bitter partisan struggle, Congress gave the administration nearly everything ("95 percent," according to Treasury
secretary Donald Regan) it asked for.

FISCAL POLICY SUCCESSES

President Reagan spelled out his tax-and-spending legislative package in a televised speech to a joint session of Congress on February
18, 1981. The president called for a 27-percent across-the-board reduction of personal income tax rates to be phased in over three years
starting July 1. In response to congressional resistance, Reagan offered a revised plan in June 1981 that trimmed back the first rate cut to
5 percent and delayed it to October 1. The revised plan won the
approval of Congress and was incorporated into the Economic Recovery Tax Act of 1981 (ERTA), which the president signed into law on
August 13, 1981. ERTA reduced personal tax rates by 23 percent, with
the initial October 1, 1981 rate cut of 5 percent followed by 10-percent
reductions on July 1, 1982 and July 1, 1983.

Additionally, ERTA immediately slashed the top rate on unearned
investment income from 70 to 50 percent and reduced the maximum
rate on capital gains (taxed at 40 percent of the investment income
rate) from 28 to 20 percent. Hence the top tax rates on income from
capital going directly to individuals were cut by a factor of 29 percent.

The bill passed by Congress also included a number of savings incentives, most notably extensions of Self-Employed Retirement Plans and Individual Retirement Accounts and the creation of "All Savers" interest income exclusions.

More important, ERTA provided for the indexing of rate brackets to inflation (the increase in the CPI during the previous year) beginning in 1985. Indexing had wide popular appeal and so was difficult to oppose openly. As a practical political matter, however, it helped lock into place a new rate structure that disproportionately benefited the rich. (The distributional impact of the Reagan administration's fiscal program is analyzed in detail below.) In the past Democratic-controlled Congresses had made ad hoc adjustments of the tax system for inflation-induced "bracket creep" in ways that favored the Democrats' below-median-income core constituency. Consequently, as we saw in Table 3.8, the progressiveness of effective federal personal income tax rates actually increased over the high-inflation 1970s. The indexing provision of ERTA would make it more difficult later on for the Democrats, when and if they regained their traditionally dominant position in the Congress, to attempt to undo ERTA's redistribution of tax burdens by using inflation as the occasion to reopen the issue of the income tax.

The tax bill proposed by the Reagan administration and passed by Congress called for a sharp reduction in effective corporate tax rates, primarily through replacement of the existing system of depreciating assets over their "useful" lives with the simplified Accelerated Cost Recovery System (ACRS), which permitted businesses to write off the value of an asset over three, five, ten, or fifteen years at an accelerated rate.[9] ACRS was so generous to business firms that the dollar value of tax deductions and credits typically exceeded the tax liabilities on the extra income produced by investment in new equipment. In other words, the effective marginal tax rate on investment in new equipment was in many cases negative. Moreover, under ERTA businesses were permitted to use their surplus tax benefits to offset tax liabilities on income from other sources and to "lease" them to other firms through sale-leaseback arrangements. The full implications of ACRS became clear shortly after ERTA was passed, and they were widely viewed as overly generous. Along with growing concern about the size of impending federal deficits, this view prompted Congress to pass—and the president to sign into law—the Tax Equity and Fiscal Responsibility Act of 1982 (TEFRA), which repealed about half the business tax reductions conferred by the 1981 ERTA legislation.[10] The rest of the Reagan administration's 1981 tax package remained in place into the president's second term, however.

President Reagan also had considerable success with the spending side of his fiscal program. The biggest victories were achieved in the first year. Thanks to feverish work at the Office of Management and Budget (OMB), directed by the brilliant David Stockman, the administration's FY 1982 budget request, along with proposed adjustments to Carter's FY 1981 spending totals, was submitted to Congress in March 1981—less than a month after Reagan entered the White House. The Reagan budget called for an FY 1982 defense expenditure increase of 7.2 billion dollars above what Carter had requested and a reduction in nondefense expenditures of 41.4 billion dollars from the Carter policy baseline. Through ingenious use of little-understood congressional budget "reconciliation" procedures, Stockman coordinated the bundling of the administration's spending proposals into one unified package, which was pushed through the Congress with breathtaking speed. The Omnibus Budget Reconciliation Act passed Congress in July 1981. It was the deepest and most widespread package of budget cuts ever passed by Congress. The president received all of the defense-spending increases he wanted and the lion's share of the requested social-spending cuts: nondefense programs were cut by about 35 billion dollars.[11] Senator Moynihan lamented: "We have undone thirty years of social legislation in three days."[12]

President Reagan was unable to repeat the great budget successes of 1981 in subsequent years, however, because many Republicans in Congress, including the Republican leadership, joined Democrats in opposing further major cuts in social spending. Mark Hatfield, Republican Senator from Oregon and chairman of the Appropriations Committee, reflected moderate Republican thinking when he told the Senate: "I think all members agree that we have reached the bone on discretionary programs so there is nothing more to cut."[13] Yet over the first term as a whole, the Office of Management and Budget estimated that the administration achieved at least one-half of the nondefense spending cuts initially called for in the 1981 budget statement. The Congressional Budget Office (CBO) estimated that by FY 1985 nondefense program spending stood about 60 billion dollars, or 1.5 percent of GNP, lower than the pre-Reagan policy baseline; the president's February 1981 announcement had envisioned FY 1985 reductions on the order of 2 to 3 percent of GNP.[14] Moreover, Reagan was successful in obtaining most of the defense spending buildup he requested. The February 1981 budget projections called for defense outlays to rise by about 1.2 percent of GNP from FY 1981 to FY 1985.[15] By the 1985 fiscal year, increases in military spending equivalent to approximately 1 percent of GNP had been achieved. These budgetary shifts were somewhat less than the president wanted, but far more than seasoned analysts thought possible when Reagan entered the White House.

MONETARY POLICY RESPONSIVENESS
Monetary policy conformed almost perfectly to President Reagan's preferences during his first term. The administration's initial monetary goals, outlined by Beryl Sprinkel, under-secretary of the Treasury for Monetary Affairs, called for the growth rate of the M1-B money supply to decelerate by about a point each year, from 7 percent per year in 1981 to 3 percent per year in 1985–1986.[16] The Federal Reserve, chaired by Paul Volcker, a highly regarded central banker well known for his anti-inflationary zeal, delivered money supply growth rates for 1981 and 1982 that corresponded closely to the administration's initial targets. The M1-B money supply was permitted to grow by 7.1 percent in 1981 and 6.5 percent in 1982, a highly restrictive policy given the prevailing growth rates of prices and nominal GNP.

Predictably, the monetary austerity of 1981–1982 created a deep, disinflationary recession. But the president "stayed the course" until late 1982, at which time double-digit unemployment rates (and, no doubt, the fact that the presidential election season loomed on the horizon) led him to abandon hard-line monetarism and push for an expansive monetary policy. Paul Volcker and the Federal Reserve proved to be as cooperative on the up side as they had been on the down side. The M1-B money supply grew at annual rates of about 11 percent in 1983 and 7 percent in 1984. Because inflation had declined sharply to between 3 and 4 percent per annum in 1983 and 1984 as a result of the deep 1981–1982 contraction, the real (inflation-adjusted) money supply growth rate soared. Real M1-B grew by more than 7 percent in 1983, which provided a big monetary stimulus to the economy and, in conjunction with enormous federal budget deficits, fueled the big 1983–1984 election-year recovery of output, incomes, and employment.[17]

On the whole, then, President Reagan was remarkably successful in obtaining the mix of fiscal and monetary policies he wanted from Congress and the Federal Reserve. At first, both the monetarists and the supply-siders were satisfied. Monetarists got the long stretch of tight money (from late 1979 to late 1982) they had been advocating to bring inflation down. The supply-siders (and high-income taxpayers) got nearly all the tax relief they had argued was necessary to revive incentives to "work, save and invest." Yet it was the administration that forged the politically convenient marriage of supply-side "fiscalism" and hard-line monetarism, which superficially reconciled an implausible combination of growth, unemployment, and inflation (and balanced budget) forecasts. The idea that supply-side fiscal policy would offset—indeed, more than offset—the contractive effects of an austere, disinflationary monetary policy by stimulating an unprecedented surge of extra work effort, investment, and output came from the administration, not from supply-side advocates or monetarists. In fact, despite well-publicized complaints about the size of federal deficits made by Martin Feldstein in 1983–1984 while he headed President Reagan's Council of Economic Advisors, macroeconomic policy during 1981 and 1982 more closely resembled the "tight money–easy fisc" policy mix Feldstein backed for many years as the key to improving investment and growth[18] (which turned the traditional Keynesian recipe of "easy money–tight fisc" on its head) than it did the position of most supply-siders.

Supply-side theorists were preoccupied with the problem of incentives and growth rather than that of inflation, though many advocated a return to the gold standard as the way to control the price level. Indeed, it was not long before the supply-siders began to complain bitterly about the administration's support for hard-line monetarism. The numbers in Table 9.1 show why.

THE ECONOMY'S "REAL" PERFORMANCE UNDER REAGANOMICS
Less than a year into the new administration's term, it was becoming obvious that President Reagan would have to choose between his inflation goals and his output-unemployment goals. The policy mix that Senate majority leader Howard Baker, a Republican from Tennessee, had colorfully described as "a river boat gamble" was not working as planned. Neither preannouncement of a monetary slowdown nor the credible application of monetary stringency nor the marriage of monetary austerity to supply-side tax cuts was succeeding in lowering inflation without imposing enormous costs in terms of lost output, lower incomes, and higher unemployment. The Phillips-curve trade-off between prices and quantities—that is, between nominal and real economic performance—remained alive and well.

As pointed out in Chapter 8, fiscal policy was expansive through-out Reagan's first term, because the loss of revenues from the tax cuts and the rise in military spending outran the reductions in social out-lays, generating large deficits (see the bottom of Table 9.1). But ex-tremely tight monetary policy overwhelmed the fiscal thrust,[19] and the surge of economic activity (and tax revenues) promised by the supply-siders failed to materialize.

Just as the partisan view of macroeconomic policy introduced in Chapter 7 would predict, the president gave clear priority to the goal of achieving significant disinflation For nearly two years the White House backed a tough monetary policy. Consequently, output growth collapsed, idle capacity rose sharply, and unemployment soared. As a result, the economy's real performance during Reagan's first four years was less favorable than during the much-maligned 1970s. The data at the top of Table 9.1 tell the story.

When Reagan entered the White House, the economy was recover-ing from the 1979–1980 OPEC shock and Carter's policy-induced re-cession. But monetary policy in 1981 and 1982 completely aborted the recovery, which had been under way since July 1980. The growth rate of real GNP was 2.5 percent in 1981, before it tumbled by more than 2 percentage points in 1982. Once monetary policy was relaxed upon the administration's urging in late 1982, growth rates responded briskly. The election-year growth of real output and incomes was especially impressive.[20] Yet over Reagan's entire first term, real GNP growth rates averaged only 2.7 percent, which is a half-point lower than the growth rate record of the 1970s and a full point lower than the average implied by the administration's forecasts. Even real dis-posable income growth rates were lower on average over 1981–1984 than during the 1970s, despite ERTA's transfer of hundreds of billions of dollars to personal incomes, which was financed by ballooning federal deficits.

The trajectory of the real economy over 1981–1984 is more accu-rately mapped by looking at movements in the gap between actual and potential real output, shown in the third row of Table 9.1. The percentage shortfall of real GNP from its sustainable level rose from 3.3 percent in 1980 to well over 8 percent in 1982 and 1983, before declining to 4.5 percent in 1984.[21] The 1982 and 1983 GNP gaps were by far the highest of the postwar period, and the average over Reagan's entire first term (−6.4 percent) was the worst of all postwar presidential administrations. Net of the 3.3-percent shortfall inherited from Carter, a gap amounting to more than 22 percent of a year's

Table 9.1 Macroeconomic goals, outcomes, and policies during Reagan's first term: annual averages by periods and years

	1970–1979	1980	1981	1982	1983	1984	1981–1984
Output, unemployment, and capacity utilization							
Real GNP growth rate							
Actual	3.2	−0.3	2.5	−2.1	3.7	6.8	2.7
Projected	—	—	1.1	4.2	5.0	4.5	3.7
GNP gap (percentage deviation of actual from natural GNP)							
Actual	−0.8	−3.3	−3.8	−8.9	−8.3	−4.5	−6.4
Growth rate of per capita real personal disposable income							
Actual	2.4	−0.6	1.7	−1.3	2.5	5.8	2.2
Percent idle capacity in manufacturing							
Actual	18.3	20.4	20.6	28.9	24.8	18.3	23.2
Unemployment rate							
Actual	6.3	7.1	7.6	9.7	9.6	7.5	8.6
Projected	—	—	7.8	7.2	6.6	6.4	7.0
Personal saving and private investment							
Personal saving as a percentage of personal disposable income							
Actual	7.3	6.0	6.7	6.2	5.0	6.1	6.0
Gross real private domestic investment as a percentage of real GNP							

Actual	17.0	14.1	15.3	13.1	14.4	17.7	15.1

Net real private nonresidential fixed investment as a percentage of real GNP							
Actual	3.0	3.0	3.2	2.3	2.2	3.8	2.9
Inflation							
Annual rate of change of GNP deflator							
Actual	6.6	8.8	9.2	5.8	3.8	3.7	5.6
Projected	—	—	9.9	8.3	7.0	6.0	7.8
Monetary and fiscal policies							
Money supply growth rate (M1-B)							
Nominal							
Actual	7.7	6.2	7.1	6.5	11.1	6.8	7.9
Projected	—	—	7.0	6.0	5.0	4.0	5.5
Budget deficit (–) or surplus (–) (for fiscal years)							
In billions of dollars							
Actual	–40	–74	–79	–128	–208	–185	–150
Projected	—	—	–55	–45	–23	+0.5	–31
As a percentage of GNP							
Actual	–1.7	–2.8	–2.7	–4.2	–6.3	–5.1	–4.6
Projected	—	—	–1.9	–1.4	–0.6	0	–1.0

Sources: Unemployment, inflation, and real GNP growth rate projections are from the White House, "America's New Beginning: A Program for Economic Recovery," February 18, 1981. Projections for the growth rate of M1-B, announced publicly in February 1981, are from Beryl Sprinkel's July 23, 1983 "Statement before the House Committee on Banking, Finance and Urban Affairs." Actual data are from *Economic Report of the President,* various years, and the Citibank Economic Database.

Note: Goals and projections are from February–March 1981.

GNP was accumulated during Reagan's first term. This translates into about 825 billion dollars' worth of 1984:4 goods and services, or close to $10,000 per household.

Manufacturing industries were hit particularly hard during the Reagan years. The Federal Reserve Board's capacity utilization data reported in Table 9.1 indicate that over 1982 idle capacity in the manufacturing sector reached almost 30 percent, the most depressed level in the postwar period. And, averaged over President Reagan's entire first term, idle capacity was 5 percentage points higher than the mean for the 1970s. Had it not been for bankruptcies, which also reached record levels during the Reagan administration, the capacity utilization data would paint an even worse picture. Despite the 1983–1984 recovery, capacity utilization during the last year of Reagan's first term was still no better than the 1970–1979 average.

Because of the human tragedies involved, in many ways the saddest aspect of the Reagan record is revealed by the unemployment statistics. Unemployment did not fall steadily from the 7.4-percent rate inherited from Carter, as the administration had claimed it would if Congress passed the Reagan tax-and-spending package. Instead, unemployment rose continuously from mid-1981 until the recovery began at the end of 1982. Joblessness peaked in December 1982 at 10.8 percent of the civilian labor force, the highest level since the Great Depression. The unemployment rate for all of 1982 and 1983 averaged close to 10 percent. During these years America experienced a phenomenon not seen since the 1930s: tens of thousands of unemployed people crisscrossing the country looking for work, ineligible for unemployment benefits, forced to rely on soup lines, and unable to apply for welfare because they had no home address.[22] And although joblessness declined steeply during the 1983–1984 period, unemployment stood no lower at the end of President Reagan's first term than it had when President Carter left office.[23]

Insofar as the real side of the economy is concerned—output, incomes, capacity utilization, and unemployment—President Reagan's program produced results that fell far short of projections and did not compare favorably to the record of earlier decades.

THE RESPONSE OF SAVING AND INVESTMENT TO THE REAGAN PROGRAM
It is clear in retrospect that the medium-run consequences of Reaganomics adversely affected the real macroeconomy. The president's program might have enhanced the economy's longer run prospects if the ERTA tax cuts had fundamentally changed the nation's

saving and investment behavior, but the empirical data in Table 9.1 indicate that this did not occur.

Chapter 3, The Costs of Inflation, pointed out that personal savings rates over the postwar years prior to the implementation of President Reagan's tax package were remarkably stable in the face of variations in inflation, interest rates, and effective tax rates. (See Tables 3.12 and 3.13 and the associated discussion.) The Economic Recovery Tax Act of 1981, which put hundreds of billions of dollars into the hands of the taxpayers (especially high-income taxpayers), produced no increase at all in aggregate personal savings rates. In fact, the data in Table 9.1 show that the average percentage of personal disposable income saved was actually lower during 1981–1984 (6 percent) than it had been during the 1970s (7.3 percent) or, for that matter, during the entire postwar period up to Reagan (6.9 percent).

ERTA unambiguously raised after-tax returns to saving, but it had no visible impact on aggregate personal saving behavior. Apparently what is called the substitution effect of higher after-tax yields, which decreases the attractiveness of current consumption relative to future consumption, was offset by the so-called income effect of increased after-tax returns, which reduces the amount of saving necessary to finance a given level of future consumption. Although raising personal savings rates was seen as a desirable objective by advocates of the president's tax package, what really counts for the long-run performance of the private economy is the rate of *investment*, personal and corporate, in the private sector. But here too Reagan fiscal policy failed to produce any improvement. Predictably, private investment declined with the deep 1981–1982 contraction and bounced back with the 1983–1984 recovery.[24] Averaged over the business cycle, however, the statistics on new investment reveal no deepening of the capital intensity of production during President Reagan's first term.

The data on gross real investment in the entire private economy as a fraction of real GNP indicate that the average for 1981–1984 (15.1 percent) was nearly 2 points lower than the corresponding mean for the 1970s (17 percent). More important than economy-wide private-sector investment (which includes investment flows to owner-occupied housing) is investment in new plant and equipment, *net* of what is necessary to offset deterioration of the existing capital stock. But there was no improvement in this critical area either. Over 1981–1984 net real private nonresidential investment as a fraction of real GNP averaged just 2.9 percent, as compared to 3 percent for the 1970s and Carter's last year. Other statistical series on investment tell a similar story: Despite a sizable reduction in tax rates on new investment, the average rate of growth of the nation's capital stock was no better under Reaganomics than it had been before; indeed, it was apparently slightly worse.

DISINFLATION DURING THE REAGAN YEARS

The principal macroeconomic success of President Reagan's first term was a substantial reduction in the rate of inflation. The annual rate of change of the GNP deflator (a better measure of the true inflation rate than changes in the CPI, as we saw in Chapter 3) was lowered by about 5 points, from the 9-percent range of 1980–1981 to under 4 percent in 1983–1984.[25] Indeed, the administration achieved more rapid disinflation than it had projected in early 1981 (see Table 9.1).

The connection of high rates of unemployment (and large GNP gaps) to lowered inflation is easy to establish. A standard "Keynesian" rule-of-thumb is that the fundamental, annual inflation rate tends to fall half a percentage point for each extra annual percentage point of unemployment. ("Extra" unemployment means deviations of the actual, official rate from the "natural," or nonaccelerating, inflation rate. In previous chapters, following convention, this deviation was referred to as the "unemployment gap.") Hence, a 1-point drop in fundamental inflation typically requires 2 extra percentage points of unemployment for a year, or 1 extra point for two years, and so on.

If we let p denote the year-on-year inflation rate and, as in earlier chapters, let U and U^N denote the actual and natural unemployment rates, respectively, the Keynesian rule implies the simple relation

$$p_t = p_{t-1} - 0.5(U_t - U_t^N) \tag{9.1}$$

Looking at the experience of the twenty-five years up to Reagan's first term by regressing p_t on p_{t-1} and the unemployment gap $(U_t - U_t^N)$ over the period 1955–1980 yields

$$p_t = 0.148 + 1.02p_{t-1} - 0.495(U_t - U_t^N) \tag{9.2}$$
$$\quad (0.30) \quad (0.11) \quad\quad (0.21)$$

where $R^2 = 0.80$, the standard error $= 1.14$, the Durbin-Watson $= 1.98$, and coefficient standard errors appear in parentheses. This formula retrieves the Keynesian rule-of-thumb relation, or Phillips curve, from empirical data on prices and unemployment.[26] Barring unusual exogenous shocks, equations (9.1) and (9.2) imply that the change in inflation between time 0 and time T is about -0.5 times the cumulative unemployment in excess of the natural rate between $t = 1$ and $t = T$. Hence,

$$p_T - p_0 = -0.5 \sum_{t=1}^{T} (U_t - U^N) \tag{9.3}$$

The standard Phillips curve, based on data from 1950 to 1980, accounts for the disinflation achieved over 1981–1984 with remarkable accuracy. Cumulative excess unemployment over 1981–1984—assuming, as most moderate Keynesians do, that the natural rate was about 6 percent in those years—amounted to 10.4 percentage points. Equation (9.3) predicts that this should have produced a decline in the annual inflation rate of about 5.2 percentage points between 1980 and 1984. As the data in Table 9.2 show, this is exactly what happened. Given that the disinflation calculations do not take into account the decline in food and especially energy prices (only some of which can be attributed to contractive U.S. monetary policy) or the appreciation of the dollar (which lowered import prices), it is perhaps surprising that inflation did not decline by a bit more than it did.

As a result of a determined commitment to a slowdown in money supply growth rates and a corresponding willingness to tolerate historically high levels of unemployment, the first Reagan administration presided over a substantial reduction of inflation in the U.S. economy. In view of the American public's distaste for inflation, this was an accomplishment of real importance. But the cost was very high. "Credibility" arguments and new classical rational-expecta-

Table 9.2 Cumulative disinflation, excess unemployment, and GNP gaps, 1981–1984

Year	Change in inflation (from 1980, GNP deflator)	Cumulative excess unemployment $(U - U^N)$	Cumulative GNP gap (percentage deviation of actual from potential)
1981	—	1.6	−3.8
1982	−3.0	5.3	−12.7
1983	−5.0	8.9	−21.0
1984	−5.2	10.4	−25.5

tions theories holding that a sustained monetary slowdown would lower inflation without imposing large losses of output and employment proved to be of no relevance empirically. Just as most Keynesians would have predicted, the 5-point reduction in the annual inflation rate took 10 extra annual percentage points of unemployment.[27] In keeping with the Okun's Law relation between output gaps and unemployment gaps, the cost of the 5 points of disinflation amounted to more than 25 percent of a year's GNP (see the last column in Table 9.2). In 1984 prices that translates into about 900 billion dollars' worth of forgone goods and services, or 180 billion dollars per point of lowered inflation.

9.2 Distributional Politics and Partisan Cleavages in Congress

PARTY DIVISIONS OVER THE REAGAN TAX-CUT PROPOSALS

The Reagan administrations' 1981–1982 fiscal program, described by Walter Fauntroy, Democratic Congressman from Washington, D.C. and chair of the Democratic Black Caucus, as "the most extraordinary attempt by any President in modern times to redistribute income from poor to rich,"[28] did indeed achieve a major redistribution of economic well-being in favor of higher income classes. The tax cuts produced much larger distributional changes than did the social spending cuts, and so we shall begin with a discussion of the struggle in Congress over the administration's tax reduction package.

The Economic Recovery Tax Act of 1981 (ERTA), which cut individual federal tax rates by 23 percent over three years, left personal income over fiscal years 1981 to 1986 nearly 600 billion dollars higher than it would have been under pre-ERTA law. ERTA, as amended the following year by the Tax Equity and Fiscal Responsibility Act of 1982 (TEFRA), also sharply reduced business taxes, largely by providing for the Accelerated Cost Recovery System and new investment tax credits. Federal taxes almost certainly would have been reduced at some point during the 1981–1984 presidential term no matter who had won the election. The high inflation of the late 1970s had substantially increased tax burdens through "bracket creep," and there was widespread support for compensatory action. In 1980 President Carter proposed that income tax credits be used to offset rising Social Security taxes, a form of tax relief that would have been especially beneficial to low- and moderate-income taxpayers. But the distribution of the tax relief enacted in 1981 was decisively influenced by Ronald Reagan's defeat of Jimmy Carter and by the Republicans' gain of 33 seats in the 1980 House races (giving them a programmatic majority) and 12 seats in the 1980 Senate contests (giving them a numerical majority in that chamber for the first time since January 1955). In the absence of these shifts in the party balance of power, the tax (and spending) changes of 1981–1982 surely would have been more limited in scope and much less favorable to the affluent.

Although the benefits of the business tax cuts embodied in ERTA/TEFRA undoubtedly flowed disproportionately to owners of capital, who naturally tend to fall at the higher end of the income distribution, the precise distributional impact of changes in corporate tax burdens is a controversial matter among professionals. Certainly it was not clear to Congress in 1981. The distributional implications of the administration's personal tax cut proposals, however, were another story. As a matter of simple arithmetic, an across-the-board tax cut—that is, an equal percentage cut in all income tax rates—necessarily would yield larger absolute benefits for the rich than for the poor, as well as larger benefits *relative* to incomes. The very poor, whose incomes fell within the zero-tax bracket range, were slated to receive nothing under the administration bill; their benefits had to trickle down. These distributional consequences were obvious immediately. And they were profound enough for the parties' core constituencies (income groups below the median for the Democrats and income groups well above the median for the Republicans) that the president's tax program unleashed a fierce struggle in Congress, creating deep partisan divisions.

In response to President Reagan's February 1981 proposal to cut personal rates cumulatively by 27 percent over three years, which was scaled back to 23 percent by the administration the following June, Democrats in the House and Senate proposed tax bills yielding smaller aggregate cuts that were targeted more heavily on lower income groups. The size of the tax cuts was important because, no matter how distributed, reductions in the federal government's most important revenue source—income tax receipts—would constrain federal spending programs later on. A dramatic reduction in the flow of federal revenues, even if not matched initially by expenditure cutbacks, would eventually begin to starve spending programs when the deficit issue had to be faced. Ronald Reagan understood this well. In fact, the president explained to the nation the strategy of using tax reduction to force control of spending in a televised speech from the Oval Office on February 5, 1981, using a "children's allowance theory" of the politics of fiscal policy to drive home the point: "Over the past decades we've talked of curtailing Government spending so that we can lower the tax burden . . . But there were always those who told us that taxes couldn't be cut until spending was reduced. Well, you know we can lecture our children about extravagance until we run out of voice and breath. Or we can cure their extravagance by reducing their allowance."[29]

Led by Dan Rostenkowski, chairman of the Ways and Means Committee, Democrats in the House tried to preserve the "allowance" of federal tax revenues, without which the Democrats' cherished social programs would be endangered, by offering an alternative one-year tax-cut proposal on April 9, 1981. The proposal called for a 40-billion-dollar fiscal 1982 cut, as compared to the 61-billion-dollar reduction embodied in just the first full year of the administration's three-year plan. All taxpayers would have received some relief under the Rostenkowski proposal, but the share of the benefits slated for those earning less than $50,000 a year was much larger than in the White House bill. The administration rejected the one-year proposal out of hand. President Reagan promptly denounced the plan as "less than half a loaf,"[30] and Treasury secretary Donald Regan called the rate reductions "puny."[31] Given the Republicans' domination of the Senate and the number of House members who were inclined to concede the tax issue to the administration, it soon became clear to Democratic House leaders that a modest, one-year tax-cut plan stood little chance of heading off the president's package.

In mid-June, after rejecting the White House's revised, 23-percent across-the-board tax-cut proposal, the Democratic majority of the House Ways and Means Committee began drafting a two-year tax cut bill in an attempt to produce a more viable plan. This Democratic alternative would have reduced average individual rates by 5 percent on October 1, 1981 and by an additional 10 percent on July 1, 1982. In contrast to the administration bill, the bill proposed by the Democrats gave those earning under $50,000 a year more than the average reduction and those earning above $50,000 less than the average reduction. Very low income earners would have benefited from increases in the zero-bracket amount and from a small increase in the earned income credit. With the exception of Representative Hance (D-Tex.), who sided with the Republicans, members of the Ways and Means Committee voted along straight party lines, passing the two-year plan on July 14, 1981.

The data in Table 9.3 give a good idea of differences in the size and redistributive impact of the Democrat's two-year tax-cut bill and the

Table 9.3   Comparing tax reductions under the Democratic and administration proposals: Tax reductions for a married couple with one earner and two dependents under the Reagan administration tax bill and the Democratic bill drafted by the Ways and Means Committee

Income	1982		1983		1984	
	Dem.	Admin.	Dem.	Admin.	Dem.	Admin.
$5,000	$50	$0	$50	$0	$50	$0
$10,000	362	52	405	78	405	83
$15,000	216	151	309	226	309	281
$20,000	250	228	385	371	385	464
$30,000	515	403	769	744	769	914
$40,000	841	639	1,275	1,188	1,275	1,438
$50,000	1,045	947	1,479	1,754	1,479	2,158
$60,000	1,199	1,255	1,633	2,370	1,633	2,928
$100,000	1,203	2,137	1,779	4,648	1,779	5,822

Source: Joint Committee on Taxation.

Note: This table assumes that all income is wage or salary and that deductible expenses are 23 percent of income.

President's revised three-year proposal.[32] The table shows the dollar cuts for one-earner, four-member households at different income levels over 1982–1984. (The distributional pattern for households with more earners and dependents is the same.) The distribution of benefits under the two proposals has the same relative shape in every year, but this shape is most easily detected by looking at the dollar cuts for 1982. During 1982 the Democratic plan provided for more tax relief, absolutely and relatively, to households with incomes of $50,000 and below and less relief to households earning more than $50,000 than did the Reagan administration's plan. Because it provided for a much larger aggregate reduction of tax revenues, by 1984 the Reagan plan reduced the absolute tax liabilities of all households earning more than $15,000 by more than did the Democratic bill. In 1984 as in 1982 and 1983, however, the Reagan plan called for distributing a larger share of the forgone revenues to households earning above $50,000 than did the Democrats' proposal. Households at the highest income ranges, $100,000 and above, were especially favored under the White House plan. Remember, however, that although the Democratic plan provided for less tax relief than did the administration plan for many middle-income and lower-middle-income households, the Democrats' bill would not have eroded federal revenues by nearly as much as did the president's bill. Therefore the Democrats' plan would have required less reduction in social spending (and/or would have produced smaller deficits). As we shall see later, the spending reductions of 1981–1982 also had distributional consequences that adversely affected the economic well-being of many lower- and middle-income households.[33]

Ultimately, the Ways and Means Committee bill was rejected on the House floor and the administration bill was passed. The showdown votes came on July 29, 1981, two days after President Reagan delivered a nationally televised public address that brilliantly made the case for the White House bill and urged the public to join him in lobbying Congress. First, the House rejected Morris Udall's substitute amendment for a one-year cut, which was similar to Rostenkowski's April proposal that the Democratic leadership earlier had decided was not viable. The key vote, however, was on Barber Conable's amendment to substitute the bill drafted by the White House (in consultation with Republicans and conservative Democrats) for the bill reported out of the Ways and Means Committee (which was drafted by the Democratic majority). The Conable amendment carried 238 to 195, sealing the president's victory in the House. The president won with essentially the same coalition of Republicans and conservative Southern Democrats (the "Boll Weevils") that gave him his spending-reduction victories, which will be discussed in the next subsection. With the lone exception of Congressman James Jeffords of Vermont, every House Republican supported the president. As the roll-call vote data reported in Table 9.4 show, the Democrats voted against the administration bill by a 4-to-1 margin, the Northern Democrats by almost 13 to 1. But the 48 Democrats who joined the Republicans in support of the Conable amendment, most of them conservative Southerners, were more than the president needed to prevail in the House.

The Senate, where the Republicans were in the majority for the first time since the 1953–1954 session of Congress, was unusually active on the tax legislation before the House completed its business. (The constitutional requirement that revenue measures originate in the House was circumvented when the Senate Finance Committee, chaired by Robert Dole, R-Kans., attached its tax package to a House-passed debt limit measure, H J Res 266.) In fact, a number of provisions written in the Senate were incorporated in the Republican bill passed by the House (the Conable amendment) and enacted into law

Table 9.4 Party cleavages in Congress on key tax-cut votes in 1981

House

HR 4242 (A one-year liberal Democratic proposal). Udall, D-Ariz., substitute amendment, to the bill, to provide a one-year reduction in income tax rates skewed to benefit
most those earning less than $50,000 per year and to provide narrowly targeted business
and investment tax incentives. Rejected 144-288, July 29, 1981.

Rep.	5-186	(3% yea)
Dem:	139-102	(57% yea)
N.Dem:	116-46	(72% yea)

HR 4242 (The Democratic two-year Ways & Means Committee bill is replaced by the
administration bill on the floor). Conable, R-N.Y., substitute amendment to reduce individual income tax rates across the board by 5 percent, 10 percent, and 10 percent over
three years, to index tax rates beginning in 1985, and to provide business and investment
tax incentives (House version of Economic Recovery Tax Act of 1981). Adopted 238-195,
July 29, 1981.

Rep:	190-1	(99% yea)
Dem:	48-194	(20% yea)
N.Dem:	12-151	(7% yea)

Senate

H J Res 266 (Indexing). Finance Committee amendment to require, beginning in 1985,
that individual income taxes be adjusted (indexed) annually to offset the effects of inflation (bracket creep). Adopted 57-40, July 16, 1981.

Rep:	43-8	(84% yea)
Dem:	14-32	(30% yea)
N.Dem:	11-20	(35% yea)

H J Res 266 (A one-year moderate Democratic proposal). Bradley, D-N.J., amendment to
limit the personal income tax cut to one year and target the relief to persons with incomes
of $50,000 or less. Rejected 24-61, July 17, 1981.

Rep:	0-43	(0% yea)
Dem:	24-18	(57% yea)
N.Dem:	22-8	(73% yea)

H J Res 266 (A three-year moderate Democratic proposal). Bradley, D-N.J., amendment
to provide a three-year personal tax cut targeted on individuals earning $50,000 or less.
Rejected 42-57, July 23, 1981.

Rep:	0-52	(0% yea)
Dem:	42-5	(89% yea)
N.Dem:	32-0	(100% yea)

Table 9.4 (*Continued*)

Senate

H J Res 266 (A three-year proposal from the liberal Democratic left). Bumpers, D-Ark., and Kennedy, D-Mass., amendment to provide a three-year personal income tax cut designed to offset increases in Social Security taxes and inflation by increasing the standard deduction and the earned income credit and reducing rates for the middle income brackets. Rejected 22-76, July 23, 1981.

Rep:	0-52	(0% yea)
Dem:	22-24	(48% yea)
N.Dem:	20-11	(65% yea)

H J Res 266 (Victory for the administration bill in the Senate). Finance Committee substitute amendment, as amended, to reduce individual income tax rates across the board by 5 percent, 10 percent, and 10 percent over three years, to index tax rates beginning in 1985, and to provide business and investment tax incentives (Senate version of Economic Recovery Tax Act of 1981). Adopted 89-11, July 29, 1981.

Rep:	52-1	(98% yea)
Dem:	37-10	(79% yea)
N.Dem:	24-8	(75% yea)

Source: Congressional Quarterly Almanac, 97th Congress, 1st Session, 1981.

after the conference committee ironed out the remaining small differences between the final House and Senate bills. By far the most important feature of ERTA to originate in the Senate was indexing, which was offered as an amendment to the Senate Finance bill by William Armstrong (R-Colo.).

Indexing was designed to offset the process of bracket creep, by which inflation (money income increases) pushes taxpayers into higher tax brackets even when there has been no growth of real (constant-dollar) income. The Armstrong proposal called for adjustment, beginning in 1985, of all income tax brackets, the zero-bracket amount (previously known as the standard deduction), the personal exemption, and capital gains, estate, and gift taxes to reflect increases in the Consumer Price Index over the previous fiscal year. As noted earlier, indexing was popular because it seemed so fair. But opponents, who came largely from the Democratic side of the aisle, pointed out that indexing would take away Congress's ability to target future inflation-based adjustments of tax rates and would tend to hold down federal revenues in subsequent years. Because Congress was about to enact a major redistribution of the federal income tax burden favoring high-income taxpayers, which at the same time would substantially shrink federal revenues, these objections were much more significant than would have been the case had indexing been attached to the pre-ERTA federal tax system. In effect, indexing would help lock the "Reagan fiscal revolution" into place. Despite these arguments (or because of them, insofar as conservatives were concerned), indexing cleared the Senate on July 16, 1981 by a vote of 57 to 40.[34] Republicans supported it overwhelmingly; Democrats opposed it by more than 2 to 1 (see Table 9.4).

With Republicans in the majority, there was never much doubt that tax cuts with the basic structure requested by the administration would pass the Senate. Nonetheless, Democratic Senators offered from the floor a number of amendments designed to scale back and redistribute the tax cuts provided by the Senate Finance Committee bill backed by the administration. Two amendments proposed by Senator Bill Bradley (D-N.J.) reflected the position of moderately liberal Senate Democrats. The first, offered on July 17, would have confined the president's tax cut to one year and would have more heavily targeted the benefits to those earning $50,000 or less. Opposed by all Republicans voting, it was defeated 24 to 61.[35] Bradley's second amendment, offered on July 23, provided for the full three-year cut but, like his first proposal, gave more relief to those earning $50,000 and below. It was defeated more narrowly than the first Bradley amendment; the vote was 42–57, with all Republican Senators in opposition and very nearly all Democrats in favor. An amendment from the left wing of the Democratic party was proposed by Senator Edward Kennedy (D-Mass.) on July 23. The Kennedy amendment, co-sponsored by Congressman Dale Bumpers (D-Ark.), called for a three-year cut targeted almost exclusively on low- and middle-income taxpayers. It was defeated handily, 22 to 76.

It was clear from these votes that the Democrats stood no chance of fundamentally altering the administration's tax proposals. The Finance Committee bill, amended to include indexing, was brought to a final vote on July 29, 1981. Not wanting to be on record as opposing a tax cut, a majority of the Democrats voted in support of the president this time, and the administration bill rolled to an 89–11 victory. The conference report was adopted on August 3 and was signed by President Reagan on August 13. The Economic Recovery Tax Act of 1981 thus became law.

PARTY DIVISIONS OVER THE REAGAN SPENDING-REDUCTION PROPOSALS
In his televised address to a joint session of Congress on February 18, 1981, President Reagan called for spending reductions to cut 41.4 billion dollars from the existing policy baseline for fiscal year 1982. Ten days later the White House announced that more cuts would be necessary to keep the deficit within the projected range, and the administration's March 10 budget message to Congress requested fiscal 1982 cuts of 48.6 billion dollars.

With support from conservative Democrats, the Republican majority completely dominated the budgetary process in the Senate. Although Democratic liberals made feeble attempts to contain social spending cuts proposed by the White House, the administration budget package sailed through the Senate with little difficulty. The only serious opposition to the president's spending proposals came in the House, where the Democrats retained a (nominal) majority.

The first round of the House budget process was controlled by the Democratic leadership and the moderate-to-liberal Democratic majority on the House Budget Committee, chaired by James R. Jones (D-Okla.). The reconciliation instructions reported out of the Budget Committee gave the president only 15.8 billion dollars in fiscal 1982 authorization cuts. The White House responded with a brilliant campaign designed to take control of the House budgetary process away from the Democratic leadership. This campaign was capped by another televised presidential address to Congress on April 28. The administration's alternative to the Budget Committee's version of the first budget resolution—known as Gramm-Latta after its sponsors Phil Gramm (D-Tex.), a right-wing junior Democratic member of the Budget Committee, and Delbert Latta (R-Ohio), the ranking minority member of the panel—called for cuts of 36.6 billion dollars in 1982 funding. The first crucial test of President Reagan's strength in the House came on May 7, when Congressman Latta moved to replace the Budget Committee reconciliation and budget instructions with the Administration-Gramm-Latta plan. Republicans supported the substitute resolution unanimously; Democrats opposed it almost 3 to 1 (see Table 9.5). But the sixty-three Democrats who joined the Republicans more than sufficed to give the president a majority, and Gramm-Latta I carried 253 to 176.

With the authorization totals established by Gramm-Latta, the budget process shifted to the authorizing committees, where the actual cuts to spending programs were crafted. The cuts, assembled by the Budget Committee and reported to the House floor as HR 3982,

Table 9.5   Party cleavages in the House on key spending-cut votes in 1981

H Con Res 115 (Gramm-Latta I). Latta, R-Ohio, substitute to the resolution reported by the Budget Committee to cut FY 1982 authorizations by 36.6 billion dollars as opposed to 15.8 billion dollars. Adopted 253-176, May 7, 1981.

Rep:	190-0	(100% yea)
Dem:	63-176	(26% yea)
N.Dem:	17-144	(11% yea)

HR 3982 (Procedural Rule requiring separate spending-cuts votes). Bolling, D-Mo., motion to order the previous question (ending debate and the possibility of amendment) on the rule (H Res 169) to provide separate program-by-program votes to achieve budget cuts required by the first FY 1982 budget resolution. Rejected 210-217, June 25, 1981.

Rep:	1-188	(0.5% yea)
Dem:	209-29	(88% yea)
N.Dem:	155-5	(97% yea)

HR 3982 (Gramm-Latta II). Latta, R-Ohio, amendments, considered en bloc, to strike parts of the authorization cuts made by eight committees and to substitute provisions endorsed by President Reagan. Adopted 217-211, June 26, 1981.

Rep:	188-2	(99% yea)
Dem:	29-209	(12% yea)
N.Dem:	3-157	(2% yea)

Source: *Congressional Quarterly Almanac*, 97th Congress, 1st Session, 1981.

came in at 37.6 billion dollars, a little higher than the total required by the Gramm-Latta reconciliation instructions. But the administration, House Republicans, and conservative Democrats complained that many of the cuts produced by the authorizing committees were "phony" and that others attacked popular programs and were unnecessarily severe (designed, perhaps, to provoke opposition on floor). More generally, they complained that the package failed to make deep enough reductions in entitlement programs, which held the key to controlling future spending. According to a GOP briefing document, "Buried within the massive House reconciliation bill and the large score-keeping savings reported for authorized programs is a critical and glaring defect: The reform and hold-down of automatic spending programs has not been achieved."[36]

Guided by the Office of Management and Budget, House Republicans and conservative Democrats therefore fashioned an alternative package, Gramm-Latta II. This plan made deeper cuts in entitlements, tightening controls on Food Stamps, school lunches, Public

Assistance, subsidized housing, Medicaid payments to the states, and student loans and phasing out student Social Security benefits and minimum Social Security benefits. At the same time it restored funding for some popular programs, such as educational impact aid. Gramm-Latta II called for cuts of 37.3 billion dollars in FY 1982; in the aggregate the cuts were not appreciably different from those of the Budget Committee package. But the sponsors claimed the cuts were targeted (on entitlement programs) in a way that would save about 20 billion dollars more than the Budget Committee bill over fiscal years 1982 to 1984.

The House Democratic leadership tried to frustrate Republican attempts to overturn the Budget Committee bill by drafting a rule for floor debate under which members would have to vote separately, program by program, on spending reductions sponsored by the administration. The Republicans wanted their budget package decided on a single up-or-down vote. The vote on the Democrats' procedural rule, introduced by Congressman Bolling on June 25, was the next big test of the president's budgetary clout in the House. The rule was narrowly rejected (210–217) after a hard core of 29 conservative Democrats joined all of the Republicans but one in supporting the president's position. It was then clear that the administration had a durable majority for its FY 1982 budget cuts in the House. Gramm-Latta II passed the following day with virtually the same coalition of Republicans and Southern "Boll Weevil" Democrats that had defeated the Democratic leadership's ground rules for debate.[37] The president's budget had prevailed in the House.

The Senate version of the budget reconciliation bill, which passed 80–15 on June 25, differed little from Gramm-Latta II. The House and Senate conferees began to work out differences on July 15 and reached agreement on July 29 without serious difficulty. The final package, which affected more than 250 programs and reduced FY 1982 spending by 35.2 billion dollars and cumulative FY 1982–1985 spending by more than 140 billion dollars, was passed by voice vote in the House on July 31 and by a vote of 80–14 in the Senate on the same day. The spending cuts became law when President Reagan signed the bill on August 13, 1981.

Less than six weeks later, on September 24, 1981, soaring deficit projections generated by high interest rates and a sagging economy prompted President Reagan to announce the need for yet more fiscal 1982 budget reductions. He called for an additional 13 billion dollars' worth of spending cuts, further tightening of nondiscretionary entitlement programs, and 3 billion dollars of new revenues. But this time Congress balked, and the President could not even rally a majority of Republicans for significant new budget savings. The White House had to settle for 4 billion dollars of new cuts. The entitlement and tax proposals were deferred.

In subsequent fiscal years, as budget deficits exceeded even the most pessimistic forecasts for 1981 and reached the 200-billion-dollar range in fiscal 1983 and 1984 (see the bottom of Table 9.), the administration redoubled its efforts to achieve deeper social spending reductions. But the hardships imposed by unprecedented postwar unemployment rates, a general feeling in the electorate that spending cutbacks had gone far enough,[38] and the Democrats' gain of 26 seats in the 1982 House elections dramatically eroded support in Congress for new austerity measures. The Democratic leadership regained control of the House, and Republicans in the Senate began to exercise a new independence of the White House. The Reagan "budget revolution" was over. Nonetheless, the administration's tax-and-spending successes of 1981 had important consequences that extended over the president's entire first term and beyond. Let us now consider the distributional consequences of these successes in detail.

9.3   Distributional Consequences of the Reagan Fiscal Program

THE TAX CUTS

Earlier I pointed out that the Economic Recovery Tax Act of 1981 (ERTA), as modified by the Tax Equity and Fiscal Responsibility Act (TEFRA) the following year, had much bigger distributional consequences than did the social spending cutbacks pushed through Congress by the Reagan administration. As we shall see in this section, both the tax cuts and the spending cuts had a similar regressive pattern. The lowest income groups benefited least from the tax cuts and were hurt most by the spending cuts. For the highest income groups the reverse was true. But the combination of the effects of ERTA and TEFRA reduced cumulative tax liabilities falling directly on households by more than 315 billion dollars over 1982–1985, whereas the reductions in spending on human resources programs achieved by the Reagan administration amounted to about 110 billion dollars over the same period.[39] The tax cuts had a larger redistributive impact than the spending cuts, then, because the dollar amounts were nearly three times as large.

The best way to begin an evaluation of the significance of the

Reagan tax cuts is to look at federal income tax burdens, by income classes, in historical perspective. Table 9.6 shows data assembled by a leading taxation expert, Joseph Minarik, on effective federal income tax rates experienced by four-person families at multiples of the median income from 1955 to 1984.[40] Movements over time in the effective rates reported in the table are accounted for by the interaction of the personal income tax code, as amended by Congress on numerous occasions,[41] with real income growth and inflation. From 1955 to 1980, the tax rate faced by the typical four-person, median-income family increased by a factor of about 1.7 (from 6.8 percent to 11.6 percent). Yet over the same period median real family income grew by 74 percent before taxes and by more than 63 percent net of federal income taxes.[42] At various times bursts of inflation raised effective rates (through inflation-induced bracket creep), especially during the late 1970s and 1980–1981. Still, as we saw in section 3.4, over the longer run inflation made virtually no contribution to the rise in aggregate tax liabilities and average tax rates; increases in real tax burdens were financed entirely out of increments to real incomes.[43] In fact, from 1955 to 1981 the total yield of the federal income tax increased only from 9.5 to 11.7 percent of total personal income.

Table 9.6   Federal income tax burdens on families at multiples of the median income, 1955–1984 (percent)

Year	Multiple of median income (in current dollars)						
	0.25	0.5	1	2	3	5	10
1955	0.0	0.0	6.8	12.4	15.2	19.3	29.2
1960	0.0	1.7	8.6	13.0	16.2	21.5	32.0
1965	0.0	2.5	7.9	12.0	15.4	20.4	30.9
1970	0.0	6.0	10.1	14.7	18.3	25.0	33.9
1975	−10.0	2.7	9.6	15.2	20.2	28.1	37.8
1980	−8.6	5.4	11.6	18.3	24.7	32.4	41.4
1981	−7.4	6.3	12.3	19.2	24.9	31.9	40.7
1982	−6.7	5.9	11.3	17.6	22.6	29.0	35.0
1983	−5.8	5.9	10.5	16.4	21.1	27.0	33.9
1984	−5.0	6.0	10.3	16.0	20.5	26.0	33.3

Source: Joseph Minarik, "Income Distribution Effects of the 1981 Tax Cuts," paper presented at the annual meeting of the National Tax Association, Nashville, Tennessee, November 26, 1984.
Note: Data pertain to four-person, husband-wife families.

The most striking feature of the historical data in Table 9.6 is the growing progressiveness of the income tax system during the 1970s.[44] For example, during the late 1950s and most of the 1960s, the difference between the tax rates experienced by families at one-half of the median income (the near-poor) and families at ten times the median (the very rich) oscillated, without trend, between 28 and 30 percentage points. By 1970 the difference between the effective rates faced by the near-poor and the very rich began to trend upward quite steadily, peaking in 1980 at 36 percentage points.[45] Comparing the tax burdens of, say, families with incomes right at the median (literally, the middle class) and those with incomes at five times the median (the very well off) reveals a similar pattern. In this case the differences in effective rates ranged, again without trend, between 12 and 13 percentage points in the 1950s and 1960s, but then began to drift upward, reaching almost 21 points in 1980.

When the same comparison of tax rates is made for families at only one-quarter of the median income (the poor) and very high income families, the pattern is even more pronounced because of the introduction of the earned income credit in 1975. Prior to 1975, families earning one-quarter of the median income or less usually paid no federal income taxes. (Their effective rate was 0 percent, as shown in Table 9.6.) After the earned income credit was enacted, however, the typical poor family faced a *negative* tax rate and therefore received a lump sum payment from the Treasury each year.[46] Hence the gap in the rates between the poor and the very rich rose from the 30 to 32 percentage-point range prevailing in the 1950s and 1960s to 50 percentage points in 1980.

As noted in Chapter 3, the reason for the dramatic increase in the degree of progression of the federal income tax system during the 1970s was that the changes legislated by Congress to offset inflation-induced increases in tax burdens were primarily in the form of increased personal exemptions and standard deductions, as well as the earned income tax credit just described.[47] All of these changes disproportionately benefited low-income groups; for the rich and near-rich they were of very little consequence. After 1970, therefore, relative income tax burdens shifted from low-income families to families further up the income ladder, particularly those at twice the median income and above. As the data in Table 9.6 for 1981–1984 indicate, the Economic Recovery Tax Act of 1981, which made no adjustments to the personal exemption, standard deductions (zero-bracket amounts), or the earned income credit, reversed the egalitarian trend of the previous decade at a stroke. By 1984 (the first year in which the full impact of the three-stage ERTA tax cuts was felt) the tax rates faced by the well heeled and the overall level of progressiveness of the federal income tax system had reverted to what they had been in the late 1960s.

A more detailed picture of the full impact of ERTA is provided by Table 9.7, which shows the actual 1984 income tax rates along with the rates that would have prevailed in 1984 under the pre-ERTA 1980 rate structure.[48] Comparisons between 1980-law effective tax rates projected to 1984 and actual 1984 effective rates under ERTA are somewhat misleading because, as was pointed out earlier, some reduction of tax burdens almost certainly would have been legislated during the 1981–1984 presidential term, no matter what the outcomes

Table 9.7   Effective 1984 federal income tax rates under 1980 law (hypothetical) and under the Economic Recovery Tax Act of 1981 (actual)

Adjusted gross income class (in dollars as defined by 1980 law)	Percentage of total taxpayers in income class	Effective tax rates in 1984		Tax reduction (percentage of adjusted gross income after tax, relative to 1980 law)
		Under 1980 law (hypothetical)	Under 1981 law (actual)	
0–$5,000	19.7	1.3	1.0	0.3
$5,000–$10,000	18.5	6.9	5.3	1.8
$10,000–$15,000		10.5	7.9	2.9
$15,000–$20,000	36.0	12.8	9.6	3.6
$20,000–$25,000		14.3	10.6	4.2
$25,000–$50,000	21.6	16.4	12.0	5.2
$50,000–$100,000	3.6	23.4	17.3	8.0
$100,000–$200,000	0.5	33.7	24.3	13.6
$200,000–$500,000	0.1	40.8	30.9	16.8
$500,000–$1,000,000		44.9	33.4	21.0
$1,000,000 and over	0.02	47.2	33.5	26.1
All classes (aggregate)		18.3	13.6	5.9

Sources: Tax rate data are from John Karl Scholz, "Individual Income Tax Provisions of the 1981 Tax Act," in Joseph Pechman, ed., *Setting National Priorities: The 1983 Budget* (Washington, D.C.: Brookings, 1982), tables A2, A3, pp. 252, 255. Data on the distribution of taxpayers by income classes are from Joseph Pechman, *Federal Tax Policy* (Washington, D.C.: Brookings, 1983), table D-9.

of the 1980 presidential and congressional elections. Although we have no way of knowing precisely what sort of tax reduction would have been enacted had the Republicans not done so well in the 1980 elections, alternatives sponsored by the Democrats surely would have targeted tax relief more heavily on lower income households and given up less federal revenue than did the Reagan plan. (See, for example, Table 9.3 and the associated discussion in Section 9.2.) In the absence of a specific, highly probable counterfactual to the administration's tax policy, however, it is natural to use the 1980 rate structure as the benchmark from which to assess the magnitudes and distribution of the tax cuts achieved by President Reagan during his first term.

The best way to express the ERTA cuts is in percent of adjusted gross income after tax, as in the last column of Table 9.7. This yields the change in disposable incomes applicable to taxpayers in various income classes. ERTA's uniform (across-the-board) reduction of rates, applied to the progressive 1980 federal income tax system, necessarily meant that relative as well as absolute benefits would rise with income. Therefore, it comes as no surprise that the reductions in tax liabilities (shown in Table 9.7 in percent of after-tax incomes) increase monotonically with adjusted gross incomes. What may seem surprising, however, is just how "top heavy" the disposable income increases generated by ERTA were.

For that tiny fraction of taxpayers with adjusted gross incomes of half a million dollars and over (about 0.2 percent, or 20,000, of the nearly 100 million people filing tax returns in the early 1980s), the benefits of ERTA were truly breathtaking. Their disposable incomes were 21 to 26 percent higher in 1984 than they would have been had 1980 tax law remained in place. The main reason that the benefits enjoyed by the super-rich were so large was that ERTA slashed the top tax rates on unearned income and capital gains by 29 percent. By contrast, for the 38 percent of the taxpaying population with adjusted gross incomes of $10,000 and below, disposable incomes in 1984 were only 0.3 to 1.8 percent higher as a result of the ERTA cuts of 1980 tax rates. The disposable income gain of the median-income taxpayer under ERTA, again relative to what 1984 after-tax income would have been under 1980 law, was in the vicinity of 3.5 percent.[49] Clearly, the Economic Recovery Tax Act of 1981 conferred rather modest benefits on the low- and middle-income classes. The big gainers, as the data in Table 9.7 show, were those in the highest ranges of the income distribution.[50]

THE SPENDING CUTS

The Omnibus Budget Reconciliation Act of 1981 (OBRA) gave President Reagan almost all the social spending cuts he had requested for fiscal 1982 in his February 1981 budget plan. Aside from the Social Security Amendments of 1983, however, few additional cuts were achieved during the remaining fiscal years of Reagan's first term.[51] Nonetheless, as a result of the budget changes embodied in OBRA, social-program spending reductions tended to grow in each succeeding fiscal year, both absolutely and relative to projected outlays under pre-Reagan policies. The principal exception to this pattern was Unemployment Insurance (UI) benefit payments. After declining (relative to the pre-Reagan policy base) in fiscal 1982, UI outlays rose sharply in fiscal 1983 because of the extraordinary unemployment rates of late 1982 and early 1983.[52] Thereafter, UI spending declined pretty much in step with the administration's budget proposals.[53]

Table 9.8 shows the Congressional Budget Office estimates of the magnitudes and distribution, by program, of the social spending reductions achieved by fiscal year 1985 (the last budget of President Reagan's first term). Programs providing cash benefits and in-kind benefits that the Congressional Budget Office was able to allocate to households by income level are distinguished from other social programs for which such an allocation could not be accurately made. As the totals at the bottom of the table indicate, by FY 1985 the Reagan administration had obtained about one-half of the cuts it wanted. Reductions amounting to 17.2 percent of projected outlays under pre-Reagan policy had been proposed; cuts of 8.8 percent had been enacted.

When he first announced his budget plan to a joint session of Congress on February 18, 1981, President Reagan declared that the "social safety net" of programs benefiting the "truly needy" who "depend on the Federal Government for their very existence" would be "exempt from any cuts."[54] The changes actually proposed in administration budget messages to Congress were only partly consistent with the president's declaration, however.[55] Generally speaking, the administration sought and received the largest cuts for employment and training programs, social services programs, and education and student aid programs. The income levels of most beneficiaries of these programs are difficult to identify, because all except those providing benefits to postsecondary students represent federal grants to states and localities, rather than payments to identifiable individuals and families. It is unlikely that very many of those affected by the

Table 9.8 Federal social spending changes in fiscal 1985 resulting from Reagan administration proposals and congressional actions over fiscal years 1982–1985

Programs	Projected FY 85 outlays under pre-Reagan policy (in billions of dollars)	Changes proposed by Reagan (percent of projected pre-Reagan policy outlays)	Changes enacted (percent of projected pre-Reagan policy outlays)
Cash benefit programs (allocated to households)			
Social Security	$200.6	−10.4	−4.6
Veterans' compensation and pensions	14.5	−6.9	−1.5
Supplemental Security Income (SSI)	8.1	−2.5	+9.0
Unemployment Insurance (UI)	29.9	−19.1	−17.6
Aid to Families with Dependent Children (AFDC)	9.8	−28.6	−14.0
Low-income energy assistance	2.4	−37.5	−9.7
In-kind benefit programs (allocated to households)			
Medicaid[a]	24.9	−15.7	−2.8
Medicare[b]	80.4	−11.2	−6.9
Food Stamps[c]	14.5	−51.7	−14.1
Child nutrition	5.0	−46.0	−28.5
Housing assistance	12.3	−19.5	−11.5
Guaranteed student loans	4.1	−22.0	−39.0
Other student assistance	4.5	−68.9	−16.1
Other social problems (not allocated to households)			
Compensatory education	4.1	−61.0	−18.9
Social services block grants	3.4	−41.2	−23.5
General employment and training	5.7	−43.9	−38.5
Public service employment	4.8	−100	−100
Totals[d]	$436.6	−17.2%	−8.8%

Sources: Congressional Budget Office, "Major Legislative Changes in Human Resources Programs since January 1981, Special Study, August 1983; and D. Lee Bawden and John L. Palmer, "Social Policy," in John L. Palmer and Isabel Sawhill, eds., The Reagan Record (Cambridge, Mass.: Ballinger, 1984), table 6.1.

a Includes 69 percent of outlays allocated to households.
b Includes 31 percent of outlays allocated to households.
c Includes 94 percent of outlays allocated to households.
d Includes small programs not listed.

cutbacks to education, social services, and employment programs depended on the government for "their very existence." On the other hand, funding reductions proposed (and enacted) for retirement programs,[56] whose benefits flow to the affluent and the broad middle classes as well as to the "truly needy," in general were smaller than those falling on means-tested income security programs ("welfare"), which benefit primarily the poor and the near-poor.

The major social programs most heavily targeted to households below the poverty line are Supplemental Security Income (which provides benefits to low-income aged, blind, and disabled persons), Aid to Families with Dependent Children (which provides benefits to low-income single-parent families[57]), Medicaid (which finances medical care for low-income persons who are blind, aged, or disabled or who belong to families with dependent children), and Food Stamps (which provides low-income individuals and families with coupons redeemable for food).[58] Over fiscal years 1982–1985, administration budget plans called for above-average spending cuts for AFDC and Food Stamps and below-average cuts for SSI and Medicaid. Reductions proposed for the SSI program, which provides cash transfers to the "dependent poor" outside the labor force, were quite small: 2.5 percent of the pre-Reagan base by FY 1985. But even this proposal was ignored by Congress, and by the last fiscal year of the president's first term the CBO estimated that outlays enacted for SSI actually would stand about 9 percent above projected outlays under pre-Reagan policy. The Medicaid program, which, like SSI, is of great importance to the "dependent poor," also fared comparatively well. The administration sought cutbacks amounting to about 15.7 percent of projected FY 1985 expenditures under the pre-Reagan policy regime. But the reductions legislated by Congress were estimated to equal about 2.8 percent, which was well below the average social-program cut of 8.8 percent that the administration would achieve in fiscal 1985.

From the point of view of low-income households, the most painful cuts were those made to the AFDC and Food Stamp programs. In comparison to the SSI and Medicaid programs, AFDC payments and Food Stamps benefits flow to much larger numbers of the "working poor"—that is, people who hold jobs but have incomes near the poverty line. In fiscal 1985 the spending cuts proposed by the Reagan administration for the AFDC program (the purest "welfare" program in the American income maintenance system) amounted to a hefty 28.6 percent of projected funding levels under pre-OBRA law. The

CBO put the spending reductions legislated by Congress at 14 percent. The cuts that were enacted under pressure from the White House, however, took a curious form indeed for an administration ostensibly committed to enhancing supply-side incentives.

Prior to OBRA, low-income working mothers could exclude the first $30 of monthly earnings and one-third of the remainder from consideration in the determination of AFDC benefits (the thirty-and-a-third rule). Child care, transportation, and some other work-related expenses could also be deducted from "countable" earnings. In other words, AFDC mothers had a financial incentive to obtain employment; they faced an implicit tax rate, in the form of reduced AFDC benefit payments, of just under 33 percent of net income from employment. Consequently, in most states working AFDC recipients had disposable incomes 25 to 35 percent higher than those of nonworking mothers receiving benefits from the same program.[59]

OBRA terminated the thirty-and-a-third exclusion after the fourth month of earnings, reduced deductions of work-related expenses from countable earnings, and figured in the earned income tax credit as monthly income. Hence under OBRA working AFDC recipients' earnings were taxed at about 60 percent—a higher marginal rate than that faced by millionaires under the ERTA income tax schedule! As a result of OBRA, the average difference in the monthly disposable incomes of nonworking and working AFDC mothers declined in most states from the 25-to-35-percent range prevailing in 1981 to under 10 percent. In some cases the difference vanished. Of the half a million households with earnings receiving AFDC benefits at the time of OBRA's enactment, it is estimated that 90 percent either became ineligible for the program or else experienced a reduction in benefits. Another 200,000 recipient households without income from employment shared the same fate in the wake of other changes to AFDC mandated by the OBRA legislation.[60] And families cut off completely from AFDC also lost their rights to Medicaid.

The Food Stamp program was targeted by the Reagan administration for very severe cuts. In fiscal 1985 the proposed funding reductions equaled almost 52 percent of projected spending under pre-Reagan policies. Congress legislated a 14-percent cut—much less than the administration wanted, but painful nonetheless for many low-income households. In the end about 1 million people were eliminated from the program, primarily by making ineligible those households with gross monthly incomes exceeding 130 percent of the federal poverty-line income.

Overall, the social-spending cutbacks sponsored by the Reagan administration fell less heavily on the middle-class entitlement programs (the most important being Social Security) and federal transfers to the dependent poor than on programs that helped improve the economic situation of the working poor. Consequently, the changes in domestic spending achieved by President Reagan during his first term greatly sharpened the distinction between work and welfare in the American income security system. Let us now see quantitatively just how the combination of spending cuts and personal tax cuts affected the economic well-being of households in different income classes.

THE COMBINED EFFECTS OF THE TAX AND SPENDING CUTS

Estimates of average changes in taxes, cash benefits, and in-kind benefits experienced by households at different income levels in calendar year 1984 are reported in Table 9.9. It is important to remember that although the changes in benefits reported in the table are averages for all households in each income class, only some households were affected by any one benefit change. Hence some households were affected much more by the benefit cuts than the per-household estimates imply, and others were affected less or not at all.[61] This problem does not arise to nearly the same degree with respect to the per-household changes in taxes, except in the case of the top income class shown (the $80,000-and-over category).[62] Within this highest adjusted gross income class, there probably are substantial cross-household differences in unearned income and capital gains receipts (on which ERTA slashed the top rates by 29 percent) and, therefore, correspondingly large variations around the average reduction in taxes.[63] Despite these limitations, the data in Table 9.9 yield the most accurate picture we have of the direct distributional consequences of Reagan's fiscal policies by the last year of his first term.[64]

The changes in tax liabilities per household in Table 9.9 simply reinforce the pattern already illustrated several times. The dollar (and percentage) improvements to household incomes from the tax cuts rise with adjusted gross incomes. Households in the under-$10,000 class, which corresponds roughly to the bottom quarter of the adjusted gross income distribution, typically experienced a very small gain. The $10,000-to-$20,000 class, which essentially comprises the second quarter of the distribution, received larger but still comparatively modest increases in income as a result of the tax cuts. The big winners from ERTA were households in the upper half of the income

Table 9.9 Changes in per-household taxes, benefits, and net income position, by adjusted income level in calendar year 1984, as a result of the Reagan administration's fiscal program

Category of change	Household adjusted gross income class in 1982 dollars (percent of all households)					Average for all 83.8 million households
	Less than $10,000 (24.1%)	$10,000– $20,000 (25.7%)	$20,000– $40,000 (34.0%)	$40,000– $80,000 (14.7%)	$80,000 and over (1.7%)	
Taxes	+20	+330	+1,200	+3,080	+8,390	+1,090
Cash benefits	−250	−210	−130	−90	−90	−170
In-kind benefits	−160	−90	−60	−80	−40	−100
Net	−$390	+$30	+$1,010	+$2,900	+$8,270	+820
Net as percent of income	−15.4%	+0.2%	+3.3%	+5.3%	+6.0%	+3.4%

Sources: Congressional Budget Office, "The Combined Effects of Major Changes in Federal Taxes and Spending Programs since 1981," staff memorandum, April 1984. Net percentage figures were derived by the author as described in the table notes.

Notes: Tax changes include effects on individuals of the Economic Recovery Tax Act of 1981 (ERTA) and the Tax Equity and Fiscal Responsibility Act of 1982 (TEFRA). Benefit changes include the effects of the Omnibus Budget Reconciliation Act of 1981 (and subsequent modifications) that can be allocated to households and the Social Security Amendments of 1983. (The most significant programs allocated to households are listed in Table 9.8). The data are in current (1984) dollars except when expressed as a percentage of 1982 incomes. The net percentage figures were computed after converting the 1984 dollar amounts to 1982 dollars using the personal consumption expenditures (PCE) deflator.

distribution. For households at $80,000 and above, the top 1.7 percent of the adjusted distribution, the tax cuts brought a genuine windfall gain.

The cuts in benefit programs—which, as was emphasized earlier, were much smaller in magnitude than the tax cuts[65]—exhibit just the opposite distributional pattern. The loss from the spending reductions rises as household income declines. Given that low-income households generally receive more cash and in-kind transfers than do households with higher incomes, it follows naturally that the former are the principal victims of cuts in social spending. Conversely, many high-income households receive no benefits from federal transfer programs, and so they literally have nothing to lose from the budget cuts. But the distributional pattern of the domestic spending cuts also reflects the fact that the percentage reductions in outlays for means-tested benefit programs, which are heavily targeted on low-income households, were twice as large as the cutbacks of non-means-tested programs, whose beneficiaries are more likely to fall in the higher income classes.

The net impacts of the Reagan tax and spending cuts, in dollar and percentage terms, are shown at the bottom of Table 9.9. By calendar year 1984, the combination of tax and spending changes, averaged across all households, had yielded a net gain of about $820 per household, or 3.4 percent of household adjusted gross income. The all-household average change is positive because the benefit reductions absorbed by individuals and families, viewed relative to projected outlays under pre-Reagan domestic spending policy, were more than offset by gains in the form of lower tax burdens, calculated relative to projected liabilities under pre-Reagan tax policy. Looked at from the vantage point of the Treasury Department, the implicit revenue gains to the federal government from the spending cuts did not begin to offset the revenue losses from the tax cuts. The difference was financed by federal deficits (borrowing), which in 1983 and 1984 reached 200 billion dollars per annum (see Table 9.1, bottom).

The all-household averages obscure large variations across income classes in the net direct impact of changes in fiscal policy in place by the last year of President Reagan's first term.[66] For the typical household with an adjusted gross income below $10,000 (the bottom quarter of the distribution), the loss of benefits overwhelmed the tax cuts. Reagan policies depressed the average income of households in this class by more than 15 percent. In the next quarter of the distribution (the $10,000-to-$20,000 class), the tax-and-spending cuts were almost offsetting. On average, households in this category experienced a tiny (0.2-percent) improvement of their real income by 1984 as a result of fiscal policy changes under Reagan. The $20,000-to-$40,000 adjusted gross income category, which includes the upper tier of the American middle class, enjoyed an improvement in real income of about 3.3 percent, almost exactly equal to the average impact of the tax-and-benefit changes across all households. Affluent households got the best deal from the changes in tax and spending policies: The real incomes of households at $40,000 and above (the top 16 percent of the 1982 adjusted gross income distribution) were improved on average by 5.3 to 6 percent. Compared to the experiences of households in the bottom half of the distribution, where Reagan's fiscal policies generally affected real incomes adversely or left them flat, this was a dramatic improvement.

The changes in household incomes discussed above and reported in Table 9.9 describe the effects of Reagan fiscal policies calculated relative to a *counterfactual* baseline of projected 1984 taxes and transfers under pre-Reagan policies. *Actual* changes in the level and distribution of disposable incomes over President Reagan's first term, however, were determined by actual changes in taxes and transfers between 1980 and 1984, in conjunction with macroeconomic fluctuations affecting wages, salaries, and other sources of personal income over the same period. We saw earlier in this chapter that Reagan's fiscal and monetary policies profoundly affected the macroeconomy. The administration's policies achieved substantial disinflation, but at the cost of very high unemployment and large gaps between actual and potential real output. More than 5 points were chopped off the inflation rate during Reagan's first term. By 1984, however, cumulative excess unemployment was 10.4 percentage points and the cumulative GNP gap was more than 25 points (see Table 9.2). The analyses of the distributional consequences of unemployment and inflation in Chapters 2 and 3 indicated that such a macroeconomic scenario, particularly the extra unemployment, would hit low-income groups especially hard.

Estimates of actual changes in real family disposable incomes from 1980 to 1984 are given in Table 9.10 for quintiles of distribution.[67] During 1980, President Carter's last year, constant (1982) dollar disposable income for families averaged $20,333. By 1984, the last year of President Reagan's first term, the average had risen to about

Table 9.10 Actual percentage changes from 1980 to 1984 in real disposable family income, by quintiles of the distribution

Quintile	Percentage change
Bottom 20%	−7.6
Second 20%	−1.7
Third 20%	+0.9
Fourth 20%	+3.4
Top 20%	+8.7
All families (average)	+3.5

Source: Marilyn Moon and Isabel Sawhill, "Family Incomes: Gainers and Losers," in John L. Palmer and Isabel Sawhill, eds., *The Reagan Record* (Cambridge, Mass.: Ballinger, 1984), table 10.5, p. 329.

$21,038—a gain of 3.5 percent, as reported in the last column of Table 9.10.[68] Growth over the period reflected macroeconomic events (1980 was a recession year, 1984 a year of brisk recovery) and actual changes in federal government transfers and taxes directly affecting persons. Despite the large personal tax cuts, which raised disposable incomes at the cost of a ballooning federal deficit, the 1980–1984 gain was not large in comparison to four-year increases in average real family incomes of 5.1 percent in the 1970s and 11.3 percent in the 1960s. And the variation around the average 3.5-percent gain across families at different income levels was extremely lopsided.

Between 1980 and 1984 real disposable incomes for families in the bottom 20 percent of the distribution fell, on average, by about 7.6 percent.[69] Adjusted for inflation, taxes, and transfers, the average income of families in the next quintile of the distribution was also lower in 1984 than in 1980. Urban Institute calculations indicate that the average decline for this group was approximately 1.7 percent. The remaining quintiles of the family income distribution had experienced varying degrees of improvement in their real disposable incomes by the end of President Reagan's first term. The average family in the third quintile of the distribution was just a little under 1 percent better off in 1984 than in 1980. The fourth quintile enjoyed a more sizable average gain of around 3.4 percent. Once again, as all the data presented earlier showed, the really big winners were those in the top income class. The real incomes of families in the highest quintile grew on average by 8.7 percent over the first Reagan administration.

When asked during the October 8, 1984 preelection presidential debate whether the country was better off than it had been four years earlier, Walter Mondale replied: "If you're wealthy, you're better off. If you're middle income, you're about where you were, and if you're of moderate income, you're worse off."[70] Data from a variety of sources on distributional outcomes during President Reagan's first term show that Mr. Mondale was right on target. The problem for Mondale and the Democrats in 1984 was that low-income voters do not go to the polls in nearly the same proportions as high-income voters; also, the electorate as a whole weighted the unusually favorable growth rate performance of 1983–1984 much more heavily than they did the miserable performance of 1981–1982. (See Chapters 5, 6, and 8.)

AGGREGATE FISCAL REDISTRIBUTIONS

The Reagan administration's fiscal policy has at times been called "revolutionary," but this is an exaggeration. Judged in relation to the

1980–1981 fiscal year budgets inherited by the administration, Reagan budget policy achieved changes in federal tax burdens and spending priorities equivalent to between 1.5 and 2 percent of GNP. Table 9.11 puts these aggregate budget shifts in historical context.

Over fiscal years 1960 to 1980–1981, federal spending as a fraction of GNP grew by 4.7 percentage points, from 18.5 to 23.2 percent. Accompanying the growth in the aggregate size of the federal budget in GNP were important changes in federal spending priorities. The share of GNP going to nondefense programs more than doubled, rising from 8.8 percent to 17.9 percent. At the same time, the fraction of GNP devoted to defense declined by more than 4 points, from 9.7 to 5.3 percent. As the data in the top frame of Table 9.11 show, the Reagan administration managed to slow down a bit (but not reverse) the rate of growth of aggregate federal spending as a percent of GNP. More significantly, the administration succeeded in altering the trend of more than two decades in federal budget priorities.

After three complete Reagan budgets covering fiscal 1982, 1983, and 1984,[71] the federal spending share of GNP was 23.8 percent—six-tenths of a percentage point higher than it had been in fiscal 1980–1981. Although the president's February 1981 budget statement called for federal outlays as a percentage of GNP to decline by 2 points by fiscal 1984, three powerful countervailing forces dashed the plan.

Table 9.11 Federal budget outlays and receipts, as percent of GNP, for selected fiscal years from 1960

Budget component	Fiscal years			
	1960	1970	1980–1981	1984
Total outlays[a]	18.5%	20.2%	23.2%	23.8%
Nondefense	8.8	11.8	17.9	17.4
Nondefense, noninterest	7.4	10.3	15.7	14.3
Nondefense, noninterest nonOASDHI	5.1	6.5	9.7	7.8
Total receipts	18.6%	19.9%	20.5%	18.6%
Corporate income taxes	4.3	3.4	2.3	1.6
Social insurance	2.1	3.9	5.5	6.8
Individual income taxes	8.5	9.7	9.7	8.3

Sources: Economic Report of the President, February 1985, tables B-71, B-76; February 1984, table 1-1.
    a. Outlays include "off-budget" items.

First, in the face of overwhelming popular and congressional resistance, the administration was unable to trim substantially Social Security and Medicare (OASDHI) spending. Outlays for OASDHI actually rose from 6.2 to 6.6 percent of GNP from fiscal 1980–1981 to fiscal 1984. Second, despite misgivings in Congress, especially on the Democratic side of the aisle, the administration itself was determined to raise defense spending sharply. The share of GNP going to the Pentagon was increased from 5.3 to 6.4 percent over the period. Third, right from the start the administration gave higher priority to reducing taxes than to balancing the federal budget, and was more committed to achieving disinflation than to reviving employment and output growth. The anti-inflation monetary policy backed by the White House reduced the supply of credit and pushed interest rates up. And as the revenue losses from the tax cuts outran the budget savings from the social-program cuts, federal deficits ballooned, adding to the demand for credit and pushing interest costs even higher. The intersection of large Treasury borrowing requirements and high interest rates yielded dramatic increases in federal debt service outlays. From fiscal 1980–1981 to fiscal 1984, federal interest payment obligations grew from 2.4 to 3.1 percent of GNP.

Although Reagan budget policy did not succeed in reducing the overall federal spending share of GNP, a substantial redistribution of spending priorities was achieved. The big winners, as we have seen, were the Pentagon and the recipients of federal interest income. In fact, those who had the inclination and resources to purchase U.S. Treasury securities during 1982–1984 received the highest inflation-adjusted returns available from the federal government during the postwar era. The principal losers from the shift in federal spending priorities were the beneficiaries of nondefense programs other than Social Security pensions and Medicare. As the data on the fourth row of Table 9.11 indicate, Reagan's fiscal policy reduced the share of nondefense, non-OASDHI outlays in GNP, exclusive of interest payments, by almost 2 percentage points (from 9.7 to 7.8 percent). This was not a revolutionary change, but it did amount to a cutback of 70 billion FY 1984 dollars,[72] and it reversed the trend of more than two decades. As we saw in the previous section, this shift in budgetary priorities from social spending to defense fell especially hard on low- and moderate-income people in the labor force.

President Reagan did achieve his first-term goal of reducing the share of federal tax receipts in GNP by about 2 percentage points. Federal revenues fell from 20.5 percent of GNP in fiscal 1980 and 1981 to 18.6 percent in fiscal 1984—the same revenue share as in 1960. Along with the shift toward a reduced federal tax share in GNP, the administration presided over important changes in the composition of federal taxes. By fiscal 1984, federal revenues were drawn much less heavily than before from progressive tax sources.

The administration-sponsored ERTA and TEFRA legislation accelerated the decline of the contribution of corporate tax revenues to federal receipts. Corporate income taxes, which ultimately are borne disproportionately by (wealthy) owners of capital, declined from 2.3 percent of GNP in fiscal 1980 and 1981 to 1.6 percent in fiscal 1984. During the same period social insurance taxes, which are regressive over the entire income range, rose from 5.5 percent of GNP to 6.8 percent. The Reagan administration was not responsible for the rise in Social Security tax burdens, however. Social insurance taxes had been rising for several decades in order to finance the increasingly generous benefits legislated by Congress. The Social Security Amendments of 1983, which raised the additional revenues necessary to keep the system solvent, had strong bipartisan support. Advocates of changing the financing of the system—from pay-as-you-go trust funds based on proportional-regressive payroll taxes[73] to general revenues based on progressive income and corporate taxes—are small in number and found largely among the left wing of the Democratic party.

At the same time that Social Security taxes were increased and corporate taxes were lowered, individual income taxes—the most progressive source of federal revenues—were reduced. The income tax share of GNP fell from 9.7 to 8.3 percent. And, as the evidence presented earlier in this chapter showed, the distribution of the personal tax cuts made the individual income tax system less progressive. As a result of these shifts in the scale and composition of federal taxes, by the end of President Reagan's first term the tax load on high-income Americans was more favorable than it had been since the late 1960s.

9.4 The Legacy of Reaganomics to the American Political Economy

I have no way of knowing whether Ronald Reagan and his advisers ever took seriously the idea that a policy mix of big tax cuts and restrictive credit conditions had a realistic chance of yielding the administration's extremely optimistic macroeconomic projections, which were so important to the success of president's fiscal legislation in Congress. Thanks to William Greider's reporting, we can be sure that David Stockman did not.[74] Neither did many of the president's supporters in the financial community. But for Wall Street and high-income people generally, the direct income benefits of the tax cuts, which were worth hundreds of billions of dollars to the upper middle class and the rich, were more than ample reason to endorse Reagan fiscal policy. What we do know in retrospect is that instead of simultaneously producing a decline in inflation and unemployment and a big surge in investment and growth, Reaganomics delivered a crushing disinflationary contraction. When the recovery did come in 1983–1984, it had a classically Keynesian character: The rebound was led by consumer spending based on huge deficits and easier credit.

The experience of Reagan's first term put to rest, probably for good, the claim of some economic theorists that a preannounced and determined commitment to a stringent, anti-inflation monetary policy would quickly prompt producers to post lower price increases, workers to settle for lower wage increases, and lenders to accept lower interest rates without the pressure of a severe recession. Supply-side ideas also did not fare well during these years. It is fair to say that supply-siders generally did not advocate a highly restrictive monetary policy for 1981–1982. In fact, few supply-side proponents initially expressed much interest in the tough monetary policy backed by the administration; apparently most of them believed that fiscal policy would in any event dominate the economy. They soon learned otherwise. As Alan Reynolds, chief economist at Polyconomics, a supply-side consulting firm, lamely admitted: "It is fair to say we didn't recognize that the monetary policy would dominate."[75]

Although the tax cuts clearly did not unleash the dramatic surge of economic activity predicted so confidently by radical supply-side theorists, I think the main intellectual casualty of the Reagan experience was the idea, forcefully promoted over many years by Martin Feldstein, that the combination of tight money and tax concessions for saving and investment was the key to raising business investment and growth. Despite the immediate 29-percent reduction of tax rates on individual capital income, the enormous concessions to business investment in the form of accelerated cost recovery allowances, and the three-stage reduction of earned income tax rates that heavily favored high-income, investment-oriented taxpayers, monetary stringency crippled aggregate demand in 1981 and 1982, which in turn depressed investment and growth. (See Table 9.1 and the associated discussion.) Only after monetary policy was relaxed in late 1982 did demand, investment, and growth revive.

More important than the intellectual casualties of Reagan economic policy were the human victims. The Reagan administration's commitment to disinflation meant that the initial stimulative impact of the tax cuts was neutralized, creating a prolonged period of high unemployment and leaving only the redistributive effects of the Reagan fiscal package. As we saw earlier, this produced windfall gains for the rich and a sizable deterioration of the absolute and relative economic well-being of those with modest incomes. Indexing of the new tax structure helped lock the fiscal changes in place. The point was made well by Robert H. Michel, the House Republican leader, when, just after the president's big tax and budget victories in Congress in July 1981, he said: "Part of the Great Society program has been repealed and because we have indexed the tax cuts to inflation and thus made them permanent, these social programs can't be reinstated except deliberately. We can't back our way into them any more on the back of tax-bracket creep."[76] Two and a half years later, Senator Ernest Hollings of South Carolina, the ranking Democrat on the Budget Committee, drew essentially the same conclusion when he complained in a speech to the Association for a Better New York that Reagan "intentionally created a deficit so large that we Democrats will never have enough money to build the sort of government programs we want."[77] President Reagan's "allowance theory" of spending control was working as planned.

The remarks of Congressman Michel and Senator Hollings touched on what I believe will be the most enduring consequences of the Reagan years. More significant than the initial effects of the reversal of the two-decade-long upward trend of social spending, the reduction in the scale and shift in the composition of federal taxes, or even than the lopsided distribution of the tax-and-spending cuts, which so heavily favored already wealthy households, were the changes achieved by the president in the broader fiscal and political environments constraining future economic and social policy choices. The permanent federal revenue loss imposed by tax-rate reduction and tax-bracket indexing meant, as a practical matter, that Ronald Reagan moved the terms of the economic debate significantly to the right. He made it more difficult than it had been at any time since the 1950s (perhaps since the 1920s) to initiate new federal tax and social-spending measures designed to improve directly the economic well-being of low- and moderate-income citizens.

Moreover, in Washington a policy philosophy emphasizing economic efficiency (as conceived in market terms) now clearly prevails over the idea that the federal government has an obligation to pursue redistributive activities geared to enhancing equity and social justice. The influence on policy of the liberal Democratic spirit of the New Deal and the Great Society, which for the most part had come to be accepted even by Republican officials in the traditional mainstream of the party, has been severely weakened. No one can say with confidence how long this market-oriented philosophy will occupy the center stage of national economic and social policy debates. Perhaps it will not survive a single major electoral victory by the Democrats. For years to come, however, less prosperous Americans may have to be content with what "trickles down."

Yet the Reagan experience also increased the salience of, and sharpened party cleavages over, the great economic and distributional issues that are the heart of class-based politics in America. Such crosscutting issues as civil rights, the counterculture, the environment, and women's liberation, which for a time obscured traditional economic lines of partisan conflict, have been pushed into the background. Under President Reagan the Republican party became more squarely aligned than ever before with the economic interests of the affluent. Galvanized by the Reagan economic program, the Democratic party, although shaken by recent Republican election successes, became just as squarely identified with the interests of moderate- and low-income Americans. Not since the New Deal era of the 1930s have competing economic interests of the classes been more clearly represented by the parties or has the balance of power between the parties been more important to the future shape of macroeconomic and distributional outcomes in the American political economy.

Notes

Index

Notes

Introduction

1. This conceptualization owes much to Robert J. Gordon's remarkable paper, "The Demand for and Supply of Inflation," *Journal of Law and Economics* 18 (1975), 807–857, and to the work of Bruno Frey and his colleagues, which is reviewed in Bruno Frey, "Politico-Economic Models and Cycles," *Journal of Public Economics* 9 (1978), 203–220. Also see Melvin Reder's seminal article, written almost forty years ago, "Theoretical Problems of National Wage-Price Policy," *Canadian Journal of Economics and Political Science* 14 (1948), 46–61; and Douglas A. Hibbs, Jr., "Contemporary Political Economy: An Overview," in Hibbs and Heino Fassbender, eds., *Contemporary Political Economy* (Amsterdam: North Holland, 1981), pp. 3–9.

2. Publicly, of course, politicians and their official economic advisers often speak as if all good things could be achieved simultaneously.

3. Because all presidents to date have been males, I use the male pronoun throughout when referring to the chief executive.

4. Gordon, "Demand for Inflation," p. 807.

5. Ray C. Fair, "The Sensitivity of Fiscal Policy Effects to Assumptions about the Behavior of the Federal Reserve," *Econometrica* 46 (September 1978), 1177.

6. An eloquent case for activism is made by Franco Modigliani, "The Monetarist Controversy or, Should We Forsake Stabilization Policies?" *American Economic Review* 67 (March 1977), 1–19.

7. America's "central bank" consists of the Federal Reserve Board (FRB) in Washington, whose seven governors are appointed by the president with the consent of the Senate for overlapping fourteen-year terms, and whose twelve presidents of the regional reserve banks are elected by their respective boards of directors, subject to FRB veto. The Federal Reserve System's activities are financed by interest receipts from its portfolio of government securities; it receives no budget from Congress. The system's most important function is regulation of the money supply. The growth of the money supply influences the availability of and rate of interest on credit, which in turn profoundly affects macroeconomic activity. The money supply is controlled primarily by the purchase and sale of government securities in the Federal Reserve's portfolio, in accordance with the monthly instructions of the Federal Open Market Committee, which is composed of the seven FRB gover-

nors, the president of the New York Reserve Bank, and four of the remaining reserve bank presidents serving in rotation.

8. See Chapter 8. Federal Reserve governors are aware of the fate suffered by the Bank of Canada (which performs functions equivalent to those of the American Federal Reserve) in 1961, when it refused to carry out the Canadian Cabinet's preferred policies. The office of head of the Bank of Canada, held at the time by Paul Coyne, was declared "vacant" by an act of Parliament, and the bank was stripped of its formal autonomy and put under the direct control of the government.

9. Robert Weintraub, "Congressional Supervision of Monetary Policy," *Journal of Monetary Economics* 4 (1978), 357. The "accord" Weintraub referred to was the March 1951 agreement between the Federal Reserve and the Treasury that relieved the Fed of its obligation to support prices of government bonds by purchasing at par value prices any notes the public would not buy. Although the accord has sometimes been viewed as a victory of the Fed over the Treasury, its main significance is that it made possible an activist monetary policy that greatly facilitated government influence on macroeconomic outcomes in subsequent years.

10. Robert J. Shapiro, "Politics and the Federal Reserve," *Public Interest* 66 (Winter 1982), 126. Also see Sandford Borins, "The Political Economy of the Fed," *Public Policy* 20 (1972) 175–198; Edward J. Kane, "Politics and Fed Policymaking," *Journal of Monetary Economics* 6 (1980), 199–211; James L. Pierce, "The Political Economy of Arthur Burns," *Journal of Finance* 34 (May 1979), 485–504; Sherman Maisel, *Managing the Dollar* (New York: Norton, 1973); John Woolley, *Monetary Politics* (London: Cambridge University Press, 1984); and John Woolley, "Central Banks and Inflation: Influence and Independence," in Leon Lindberg and Charles Maier, eds., *The Political Economy of Global Inflation and Stagnation* (Washington, D.C.: Brookings, 1985).

11. Robert J. Samuelson, "The Fed's Illusionary Independence," *National Journal* (January 21, 1978), 108.

12. One is reminded of President Nixon's remark after administering the oath of office to Arthur Burns, the new chairman of the Federal Reserve, in 1971: "I hope that independently he will conclude that my views are the ones that should be followed." *Time*, "The Economy: Arthur the Independent," March 1, 1971, p. 70. Ironically, although Burns was one of the most accommodating Reserve chairmen in the Fed's history, serving Nixon's interests exceedingly well (see Chapter 8), through artful posturing and forceful statements of intent he managed to maintain an image of fierce independence.

1. Postwar American Macroeconomic Performance in Historical Perspective

1. In 1984 dollars the corresponding real per capita GNP numbers for 1890 and 1980 are $2,800 and $14,300, respectively.

2. Some would argue, with good reason, that the 1981–1983 contraction, which was intentionally induced by the Reagan administration to fight infla-

tion, qualifies as "major." Macroeconomics during Reagan's first term is treated separately in Chapter 9.

3. Data assembled by Arthur Lewis show that the same can be said of the 1870s. See his *Growth and Fluctuations 1870–1913* (London: Allen and Unwin, 1978).

4. During President Reagan's first term the long-standing convention was modified. Now the official unemployment rate is defined as the number of unemployed as a fraction of the total labor force (civilian plus military). This new definition yields an official rate about a tenth of a percentage point lower than that yielded by the old one.

5. The unemployment rate during the first Reagan administration (discussed in Chapter 9) was exceptionally high by postwar standards. Unemployment averaged 7.6 percent in 1981, 9.7 percent in 1982, 9.5 percent in 1983, and 7.6 percent in 1984.

6. Robert Solow, "The Intelligent Citizen's Guide to Inflation," *Public Interest* (Winter 1975), 31.

7. Chapter 3 gives details of the Consumer Price Index and analyzes alternative measures of the price level.

8. *Deflation* means a decline in the price level; *disinflation* refers to a decline in the rate of increase of the price level—in other words, a decline in the inflation rate.

9. For a review of the transition from the small, single-product, geographically bounded, owner-managed, and perhaps more competitive firm of the mid-nineteenth century to the corporate giant of the mid-twentieth century, see Michael Best and William Connolly, *The Politicized Economy*, 2nd ed. (Lexington, Mass.: D. C. Heath, 1982), p. 161ff; and especially Alfred D. Chandler, *The Visible Hand* (Cambridge, Mass.: Harvard University Press, 1977).

In principle there is no necessary monotonic association between price flexibility and industrial competitiveness. A monopolist might quickly adjust prices (upward or downward) to demand in a manner consistent with the extraction of monopoly profits.

10. Evidence showing a similar pattern in the response of wholesale prices and manufacturing wages to cyclical downturns is presented in Jeffrey Sachs's important study "The Changing Cyclical Behavior of Wages and Prices: 1890–1976," *American Economic Review* (March 1980), 78–90. Also see Philip Cagan, *Persistent Inflation* (New York: Columbia University Press, 1979), chap. 3.

Annual data available on nominal (money) compensation per worker in the private nonfarm economy during the 1929–1980 period show that prior to World War II there were five years in which the money wage actually declined (1930, 1931, 1932, 1933, 1938, and 1939), but since the war nominal compensation per worker has never declined.

11. Sachs's more elaborate analyses of manufacturing wage inflation data yielded comparable results (see Sachs, "Wages and Prices," p. 83). Using an unemployment gap variable in place of the output gap term also gives results similar to those in Table 1.2.

12. Sharper estimates of the costs of disinflation based on better measures of gaps in output and unemployment are given in subsequent chapters. A simple model and a crude output gap measure are used here to permit prewar and postwar comparisons.

13. Joseph W. Garbarino, *Wage Policy and Long-Term Contracts* (Washington, D.C.: Brookings, 1962), p. 77ff. Major contracts are defined as those covering more than 5000 workers.

14. Flanagan's study of union versus nonunion wages indicates, however, that most of the cyclical inflexibility of negotiated (union) wages stems from the duration of rather than the staggering of contracts: "First year negotiated wages are almost as sensitive to labor market pressures as non-union wages. Most of the inertia in negotiated wages is a by-product of multi-year labor agreements." Robert J. Flanagan, "Wage Interdependence in Unionized Labor Markets," *Brookings Papers on Economic Activity*, 1967 (3), 673. Also see John Taylor, "Union Wage Settlements during a Disinflation," *American Economic Review* 73 (December 1983), 981–993.

15. Garbarino, *Wage Policy*, p. 77ff. Also, Sachs ("Cyclical Behavior of Wages and Prices") presents data for 1972 showing that 83 percent of labor agreements covering 1000 workers or more had a duration of two or more years.

16. Garbarino, *Wage Policy*, p. 80.

17. Clark Kerr, "Governmental Wage Restraints: Their Limits and Uses in a Mobilized Economy," *American Economic Review* 42 (May 1952), 370; emphasis added.

18. See Robert Flanagan, "Wage Concessions and Long-Term Union Wage Flexibility," *Brookings Papers on Economic Activity*, 1984 (1), 183–216; and Daniel Mitchell, "Shifting Norms in Wage Determination," *Brookings Papers on Economic Activity*, 1985 (2), 523–574.

19. There are, of course, significant exceptions: for example, trends in the prices of electronic calculators, computers, and related goods. Also, commodity and raw-material (food, oil) prices are highly volatile, exhibiting sharp rises and declines.

20. For a comprehensive, factual, institutional history of the evolution of government involvement in the economy through the 1950s, see Merle Fainsod et al., *Government and the American Economy*, 3rd ed. (New York: W. W. Norton, 1959).

21. In the view of some economists, monetary instability was (and is) the primary cause of business cycles. See, for example, Milton Friedman and Anna Schwartz, *A Monetary History of the United States, 1867–1960* (Princeton: Princeton University Press, 1963). For a contrary view that the growth of government (discussed later in this chapter) has been a more important source of macroeconomic stabilization than have changes in the monetary system, see J. Bradford De Long and Lawrence Summers, "The Changing Cyclical Variability of Economic Activity in the United States," in Robert Gordon, ed., *The American Business Cycle: Continuity and Change* (Chicago: University of Chicago Press, 1986).

The M2 measure of money used in Figure 1.7 includes currency plus demand deposits (M1-A) plus other checkable deposits at banks and thrift institutions (M1-B) plus overnight repurchase agreements and Eurodollars, money-market mutual-fund shares, and savings and small-denomination time deposits at commercial banks and thrift institutions.

22. Milton Friedman, in his 1954 lecture delivered in Stockholm, "Why the American Economy Is Depression-Proof," emphasized the importance of federal deposit insurance in stabilizing the supply of money and credit. Reprinted in Friedman, *Dollars and Deficits* (New York: Prentice-Hall, 1968).

23. Benjamin Friedman, "Postwar Changes in American Financial Markets," in Martin Feldstein, ed., *The American Economy in Transition* (Chicago: University of Chicago Press, 1980), p. 66.

24. Robert D. Hershey, Jr., "U.S. Insurance: Critics Grow," *New York Times*, June 8, 1982, p. D1.

25. Friedman, "Postwar Changes," p. 66.

26. Stockman's projections for 1982 are reported in "White House Urging Sizeable Reductions in Loan Guarantees," *New York Times*, March 9, 1981, p. 1, D3. A more dispassionate analyst, Elisabeth Rhyne of Brookings, later estimated that closer to a fifth of all credit advanced in 1982—about 88 billion dollars—flowed through federal credit programs. See Rhyne, "Federal Credit Programs," in Joseph A. Pechman, ed., *Setting National Priorities: The 1984 Budget* (Washington, D.C.: Brookings, 1983), appendix B, p. 231. Trends in the share of credit flowing through federal programs, which rose from about 15 percent in the 1970s to 23 percent in Carter's last year before falling under Reagan, are also discussed in Andrew Carron, "Fiscal Activities outside the Budget," in Joseph A. Pechman, *Setting National Priorities: The 1982 Budget* (Washington, D.C.: Brookings, 1981), appendix A, pp. 261–269.

27. Albert Wojnilower, "The Central Role of Credit Crunches in Recent Financial History," *Brookings Papers on Economic Activity*, 1980 (2), 299–339.

28. See, for example, Edward M. Bernstein's essay "Back to the Gold Standard?" *Brookings Bulletin* (Fall 1980), 8–12 and the essays in Barry Eichengreen, ed., *The Gold Standard in Theory and History* (New York: Methuen, 1985).

29. On the populist movement and bimetallism see James Sundquist, *Dynamics of the Party System* (Washington, D.C.: Brookings, 1973), pp. 85–109; and Richard Hofstadter, *The Age of Reform* (New York: Vintage, 1955), pp. 85–109.

30. For a convenient historical summary of the international gold standard, see Leland B. Yeager, *International Monetary Relations*, 2nd ed. (New York: Harper and Row, 1976).

31. Because the growth rate of the money supply affects inflation and output in current and future years, the inflation rate and the real output gap terms appear with a one-period lag in the feedback equations.

32. Martin Neal Baily, "Stabilization Policy and Private Economic Behavior," *Brookings Papers on Economic Activity*, 1978 (1), 11–50.

33. Computations from data in the March 1979 *Current Population Survey*

indicate that 42 percent of all households received one or more government cash transfers and that such transfers averaged 14 percent of the total money income of households.

34. Nonetheless, as noted in the previous discussion of monetary activism, discretionary countercyclical fiscal actions may contribute indirectly to stabilization by influencing private expectations and behavior.

35. Arthur M. Okun, "Postwar Macroeconomic Performance," in Martin Feldstein, ed., *The American Economy in Transition* (Chicago: University of Chicago Press, 1980), p. 163.

36. Walter Galenson and Robert Smith, "The United States," in John Dunlop and Walter Galenson, eds., *Labor in the Twentieth Century* (New York: Academic Press, 1978), table 1.41, p. 76; and Gary Burtless, "Why Is Insured Unemployment So Low?" *Brookings Papers on Economic Activity,* 1983 (1), 225–253.

37. Joseph E. Hight, "Trends in Unemployment Insurance Wage Replacement, United States 1950–1977," Office of the Assistant Secretary for Policy, Evaluation and Research Office of Income Maintenance, Department of Labor, July 1980. Using slightly different measurement techniques, George Perry concluded that unemployment wage replacement rose from about 39 percent in 1951–1955 to 47 percent in 1977. George L. Perry, "Slowing the Wage Price Spiral: The Macroeconomic View," *Brookings Papers on Economic Activity,* 1978 (2), 283. Between 1939 and the early 1950s, however, wage replacement declined. See Raymund Munts, "Policy Development and Unemployment Insurance," in Goldberg et al., eds., *Federal Policies and Worker States since the 1930s* (Madison, Wis.: Industrial Relations Research Association, 1976).

38. Although public transfers to the unemployed have in recent decades provided a significant cushion against unemployment-induced income losses, this should not be interpreted to mean that recessions confer no economic (or psychological) pain on those affected most directly. See the discussion in Chapter 2.

39. Robert J. Gordon, *Macroeconomics,* 2nd ed. (Boston: Little, Brown, 1981), p. 510; and Robert J. Barro and Chaiput Sahaskul, "Measuring the Average Marginal Tax Rate from the Individual Income Tax," National Bureau of Economic Research, Working Paper No. 1060, July 1983.

40. The sensitivity today of government revenue to changes in output (as well as to changes in inflation and interest rates) is the reason why the Reagan administration, only *weeks* after having achieved passage of 95 percent of their economic program, had to accept dramatically higher estimates of the 1982 fiscal year deficit and felt it necessary to modify the 1982 budget by seeking additional expenditure cuts. See Chapter 9.

41. Using a somewhat different approach, Gordon in *Macroeconomics* arrived at different estimates of the contribution of government size and tax-and-transfer progressivity to the net marginal tax rate.

42. These estimates of course are very much "back of the envelope" and probably should be scaled down somewhat by making investment endogenous through, for example, an IS-LM model. See Alan Blinder and Robert

Solow, "Analytical Foundations of Fiscal Policy," in Alan Blinder et al., *The Economics of Public Finance* (Washington, D.C.: Brookings), pp. 3–115. Yet such estimates are consistent with calculations based on more sophisticated econometric models of the U.S economy. See, for example, Bert G. Hickman and Robert M. Coen, *An Annual Growth Model of the U.S. Economy* (Amsterdam: North-Holland, 1976), table 9.6, p. 194.

43. In a provocative book that attracted a great deal of attention, *The Zero Sum Society* (New York: Basic Books, 1980), Lester Thurow claimed that the growth of economic security has (a) undercut capitalism, (b) reduced the rate of real growth, and (c) weakened American democracy. The first claim is surely true: market forces are no longer unrestrained. The second claim is doubtful in view of the growth record in the postwar period relative to the prewar period, though the counterfactual experience (what growth we might have experienced during the postwar years had an unrestrained market regime remained in place) is difficult to assess—certainly Thurow makes no serious attempt to do so. The third claim amounts to the assertion that democracy is destroying itself; after all, the development of economic security represents the articulation of the American democratic process, with its popular as well as its elitist and special-interest aspects. Thurow's observation seems to rest on the belief that a democracy could deal more effectively with economic problems if the government supplied less security to its citizens, who as a result would be more concerned but disinterested and thus would "make the democratic process work" (p. 24). Thurow's views on this score seem to me to be misguided.

2. The Costs of Unemployment

1. The most divisive issue has been the level at which to peg the "full unemployment" rate of employment. A typical trade union view appears in Nat Goldfinger, "Full Employment: The Neglected Policy," *American Federationist* 79 (November 1972), 7–13. For arguments that measured unemployment is a less serious problem than is something thought, see Martin Feldstein, "The Economics of the New Unemployment," *Public Interest* 33 (Fall 1973), 3–42; and Kenneth W. Clarkson and Roger E. Meiners, "Government Statistics as a Guide to Economic Policy: Food Stamps and the Spurious Increase in Unemployment Rates," *Policy Review* (Summer 1977), 27–54. The most recent major review of unemployment measurement questions sponsored by the federal government is *Counting the Labor Force* (Washington, D.C.: National Commission on Employment and Unemployment Statistics, 1979). Understandably, the commission chose not to confront directly the politically sensitive issue of the full employment rate of unemployment. Also see Helen Ginsburg, *Full Employment and Public Policy* (Lexington, Mass.: D. C. Heath, 1983), and the articles in S. Moses, ed., *Planning for Full Employment, the Annuals of the American Academy of Political Science*, March 1975.

2. Chapter 9 reports evidence on the short-run unemployment-inflation trade-off.

3. Prior to 1966 the age threshold was 14 years and over. During President Reagan's first term, the denominator of the "official" unemployment rate was changed to include the *total* labor force, civilian plus military. The new official rate generally runs about one-tenth of a percentage point below the old rate. Throughout this volume the traditional civilian-rate concept of official unemployment is used.

4. Quoted in Kay L. Schlozman and Sidney Verba, *Injury to Insult* (Cambridge, Mass.: Harvard University Press, 1979), p. 32.

In a detailed investigation of unemployment measurement, a leading macroeconomist, Robert E. Hall, complained that the procedures used to assess job-seeking activity permit "almost meaningless activities like 'checked with friends and relatives' . . . to count a person as unemployed." Robert E. Hall, "The Nature and Measurement of Unemployment," National Bureau of Economic Research, Working Paper no. 252, July 1978, p. 23. Perhaps so, but when *New York Times* reporters interviewed some of the 26,200 people in Baltimore who lined up in September 1981 to apply for 75 entry-level clerical and blue-collar positions with the Social Security Administration—jobs paying between $7000 and $12,000 annually—most respondents indicated that they had learned of the jobs by word of mouth. "Officials Say 26,200 Applied for 75 Jobs in Baltimore," *New York Times*, September 21, 1981, p. 38. Similarly, the "word spread fast" in Hempstead, Long Island, in September 1982 when 4508 people, many of them "highly over-qualified," formed lines in the predawn darkness for several days to apply for 296 jobs, ranging from dishwasher to desk clerk, at a new Marriott hotel. Interestingly, the official unemployment rate in suburban Nassau and Suffolk counties at the time of this episode was 6.8 percent—well below the corresponding national rate of 9.8 percent. "4,508 Line Up for 296 L.I. Jobs from Dishwashers to Clerks," *New York Times*, September 28, 1982, p. 1. No doubt informal checking-around also helped boost to about 20,000 the turnout of applicants in January 1983 for 200 openings at a suburban Milwaukee auto plant. The crowd was so large that the company processed the job seekers at State Fair Park. "Looking for Work," *New York Times*, January 18, 1983. In these and a great many other similar cases, casual job-seeking activity prompted quite impressive demonstrations of available labor supply.

5. Analysis of data from the 1970s by Kim Clark and Laurence Summers in "Labor Market Dynamics and Unemployment: A Reconsideration," *Brookings Papers on Economic Activity*, 1979 (1), 13–72, indicates that only about half of those reporting layoff unemployment return to jobs in the same occupation and industry.

6. Robert E. Hall, "Why Is the Unemployment Rate So High at Full Employment?" *Brookings Papers on Economic Activity*, 1970 (3), 369–402. As the reference in note 4 makes plain, Hall has shifted from a moderate liberal position to quite a conservative position on the "meaning" of unemployment statistics.

7. A similar range of unemployment indicators was proposed by Julius Shiskin in "Employment and Unemployment: The Doughnut or the Hole," *Monthly Labor Review* (February 1976), 3–10.

8. What follows is based on the comprehensive reports in the March 1979 issue of the *Monthly Labor Review*, pp. 13–52.

9. Established by the Social Security Act of 1935 and financed by federal and state payroll taxes assigned to the UI trust fund administered by the Department of Labor, the basic federal-state system of unemployment insurance provides twenty-six weeks of benefit payments. As noted in the Introduction, UI wage replacement now averages between 40 and 50 percent of posttax earnings, although there is great variation across states in benefit levels.

The Amendments of 1970 established a "permanent" program allowing states to extend benefits for thirteen additional weeks when the state unemployment rate among insured workers exceeds 4 percent or when the national rate among insured workers exceeds 4.5 percent. Costs are shared equally by the federal government and the states. Congress must allocate special funds for payments to continue after thirty-nine weeks. This happened during the 1974–1975 recession, when an additional twenty-six weeks of eligibility was authorized, which extended benefits to sixty-five weeks at a cost of about 6.2 billion dollars from 1975 to 1977.

The Amendments of 1976 made coverage of wage and salary workers nearly universal, but because entrants new to the labor force and those who leave jobs voluntarily are not eligible and because the long-term unemployed exhaust their benefits, effective coverage of the unemployed is less than universal. For example, in the second half of 1982 only about 45 percent of those officially unemployed received benefits, and in 1983 only 39 percent received benefits. This represents a substantial decline from earlier coverage levels (the effectiveness of the UI system peaked during the 1975 recession, when nearly 78 percent of the unemployed received benefits) and reflects the Reagan administration's successful efforts to trim back both coverage and benefit extensions. The Omnibus Budget Reconciliation Act of 1981 (the vehicle for most of the Reagan administration's 1982 budget cuts) made it very difficult for states to qualify for extended benefits. This act raised the threshold to 5 percent unemployment among insured workers and excluded from the calculation of insured (threshold) rates those unemployed who had exhausted twenty-six weeks of regular benefits. In August 1982, however, amid soaring unemployment rates, Congress created a 2.2-billion-dollar temporary program of supplemental benefits that provided extra compensation for six to ten weeks, depending on the circumstances of individual states. The program cushioned some of the effects of the 1981 cutbacks.

More details of the UI system are provided in Daniel S. Hamermesh, *Jobless Pay and the Economy* (Baltimore: Johns Hopkins University Press, 1977); Guy Burtless, "Why Is Insured Unemployment So Low?" *Brookings Papers on Economic Activity*, 1983 (1), 225–254; and Congressional Budget Office, *Promoting Employment and Maintaining Incomes with Unemployment Insurance*, March 1985.

10. As young and inexperienced workers grow older and acquire desired job skills and experience during the next decade, and as the proportion of younger and unskilled workers in the labor force declines, demographic pressure on unemployment will decrease.

11. Schlozman and Verba, *Injury to Insult*.

12. M. Harvey Brenner, *Estimating the Social Costs of National Economic Policy: Implications for Mental and Physical Health, and Aggression* (Washington, D.C.: Government Printing Office, 1976); and idem, *Mental Illness and the Economy* (Cambridge, Mass.: Harvard University Press, 1973).

13. Arthur Okun, "Potential GNP: Its Measurement and Significance," American Statistical Association, *Proceedings of the Business and Economics Statistics Section*, 1962.

14. Recall that the difference of natural logarithms, say $\ln X_t - \ln X_{t-1}$, gives proportional changes in X that are symmetrical about 0. Hence Q appears in log difference form in equations (2.1) and (2.2).

15. Data on Q^N and U^N were taken from the spring 1983 revision sheet for table B-1 of Robert J. Gordon's *Macroeconomics* (Boston: Little, Brown, 1981). Gordon calls Q^N and U^N the "natural" levels of real output and unemployment. Appendix C of Gordon's book describes the methods used to construct the natural unemployment and natural real output series. The Q^N series is similar to the Y^* data (trend per capita real output) used in Chapter 1 here. The U^N series allows for the secular increase in noncyclical unemployment discussed in the last section. From the mid-1970s on, Gordon estimates U^N to be 6 percent. Therefore, unemployment rates held below 6 percent now tend to generate ever-increasing inflation rates. See the estimates of the Phillips-curve unemployment-inflation trade-off in Chapter 9.

16. This estimate is probably on the conservative side. Two percent is the lower bound of contemporary estimates of the Okun's Law multiplier, which ranges between 2.0 and 2.5. Okun's original estimate was about 3.0 percent, now generally considered to have been too high. For statistical reasons not worth developing here, one obtains a somewhat higher implied multiplier by regressing movements in unemployment on real output changes and taking the inverse of the slope coefficient. For a discussion of these issues see George L. Perry, "Potential Output and Productivity," *Brookings Papers on Economic Activity*, 1977 (1), 11–47, and especially the comments on this paper; and John A. Tatum, "Economic Growth and Unemployment: A Reappraisal of the Conventional View," *Federal Reserve Board of St. Louis Review* (October 1978), 16–22.

17. Gordon attempted to quantify the amount by which the real output cost of unemployment should be discounted for the imputed value of the leisure time "enjoyed" by the unemployed. He estimated that the net social welfare loss of each extra percentage point of unemployment is perhaps 75 percent of the gross cost discussed in the text. Robert J. Gordon, "The Welfare Cost of Higher Unemployment," *Brookings Papers on Economic Activity*, 1973 (1), 133–195.

18. For a more detailed discussion of this issue see Arthur M. Okun, *Prices and Quantities* (Washington, D.C.: Brookings, 1981), chap. 7.

19. This trend is documented in Richard B. Freeman, "The Evolution of the American Labor Market," in Martin Feldstein, ed., *The American Economy in Transition* (Chicago: University of Chicago Press, 1980), pp. 349–396.

20. Martin Feldstein, "The Private and Social Costs of Unemployment," *American Economic Review, Papers and Proceedings* 68 (May 1978), 155–158; emphasis added.

21. Martin Feldstein, "The Effect of Unemployment Insurance on Temporary Layoff Unemployment," *American Economic Review* 68 (December 1978), table 1, p. 840. For the early 1980s the Congressional Budget Office estimated the average net wage replacement rate to be 45 to 50 percent. See CBO, *Promoting Employment*, p. 79.

22. Edward Gramlich, "The Distributional Effects of Higher Unemployment," *Brookings Papers on Economic Activity*, 1974 (2), 293–341; and Edward Gramlich and Deborah Laren, "How Widespread Are Income Losses in a Recession?" in D. Lee Bawden, ed., *The Social Contract Revisited* (Washington, D.C.: Urban Institute, 1984), pp. 157–180.

23. Notice in Table 2.4 that when income is controlled the probability of unemployment is lower for females than for males.

24. This is smaller than the aggregate income and output costs discussed earlier in this chapter—a loss of 2.0 percent or more of GNP for each extra percentage point of unemployment—because the income concept considered here (earned personal income) is narrower. Labor income is less responsive to contractions than is aggregate output.

25. It should be mentioned that each dollar of transfer income therefore offsets more than a dollar of lost pretax earned income because transfers are not fully taxed. How much more depends on the applicable marginal tax rate. The average marginal rate in the late 1970s and early 1980s was in the vicinity of 30 percent; it was somewhat less for low-income groups and, of course, greater for high-income groups. Before 1979 unemployment compensation was exempt from taxation as a result of a series of Internal Revenue Service rulings. The Revenue Act of 1978 specified that benefits were to be taxed when benefits plus other earnings exceeded $20,000 per year for individuals and $25,000 for couples. In 1982 Congress lowered the thresholds to $12,000 and $18,000, respectively. These changes are significant for seasonal workers (for example, those in the construction trades) and for families in which both spouses work.

26. Evidence on the response of the income distribution to movements in unemployment (and inflation) is presented in Chapter 3.

3. The Costs of Inflation

1. A useful history of the CPI is given in Bureau of Labor Statistics, *The Consumer Price Index: History and Techniques*, Bulletin No. 1517.

2. Not surprisingly, workers with longer contracts are more likely to be covered by inflation escalators. In 1978 more than 70 percent of workers in bargaining units with three-year contracts were covered by cost-of-living escalators, whereas only about 9 percent of workers in units with one-year agreements were covered by escalator clauses. For more detailed information, see "Indexation of Wages and Retirement Income in the United States,"

Federal Reserve Bank of New York *Quarterly Review*, Autumn 1978. The big 1981–1982 construction (discussed in Chapter 9) weakened unions substantially and reduced COLA coverage.

3. An adjustment is made only in years when the CPI is at least 3 percent higher than it was in the time of previous adjustment. Legislation signed into law on April 20, 1983 (the bipartisan Social Security rescue plan) deferred to January 1 cost-of-living benefit increases that had previously gone into effect in July. Because of a curious congressional oversight, for several years following enactment of the policy change in 1972 the benefits promised to active workers were actually overindexed to inflation by a substantial margin. Active workers' promised benefits rose along with their nominal wages (which of course reflected inflation) and then were *additionally* increased with each 3-percent rise in the CPI. Real promised benefits therefore rose in proportion to the rate of money wage inflation *plus* price inflation. The 1977 amendments to the Social Security Act corrected this bizarre legislative error. An account of this episode and a general history of the Social Security system appear in Martha Derthick, *Policymaking for Social Security* (Washington, D.C.: Brookings, 1979).

4. Notice that the CPI may also be expressed as the weighted average of current item prices relative to base period prices, with weights corresponding to the reference period expenditure shares of each commodity (that is, corresponding to the average expenditure for each item in the survey population during the reference period):

$$\text{CPI}_t = \sum_i w_{i0} \frac{P_{it}}{P_{i0}}, \qquad \text{where } w_{i0} = \frac{q_{i0}P_{i0}}{\sum_i q_{i0}P_{i0}}$$

In practice the CPI is occasionally rebased so that the base period for the item prices, P_{i0}, is different from the expenditure survey reference period for the commodity bundle, $\sum_i q_{i0}$.

5. Prior computations of the CPI were based on 1960–1961, 1947–1949, and 1934–1936 surveys of the expenditures of urban wage and clerical workers (about 45 percent of the population in the 1970s). BLS continues to publish the wage and clerical earners index (CPI-W), which is the basis for most indexing agreements, but it differs very little from the all-urban index (CPI-U) used in Table 3.1 and later calculations. When the underlying market basket is revised, the revised index is simply linked to prior ones to form a continuous series. Bureaucratic inertia seems to be the only explanation for the fact that the most recent 1972–1973 expenditure weights were not incorporated into the index until 1978. In some respects it is unfortunate that the 1972–1973 weight revision just missed registering the reduction in energy consumption following the October 1973 OPEC-induced quadrupling of world oil prices.

6. It is possible to estimate the orders of magnitude involved by making strong assumptions about consumers' indifference curves based on the the-

ory of consumer demand. A good illustration appears in Steven Braithwait, "The Substitution Bias of the Laspeyres Price Index: An Analysis Using Estimated Cost-of-Living Indexes," *American Economic Review* 70 (March 1980), 64–77. Over the period 1958–1973, Braithwait estimates that the upward cost-of-living bias in the fixed-weights (Laspeyres) price index averaged only 0.1 percent per year. In subsequent years of higher inflation and higher relative price changes (see the discussion ahead), the upward bias undoubtedly has been greater.

7. For detailed discussion see Alan Blinder, "The Consumer Price Index and the Measurement of Recent Inflation," *Brookings Papers on Economic Activity* 1980 (2), 539–565; Phillip Cagan and Geoffrey Moore, *The Consumer Price Index: Issues and Alternatives* (Washington, D.C.: American Enterprise Institute, 1981); Ann Dougherty and Robert Van Order, "Inflation, Housing Costs and the Consumer Price Index," *American Economic Review* 72 (March 1982), 154–164; and Robert J. Gordon, "The Consumer Price Index: Measuring Inflation and Causing It," *Public Interest* 63 (Spring 1981), 112–134.

8. Between 1953 and 1964 all mortgage interest costs were included.

9. The contribution of interest rates to the "cost of living" is also distorted, because the deductibility of nominal interest payments from taxable income is not taken into account. The net-of-tax real cost of borrowed funds has actually been negative for many high-income mortgagees in an era of high inflation and, hence, high nominal interest rates. This is one of the chief reasons why real property has been such an attractive investment for the rich. Further discussion of this important point appears later in this chapter.

10. The data assembled by the Bureau of Labor Statistics back to 1967 on the revised CPI, which incorporates the same rental equivalence method of measuring home ownership costs used in constructing the PCE deflator, confirm that the behavior of the traditional CPI is correctly attributed to its peculiar treatment of housing.

11. The PCE implicit-price deflator may also be written as the weighted average of current prices relative to base-period prices, with weights corresponding to the implied reference period expenditure shares of the current consumption bundle:

$$\text{PCE}_{t(\text{current weights})} = \sum_i w_{it} \frac{P_{it}}{P_{i0}}, \quad \text{where } w_{it} = \frac{P_{i0}q_{it}}{\sum_i P_{i0}q_{it}}$$

The base or reference period for the P_{i0} is currently 1972.

12. Strictly speaking, a current-weights price index should only be used to assess *cumulative* inflation after the reference period. For a technical analysis of this often overlooked point, see Jack E. Triplett, "Reconciling the CPI and the PCE Deflators," *Monthly Labor Review* (September 1981), 3–15. But the current-weights PCE (and GNP) deflators are so often used to measure pre– and post–reference period inflation rates that rises in these indexes over the entire 1950–1981 range are shown in Table 3.1.

13. The natural employment surplus/deficit is the difference that would have existed between federal tax revenues and federal expenditures if the economy were operating at the natural rate of output and unemployment—that is, the rate of output and unemployment sustainable without accelerating inflation. The natural employment surplus/deficit registers the fiscal stimulus—expansionary when negative (deficit) and contractive when positive (surplus)—to economic activity. Comparisons over time in a growing economy are facilitated by taking the natural employment surplus/deficit as a percentage of natural employment output (natural GNP). The natural employment surplus/deficit and natural employment output data are taken from the spring 1981 revision sheet for table B-2 of Robert J. Gordon's *Macroeconomics* (Boston: Little, Brown, 1981).

14. The real money supply growth rate is simply the nominal money supply growth rate less the inflation rate (here the traditional CPI rate). When the real money supply growth rate is persistently positive, the authorities are accommodating inflation, which tends to stimulate economic activity; when it is persistently negative, policy is leaning against inflation, which tends to contract economic activity.

15. A useful rule of thumb for the postwar period is that each extra percentage point of unemployment sustained for a year yields a decline of approximately 0.5 percentage point in the underlying inflation rate.

16. Quoted in *Business Week*, May 22, 1978, p. 109.

17. Conventional inflation measures naturally declined by a greater amount (from about 10 percent per annum in 1974 to 5–6 percent per annum in 1976) because the big food and energy shocks—relative price increases—passed through the economy and were not repeated immediately.

18. Monetarists correctly identify the proximate source of inflation as sustained growth in the money supply in excess of the growth rate of the natural GNP. In their view disinflation requires nothing more than a "tight" monetary policy—that is, a decelerating growth rate of the nominal (and hence the real) money supply. The problem is that monetarists by and large have underestimated the reduction of output and employment and overestimated the decline of inflation initially produced by monetary decelerations.

19. The distribution of income for all households—families and unrelated individuals—exhibits a pattern very similar to that shown for families alone in Table 3.2. Over time "families" is a more comparable concept, and so the analysis here is confined to family income shares.

The income concept in Tables 3.2 and 3.3 (known as "census income") lies halfway between market income (which is primarily what we are interested in here) and net or "final" income. Census income includes cash transfers, but does not include in-kind transfers, the implicit value of public goods (for example, education), or tax liabilities. Chapter 7 presents analyses of movements in the distribution of net income in relation to partisan political forces. The distribution of income shifted dramatically toward the rich in years after 1980 under the macroeconomic and distributional policies of President Reagan. See Chapter 9.

20. For analyses spanning a much longer time period, over which there were significant secular trends, see Alan Blinder, "The Level and Distribution of Economic Wellbeing," in Martin Feldstein, ed., *The American Economy in Transition* (Chicago: University of Chicago Press, 1980). Using a slightly different income concept, Blinder reports some consistent data spanning the late 1920s and the early 1960s. Also see Jeffrey G. Williamson and Peter H. Lindert, *American Inequality: A Macroeconomic History* (New York: Academic Press, 1980). Including in-kind transfer benefits in personal income yields a modest trend toward greater equality. See Douglas Hibbs, Jr., and Christopher Dennis, "The Politics and Economics of Income Distribution Outcomes in the Postwar U.S.," November 1986, unpublished.

21. See Blinder's review in "The Level and Distribution of Economic Wellbeing."

22. In other words, if income distribution data could be accurately adjusted for demographic changes, there probably would be a trend toward greater equality that is masked by the raw numbers. Also, if it could be unambiguously measured, the distribution of *lifetime* incomes would undoubtedly show a stronger trend toward more equality than does the measured distribution of annual incomes. For discussion of these issues, see Morton Paglin, "The Measurement and Trend of Inequality: A Basic Revision," *American Economic Review* 65 (September 1975), 598–609; and Sheldon Danziger et al., "The Measurement and Trend of Inequality: Comment," *American Economic Review* 67 (June 1977), 505–512.

23. Alan Blinder and Howard Esaki, "Macroeconomic Activity and Income Distribution in the Postwar United States," *Review of Economics and Statistics* (November 1978), 604–609. Also see Alan Blinder and Rebecca West, "Macroeconomics, Income Distribution and Poverty," National Bureau of Economic Research, Working Paper No. 1567, February 1985.

24. Notice that ordinary least-squares estimation automatically imposes these cross-equation constraints:

$$\sum_1^5 (a_{0i} + a_{1i}) = 1.0$$

$$\sum_1^5 b_{1i} = \sum_1^5 b_{2i} = \sum_1^5 (c_{1i} + c_{2i}) = \sum_1^5 e_{i(t)} = 0$$

25. Regression estimates using alternative measures of price inflation (for example, the rate of change of the GNP deflator) are very similar to those in Table 3.3. Purging the equations of autocorrelated errors using autoregressive-generalized least-squares estimation (which of course nullifies the cross-equation constraints listed in note 24) also yields estimates very similar to those reported in Table 3.3. The most pertinent coefficient estimates for the GLS equations are as follows:

Variable	Lowest quintile	Second quintile	Third quintile	Fourth quintile	Highest quintile
Unemployment	−0.098**	−0.105**	−0.026	0.041	0.224**
	(0.027)	(0.018)	(0.013)	(0.021)	(0.043)
Inflation	0.021	0.008	−0.003	−0.008	−0.006
	(0.011)	(0.008)	(0.007)	(0.009)	(0.020)
Autoregressive correction (AR_q)	AR_2	AR_3	AR_4	AR_1	AR_3

** Significant at the 0.01 level, two-tail test.

26. Previous empirical studies using a variety of methods applied to income distribution data available through the 1960s and early 1970s reach similar conclusions about the distributional impact of inflation and unemployment. See Charles Metcalf, *An Econometric Model of the Income Distribution* (Chicago: Markhorn, 1972); Thad Mirer, "The Effects of Macroeconomic Fluctuations on the Income Distribution," *Review of Income and Wealth* 19 (December 1973), 214–224; Paul Schultz, "Secular Trends and Cyclical Behavior of Income Distribution in the United States, 1944–1965," in L. Soltow, ed., *Six Papers on the Size Distribution of Wealth and Income* (New York: Columbia University Press, 1968); and Lester Thurow, "Analyzing the American Income Distribution," *American Economic Review* 60 (May 1970), 261–269.

27. Recall the rule of thumb given in note 15.

28. As the great nineteenth-century British economist Alfred Marshall put it, "The same change of prices affects the purchasing power of money to different persons in different ways. For him who can seldom afford to have meat, a fall of one-fourth in the price of meat accompanied by a rise of one-fourth in that of bread means a fall in the purchasing power of money; his wages will not go so far as before. While to his richer neighbour, who spends twice as much on meat as on bread, the change acts the other way."

29. Robinson G. Hollister and John L. Palmer, "The Impact of Inflation on the Poor," in K. E. Boulding and M. Pfaff, eds., *Redistribution to the Rich and the Poor* (Belmont, Calif.: Wadsworth, 1972), 240–270. Palmer and Michael Barth carry this sort of analysis forward to 1974 in "The Distributional Effects of Inflation and Higher Unemployment," in M. Moon and E. Smolensky, eds., *Improving Measures of Economic Wellbeing* (New York: Academic Press, 1977), 201–239. For this more recent period, however, they continue to use 1960–1961 income group–specific consumption bundles. Analysis based on the most recently available 1972–1973 consumption bundles appear later in this chapter.

30. In 1960 the official level of poverty income for a family of four (two parents plus two children) was $3022.

31. Computed from Hollister and Palmer, "Impact of Inflation," table 4, p. 245.

32. Data for what corresponds roughly to the second and fourth quintiles

of the expenditure survey sample were omitted from Table 3.4 (and Table 3.6) to conserve space. The expenditure patterns (Table 3.4) and inflation experiences (Table 3.6) for the omitted classes, however, are consistent with the relationship reported.

Because the average size of low-income households is smaller than that of high-income households, per capita household incomes are less unequal than those shown in the tables. Average size rises monotonically from 1.9 persons per household in the $3000–$3999 class to 3.8 persons per household in the $20,000–$24,999 class. The corresponding per person incomes therefore range from approximately $1800 in the lowest income class to $5800 in the next-to-highest income class. Per capita household income is not clearly a superior comparative index of real financial well-being, however. Household economies of scale, division of labor, family ("public") goods, and other factors make real income comparisons across households of varying size a very tricky business. For further discussion of this point, see Edward P. Lazerar and Robert T. Michael, "Family Size and the Distribution of Real Per Capita Income," *American Economic Review* 70 (March 1980), 91–107.

33. See, for example, Leslie E. Nultz, "How Inflation Hits the Majority," *Challenge* (January/February 1979), 32–38; and Gar Alperovitz and Jeff Faux, "Controls and the Basic Necessities," *Challenge* (May/June 1980), 21–29. These and many other analyses exaggerate inflation of the "necessities" primarily because home ownership is included in the necessities consumption bundle. Shelter is certainly a necessity; ownership of a home is not. Indeed, as pointed out earlier, acquisition of real property was a major form of investment for the middle class and especially the upper middle classes during the 1970s. According to the Bureau of Labor Statistics, *Consumer Expenditure Survey: Interview Diary and Interview Survey Data, 1972–73*, Bulletin 1992, 1978, table 1, pp. 24–25, for example, only 5.7 percent of the households with incomes under $3000 were amortizing home mortgage debt. The percentage rises steadily with income, peaking at 64 percent for households with 1972–1973 average incomes exceeding $25,000.

An enlightened discussion of the necessities/nonnecessities issue appears in Joseph Minarik, "Inflation in the Necessities," *The Brookings Bulletin* 16 (Spring 1980), 8–10.

34. It is important to understand that the income class–specific price indexes and inflation rates shown in Table 3.6 are not in any way influenced by my designation of the goods and services in the CPI consumption bundle as "necessities" and "nonnecessities."

35. Indeed Robert Michael's analysis of micro-household data over the period 1967–1974 indicates that the dispersion of inflation rates *within* socio-economic groups far exceeds the between-group dispersions. His analysis of income group–specific inflation rates in consistent with the results reported here. See Robert Michael, "Variation across Households in the Rate of Inflation," *Journal of Money, Credit and Banking* 11 (February 1979), 32–46.

36. Recall also that the CPI fails to take account of the tax deductability of home mortgage interest payments and during the sample period confused

home asset appreciation with owned shelter costs. These factors biased the index upward disproportionately for high-income groups, who tend to have heavy home expenditures and investments. See the detailed analysis of Ann Dougherty and Robert Van Order, "Inflation, Housing Costs and the Consumer Price Index," *American Economic Review* 72 (March 1982), 154–164.

37. Inflation also has not been higher for the aged. A study by Michael Boskin and Michael Hurd, "Are Inflation Rates Different for the Elderly?" National Bureau of Economic Research, Working Paper No. 943, July 1982, shows negligible differences across age groups in cumulative and annual inflation over 1961–1981.

38. See Joseph Minarik, "The Size Distribution of Income during Inflation," *Review of Income and Wealth* 25 (December 1979), 377–392. A less technical report of this research appears in Minarik's "Who Wins, Who Loses from Inflation?" *Challenge* (January/February 1979), 26–31.

39. This is a much broader measure of financial well-being than the census income data used in Tables 3.2 and 3.3. It includes census income (defined in Table 3.2) less all taxes plus income-in-kind plus changes in the value of assets (such as bonds, stocks, and real property). The comprehensive income concept therefore includes changes in *wealth* or net worth as well as household consumption.

40. Minarik also undertook simulations of the effects of bigger inflationary surges (an increase of 5 percentage points in the inflation rate) and of the impact of extra inflation concentrated in food and fuel. The results of these experiments were similar to those reported here. Analogous simulations of the impact of increased inflation on census incomes (a narrower income measure than accrued comprehensive incomes) showed greater adverse effects on low-income groups. A sustained 2-percentage-point increase in inflation reduced the average real census income of low-income groups by 0.6 percent, had little effect on middle-income households, and had the largest adverse impact on the upper-income classes.

41. Hollister and Palmer, "Impact of Inflation," p. 255.

42. An illustration of what I have in mind here is Robert Pear's front page *New York Times* article entitled "Inflation Wiped Out Gains in Earnings in 70's" (April 25, 1982, p. 1), which appeared along with many similar stories after income data from the 1980 census were released by the Census Bureau. I shall provide no systematic analysis of media coverage of the impact of inflation on real income, but by scanning the relevant digests readers readily may confirm that the *Times* headline above is quite typical of press reports since the mid-1970s.

43. The connection is exaggerated for two reasons. First, personal disposable income—market income plus cash transfers less tax payments and social insurance contributions—is a conservative measure of economic well-being, though probably the best one available. It is conservative because it does not include the market value of such targeted noncash benefits as Medicaid, Medicare, food stamps, subsidized credit, and housing assistance and also because it excludes the contribution to standards of living of such quasi-public goods as public hospitals and public education, as well as of such pure

public goods as national defense, police and fire services, public utilities, and so on. Inasmuch as the value of these excluded goods has almost certainly increased relative to measured disposable income during the last decade, the latter underestimates the growth in "true" standards of living.

Second and more important, as I explained earlier in this chapter, the traditional CPI-based inflation rate exaggerated increases in the "true" cost of living until the revisions of 1983 and 1985. Hence, when it is used to deflate nominal disposable income, the real income growth rate is biased downward. I use the traditional CPI because during the postwar period it has been the most closely watched price index (by the media, voters, and politicians), and because it puts assertions about the costs of inflation on the strongest possible footing.

44. Households in which pretax incomes do not rise with inflation experience a decline in real income without any decline in tax burdens. From January 1985 to January 1987 federal tax rates were indexed to changes in the CPI during the previous year.

45. For details see Eugene Steurle and Michael Hartzmark, "Individual Income Taxation, 1947–79," *National Tax Journal* 34 (June 1981), 145–166. Also see Table 3.8 and Chapter 9.

46. Adjusted gross income, as the notes in Table 3.8 indicate, is a somewhat narrower concept of income than total personal income. Also, Table 3.8 deals only with federal income taxes. The tax rates in this table may therefore appear a little higher than those implied by the average rates in column 2 of Table 3.7, which are based on all tax and social insurance payments as a fraction of total personal income.

47. Effective income tax rates, which account for about 70 percent of total taxes on personal income, also increased over the period from 11 percent of personal income in 1960–1964 (the first subperiod for which data on federal plus state income tax payments are available) to 13.8 percent in 1981–1982.

48. The average effective tax rate on personal incomes is equal to [(GPTX + GPSIN)/GPY], as in column 1 of Table 3.7. Note that in the regressions the tax rates are expressed as proportions, not percentages.

49. Real personal income per capita increased from 1,971 1967 dollars in 1947 to 3,985 1967 dollars in 1979.

50. These results and conclusions are consistent with the extensive analysis of Emil M. Sunley and Joseph A. Peckman, "Inflation Adjustment for the Individual Income Tax," in Henry J. Aaron, ed. *Inflation and the Income Tax* (Washington, D.C.: Brookings, 1976), pp. 153–167.

51. Disposable personal income, GYD, equals personal income, GPY (which in the national accounts includes cash transfers to persons, GPT), less personal tax payments and social insurance contributions (GPTX + GPSIN). Personal disposable income can therefore be expressed in the usual way as personal income times 1 minus the conventional tax rate,

$$GYD = \left[1 - \left(\frac{GPTX + GPSIN}{GPY} \right) \right] \cdot GPY$$

or as personal income less transfers times the transfer-adjusted net tax rate,

$$GYD = \left[1 - \left(\frac{GPTX + GPSIN - GPT}{GPY - GPT}\right)\right] \cdot (GPY - GPT)$$

52. For a detailed and critical review of such thinking, see Edmund S. Phelps, *Inflation Policy and Unemployment Theory* (London: Macmillan, 1972), chap. 5.

53. Partitioning income between labor and capital is difficult for unincorporated business and is not relevant for the public sector.

54. All variables in equation (3.4) are defined as in columns 1, 4, 6, and 7 of Table 3.7 and are expressed in percentage points.

55. This is about twice the magnitude of the energy weight in the CPI and reflects the indirect as well as the direct effects of the energy price shocks on incomes.

56. This partitioning of the real income slowdown between energy shocks and (policy-induced) output contractions is virtually identical to that arrived at by Michael Bruno in his comparative study of the productivity slowdown in industrial countries. See Michael Bruno, "World Shocks, Macroeconomic Response, and the Productivity Puzzle," National Bureau of Economic Research, Working Paper No. 942, July 1982. In the medium run moves in real incomes and productivity are virtually one to one, so the results are complementary.

57. The relation between profit shares and rates of return is given by the identity $\pi/Y = (\pi/K) \cdot (K/Y)$, where π/Y is the profit share, π/K is return on capital, and K/Y is the capital-output ratio.

58. Although I refer to the resulting series as "profits," the sum of corporate profits and net interest payments to corporate bondholders in fact yields total capital income. The inclusion of net interest softens the profits slide since the late 1960s (discussed later) because of the growth of corporate debt finance that was encouraged by the interaction of the corporate tax structure and inflation.

59. For extensive discussions of these and related profit data series, see Daniel M. Holland and Stewart C. Myers, "Trends in Corporate Profitability and Capital Costs," in R. Lindsay, ed., *The Nation's Capital Needs: Three Studies* (New York: Committee for Economic Development, 1979); Michael C. Lovell, "The Profit Picture: Trends and Cycles," *Brookings Papers on Economic Activity* 1978 (3), 769–788; William Nordhaus, "The Falling Share of Profits," *Brookings Papers on Economic Activity* 1974 (1), 169–217; and Martha S. Scanlon, "Postwar Trends in Corporate Rates of Return," *Public Policy and Capital Formation* (Washington, D.C.: Board of Governors, Federal Reserve, 1981), pp. 75–84. Most studies of corporate profits deal with the nonfinancial corporate sector; however, the data on the total corporate sector mimic closely the series for nonfinancial corporations. Therefore the results reported here are comparable to those of other studies.

60. Some of the most intriguing conjectures appear in Nordhaus, "Falling Share of Profits."

61. Because corporate product comes largely from the manufacturing sector, manufacturing capacity utilization is a better indicator of the business cycle here than is the GNP gap used earlier.

62. Walter Y. Oi, "Labor as a Quasi-Fixed Factor," *Journal of Political Economy* 70 (December 1962), 538–555.

63. Any decline in profit income depresses the rate of return in the short run, because the stock of physical capital is fixed—it represents a sunk cost. That is why the regression results show that the rate of return is more sensitive to business cycle fluctuations than is the profit share.

64. It has long been understood that the movement of wage and profit shares over the business cycle is in large part due to cyclical movements in labor costs. See, for example, Albert Burger, "Relative Movements in Wages and Profits," *Federal Reserve Bank of St. Louis Review* 55 (February 1973), 8–16; Edwin Kuh, "Income Distribution and Employment over the Business Cycle," in J. Duesenberry et al., eds., *Brookings Quarterly Econometric Model of the United States* (Chicago: Rand McNally, 1965). 227–278; and Thor Hultgren, *Costs, Prices and Profits: Their Cyclical Relations* (New York: National Bureau of Economic Research, 1965). These issues are analyzed from a Marxist point of view in Thomas Weisskopf, "Marxist Crisis Theory and the Rate of Profit in the Postwar U.S. Economy," *Cambridge Journal of Economics* 3 (1979), 341–378.

65. In setting up the regressions in Table 3.10 that underlie this conclusion, I assume that profits affect output (via investment) primarily in subsequent years. In other words, there is little simultaneous feedback from profits to output in the annual data series.

66. The tax legislation introduced by the Reagan administration and passed by Congress in 1981 changed the situation significantly. See Chapter 9.

67. One interesting speculation is that FIFO accounting was (and to some extent still is) widely retained because bonus arrangements and other forms of executive compensation often are tied to reported nominal pretax profits. This would appear to be an irrational compensation system under inflation, however, and we are left with the mystery of why it survived.

68. Because bondholders are taxed on nominal interest income, however, the net impact on the effective rate of tax on *capital* income as a whole depends on the difference between corporate and personal tax rates. Although corporate tax rates during the postwar period generally exceeded personal rates, the effective rate reduction via the treatment of interest payments and income clearly was less for total capital income than for corporate income. It should also be emphasized that inflation, strictly speaking, cannot be treated as exogenous to tax rates. After all, changes in the tax law enhancing after-tax profits were made in response to inflation. See the discussion later in this chapter.

69. Notice that the tax rate data in Table 3.9 pertain to corporate income, not total capital income. Capital income tax rates are higher, and hence post-tax returns to capital are lower than shown because dividends, bond interest, and capital gains accruing to individuals are also taxed. Feldstein et al., "The Effective Tax Rate and the Pretax Rate of Return," National Bureau of Eco-

nomic Research, Working Paper No. 740, August 1981, estimated that effective tax rates on total capital income in the nonfinancial corporate sector averaged 69.6 percent in the 1950s, 59.6 percent in the 1960s, and 68.7 percent in the 1970s. These estimates appear to be extreme, however. In a more recent study Don Fullerton and Yolanda Henderson put the overall tax on capital in the corporate sector under 1980 law (that is, prior to the Reagan tax reduction package) at just 34.5 percent. Don Fullerton and Yolanda Henderson, "Incentive Effects of Taxes on Capital Income," National Bureau of Economic Research, Working Paper No. 1262, June 1984. Also see Eugene Steurele, "Is Income from Capital Subject to Individual Income Taxation?" *Public Finance Quarterly* 10 (July 1982), 282–303. Returns to total capital income may be more relevant than corporate returns for the savings and investment decisions of households, an important topic that is treated in the next section.

70. A useful review and evaluation of various (inadequate) explanations appears in William Brainard et al., "The Financial Valuation of the Return to Capital," *Brookings Papers on Economic Activity* 1980 (2), 453–511.

71. Zvi Bodie, "Common Stocks as a Hedge against Inflation," *Journal of Finance* 31 (May 1976), 459–470; E. F. Fama and G. W. Schwert, "Asset Returns and Inflation," *Journal of Financial Economics* 5 (November 1977), 115–146; John Lintner, "Inflation and Security Returns," *Journal of Finance* 30 (May 1975), 259–280; Franco Modigliani and Richard Cahn, "Inflation, Rational Valuation, and the Market," *Financial Analysts Journal* (March–April 1979), 24–44; and Charles Nelson, "Inflation and Rates of Return on Common Stocks," *Journal of Finance* 31 (May 1976), 471–487.

72. Martin Feldstein, "Inflation and the Stock Market," *American Economic Review* 70 (December 1980), 839–847; idem, "Inflation, Tax Rules and the Stock Market," *Journal of Monetary Economics* 6 (July 1980), 309–331; and Lawrence Summers, "Inflation and the Valuation of Corporate Equities," National Bureau of Economic Research, Working Paper No. 824 (December 1981). Eugene Fama, "Stock Returns, Real Activity, Inflation and Money," *American Economic Review* 71 (September 1981), 545–565, tries to explain the negative correlation by an alleged adverse impact of inflation on real activity generally. Also see Jason Benderly and Burton Zwick, "Inflation, Real Balances, Output and Real Stock Returns," *American Economic Review* 75 (December 1985), 1115–23.

No empirical study of stock performance that I am aware of has claimed to explain more than half of the 1969–1981 market plunge.

73. The inflation rate is negative and significant in regressions of stock prices on the pretax, instead of the after-tax, rate of return, which is consistent with the idea that inflation's adverse effects on market performance operate through the corporate tax system, as Feldstein and Summers have argued. Using profit shares as the measure of profitability in stock prices regressions produced essentially the same results as those discussed for rates of return.

74. The ratio ln(real stock price index 1979/real stock price index 1968) =

−0.65, that is, a 65-percent decline. Because the natural log of real stock prices is the dependent variable in the regression, the coefficients of the after-tax rate of return variables give the implied proportional response of the market to percentage point movements in profitability. Only the contemporaneous rate of return variable is significant in the ln real stock prices regression results, and allowing a 6-point decrease in the former variable (−6 · 0.045 = −0.27) gives −0.27/−0.65 = 0.42, which means that the deterioration of profitability accounts for about four-tenths of the decline in real stock prices. If we ignore the fact that the lagged rate of return variable is insignificant and sum the coefficients [−6 · (0.045 + 0.020) = −0.39], we get 0.60 as the upper bound of the fraction of the decline in real stock prices attributable to the after-tax profitability decline: −0.39/−0.65 = 0.60.

75. Some forms of savings income are not subject to taxation, but this does not affect the main point.

76. In 1980 a married couple with (above median) taxable income of $30,000 faced a marginal federal income tax rate of about 37 percent.

77. One might suppose that interest rates would reflect taxes as well as inflation, so real returns to savings would not be affected by the interactions of taxation and rising prices. Empirical research on interest rates, however, indicates that tax effects on interest yields have been relatively small or nonexistent. Indeed, until the late 1970s interest rates did not even fully reflect inflation. See Vito Tanzi, "Inflationary Expectations, Economic Activity, Taxes, and Interest Rates," *American Economic Review* 70 (March 1980), 12–21; Joe Peek, "Interest Rates, Income Taxes, and Anticipated Inflation," *American Economic Review* 72 (December 1982), 980–991; and Lawrence Summers, "The Nonadjustment of Nominal Interest Rates: A Study of the Fisher Effect," in James Tobin, ed., *A Symposium in Honor of Arthur Okun* (Washington, D.C.: Brookings, 1983), pp. 201–241.

78. In addition to being a professor of economics at Harvard and president of the National Bureau of Economic Research, Martin Feldstein was Murray Weidenbaum's successor as chairman of the Council of Economic Advisors during President Reagan's first term.

79. The argument is spelled out in nontechnical terms in Martin Feldstein, "Tax Rules and the Mismanagement of Monetary Policy," *American Economic Review, Papers and Proceedings* 70 (May 1980), 182–186. The theoretical foundation is developed in Feldstein's "Inflation, Tax Rules and the Accumulation of Residential and Nonresidential Capital," *Scandinavian Journal of Economics* 84 (2), (1982), 293–311.

80. This may be why Feldstein was invited to head the Council of Economic Advisors when Murray Weidenbaum resigned in the fall of 1982.

81. Equally skeptical conclusions were reached by Barry Bosworth in "Capital Formation and Economic Policy," *Brookings Papers on Economic Activity* 1982 (2), 273–326, based on an analysis of data similar to those in Table 3.12.

82. The tax rates cited here pertain to federal, state, and local income tax revenues as a percentage of total personal income before the adjustments,

exemptions, and so on permitted by the tax codes. The rates may therefore appear low. Marginal tax rates are higher, but over time they track the rise in average effective rates even though, as shown earlier, the personal income tax rate structure became somewhat more progressive in the 1970s.

83. Indeed this pattern persists back at least to the turn of the century, at which time personal savings rate data first became available. The main variations about a rather stable level occur during the Great Depression, when the massive decline in income depressed the savings rate, and during World War II, when consumption goods were unavailable. See the data reported in Robert J. Gordon, *Macroeconomics*, 2nd ed. (Boston: Little, Brown, 1981), figure 13-2, p. 396.

Gross savings (public plus private) and gross private savings as a percentage of GNP also have been remarkably stable over the postwar period, varying between about 15.4 percent and 17.3 percent and exhibiting no apparent connection with surges and declines in inflation.

84. Here as in the other regressions, the main conclusions implied by the statistical results were not sensitive to the price index used to measure inflation or to the indicator used to track the business cycle.

85. For a more detailed investigation of savings rates over the 1951–1974 period that extends far beyond our interest here in savings and inflation, see E. Phillip Howrey and Saul H. Hymans, "The Measurement and Determination of Loanable-Funds Saving," *Brookings Papers on Economic Activity* 1978 (3), 655–685.

86. A better evaluation of the permanent income hypothesis requires analysis of the behavior of conventional savings plus expenditures for consumer durables, because, as noted earlier, the latter are a form of household savings.

87. Ironically, although Martin Feldstein has been among the most vigorous advocates of the idea that disinflationary, tight-money policies are likely to increase saving and investment, he has supplied perhaps the most elegant demonstration that connections among inflation, the real rate of return, saving, and investment are indeterminate theoretically and, hence, may only be resolved empirically. See his "The Rate of Return, Taxation and Personal Savings," *Economic Journal* 88 (September 1978), 482–487. In an earlier paper, "Inflation, Income Taxes, and the Rate of Interest: A Theoretical Analysis," *American Economic Review* 66 (December 1976), 809–820, Feldstein concluded that when the corporate tax rate exceeds households' personal tax rate (which has been true with respect to the great majority of households), inflation induces an *increase* in the savings rate.

88. But recall that, as the tax rate regressions reported in the previous section illustrated, the average effective rate of taxation of personal income over the postwar period as a whole increased with real rather than nominal income rises, as a result of periodic discretionary tax rate adjustments legislated by Congress. Federal income tax brackets were indexed formally to inflation beginning in 1985.

89. Net investment is defined as gross investment less capital consumption allowances with capital consumption adjustment. The net figures, then,

give the increment to residential investment above that necessary to offset depreciation of the housing capital stock.

90. Residential investment during this period reflects the 1971–1973 boom in housing construction.

91. Toward the end of the 1970s, innovations in mortgage financing by home sellers and mortgage banks began to overcome the fixed-rate front loading. During the 1960s and early 1970s, adjustable interest rate mortgages (which tend to smooth real debt services as a percentage of the loan) were unknown. Over the years 1981 to 1984 the fraction of all mortgages with adjustable rates varied between 25 and 55 percent. (See the data reported in Peter Kilborn, "Playing the Odds on Mortgages," *New York Times*, January 24, 1984, p. D1.) Also, in accordance with the Depository Institutions Deregulation and Monetary Control Act passed by Congress in March 1980, by late 1982 significant deregulation of the banking industry had been implemented that allowed institutions making mortgage loans to compete more successfully with money market funds and other instruments for deposits. These developments are gradually modifying the depressing impact of inflation on the housing sector.

92. See Martin Feldstein, "Inflation, Tax Rules and Investment: Some Econometric Evidence," *Econometrica* 50 (July 1982), 825–862. In this major empirical study Feldstein flatly concludes that "the rising rate of inflation has, because of the structure of existing U.S. tax rules, substantially discouraged [net private fixed nonresidential] investment in the past 15 years" (p. 860). But Feldstein's regressions show no direct link from inflation to investment. His conclusions about inflation are based on circumstantial reasoning, and they are not supported by the econometric results discussed later in this chapter that directly estimate the impact of inflation on private investment rates.

93. Gross and net real private domestic investment per nonagricultural worker in the private sector also exhibited no tendency to fall with rising inflation rates during the postwar period, though both declined sharply during business contractions. Gross real private investment per private-sector nonagricultural worker rose from an average of $2132 in 1950–1954 to $3087 in 1970–1974 (1972 dollars). Except for surges during expansions, it has not continued upward since that time because of the great expansion of the active labor force and repeated (policy-induced) contractions. Net real investment per worker increased from about $1000 in the early 1950s to over $1400 in the late 1960s and early 1970s but then fell back to the level of the 1950s as a result of the 1974–1975, 1979–1980, and 1981 recessions and the expansion of the labor force.

94. The association between the variability of relative prices and the total inflation rate shown in Figure 3.4 remains strong after allowing for the dependence of current inflation on past inflation (price inertia). Substituting estimated values for 1967:1 through 1981:4 into the equation

$$DP_t = a_0 + \sum_{i=1}^{3} b_i DP_{t-i} + c\sigma(DP_{it})$$

where DP is the annualized Divisia consumer price inflation rate and $\sigma(DP_{it})$ is the sample standard deviation of relative prices, yields

$$a_0 = 0.20, (0.35), \qquad \sum_i b_i = 0.70, \qquad c = 0.58$$
$$(0.35) \qquad\qquad\qquad (0.08) \qquad\quad (0.15)$$

where $R^2 = 0.79$, standard error of the regression = 1.34, Durbin-Watson = 1.76, and standard errors appear in parentheses.

A unit increase in the standard deviation of relative prices is therefore associated with an increase of 0.6 percentage point in the total inflation rate contemporaneously, and with an increase of about 2 percentage points [0.58/(1 − 0.7)] after all lags of adjustment.

95. This appears to be the implication of Robert Barro's article "Rational Expectations and the Role of Monetary Policy," *Journal of Monetary Economics* (January 1976), 1–32, and underlies the empirical analysis of Richard Parks's article "Inflation and Relative Price Variability," *Journal of Political Economy* 86 (February 1978), 79–95.

On the difficulty of determining causal ordering statistically, see Stanley Fischer, "Relative Shocks, Relative Price Variability, and Inflation," *Brookings Papers on Economic Activity* 1981 (2), 381–431. Additional postwar empirical evidence and a review of earlier studies appear in Daniel Vining and Thomas Elwertowski, "The Relationship between Relative Prices and the General Price Level," *American Economic Review* 66 (September 1976), 699–708.

96. For example, not one of the price indexes for the fifteen broad consumer commodity groups used in the computations for Tables 3.4 and 3.5 and Figure 3.4 declined from one year to the next during 1967–1981. There was of course considerable dispersion of the (positive) commodity group–specific inflation rates.

97. A study by Frederick Mills undertaken more than fifty years ago indicates that early in the twentieth century, when deflation was as common as inflation, relative price variability was closely associated with the *absolute value* of changes in the general price level. See Frederick Mills, *The Behavior of Prices* (New York: National Bureau of Economic Research, 1927), p. 284. Prior to the postwar era of continuous inflation, relative price realignments apparently were just as likely to contribute to a falling general price level as to a rising one. This may be one reason that prior to World War II deflation was viewed by the public with at least as much alarm (and perhaps more) as inflation is today.

98. James Tobin, "There Are Three Types of Inflation: We Have Two," *New York Times*, September 6, 1974, p. 33.

99. Arthur M. Okun, "Inflation: Its Mechanics and Welfare Costs," *Brookings Papers on Economic Activity* 1972 (2), 383; and idem, *Prices and Quantities* (Washington, D.C.: Brookings, 1981), p. 160.

If the total inflation rate is positively related to the variance of the *total* rate, and if the latter is taken to be an indicator of uncertainty about inflation, then higher inflation imposes costs in the form of higher uncertainty. This does not appear to have been the case during the postwar era in the United States, however. Regressing the variance of the CPI inflation rate [Var(DCPI)] on the mean of the CPI inflation rate ($\overline{\text{DCPI}}$) defined for nonoverlapping 12-quarter periods, $t = 1 = 1949{:}1{-}1951{:}4$, $t = 2 = 1952{:}1{-}1954{:}4, \ldots, t = 11 = 1979{:}1{-}1981{:}4$, yields the essentially null result

$$\text{Var(DCPI)}_t = \underset{(4.40)}{4.44} + \underset{(0.84)}{0.142} \, \overline{\text{DCPI}}_t$$

where $R^2 = 0.003$, SER $= 5.02$, and standard errors are shown in parentheses. The same analysis applied to the GNP current-weights deflator also shows that there is no association between the mean and the variance of the inflation rate.

Similar analyses reported by Stanley Fischer in "Towards an Understanding of the Costs of Inflation: II," in K. Brunner and A. Meltzer, eds., *The Costs and Consequences of Inflation* (Amsterdam: North-Holland, 1981), pp. 5–41, yield results indicating significant positive associations between inflation and survey-based price expectations. Fischer, however, applies autoregressive corrections for residual time dependence, which in a number of cases amounts to investigating the association between the first differences of the means and variances constructed for nonoverlapping periods. Consequently, his regressions pick up the artifactual scale-dependence of the mean and variance—mean $(AX) = A\bar{X}$, Var $(AX) = A^2$ Var X, for any constant A—rather than nonartifactual empirical associations in the data.

100. Seymour M. Lipset and William Schneider, *The Confidence Gap* (New York: Macmillan, 1981).

101. James Tobin, "Inflation Control as Social Priority," paper delivered to the conference on the Political Economy of Inflation and Unemployment in Open Economies, Athens, Greece, 1976.

102. See George Katona, "The Psychology of Inflation," in Richard T. Curtin, ed., *Surveys of Consumers 1974–1975* (Ann Arbor: Survey Research Center, University of Michigan) for discussion of this point.

103. Known as "money illusion" to professional analysts, this phenomenon is put into even sharper focus by remembering that most salary earners receive annual income increases, and cost-of-living adjustments aside, many hourly wage earners in organized industries receive increases once every two to three years. Employees therefore receive discrete jumps in their standard of living that they subsequently see being "taken away" by rises in the price level until the next wage or salary adjustment round. The fact that in periods of high price inflation high money wage and salary increases are largely dependent on the rates of past, current, and expected future inflation may not be fully understood by many individuals, leading to frustration and disappointment.

104. Lack of sophistication in such matters is not wholly confined to the ordinary citizen. Over the 1970s real, price-deflated salaries of tenured professors at Harvard fell on average by nearly 15 percent, though their money incomes rose substantially. Many of my former colleagues, all wise and intelligent people, blamed this on "inflation." Inflation played virtually no role in

this unhappy story. Although as consumers of energy they did experience some real loss, the fundamental explanation of the deterioration of my colleagues' standard of living resides in the almost continuous national excess supply of academics since the boom years of the middle and late 1960s. Alas, not even tenured Harvard professors were immune as a group to such strong market forces.

105. Recessions during this period are, then, seen as the intentional consequences of macroeconomic policy, partly indirect because the authorities refused to take actions offsetting the adverse impact of external shocks on aggregate demand and partly direct when the authorities actively attempted to depress effective demand.

106. Estimates of cumulative forgone output (here tallied for 1973–1982) vary with the time range analyzed. The cumulative output loss was 461 billion (1982:4) dollars for 1947–1982, as opposed to 715 billion for 1973–1982, because of the large, unsustainable (and inflationary) output levels and associated low rates of unemployment that were achieved during 1965–1969.

4. Public Concern about Inflation and Unemployment

1. The *Gallup Reports* use "inflation" and "the high cost of living" interchangeably. A further hint of how deep the problem runs at Gallup is given by the following question asked in the October 1970 survey: "When people around here go to vote on November 3rd for a candidate for Congress, how important will inflation—the high cost of living—be in their thinking?" *Gallup Opinion Index*, November 1978, Report 160, pp. 13–20.

2. The alternative wording in brackets was used in the 1971:3, 1971:4, and 1972:1 surveys. Richard Curtin of the Institute for Social Research at the University of Michigan kindly supplied the data to me.

3. More data illustrating this point appear in Paul Peretz, *The Political Economy of Inflation in the United States* (Chicago: University of Chicago Press, 1983), table 29, p. 134; figure 32, p. 185; and figure 33, p. 186. Chapter 4 of Peretz's book explores a great many other aspects of public perceptions of inflation.

4. See Donald R. Kinder and D. Roderick Kiewiet, "Economic Discontent and Political Behavior: The Role of Personal Grievances and Collective Economic Judgments in Congressional Voting," *American Journal of Political Science* 23 (August 1979), 495–527; and Kinder and Kiewiet, "Sociotropic Politics: The American Case," *British Journal of Political Science* 11 (April 1981), 129–161.

5. Gerald Kramer, "The Ecological Fallacy Revisited: Aggregate- versus Individual-Level Findings on Economics and Elections, and Sociotropic Voting," *American Political Science Review* 77 (March 1983), 92–111.

6. A large majority of the general public believes there is a trade-off between unemployment and inflation. For example, despite years of stagflation (high unemployment *and* inflation) in the wake of the OPEC shocks, responses in an April 1979 Yankelovich, Skelley, and White survey to the

question "Will you tell me . . . whether you feel this is or is not a choice the American people will have to make in the next few years . . . either high inflation or high unemployment?" were "is," 62%; "is not," 22%; and "not sure," 16%. It is unclear from such data whether people distinguish the long run from the short run.

7. Patterns in the responses to the University of Michigan survey question are consistent with those for parallel questions in the Harris and *New York Times*/CBS News polls, although data from the latter surveys are not available for as long a time range. Gallup data on concern about inflation and unemployment are out of line with those of the other surveys probably because, as noted above, Gallup polls confuse high prices with rising prices and perhaps also because the Gallup question assesses concern about noneconomic as well as economic issues. Results from the various polls are compared in Stanley Fischer and John Huizanga, "Inflation, Unemployment, and Public Opinion Polls," *Journal of Money, Credit and Banking* 14 (February 1982), 1–19.

8. Earlier analyses of the response of public concern about inflation in the United States to economic events and perceptions include Fischer and Huizanga, "Inflation, Unemployment, and Public Opinion Polls"; Douglas A. Hibbs, Jr., "The Mass Public and Macroeconomic Performance: The Dynamics of Public Opinion Toward Unemployment and Inflation," *American Journal of Political Science* 23 (November 1979), 705–731; idem, "Public Concern about Inflation and Unemployment in the United States: Trends, Correlates, and Political Implications," in Robert Hall, ed., *Inflation: Causes and Effects* (Chicago: University of Chicago Press, 1982), chap. 10, pp. 211–231; and Peretz, *The Political Economy of Inflation*.

9. Results from regressions with this index of Inflation Concern are therefore symmetrical with respect to concern about inflation and unemployment. A 1-point increase in the index represents a 1-point increase in concern about inflation and a 1-point decrease in concern about unemployment; the converse is true of decreases in the index.

10. See the discussion of Ugap in Chapter 2. The value of U^N increases monotonically from 5 percent in the 1950s to 5.6 percent in the late 1960s and early 1970s (the beginning of the regression time range) to 6 percent in the mid-1970s, after which it is constant at 6 percent through 1984.

11. Recall from Chapter 2 that the fraction of the labor force experiencing one or more spells of unemployment during a year (4 quarters) is between 2.5 and 3.0 times the official unemployment rate. Indeed, the memory of past unemployment or, more likely, the fear of future unemployment may create more anxiety than does contemporaneous personal experience.

12. The University of Michigan's May-June 1964 Survey of Consumer Finances supplies a bit of information about relative magnitudes. During a period when unemployment was running at about 5.6 percent of the civilian labor force, 20 percent of the wage and salary earners in the survey reported having experienced one or more spells of unemployment over the preceding 42 months. Another 20 percent were aware of unemployment over the same

period among relatives, friends, or neighbors. Altogether between 35 and 40 percent of the employees interviewed either had experienced unemployment themselves or knew someone else who had been unemployed.

13. Aside from the constant term, the estimation results obtained from entering the simple unemployment rate rather than the unemployment gap in the "inflation concern" equations are nearly identical to those reported in the text. From a theoretical point of view, however, the unemployment gap is probably a more appropriate indicator of slack in the labor market.

14. The fraction of the electorate tying perceived declines in financial well-being to inflation, however, rises with the inflation rate when people are not constrained to choose between inflation and unemployment as sources of hardship. See Peretz, *The Political Economy of Inflation*, table 8, p. 94.

15. See Jeffrey Sachs, "The Oil Shocks and Macroeconomic Adjustment in the United States," *European Economic Review* 18 (1982), table 1, p. 244.

16. E. J. Dionne, Jr., "The New Politics of Jobs," *Public Opinion* (March/April 1978), 53.

17. No attempt was made to create constant-dollar income classes, despite the substantial inflation over the period 1974–1981. A more rigorous analysis of such data would require adjustment of income categories.

18. I implicitly assume here that party affiliation stems from economic interests and preferences, and not the reverse.

5. Macroeconomic Performance and Mass Political Support for the President

1. Broad reviews of the professional literature appear in Kristen Monroe, "Econometric Analyses of Electoral Behavior: A Critical Review," *Political Behavior* 9 (1979), 137–173; Monroe, *Presidential Popularity and the Economy* (New York: Praeger, 1984); and Martin Paldam, "A Preliminary Survey of the Theories and Findings on Vote and Popularity Functions," *European Journal of Political Research* 9 (1981), 181–199.

2. This chapter extends my earlier work on the United States in Douglas A. Hibbs, Jr., with Douglas Rivers and Nicholas Vasilatos, "On the Demand for Economic Outcomes: Macroeconomic Performance and Mass Political Support in the United States, Great Britain and Germany," *Journal of Politics* 44 (May 1982), 426–462; and Douglas A. Hibbs, Jr., with Nicholas Vasilatos, "The Dynamics of Political Support for American Presidents Among Occupational and Partisan Groups," *American Journal of Political Science* 26 (May 1982), 312–332. These and other earlier articles by me and my collaborators are collected in Douglas A. Hibbs, Jr., *The Political Economy of Industrial Democracies* (Cambridge, Mass.: Harvard University Press, 1987).

3. See Michael Lewis-Beck and I. W. Rice, "Presidential Popularity and Presidential Vote," *Public Opinion Quarterly* 46 (1982), 534–537; and Lee Sigelman, "Presidential Popularity and Presidential Elections," *Public Opinion Quarterly* (Winter 1979), 532–534. Also see Chapter 6.

4. See Samuel Kernell, "Presidential Popularity and Negative Voting: An Alternative Explanation of the Midterm Congressional Decline of the President's Party," *American Political Science Review* 72 (June 1977), 506–522; James E. Pierson, "Presidential Popularity and Midterm Voting at Different Electoral Levels," *American Journal of Political Science* 19 (November 1975), 683–693; and Edward Tufte, "Determinants of the Outcomes of Midterm Congressional Elections," *American Political Science Review* 69 (September 1975), 812–826.

5. Richard Neustadt, *Presidential Power* (New York: Wiley, 1960), p. 93.

6. Rich Jarosolvsky, "Reagan's Revolution Stalls as Policies Falter Both Here and Abroad," *Wall Street Journal,* December 23, 1982.

7. George Edwards, *Presidential Influence in Congress* (San Francisco: W. H. Freeman, 1980); and Douglas Rivers and Nancy Rose, "Passing the President's Program: Public Opinion and Presidential Influence in Congress," *American Journal of Political Science,* May 1985.

8. Donald Kinder, "Presidents, Prosperity, and Public Opinion," *Public Opinion Quarterly* 45 (Spring 1981), 1.

9. Notable exceptions are Friedrich Schneider, "Different (Income) Classes and Presidential Popularity: An Empirical Analysis," *Munich Social Science Review* (1978), 53–69; and M. Stephen Weatherford, "Economic Conditions and Electoral Outcomes: Class Differences in the Political Response to Recession," *American Journal of Political Science* (1978), 917–938.

10. It would be much better if we had a time series of responses to a question of the sort "If an election were held today, would you vote for the incumbent or for the opposition?" Remember, however, that the Gallup approval ratings correlate highly with presidential election outcomes.

11. It is assumed that U^i never exactly equals U^o; that is, $U^i = U^o$ occurs with probability 0.

12. Trying out different values of P in equation (5.5) (or taking the second derivative) will show that the slope (derivative) is maximized at $P = 0.5$. Evaluating equation (5.4) shows that this maximum corresponds to $\beta'x^*\text{diff} = 0$.

13. For a more extended discussion of the implications of this idea, see Samuel Kernell and Douglas A. Hibbs, Jr., "A Critical Threshold Model of Presidential Popularity," in Douglas A. Hibbs, Jr., and Heino Fassbender, eds., *Contemporary Political Economy* (Amsterdam: North Holland, 1981), chap. 3. Also see the discussion of empirical results later in this chapter.

14. Proof: From equation (5.4) we have

$$P_{jt} = \frac{\exp(\beta'x^*\text{diff}_{jt})}{1 + \exp(\beta'x^*\text{diff}_{jt})}$$

Hence,

$$1 - P_{jt} = 1 - \frac{\exp(\beta'x^*\text{diff}_{jt})}{1 + \exp(\beta'x^*\text{diff}_{jt})}$$

Therefore,

$$\frac{1 - P_{jt}}{P_{jt}} = \frac{1}{\exp(\beta' x_{jt}^*)}$$

$$\frac{P_{jt}}{1 - P_{jt}} = \exp(\beta' x_{jt}^*)$$

$$\ln\left(\frac{P_{jt}}{1 - P_{jt}}\right) = \beta' x_{jt}^*$$

Substituting the observed sample proportions (P_{jt}') for the true group probabilities (P_{jt}) yields equation (5.6) in the text.

15. Joseph Berkson, "Maximum Likelihood and Minimum Chi Square Estimates of the Logistic Function," *Journal of the American Statistical Association* 50 (March 1955), 130–162. For wide-ranging, synthetic treatments of specification and estimation of qualitative response models, see G. S. Maddala, *Limited and Qualitative Variables in Econometrics* (Cambridge: Cambridge University Press, 1983); and Takeshi Amemiya, "Qualitative Response Models: A Survey," *Journal of Economic Literature* 19 (December 1981), 1483–1536.

16. Morris Fiorina, "An Outline for a Model of Party Choice," *American Journal of Political Science* 21 (1977), 618.

17. Angus Campbell et al., *The American Voter* (New York: Wiley, 1960), p. 151.

18. Throughout this book I use *incumbent* to mean the party of the president. The model does not take into account the strength of the parties in Congress.

19. The most exhaustive analysis of retrospective voting in the United States is Morris Fiorina's *Retrospective Voting in American National Elections* (New Haven: Yale University Press, 1981). For an innovative attempt to build in future orientations to political support evaluation functions, see Henry Chappell and William Keech, "A New View of Political Accountability for Economic Performance," *American Political Science Review* (March 1985), 10–27.

20. Equivalently, one might assume for illustrative purposes that the matrix of performance variables, x, is held constant at $\bar{x}$ and that the vector product $\beta'\bar{x}$ is equal to -0.02.

21. For x held at some constant value $\bar{x}$ and for $0 < g < 1$, the partial sum *through* lag k of the infinite series $\beta\Sigma_{k=0}^{\infty}g^k\bar{x}$ is $\beta'\bar{x}(1 - g^{k+1})/(1 - g)$. The partial sum *from* lag k back to the indefinite past is $\beta\bar{x}g^{k+1}/(1 - g)$. Hence, the value of $\ln[P_t'/(1 - P_t')]$ implied by equation (5.15) for the example discussed in the text is

$$-0.02 \cdot 10[(1 - 0.8)/(1 - 0.8) - 0.8/(1 - 0.8)] = 0.60$$

Recall from equations (5.4) and (5.6) that the poll proportion corresponding to a logit of 0.60 is exp 0.60/(1 + exp 0.60) = 0.65, or 65 percent

22. For further discussion of this feature of the model, in the context of an analysis of Britain where $w = 1$, see Douglas A. Hibbs, Jr., "Economics Outcome and Political Support for British Governments among Occupational Classes," *American Political Science Review* 76 (June 1982), 259–279; William R. Keech's comment "Of Honeymoons and Economic Performance: Comment on Hibbs," *American Political Science Review* 76 (June 1982), 280–281; and my reply, "More on Economic Performance and Political Support in Britain: A Reply to William R. Keech," *American Political Science Review* 76 (June 1982), 282–284. Also see Jean Dominique Lafay's insightful paper "Important Political Change and the Stability of the Popularity Function before and after the French General Election of 1981," *Political Behavior*, 1985, which comments on the implications of the model for the French case, as published in Douglas A. Hibbs, Jr., "Economics and Politics in France: Economic Performance and Mass Political Support for Presidents Pompidou and Giscard d'Estaing," *European Journal of Political Research* 9 (1981), 133–145; and idem, "Performance Economique et Fonction Popularité des Présidents Pompidou et Giscard d'Estaing," *Revue d'Economie Politique* 93 (1983), 44–61.

23. See Samuel Kernell, "Explaining Presidential Popularity," *American Political Science Review* 72 (June 1978), 506–522, who uses "early term" trend variables; Douglas A. Hibbs, Jr., and Nicholas Vasilatos, "Macroeconomic Performance and Mass Political Support in the United States and Great Britain," in Douglas A. Hibbs, Jr., and Heino Fassbender, eds., *Contemporary Political Economy* (Amsterdam: North Holland, 1981), pp. 31–48; and John Mueller, "Presidential Popularity from Truman to Johnson," *American Political Science Review* (1970), 18–34, who use time-trend and time-cycle variables. The most extreme version of the exogenous trend approach to "explaining" movements in political support for presidents appears in James Stimson's work. Stimson went so far as to argue that "presidential approval may be almost wholly independent of the president's behavior in office" and instead is "a function largely of inevitable forces associated with time." Stimson, "Public Support for American Presidents: A Cycle Model," *Public Opinion Quarterly* (1976), 1.

24. All available surveys in a quarter were averaged to form the quarterly proportions.

25. There are four missing P'_{jt} observations in the regression range. Also recall that observations back to the late 1940s are used in the right-side lag functions.

26. All rates of change were formed by taking the quarter-on-quarter first differences of the natural logs and are expressed as annual rates. Hence, $\ln(X_t/X_{t-1}) \cdot 400$ gives the quarter-to-quarter percentage rate of change of X expressed as an annual rate.

27. See John Mueller, "Trends in Popular Support for the Wars in Korea and Vietnam," *American Political Science Review* 65 (June 1971), 358–375; and idem, *War, Presidents and Public Opinion* (New York: Wiley, 1973).

28. John Mueller, "Presidential Popularity from Truman to Johnson," *American Political Science Review* 64 (March 1970), 18–34; and idem, *War, Presidents and Public Opinion*. Mueller, unlike myself, scored the first period of each administration as a Rally point.

29. Nelson Polsby, *Congress and the Presidency* (Englewood Cliffs, N.J.: Prentice-Hall, 1964), p. 25.

30. Quoted in Richard Brody, "International Crises: A Rallying Point for the President?" *Public Opinion* December/January 1984), 41.

31. These remarks follow straightforwardly from the algebra of "specification error analysis" of regression models. Qualitative and casual quantitative analyses are even more likely to lead to mistaken inferences of this kind. One of the strengths of multivariate, quantitative modeling is the help it gives in sorting out the net, relative effects of correlated independent variables in nonexperimental research settings.

32. The shadow constants may also be interpreted in terms of Figures 5.1 and 5.2. Because the constants are proxies for unobserved shadow performance, $\hat{x}$, the quantity x^*diff equals $(x\text{diff} - S)$. Therefore, positive shadow constants shift the utility difference regression line in Figure 5.1 upward and the logistic probability curve in Figure 5.2 to the left. Negative constants shift these functions downward and to the right, respectively. The pro-Republican bias implies upward or leftward shifts in the functions facing Republican presidents as compared to the functions facing Democratic presidents. Hence, at any given observed relative performance outcome $\beta'x^*$diff, Republican presidents achieved a higher utility difference $(U^i - U^o)$, more approval choices $(Y = 1)$, and therefore higher approval probabilities and proportions $[P(Y = 1)]$ than Democratic presidents. One can also think of the pro-Republican bias as shifting the threshold of approval change downward from 0 in Figure 5.1 and leftward from the zero point on the horizontal axis in Figure 5.2 for Republican, as compared to Democratic, chief executives.

33. See Herbert Asher, *Presidential Elections in American Politics* (Homewood, Ill.: Dorsey Press, 1980), chap. 5, for some interesting conjectures.

34. Donald Stokes, "Some Dynamic Elements of Contests for the Presidency," *American Political Science Review* (March 1966), 19–28; Michael Kagay and Greg Caldeira, "I Like the Looks of His Face: Elements of Electoral Choice, 1952–1972," unpublished paper, 1975; and Ray Fair, "On Controlling the Economy to Win Elections," Cowles Foundation Discussion Paper No. 397, 1975.

35. Strictly speaking, given the specification of the political support model, in order to compute time profiles reflecting the net *relative* impact of sustained performance streams, one should evaluate (as the previous hypothetical examples showed) expressions of the form

$$\frac{(1 - g^{k^*+1}) - g^{k^*+1}}{1 - g} = \frac{1 - 2g^{k^*+1}}{1 - g}$$

in cases where a new president follows administrations of the out-party, and expressions of the form

$$\frac{(1 - g^{k^*+1}) + (2w - 1)g^{k^*+1}}{1 - g} = \frac{1 + (2w - 2)g^{k^*+1}}{1 - g}$$

when a new president follows administrations of his own party.

36. Another way to look at this is to remember that for $g = 0.82$, past outcomes are discounted at rate $\rho = (1 - g)/g = 0.22$, or 22 percent per quarter.

37. The first-period response (in percentage points) of P' to a unit increase in any independent variable, evaluated from a benchmark of 50 percent approval, is, however, simply the logit model regression coefficient (β) multiplied by 25. This follows from the fact that the derivative of P' with respect to each right-side variable is $P'(1 - P') \cdot \beta$, where β is the appropriate regression coefficient. Evaluating the derivative at $P' = 0.5$ and expressing the result in percentage points ($\times$ 100) implies multiplying β by 25.

38. Unless otherwise noted, the changes in approval ratings ($\Delta P'_j$) are computed from the expression

$$\Delta P'_j = F\left(\bar{y}_j^* + \beta_j \frac{1 - g_j^n}{1 - g_j} \Delta x\right) - F(\bar{y}_j^*)$$

where F is the logistic distribution function, $F(x) = \exp(x)/1 + \exp(x)$; $\bar{y}^*$ is the mean approval logit for (Democratic and Republican) presidents in partisan group j; n is the number of periods that Δx is sustained; and Δx is the magnitude of the increase in the independent variables. $\Delta P'_j$ is expressed in percentage points rather than proportions.

39. The simulation estimates are derived by comparing the approval rates for 1968:3 (the quarter in which American losses were highest), generated by simulating the political support equations holding battle fatalities fixed at 0, with the 1968:3 approval rates of the fitted equations. Other measures of the war's intensity—including draft rates, bombing activity, and war casualties as opposed to war fatalities—were also tried in the estimation equations, but these variables added little to the explanatory power of the killed-in-action rate.

40. William Lunch and Peter Sperlich, "American Public Opinion and the War in Vietnam," *Western Political Quarterly* (March 1979), 21–44.

41. Robert E. Berney and Duane E. Leigh, "The Socioeconomic Distribution of American Casualties in the Indochina War: Implications for Tax Equity," *Public Finance Quarterly* (1974), 223–235.

42. Senator Edward Kennedy's attempt to wrest the nomination from Carter suffered a major setback as a result of the rally 'round the president effect and the associated diversion of public attention from the economy, which occurred at a crucial juncture in the 1980 primary season.

43. Many commentators believed that the crises in Iran and Afghanistan actually contributed to Reagan's defeat of Carter via the "backlash" effect. But there is very little evidence of this in the poll data. See Chapter 6.

44. The aggregate estimate is obtained simply by summing the group effects, weighted by each group's share in the total electorate. It is somewhat

smaller than many press reports implied at the time. But remember that prices accelerated and real income growth rates slowed in late 1973 and 1974 following the OPEC oil price hike of October 1973. The estimates of the impact of Watergate on Nixon's mass political support discussed in the text, which I believe are more realistic, illustrate the advantage of basing inferences on a multivariate model that includes important variables that covary.

45. According to the usual statistical significance tests, only the Independents are distinctive.

46. Letting y^* denote the logit $\ln[P'/(1 - P')]$, we have the total differential

$$dy^* = (\partial y^*/\partial \text{Ugap}) \cdot d\text{Ugap} + (\partial y^*/\partial p) \cdot dp + \cdots + (\partial y^*/\partial x) \cdot dx$$

where x denotes other variables in the model.

Holding changes in other variables (dx) at 0, consider changing (exogenously) only the unemployment gap (Ugap) and inflation (p) so as to keep the political support index constant ($dy^* = 0$):

$$dy^* = 0 = (\partial y^*/\partial \text{Ugap}) \cdot d\text{Ugap} + (\partial y^*/\partial p) \cdot dp$$

Solving for $dp/d\text{Ugap}$, which means solving for the slope of the indifference curve (giving p and Ugap values that render y^* constant), we have

$$dp/d\text{Ugap}|_{y^*=\text{constant}} = \text{MRS Ugap for } p$$
$$= -(\partial y^*/\partial \text{Ugap})/(\partial y^*/\partial p) = -\beta(\text{Ugap})/\beta(p)$$

Notice, however, that matters would become more complicated if we took a dynamic view and acknowledged the endogenous, structural relationship of inflation and unemployment (the Phillips curve).

47. The induced changes are computed in the same way as the comparable changes given in Table 5.3.

48. Given the values of the decay rate parameters g_j, "indefinitely" essentially means five to six years (20 to 24 quarters).

49. Because of the nonlinearity of the response function, the effects would be a little less than twice the size of those produced by 2 extra points of unemployment.

50. To keep things consistent with the quarterly inflation rates used in the political support equations, the energy price increases I refer to are calculated as the sum of the quarter-on-quarter changes expressed at annual rates.

51. As in Table 5.3, the simulation estimates are generated by contrasting the approval percentages implied by the fitted logits with the approval percentages simulated after holding p-oil at 0.

52. Recall from equation (5.5) that the responses of P'_{jt} to marginal changes in x are proportional to $P'_{jt}(1 - P'_{jt})$. The average approval ratings shown in the first column of Table 5.4 indicate that the latter quantity is typically about 0.25 for the Independents and generally ranges between 0.18 to 0.235 for Democrats and Republicans. Hence, other things being equal, the responses of

Independents' approval proportions to changes in the economy are often magnified by factors ranging from 1.4 (0.25/0.18), which is an important magnification, to 1.06 (0.25/0.235), which is unimportant.

53. The exact value is 23.8: $0.082^0/0.82^{16} = 1.0/0.042 = 23.8$

54. The exact value is 10.8: $(1 - 0.82^4)/(0.82^{12} - 0.82^{16}) = 10.8$.

6. Economic Performance and the 1980 and 1984 National Elections

1. Three formerly Democratic House seats were vacant at the time of the election; the number of Democrats in the House on election day was there fore 273.

2. In statistical terms, the magnitude of the Democrats' seat losses in the Senate was the most unusual feature of the 1980 elections. The only other double-digit shifts in the party distribution of Senate seats since World War II were in 1946, when the Democrats lost 12 seats and the Republicans gained 13, and in 1958, when the Democrats gained 16 seats and the Republicans lost 12. The next largest shift was in 1948, when the Democrats gained and the Republicans lost 9 seats. It must be remembered, however, that the Democrats were more exposed than the Republicans in 1980: the Democrats held 24 of the 34 seats that were up for election. And even though the Republicans won 22 of the 34 Senate races, they received only 47 percent of the nation-wide senatorial vote.

By comparison, neither the presidential nor the House vote results were particularly unusual. Reagan's two-party vote share was just about equal to the postwar mean of 55 percent for presidential winners; remember, though, that Carter was the first elected incumbent to be defeated since Hoover in 1932. (Carter also presided over the worst election-year economic record since Hoover, a fact that will be discussed later in the chapter.) The 3-percent decline in the Democrats' share of the popular vote for the House was about 1 standard deviation above the mean loss in presidential years for the party losing the presidency (the postwar mean is −1.84 percent, with a standard deviation of 3 percent), as was the Democrats' loss of 33 House seats (the postwar mean seat decline for the losing party in presidential elections is about 18, with a standard deviation of 26.)

3. Although it was the largest loss experienced since 1922 by either party in its first mid-term election after winning the White House, the 1982 House seat shift against the Republicans was smaller than many had anticipated given the dismal state of the economy. For example, whereas my own fore-cast of the aggregate House vote shift (−5%) was right on the money (see Douglas A. Hibbs, Jr., "President Reagan's Mandate from the 1980 Elections: A Shift to the Right?" *American Politics Quarterly* [October 1982], table 6, p. 410], I, along with others, predicted a seat shift (−39) that proved to be much too large (see the review of 1982 forecasts in Michael Lewis-Beck and Tom Rice, "Forecasting U.S. House Elections," *Legislative Studies Quarterly* [August 1984], 475–486). Money and organization appear to be the main reasons

the Republicans were so successful at cutting their losses. The Republican party is more effective than ever at raising money, and the Republicans allocate their resources with much greater skill than do the Democrats. Intimidated by a superior Republican organization, the Democrats spent too much money (and obtained "too many" votes) in 1982 on behalf of candidates who did not need quite so much defending. Consequently, many of the potentially successful Democratic candidates were underfinanced and suffered marginal defeats at the hands of vulnerable Republicans. On this point, see the analysis of Adam Clymer, "The Economic Basis of 'Throwing the Bums Out' in the 1980 and 1982 Elections," paper delivered at the Annual Meeting of the American Political Science Association, Chicago, September 1983; Gary Jacobson, "Reagan, Reaganomics, and Strategic Politics in 1982: A Test of Alternative Theories of Midterm Congressional Elections," paper delivered at the Annual Meeting of the American Political Science Association, Chicago, September 1983; and Gary Jacobson and Samuel Kernell, "Party Organization and the Efficient Distribution of Congressional Campaign Resources: Republicans and Democrats in 1982," paper delivered at the Weingart-Caltech Conference on Institutional Context of Elections, Pasadena, California, February 1984. The Jacobson and Kernell work on campaign finance and resource allocation is truly pathbreaking.

4. Compared to the Republicans' strength in the House after the 1982 elections, the Republican gain amounted to 16 seats.

5. Representative Guy Vander Jagt of Michigan, chairman of the Republican Campaign Committee, put it more graphically. He said that unless the Republicans gained 20 to 22 seats in the House, "the Reagan revolution is over." Cited in Hedrick Smith, "Reagan Faces Difficult Task in Leading Divided Congress," *New York Times*, November 8, 1984, p. 1.

6. Kerry replaced Paul Tsongas, also a Democratic liberal.

7. With respect to 1980, examples of this view are Norman Podhoretz, "The New American Majority," *Commentary* 71 (January 1981), 19–28; Theodore White, *America in Search of Itself* (New York: Harper and Row, 1981); and (in a piece written just before the election) R. M. Scammon and Ben J. Wattenberg, "Is It the End of an Era?" *Public Opinion* (October/November 1980), 2–12.

8. The first extended development of the idea that election results often represent rational, retrospective performance judgments by the voters appears in V. O. Key, *The Responsible Electorate* (New York: Vintage, 1966). For a more modern treatment of this idea, see Morris Fiorina, *Retrospective Voting in American National Elections* (New Haven: Yale University Press, 1981), and the recent review of the literature by D. Roderick Kiewiet and Douglas Rivers, "A Retrospective on Retrospective Voting," California Institute of Technology, Social Science Working Paper 528, June 1984.

9. Studies drawing broadly similar conclusions about the sources of the 1980 election outcomes include Paul Abramson et al., *Change and Continuity in the 1980 Elections* (Washington, D.C.: Congressional Quarterly Press, 1981); Walter Dean Burnham, "The 1981 Earthquake: Realignment, Reaction or

What?" in Thomas Ferguson and Joel Rogers, eds., *The Hidden Election: Politics and Economics in the 1980 Presidential Campaign* (New York: Pantheon, 1981); Marlene Pomper, ed., *The Election of 1980* (Chatham, N.J.: Chatham House Publishers, 1981); Austen Ranney, ed., *The American Elections of 1980* (Washington, D.C.: American Enterprise Institute, 1981); *The Gallup Political Index*, Report No. 181, September 1980; and Garry Orren and E. J. Dionne, "The Next New Deal," *Working Papers* (May/June 1981). An analysis more compatible with the "shift to the right" interpretation appears in Warren Miller and Merrill Shanks, "Policy Directions and Presidential Leadership: Alternative Interpretations of the 1980 Presidential Election," *British Journal of Political Science* 12 (July 1982), 299 356.

10. The political science literature on party realignments is enormous, and I will make no attempt to review or reference it here. One of the most comprehensive studies is James Sundquist's *Dynamics of the Party System: Alignment and Realignment of Political Parties in the United States*, rev. ed. (Washington, D.C.: Brookings, 1983), which includes numerous references to the literature.

11. Sundquist, *Dynamics of the Party System*, p. 425.

12. Of the 22 Republican seats up for election in 1986, 16 were held by first-term senators.

13. Indeed, President Reagan gained fewer supporters in the House than the 16-seat shift in favor of the Republicans (14 seats, counted from the Republicans' strength just prior to the election) would suggest. Four of the new Republicans replaced Democrats who strongly supported Reagan's legislative program during his first term.

14. I refer here to four-quarter growth rates, as shown in Fig. 6.2.

15. Recall that for a lag parameter $g = 0.8$, the three quarters nearest the election contribute about 50 percent to the total weight of the cumulative average.

16. Notice that the only other sitting president to be defeated in a postwar reelection bid—Ford in 1976—also had a distinctively poor macroeconomic record.

17. The estimates in equation (6.1) indicate that Gallup approval ratings exhibit wider swings than do presidential voting outcomes: that is, people find it easier to approve or disapprove of a president's performance than to give or deny the incumbent party their presidential vote. More evidence on the connection between Gallup poll ratings and presidential election outcomes appears in Lee Sigelman, "Presidential Popularity and Presidential Elections," *Public Opinion Quarterly* (Winter 1979), 532–534; and Michael Lewis-Beck and Tom Rice, "Presidential Popularity and Presidential Vote," *Public Opinion Quarterly* (Winter 1982), 534–537.

18. The Gallup rating was not available to me at the time of writing, so I used the approval rating obtained by the *New York Times*/CBS News poll, which is based on the Gallup approval question.

19. A great many studies have found the per capita real income (or output) growth rate to be the single best predictor of election outcomes. See, for example, Robert Wescott and Miriam Goldberg, "The Economy and the 1984

Presidential Election," *Wharton Quarterly Model Outlook* (January 1984), 69–72; Ray C. Fair, "The Effect of Economic Events on Votes for President," *Review of Economics and Statistics* (1978), 159–173; and Robert J. Gordon, "Who Will Win the Election?" *Gordon Update* (Spring 1984), 4–6. Real disposable income is a very broad measure of economic well-being, inasmuch as it includes income from all sources, is adjusted for inflation and taxes, and moves with changes in unemployment.

20. By virtue of the lag-weight rate of decay parameter g, equation (6.2) is nonlinear, and so a standard nonlinear least-squares algorithm was used for estimation. An intuitive description of the nonlinear estimation procedure used in equation (6.2) might be helpful to some readers. Nonlinear estimation of equation (6.2) is equivalent to ordinary least-squares estimation of

$$V_t = \beta_0 + \beta_1 R_t^*$$

where R^* is formed from

$$R_t^* = \sum_{i=0}^{14} g^i R_{t-i-1} \left(1 \bigg/ \sum_{i=0}^{14} g^i \right)$$

and $0 \le g \le 1$.

Forming an R^* variate for every value of g in the interval 0 to 1, running an ordinary least-squares regression with each R^* so formed, and choosing the equation yielding the minimum standard error of the regression (best fit) would give estimates of β_0, β_1, and g identical to those reported in the text.

Notice that if the best-fitting least-squares regression were based on $g = 0$, then R_t^* would equal R_{t-1}, implying that election outcomes responded only to the preelection quarter (July–August–September) record. If it were based on $g = 1$, R_t^* would equal $(1/15) \cdot \sum_{i=0}^{14} R_{t-i-1}$, implying that election outcomes responded to an arithmetic average of real income growth rates during the presidential administration. The value of g producing the best fit is $g = 0.8$, which means that R_t^* is based on a cumulative geometrically weighted average of the values R_{t-i-1}, $i = 0, 1, 2, \ldots , 14$, with the lag-weight sequence $0.21(t - 1)$, $0.17(t - 2)$, $0.13(t - 3)$, $0.11(t - 4)$, $\ldots , 0.01(t - 15)$.

Finally, notice that equation (6.2) is similar in spirit to the innovative model developed by Edward Tufte, *Political Control of the Economy* (Princeton: Princeton University Press, 1978), table 5-6, p. 122, which uses the election-year change in per capita real personal disposable income and the net advantage of the incumbent party's candidate as measured by the average number of "good" versus "bad" points about the candidates' personalities mentioned by respondents in the election surveys conducted by the Survey Research Center at the University of Michigan. One problem with the net-advantage variable (which exhibits a correlation of 0.91 with the nationwide presidential vote over the 1948–1976 period) is that it may come a bit too close to being a survey-based measure of intention to vote for the candidate of the incumbent party. Another is that this variable cannot be used to forecast election outcomes because data necessary to form the net advantage index are not available until long after the election. As for the real income variable, the *cumulative* weighted-average quarter-on-quarter real income growth rate used in equation (6.2) does a better job empirically of explaining presidential voting outcomes than do election-year income changes.

21. Taking equation (6.2) literally, we see that the predicted vote share for the incumbent party's presidential candidate reaches 52 percent for a cumulative growth rate equal to just 1.7 percent: $(52 - 45.7)/3.3 = 1.7$.

22. See, for example, Lewis-Beck and Rice, "Forecasting U.S. House Elections"; and John R. Hibbing and J. R. Alford, "Economic Conditions and the Forgotten Side of Congress: A Foray into U.S. Senate Elections," *British Journal of Political Science* (July 1982), 413–421.

23. The fact that the ERA and abortion issues contributed little to Reagan's appeal comes as no surprise in view of the general distribution of public opinion on these questions, which diverged sharply from the Republican candidate's strong, well-publicized positions. For example, 1980 Gallup polls reported that only 31 percent of the public opposed the Equal Rights Amendment and only 18 percent of the public favored making abortions "illegal under all circumstances." These distributions have been quite stable since the mid-1970s. See the *Gallup Opinion Index*, Report No. 183, December 1980, pp. 2–3.

The University of Michigan's Survey Research Center National Election Study data also show that domestic economic concerns had a much bigger influence on voting decisions in 1980 than did the crisis in Iran or other issues. See the report by A. H. Miller and M. P. Wattenberg, "Policy and Performance Voting in the 1980 Election," unpublished, Center for Political Studies, University of Michigan, presented to the American Political Science Association, September 1981.

24. According to the Federal Election Commission, the various New Right organizations raised more money nationally for the 1980 elections than did the entire Democratic party. See the discussion of Frances Fitzgerald, "The Triumphs of the New Right," *New York Review of Books*, November 19, 1981, p. 19 ff. Similar data for 1984 were not available when this chapter was written.

25. Surprisingly, according to the *Los Angeles Times* exit polls, almost half the 1984 voters who felt that the federal deficit was the most important election issue supported Reagan rather than Mondale. Apparently many voters bought the Republican charge that the tax increase Mondale advocated to help reduce the enormous federal deficits opened up under Reagan would in the end, wind up being used to finance new federal spending.

26. See The Roper Center, *General Social Surveys, 1972–1980: Cumulative Codebook* (1980), pp. 71–74; and *Public Opinion* (February/March 1981), 27.

27. See the report on this survey by A. Clymer, "Public Prefers a Balanced Budget to Large Cut in Taxes, Poll Shows," *New York Times*, February 3, 1981, B9, p. 1.

28. In 1976, for example, only 37 percent of the GSS respondents felt we were spending too little or about the right amount on "welfare." See Roper

Center, *General Social Surveys, 1972–1980: Cumulative Codebook* (1980), pp. 71–74; and *Public Opinion* (February/March 1981), 27.

29. *Public Opinion* (April/May 1983), 27.

30. *Gallup Report*, November 1982, p. 16; and *Gallup Report*, February 1983, p. 20.

31. William Schneider, "The Divided Electorate," *National Journal* (October 29, 1983), 2203; and idem, "The Voters' Mood in 1986," *National Journal* (December 7, 1985), 2759. Also see Seymour M. Lipset, "The Economy, Elections, and Public Opinion," *Toqueville Review* (Fall 1983), 431–469; and idem, "Beyond 1984: The Anomalies of American Politics," *PS* (Spring 1986), 222–236.

32. Not surprisingly, Ford received the second worst rating. Only 5 percent of the respondents considered him "best on domestic affairs," and 13 percent considered him "least able to get things done." The data are reported in *Public Opinion* (February/March, 1981), 38. The University of Michigan's Survey Research Center National Election Study data show that Ronald Reagan was not very positively evaluated during the 1980 campaign. In "Policy and Performance Voting," Miller and Wattenberg, reported that over the history of the National Election Studies, which began in 1952, Reagan was evaluated less favorably than any other successful presidential candidate. But his opponent—Jimmy Carter—was seen even less favorably.

33. Reagan put a similar question to viewers of the October 28, 1980 Reagan-Carter debate, when in his closing statement he encouraged voters to ask themselves, "Are you better off than you were four years ago?"

34. The Anderson voters, who found both Reagan and Carter unappealing, appear to have hurt neither major party candidate relative to the other, and so their numbers may be ignored for the most part for the purposes of this analysis.

35. See Orren and Dionne, "The Next New Deal."

36. Indeed, the last big contractions under the Democrats were in 1893–1894 and 1895–1896 during Grover Cleveland's presidency. The Democrats led the Republicans on 37 of the 41 occasions between 1951 and 1980 when the Gallup poll asked "Which political party—the Republic or Democratic—do you think will do a better job of keeping the country prosperous?" The Democratic advantage averaged 9 percentage points in the 1950s, 24 points in the 1960s, and 17 points in the 1970s. By the fall of 1980 the Democratic lead on the prosperity issue had vanished. See *Gallup Opinion Index*, Report No. 181, September 1980, p. 8.

37. Percentages were computed from the marginal distributions in the 1976 and 1980 SRC National Election Study codebooks. The questions were "Do you think [inflation, the problems of unemployment] would be handled better by the Democrats, by the Republicans, or about the same by both?"

38. See, for example, the August/September 1984 *Gallup Report*, pp. 17–18; and *Public Opinion* (December/January 1985), p. 38.

39. I refer here to President Reagan's February 18, 1981, budget statement, "America's New Beginning: A Program for Economic Recovery," Executive Office of the President/Office of Management and Budget, 1981.

40. Cited in Lipset, "Beyond 1984," p. 236.

41. Sunquist, *Dynamics of the Party System*, p. 448.

7. Political Parties and Macroeconomic Policies and Outcomes

1. Thomas Edsall's provocative book argues that the class and income bases of the parties have become more distinct, although power within the Democratic party is increasingly exercised by an affluent "reformist" elite. See Thomas Edsall, *The New Politics of Inequality* (New York: Norton, 1984).

2. On class, parties, and voting, see Richard F. Hamilton, *Class and Politics in the United States* (New York: Wiley, 1972); and David Knoke, *Change and Continuity in American Politics* (Baltimore: Johns Hopkins University Press, 1976).

3. Occupational-class cleavages in voting show some signs of having declined among whites since the mid-1960s, although the trend is not very pronounced and is often overinterpreted. See the data and discussion in Paul R. Abramson et al., *Change and Continuity in the 1980 Elections* (Washington, D.C.: Congressional Quarterly Press, 1982), chap. 5. On the other hand, the income class bases of the parties appear to have been strengthened since the 1960s.

4. Leonard Silk and David Vogel, *Ethics and Profits: The Crisis of Confidence in American Business* (New York: Simon and Schuster, 1976), pp. 62, 63, 64.

5. Nat Goldfinger, "Full Employment: The Neglected Policy?" *American Federationist* 79 (November 1972), 7–8.

6. The results of the survey, which are reported in the *Washington Post* of September 7, 1976, were made available to me by Sidney Verba.

7. The contrasting priorities of the parties with respect to macroeconomic and distributional issues also show up in the contents of party platforms and the annual Economic Reports of the President and Reports of the Council of Economic Advisors. See the content analyses in Edward Tufte, *Political Control of the Economy* (Princeton: Princeton University Press, 1978), chap. 4.

8. These movements include: the 1953–1954, 1957–1958, and 1960–1961 contractions under Eisenhower; the 1970 recession under Nixon; the 1974–1975 recession under Ford; and the 1981–1982 contraction under Reagan. The 1979–1980 recession under Carter is the sole exception to the pattern.

9. The partisan model is based on my earlier study, "Political Parties and Macroeconomic Policy," *American Political Science Review* 71 (December 1977), 1467–1487. For the presentation here and later in this chapter, I have drawn also on Henrik J. Madse, "Partisanship and Macroeconomic Outcomes: A Reconsideration," in D. A. Hibbs, Jr., and H. Fassbender, eds., *Contemporary Political Economy* (Amsterdam: North Holland, 1981), 269–282.

10. My "partisan," or "party cleavage," view has little in common with the bulk of the work in the formal theoretical tradition for modeling party and candidate policy behavior that is based on multidimensional extensions of Downsian spatial analysis in which the parties are mere vote maximizers. See Anthony Downs, *An Economic Theory of Democracy* (New York: Harper, 1957). Although technically rigorous, this tradition is not very helpful empirically

because it does not account for well-documented systematic differences in the parties' policy stands and behavior. Under certain restrictive conditions, such theories predict that both parties will take the same policy stands (the multivariate mean of voters' most preferred policy points); under more general conditions, these theories are not able to make any firm predictions at all about party policy behavior. For discussion and citations, see Benjamin Page, "Elections and Social Choice: The State of the Evidence," *American Journal of Political Science* (August 1977), 639–668.

Lines of formal theorizing that are more in tune with the partisan framework because they acknowledge the importance of the preferences of the parties' core constituencies in the formation of policy stands appear in the work of Peter Aranson and Peter Ordeshook, "Spatial Strategies for Sequential Elections," in Richard Niemi and Herbert Weisberg, eds., *Probability Models of Collective Decision Making* (Columbus, Ohio: Charles E. Merrill, 1972), pp. 298–331; James Coleman, "The Positions of Political Parties in Elections," in Niemi and Weisberg, *Probability Models*, pp. 332–357; and the recent papers of Gary Cox et al., "Policy Choice and Electoral Investment," May 1984, unpublished; and Henry Chappell and William Keech, "Policy Motivation and Party Differences in a Dynamic Spatial Model of Party Competition," *American Political Science Review* (September 1986), 881–899. Donald Wittman's work is also relevant in this regard. Wittman sees parties and candidates as seeking distinctive policy goals rather than simply acting as vote maximizers. See Donald Wittman, "Parties as Utility Maximizers," *American Political Science Review* 67 (June 1973), 490–498; and idem, "Candidates with Policy Preferences: A Dynamic Model," *Journal of Economic Theory* 14 (February 1977), 180–189. Theoretical work in progress by Alberto Allesina of Harvard University on macroeconomic policy also is motivated by the idea that parties represent the interests of different constituencies and have different objectives. See Allesina's preliminary report, "Rules, Discretion and Reputation in a Two-Party System," Harvard University, March 1985, unpublished.

11. A limitation of this setup is that the Dem term, which is defined by the party controlling the presidency, does not take into account the partisan balance in Congress. The model is extended to include the party balance in Congress in the next section.

12. The model is written for quarterly time; therefore periods are quarters.

13. An alternative but empirically and theoretically identical interpretation of the U^T equation is that the parties have different ideas about the normal, or natural, rate of unemployment, U^N, which lead them to pursue different targets.

14. A fascinating account of this process during the early days of the Reagan administration, which hit the ground running harder than most, appears in William Greider's now famous article "The Education of David Stockman," *Atlantic* (December 1981), 27–40. A book-length version of this amusing tale was published subsequently under the title *The Education of David Stockman and Other Americans* (New York: Dutton, 1982).

15. Connolly's remarks were made in an interview with economist Pierre Rinfret.

16. Recall that because ln Q is the dependent variable in the real output equations, the parameters give the proportional responses of Q to unit movements in the independent variables. Hence, a coefficient of -0.009 indicates an initial decline of 0.9 percent in real output per unit change in the right-side variable. Given the way the Shock term is calculated, which is described at the bottom of Table 7.3, its coefficient in the log real output regressions should be in the vicinity of 0.01.

17. Take, for example, the real output model, equation (7.6). Readers familiar with discrete time dynamics will recognize that (holding ln Q^N fixed) the steady-state solution of this (stable) difference equation is

$$\ln Q = \phi_1 \cdot b_0/1 - [(1 - \phi_1 + \phi_2) - \phi_2]$$
$$+ \phi_1/1 - [(1 - \phi_1 + \phi_2) - \phi_2]\ln Q^N$$
$$+ \phi_1 \cdot b_1/1 - [(1 - \phi_1 + \phi_2) - \phi_2]\text{Dem}$$
$$+ b_2/1 - [(1 - \phi_1 + \phi_2) - \phi_2]\text{Shock}$$

and therefore

$$\ln Q^* = b_0 + \ln Q^N + b_1 \text{ Dem} + b_2/\phi_1 \text{ Shock}$$

where ln Q^* denotes the steady-state solution.

Analogous steady-state results hold for the unemployment model:

$$U^* = b_0 + U^N + b_1 \text{ Dem} + b_2/\phi_1 \text{ Shock}$$

It is not realistic to evaluate the steady-state effects of Shock, because that variable cannot remain nonzero indefinitely. Also, as will be pointed out later, partisan effects are bounded if U^N is a true natural unemployment rate.

18. In turn this implies (by Okun's Law) a percentage gap 2 to 3 times larger in the real output targets of the parties.

19. In the concluding section of Chapter 8 I suggest that this is one important source of cycles in partisan control of the presidency. Also see the discussion later in this chapter about the relaxation of unemployment targets with increasing inflation.

20. The results graphed in Figures 7.2 and 7.3 were obtained by simulating the equations with Dem held at $+1$ for thirty-two periods and then held at 0 for thirty-two periods for enough cycles to dissipate completely transitory initial conditions. In the simulation runs exogenous and stochastic shocks were kept at 0, and normal unemployment (U^N) and normal log output (ln Q^N) were held fixed at their 1983:2 values. The unemployment results are reported as deviations from U^N and are in percentage points. The log real output results are deviations from (and, hence, percentages of) ln $Q^N + b_0$.

21. The thirty-two-quarter interparty unemployment difference is consis-

tent with the results of my 1977 article, which used a more empirical (less theoretical) Box-Jenkins-Tiao methodology to approach the same issue. The partisan difference of 2.36 percentage points reported in that paper would have been 2.08 points (and, hence, even closer to the estimate obtained here) had I simulated the model long enough to nullify arbitrary initial conditions. (See Douglas Hibbs, Jr., "Political Parties and Macroeconomic Policy.") The substantive specification and ARIMA equation methodology of my 1977 article is extended in several important respects in James Alt, "Party Strategies, World Demand, and Unemployment in Britain and the United States, 1947–1983," *American Political Science Review* (December 1985), 1016–40. Results compatible with those in my earlier article and here also appear in Henry Chappel and William Keech, "Party Differences in Macroeconomic Policies and Outcomes," *American Economic Review* 76 (May 1986), 71–74; Alberto Allesina and Jeffrey Sachs, "Political Parties and the Business Cycle in the United States, 1948–1984," National Bureau of Economic Research, Working Paper No. 1940, 1986; and Douglas A. Hibbs, Jr., and Christopher Dennis, "The Politics and Economics of Income Distribution Outcomes in the Postwar United States," November 1986, unpublished.

22. For unemployment the proportion of the thirty-two-quarter partisan impact achieved by the sixteenth period is about 0.98; for real output it is a bit smaller—about 0.90.

23. Because of adjustment lags in the realization of economic goals, one cannot draw sound conclusions about partisan differences by contrasting mean performance computed over all Democratic years with the average for all Republican years, as is commonly done in the literature. See, for example, the discussions of interparty differences in unemployment priorities and performance in Benjamin Page, *Who Gets What from Government* (Berkeley: University of California Press, 1983), pp. 185–186; and in Paul Peretz, *The Political Economy of Inflation in the United States* (Chicago: University of Chicago Press, 1983), pp. 204–207.

A simple illustration will clarify this point. Suppose we observed the following sequence of annual unemployment rates during a four-year Democratic administration followed by a four-year Republican administration.

8, 7, 6, 5 | 5, 6, 7, 8

Contrasting the arithmetic means (6.5 in each case) would indicate no interparty difference in performance, but obviously such a comparison yields a distorted picture of the impact of variations in party control of the presidency on the time path of unemployment.

Similarly, if one were to contrast the average Democratic and Republican unemployment performance over the first sixteen quarters of each partisan cycle shown in Figure 7.2, the implied interparty difference would be negligible. Computing arithmetic means over the entire thirty-two quarters of each partisan cycle in Figure 7.2 would show a partisan difference in the correct direction, but it would be understated.

24. I know of no instance, however, in which favorable performance early in a first term was credited by a president to the previous administration. A recent and unusually stark illustration of such asymmetry was President Reagan's attempt to tie the deep 1981–1982 contraction to the policies of Carter while simultaneously claiming full credit for the disinflation that the recession (along with very good luck in food and energy prices) produced.

25. Chapter 5 supplied indirect evidence that voters understand this, or at least behave as if they did. When political support was modeled explicitly as a function of interadministration and interparty economic performance comparisons, estimates of the backward-looking discount rate (the weights given current and past performance outcomes) used to form contemporaneous political judgments indicated that after sixteen quarters fluctuations in a president's support was based entirely on his own record, as opposed to his record in comparison to that of previous administrations.

26. This is the main point of Nathaniel Beck's article "Parties, Administrations and American Macroeconomic Outcomes," *American Political Science Review* 76 (March 1982), 83–93. Although marred by misunderstandings of difference equations and, hence, miscalculations of dynamic impacts, this article indicates that autoregressive unemployment models with administration-specific terms yield corrected R^2s slightly higher than those of parallel models that include only party terms. I discuss this and related points in Douglas Hibbs, Jr., "Comment on Beck," *American Political Science Review* 77 (June 1983), 447–451.

27. During the period studied here the Republicans have enjoyed outright majorities in the House only once (1953–1954) and in the Senate only three times (1953–1954, 1981–1982, and 1983–1984).

28. The possibility that the speed of adjustment to targets, as opposed to the magnitudes of targets, is conditioned by the balance of party forces in Congress was also evaluated by allowing ϕ_1 to be variable and writing it as a function of terms measuring the partisan balance. This led to much more complicated nonlinear equations than those discussed in this book, but the data were not rich enough for them to be estimated successfully.

29. The coding for Korea applies only to three periods in the regression range: 1953:1–1953:3.

30. An unusually candid admission of this may be found in Barry Goldwater's Op-Ed page essay attacking the Democratic ticket just prior to the 1976 election. After warning of the dire fiscal and inflationary consequences of a victory by Carter and the Democrats ("an alliance between an arrogant liberal majority in Congress and a labor President"), Goldwater observed: "Jimmy Carter and his running mate, Senator Walter F. Mondale, know as we do that a full-employment economy has never been achieved in this country and probably never will be. The closest we have ever come was in the midst of an all-out war when many in the labor force were in the military and our munitions industries were running at capacity." Barry Goldwater, "The Future with Ford," *New York Times*, November 1, 1976, p. D1.

31. The war-related fiscal thrusts in the regression range are concentrated

during Johnson's presidency (Vietnam). Because this was a period of especially vigorous growth and low unemployment, adding the War term tends
to diminish, probably by too great a margin, the estimated partisan effects (b_1
Dem).

32. George J. Stigler, "General Economic Conditions and National Elections," *American Economic Review, Papers and Proceedings* 63 (May 1973), 167.

33. Nor is it true that Republican and Democratic administrations are not
distinguished by the priority they give to unemployment, as the evidence
presented plainly shows.

34. In 1976, prior to the changes pushed through by the Reagan administration, average effective rates peaked at 33 percent for incomes between
$200,000 and $500,000, and then declined to 28 percent at the highest income
levels. Not only were the effective rates higher than they are now, but the
rate schedule was more progressive. See Joseph A. Pechman, *Federal Tax
Policy*, fourth ed. (Washington, D.C.: Brookings, 1983) and earlier editions;
and see Henry J. Aaron and Michael J. Boskin, eds., *The Economics of Taxation*
(Washington, D.C.: Brookings, 1980). Also see Chapter 9 of this book.

35. Unemployment Insurance payroll taxes are borne directly by employers alone; Social Security payroll taxes are shared equally by employees and
employers. Much evidence indicates, however, that employers shift their
payroll tax contributions to employees in the form of lower wages, and so
for practical purposes these contributions probably are more accurately
treated entirely as taxes on personal incomes. It must also be remembered
that although Social Security taxes reduce the progressivity of the tax system,
Social Security benefits increase after-tax income equality.

36. On the other hand, state and local taxes are largely either proportional
or regressive, and hence tend to offset much (perhaps nearly all) of the
progressivity of federal taxes. It is federal fiscal activity over time in relation
to partisan control of the federal government that concerns us here, however.
To get an idea of the (modest) direct impact of federal personal taxation
(income plus payroll taxes) on the distribution of income among families at a
point in time, consider Radner's data for 1972:

Effect of federal personal taxes on the distribution of family
income, 1972

Quintile	Before tax	After tax	Change
Lowest fifth	4.92	5.26	+0.34
Second fifth	11.59	12.23	+0.64
Middle fifth	17.22	17.69	+0.47
Fourth fifth	23.57	23.87	+0.30
Highest fifth	42.70	40.95	−1.75

Source: As reported in Alan S. Blinder, "The Level and Distribution of Economic Well-Being," in M. Feldstein, ed., *The American Economy in Transition* (Chicago: University of Chicago Press,
1980), table 6.17, p. 443.

37. The evolution of the federal transfer system is reviewed insightfully by Norman Furniss and Timothy Tilton in *The Case for the Welfare State* (Bloomington: Indiana University Press, 1979).

38. *Complete Presidential Press Conferences* (New York: DaCapo Press, 1972), vol. 9, pp. 437–438, cited in Furniss and Tilton, *The Case for the Welfare State*, p. 239.

39. Actually, the program initiated by the Johnson administration in 1965 was Aid to the Blind, Aid to the Permanently Disabled, and Old Age Assistance. This program, combined with the extensions enacted in 1972, is now known as Supplemental Security Income.

40. The "dependent" poor who are not available for work include most AFDC mothers, the blind, the disabled, and so on.

41. The official poverty level is adjusted each year to reflect changes in the Consumer Price Index. In 1983 individuals with cash incomes below $5061 and families of four with incomes below $10,178 were classified as poor.

42. See Chapter 3, Table 3.2 for data on quintile income shares. Also see Radner's data in note 36 above.

43. See Timothy Smeeding, "The Antipoverty Effectiveness of In-Kind Transfers," *Journal of Human Resources* 12 (Summer 1977), 360–378; and idem, "On the Distribution of Net Income: Comment," *Southern Economic Journal* 46 (January 1979), 932–944.

44. The change in the numbers, then, comes from adjusting the value of Medicaid expenditures downward from 1.3 percent of total pretransfer personal income to $0.7 \cdot 1.3 = 0.9$ percent. Also, remember that the actual redistributions should be evaluated in terms of posttax and posttransfer income and therefore depend on the distribution of taxes paid as well as that of transfers received. The data on "net" income shares analyzed later take this into account, but the numbers used above yield an accurate picture of the magnitudes involved.

45. Sheldon Danziger et al., "How Income Transfer Programs Affect Work, Savings and the Income Distribution: A Critical Review," *Journal of Economic Literature* 14 (September 1981), 1019.

46. Unfortunately, revised data covering the Carter and Reagan periods were not available to me at the time of writing. An analysis of revised data through 1983 by Christopher Dennis of California State University, Long Beach and me appears in "Politics and Economics of Income Distribution."

47. Recall from Table 3.3 that movements in unemployment are associated with income shifts between the bottom 40 percent and the top 20 percent of the "census" income distribution.

48. Cited in Francis Piven and Richard Cloward, *Regulating the Poor: The Functions of Public Welfare* (New York: Random House, 1971), p. 53.

49. Dwight D. Eisenhower, *Mandate for Change* (New York: Doubleday, 1963), pp. 441–442.

50. Hugh Heclo, "The Welfare State: The Costs of American Self-Sufficiency," in Richard Rose, ed., *Lessons from America: An Exploration* (London: Macmillan, 1974), p. 259.

51. David Stockman, "The Social Pork Barrel," *Public Interest* (Spring 1975), 3–30.

52. Benjamin Page draws the same conclusion from his review of postwar income maintenance and welfare policy: "American political history in recent years has tended to follow a cyclical pattern, in which Democratic social welfare activism has been followed by Republican quiescence and then a new outpouring of Democratic activism." See Page, *Who Gets What*, p. 92. Page is much more critical and pessimistic than I am, however, about what has been achieved to improve equality.

53. There is a great body of comparative and international evidence that the strength of Left parties (in the context of American domestic politics, the Democratic party is the party of the Left) yields improvements in income equality. See J. Corina van Arnhem and Geurt Schotsman, "Do Parties Affect the Distribution of Incomes?" in Francis Castles, ed., *The Impact of Parties* (Beverly Hills: Sage, 1982); David Cameron, "The Expansion of the Public Economy: A Comparative Analysis," *American Political Science Review* 72 (December 1978), 1243–1261; J. Dryzek, "Politics, Economics and Inequality: A Cross-National Analysis," *European Journal of Political Research* 6 (1978), 399–410; and C. Hewitt, "The Effect of Political Democracy and Social Democracy on Equality in Industrial Societies: A Cross-National Comparison," *American Sociological Review* 42 (1977), 450–464.

54. Because we are dealing with annual data, higher order adjustment dynamics, such as the second-order schemes used for the quarterly unemployment and real output series, are not necessary.

55. Appropriate interaction models were estimated but are not shown in Table 7.6. In a subsequent analysis (Dennis and Hibbs, "Politics and Economics of Income Distribution"), I show that the Democrats' strength in the Congress exerts influence on income distribution by boosting the flow of funds to transfer programs.

56. Notice that because I_{t-1} appears on the right side of the model with (implicit) unit coefficient, the implied impact of Dem accumulates indefinitely by $\phi \cdot b_1$ per year. Obviously, the effects are in principle bounded (inequality cannot decline or equality increase without limit), but an unbounded model describes the postwar data well.

57. Arthur Okun, *Equality and Efficiency: The Big Tradeoff* (Washington, D.C.: Brookings, 1975).

58. Raymond Wolfinger and Steven Rosenstone, *Who Votes?* (New Haven: Yale University Press, 1980), fig. 2.2.

59. Page, *Who Gets What*, pp. 51, 97. Also see Wolfinger and Rosenstone, *Who Votes?* table 6.3.

60. For a start on these matters, see Daniel Bell, "The End of American Exceptionalism," in Nathan Glazer and Irving Kristol, eds., *The American Commonwealth 1976* (New York: Basic Books, 1976); Donald J. Devine, *The Political Culture of the United States* (Boston: Little, Brown, 1972); Louis Hartz, *The Liberal Tradition in America* (New York: Harcourt, 1955); Samuel Huntington, *American Politics: The Promise of Disharmony* (Cambridge, Mass.: Harvard University Press, 1981); Seymour Martin Lipset, "American Exception-

alism in North American Perspective," in E. M. Adams, ed., *The Idea of America* (Cambridge, Mass.: Ballinger, 1977), pp. 107–161; Lipset, "Why Is There No Socialism in the United States?" in Seweryn Bialer and Sophia Sluzar, eds., *Sources of Contemporary Radicalism* (Boulder, Colo.: Westview Press, 1977), pp. 31–149, 346–363; and Werner Sombart, *Why Is There No Socialism in the United States?* (London: Macmillan, 1976; first published in 1906). For some ideas derived from highly stylized models about why the tax system produced by electoral politics is not more progressive, see Gerald Kramer and James Snyder, "Fairness, Self-Interest, and the Politics of the Progressive Income Tax," unpublished, June 1983.

61. To gain an idea of just how complicated the measurement of fiscal thrust is, see Alan Blinder and Robert Solow, "Analytical Foundations of Fiscal Policy," in Alan Blinder et al., *The Economics of Public Finance* (Washington, D.C.: Brookings, 1974), 3–115.

62. Monetary policy was once viewed as a rather arcane matter, well beyond the ken of the average citizen. Even John F. Kennedy, while a Senator, is said to have been unable to distinguish monetary from fiscal policy. For many people monetary issues no doubt remain somewhat mysterious, but following the money supply-led contractions of the 1970s, interest in and knowledge of the topic percolated down to the grass roots. A story told by E. Gerald Corrigan, formerly president of the Federal Reserve Bank of Minneapolis and now head of the Federal Reserve Bank of New York, illustrates the point vividly. After speaking to a group of local steelworker union leaders in northeastern Minnesota in 1981, Corrigan remembers expecting hostile remarks about high interest rates and unemployment: "After I got through talking, there was an ominous silence. Then, a tough-looking man in a corner of the room raised his hand: 'Mr. Corrigan, I got a question for you. Why was M1 down 3 billion dollars last week?'" The anecdote appears in Tom Herman and Alan Murray, "M1 Mania Irks Fed, but Monetary Data Still Rattle Markets," *Wall Street Journal*, January 24, 1984, pp. 1, 19.

63. See Jerome Stein, "Monetarist, Keynesian, and New Classical Economics," *American Economic Review* 71 (May 1981), 139–144; and John Taylor, "Stabilization, Accommodation, and Monetary Rules," *American Economic Review* 71 (May 1981), 145–149.

64. Here and later in this chapter, all growth rates are formed as the first difference of the natural logarithms and are expressed at annual rates. Hence $m = \ln(M1_t/M1_{t-1}) \cdot 400$. After 1959:1, money supply growth rates are based on the "new" M1.

65. Thus $c\bar{p}$ denotes the weighted sum of recent past inflation rates: $c_1 p_{t-2} + c_2 p_{t-1} + \ldots + c_j p_{t-j}$.

66. An alternative view is that money supply growth relative to *expected* inflation is what affects unemployment and real output. If expected inflation is based on lagged inflation (which to a great extent is the case, given the inertia of wages and prices), the two views have identical empirical implications. Therefore the expectations view is also embodied in the rest of the equations estimated in this section.

67. Adding interaction terms of the form $(\bar{p} \cdot Dem_t)$, where, as earlier,

Dem is +1 for Democratic administrations and 0 for Republican ones, would allow interparty differences in the sensitivity of monetary targets to inflation that are independent of cross-party differences in unemployment targets. See the discussion later in this chapter.

68. The only difference between equations (7.1) and (7.12) is that Dem appears without any lag. The lag is dropped here because, in principle, monetary policy can respond immediately (within a quarterly time frame) to an administration's preferences.

69. If FCABR denotes federal cyclically adjusted budget revenues and FCABE denotes federal cyclically adjusted budget expenditures (seasonally adjusted at annual rates), then Fisc is formed: Fisc = ln (FCABR/FCABE)·100. Both FCABR and FCABE are also seasonally adjusted and are expressed at annual rates. Standardizing the cyclically adjusted surplus/deficit to a revenue/expenditure base, as opposed to a GNP base, allows analysis of fluctuations in fiscal thrust that are not influenced by trends in the federal tax and spending share of GNP. The cyclically adjusted budget data series are described in Frank de Leeuw and Thomas Holloway, "Cyclical Adjustment of Federal Budget and Federal Debt," *Survey of Current Business* (December 1983).

70. Estimates of $c\bar{p}$ therefore reflect both automatic responses of the adjusted surplus/deficit to inflation (c_2) and discretionary fiscal policy reactions to rising prices ($\phi_1 \cdot c_1$).

71. Recall from equation (7.10) that

$$m_t - m_{t-1} = \phi_1(m_t^T - m_{t-1})$$

Hence

$$m_t = (1 - \phi_1)m_{t-1} + \phi_1 m_t^T$$

$$= \phi_1 \sum_{i=0}^{\infty} (1 - \phi_1)^i m_{t-1-i}^T$$

And at steady state (after all adjustment lags) we have, for fixed m^T,

$$m = \phi_1/[1 - (1 - \phi_1)]m^T = m^T$$

After i lags the percentage of the adjustment of m to m^T is $[1 - (1 - \phi_1)^{i+1}]$, which for $\phi_1 = 0.63$ is 0.86, or 86 percent, when $i = 1$ (two periods, $i = 0, 1$) and 0.94, or 94 percent when $i = 2$ (three periods, $i = 0, 1, 2$).

72. Notice also that if the economy is in a deflationary spiral (that is, if $\bar{p} < 0$), the influence of $\bar{p}$ on the real money supply growth rate goes the other way. We have no empirical observations of this situation in the postwar period, however.

73. This was established by empirical results not reported.

74. In the annual unemployment model presented in Hibbs and Dennis, "Politics and Economics of Income Distribution," the impact of inflation on

the parties' unemployment goals is statistically significant and is estimated to be nearly 0.30 per extra point of inflation. The interparty unemployment performance difference for eight-year presidential regimes reported in Hibbs and Dennis, however, is nearly identical to the results discussed in this chapter.

8. Political Business Cycles

1. The seminal theoretical statement of the electorally induced economic cycle is William Nordhaus's "The Political Business Cycle," *Review of Economic Studies* 42 (April 1975), 169–190. The first sustained empirical treatment for the United States, which includes fascinating anecdotal reports along with numerous statistical analyses, is Edward Tufte's *Political Control of the Economy* (Princeton: Princeton University Press, 1978). Subsequent studies, which yield only mixed support for the basic political business cycle argument, include Kabir U. Ahmad, "An Empirical Study of Politico-Economic Interaction in the United States: A Comment," *Review of Economics and Statistics* (February 1983), 173–178; Nathaniel Beck, "Does There Exist a Political Business Cycle: A Box-Tiao Analysis," *Public Choice* 38: 2 (1982), 205–209; Thad A. Brown and Arthur A. Stein, "The Political Economy of National Elections," *Comparative Politics* 14 (July 1982), 479–497; David Cameron, "Taxes, Spending, and Deficits: Does Government Cause Inflation?" in Leon Lindberg and Charles Maier, eds., *The Politics and Sociology of Global Inflation and Stagnation* (Washington, D.C.: Brookings, 1985); Bruno S. Frey and Freidrich Schneider, "An Empirical Study of Politico-Economic Interaction in the U.S.," *Review of Economics and Statistics* 60: 7 (1978), 174–183; David G. Golden and James M. Poterba, "The Price of Popularity: The Political Business Cycle Reexamined," *American Journal of Political Science* 24 (November 1980), 696–714; L. O. Laney and T. D. Willett, "Presidential Politics, Budget Deficits, and Monetary Policy in the United States; 1960–1965," *Public Choice* 40 (1983), 53–69; Dudley Luckett and Glenn Potts, "Monetary Policy and Partisan Politics," *Journal of Money, Credit and Banking* 12 (August 1980), 540–546; C. Duncan Macrae, "A Political Model of the Business Cycle," *Journal of Political Economy* 85 (1977), 239–263; idem, "On the Political Business Cycle," in Douglas A. Hibbs, Jr., and H. Fassbender, eds., *Contemporary Political Economy: Studies in the Interdependence of Politics and Economics* (Amsterdam: North Holland, 1981), pp. 169–184; B. T. McCallum, "The Political Business Cycle: An Empirical Test," *Southern Economic Journal* (January 1978), 504–515; Kevin Maloney and Michael Smirlock, "Business Cycles and the Political Process," *Southern Economic Journal* 48 (1981), 377–392; Stephen M. Weatherford, "Do Presidents Try to Control the Economy to Win Elections?" paper delivered at the 1982 Annual Meeting of the American Political Science Association, Denver, September 2–5, 1982; Richard Winters et al., "Politics and American Public Policy: The Case of the Political Business Cycle," in Samuel Long, ed., *Handbook of Political Behavior* (New York: Plenum, 1981), pp. 39–111; and John Wooley, *Monetary Politics, the Federal Reserve and the Politics of Monetary Policy* (Cambridge: Cambridge University Press, 1984).

2. Nordhaus, "The Political Business Cycle," p. 187.

3. This assumption might be modified to say that incumbents seek a comfortable margin of victory. Given uncertainty about projected electoral outcomes, however, in practice this would amount to nearly the same thing as vote maximization. The "incumbent" party in Congress is normally defined to be the party of the president rather than the majority party in the House or Senate.

4. The "size" and political significance of this window depend on how rapidly inflation responds to lowered unemployment (the slope of the short-run Phillips curve) and on the weight the electorate gives current inflation as compared to unemployment (the marginal rate of substitution discussed in Chapter 5). Strictly speaking, if there is a Phillips curve, an incentive to pursue election-cycle policies exists even if voters weight past outcomes equally and only discount the future. Theoretical analyses of various election-cycle patterns generated by a stylized model in which the discount rate, time horizon, and other constraints are varied appear in Henry Chappell and William Keech, "Welfare Consequences of the Six-Year Presidential Term Evaluated in the Context of a Model of the U.S. Economy," *American Political Science Review* 77 (March 1983), 75–91.

5. For a good nontechnical discussion of the policy implications of rational-expectations theory, see Bennett McCallum, "The Significance of Rational Expectations Theory," *Challenge* (January–February 1980), 37–43. An elegant, more theoretical treatment is given by Robert J. Gordon in "Recent Developments in the Theory of Inflation and Unemployment," *Journal of Monetary Economics* 2 (1976), 185–219. New classical models grant that anticipated fiscal policies have substantial effects.

6. See Chapters 5 and 6. The (often implicit) assumption that the electorate is oblivious to or steeply discounts the future consequences of current macroeconomic policy actions is more difficult to evaluate empirically and remains ambiguous in the literature. For a clever investigation of this question, see Henry Chappell, Jr., "Presidential Popularity and Macroeconomic Performance: Are Voters Really So Naive?" *Review of Economics and Statistics* 65 (3) (August 1983), 385–392; and Henry Chappell, Jr., and William Keech, "A New View of Political Accountability for Economic Performance," *American Political Science Review* 79 (June 1985), 10–27.

7. See R. Douglas Rivers and Nancy Rose, "Passing the President's Program: Public Opinion and Presidential Influence in the Congress," *American Journal of Political Science* 29 (May 1985), 183–196. Among the first to call attention to the importance of popular support in the polls for presidential prestige, effectiveness, and power was Richard Neustadt in his classic study *Presidential Power* (New York: Wiley, 1960).

8. Remember that these electorally motivated effects are illustrated net of the partisan effects. The pattern of actual election-period outcomes under the conjunction of the partisan and political business cycle hypotheses would depend on which party controlled the presidency. For example, if both hypotheses have merit, the election-year push would begin (and end) at a lower

unemployment level under a typical Democratic administration than under a typical Republican one. Because of the dynamic structure of the economy, an election-oriented economic push that peaks at t^* (the election quarter) will carry over to postelection periods before dying out, unless special austerity measures are taken just after the election.

9. The time profiles would resemble those of the partisan effects graphed in Figures 7.2 and 7.3 (that is, they would resemble first-order dynamic growth or decay), although the dynamic paths would be truncated at four rather than thirty-two periods.

10. The test equations for the M1 money supply growth rate and the adjusted surplus/deficit are based on models 2 and 4, respectively, of Table 7.7, augmented to include election-cycle terms as described earlier. The election-cycle equation for the growth rate of per capita real personal disposable income is derived in the same way as the unemployment and real output equations. Letting r denote the real income growth rate (computed by the first difference of the logarithms and expressed at annual rates), we have the target function

$$r_t^T = b_0 + c_1 q_t^N + b_1 \text{Dem}_{t-1} + a_1 \text{Elect}_t \tag{i}$$

where q^N denotes the growth rate of Q^N (natural real output). Hence the targets of both parties are proportional to (constrained by) the natural real output growth rate, and both parties are assumed to attempt election-period real income accelerations proportional to a_1 Elect. As before, real income growth rate goals vary across the parties by a factor equal to b_1. Clearly, to be consistent with earlier results, b_1 should be greater than 0.

The adjustment-to-target function for r is

$$r_t - r_{t-1} = \phi_1(r_t^T - r_{t-1}) + b_2 \text{Shock}_{t-1} + e_t \tag{ii}$$

Because r is a quarter-to-quarter growth rate, there is less structural inertia than in the cases of unemployment and real output levels. Consequently, the adjustment equation is first order. And inasmuch as growth rates are more easily adjusted to targets than are levels or flows, the magnitude of ϕ_1 is likely to be much closer to 1 in the equations for r than in the comparable equations for U or Q.

Substituting equation (i) into equation (ii) and solving for r gives the dynamic estimating equation

$$r_t = \phi_1 \cdot b_0 + (1 - \phi_1)r_{t-1} + \phi_1 \cdot c_1 q_t^N + \phi_1 \cdot b_1 \text{Dem}_{t-1} \tag{iii}$$
$$+ \phi_1 \cdot a_1 \text{Elect}_t + b_2 \text{Shock}_{t-1} + e_t$$

The estimates for r in Table 8.1 are based on equation (iii).

11. See especially Tufte, *Political Control of the Economy*.

12. Monetary expansions—and, to a lesser degree, fiscal expansions—occurring in an election quarter would not begin to have large impacts on

incomes, output, and employment until periods after the election. Therefore, money supply growth rate equations and fiscal equations in which the election-cycle variables were lagged 1 and 2 quarters were also estimated. None of these experiments, however, produced results appreciably different from those reported in Table 8.1. I also estimated election-cycle equations for unemployment and real output that included lagged inflation rates. These models, which incorporate the assumption that high inflation rates prompt administrations to pursue less ambitious unemployment and real output targets, yielded results similar to those reported in Table 8.1.

13. Nordhaus, "The Political Business Cycle."

14. See, for example, Howard S. Bloom and H. Douglas Price, "Voter Response to Short-Run Economic Conditions: The Asymmetric Effect of Prosperity and Recession," *American Political Science Review* 66 (December 1975), 1240–54; Saul Goodman and Gerald H. Kramer, "Comment on Arcelus and Meltzer, the Effect of Aggregate Economic Conditions on Congressional Elections," *American Political Science Review* 69 (December 1978), 1255–65; John R. Hibbing and John R. Alford, "The Electoral Impact of Economic Conditions: Who Is Held Responsible?" *American Journal of Political Science* 25 (August 1981), 423–439; John R. Hibbing and John R. Alford, "Economic Conditions and the Forgotten Side of Congress: A Foray into U.S. Senate Elections," *British Journal of Political Science* (July 1982), 413–421; Tufte, *Political Control of the Economy*, chap. 5; and M. Stephen Weatherford, "Economic Conditions and Electoral Outcomes: Class Differences in the Political Response to Recession," *American Journal of Political Science* 22 (November 1978), 917–938.

15. More precisely, any president seeking election has a special incentive, including Johnson, who assumed office after Kennedy's assassination, and Ford, who was elevated to the vice presidency as a result of Agnew's forced resignation and to the presidency because of Nixon's.

16. The 1972 episode is described in Maisel, *Managing the Dollar*. Also see Sandford Rose, "The Agony of the Federal Reserve," *Fortune* 90 (July 1974); Tufte, *Political Control of the Economy*, chap. 2; and Wooley, *Monetary Politics*, chap. 8.

17. Calculated on a year-on-year basis, the M1 deflated by the GNP deflator grew by a healthy 2.8 percentage between 1971 and 1972.

18. The rate of growth of output and real income was also higher in 1973 than in 1972, indicating that the monetary expansion came a little late to have maximum effect prior to the election.

19. Tufte, *Political Control of the Economy*, p. 57.

20. The time path of real output under Reagan closely mimics that of unemployment, which was shown along with real income growth rates in Figure 6.2.

21. As it turned out, Johnson hardly needed the assistance of an election-year fillip in real income growth; the Republicans supplied him with the eminently beatable Barry Goldwater for an opponent. Nixon's efforts in 1972 to generate an election-year boom proved to be equally unnecessary; the Democrats supplied him with George McGovern. In neither of these cases,

therefore, is it likely that electorally inspired economic policies altered the presidential outcome. The 1984 election is another matter, however.

22. G. L. Bach, *Making Monetary and Fiscal Policy* (Washington, D.C.: Brookings, 1971), p. 116.

23. Cited in F. R. Dulles, *Labor in America* (New York: Crowell, 1966), p. 394.

24. Recall that "long-run" goals are for practical purposes fully realized by the end of sixteen quarters, or one full presidential term.

25. As noted previously, it is appropriate to start with elections after the 1951 Treasury–Federal Reserve Accord, which made possible coordinated policy and some degree of genuine "political control" of the economy. (Recall that I began the earlier empirical analyses with 1953:1.) It surely would not be appropriate to begin a postwar political analysis of macroeconomic developments with any year before 1948. Between 1945 and 1948, adjustment to the massive demobilization following Japan's surrender was the main force driving the economy.

26. This is why after the war Eisenhower was for a time being courted by both parties as a possible presidential standard bearer. As noted in Chapter 5, in 1952 the Democrats were also burdened with responsibility for the Korean War.

27. Truman acted true to form. In 1948 he vetoed a Republican-initiated tax-cut bill, as he had done twice before in 1947. The veto was overridden by the Republican-controlled Congress. Ironically, the ensuing tax reduction helped reduce unemployment and fueled a brisk election-year growth of real disposable incomes, which undoubtedly contributed to Truman's defeat of Dewey and to the restoration of Democratic majorities in the House and Senate. The 1948 episode, therefore, cannot reasonably be taken as evidence of electorally inspired presidential stimulation of the economy.

28. Most notably by Tufte in *Political Control of the Economy.*

29. Dwight D. Eisenhower, *Waging Peace* (Garden City, N.Y.: Doubleday, 1965), pp. 461, 462.

30. *Economic Report of the President* (Washington, D.C.: Government Printing Office, 1956), p. 28.

31. Dwight D. Eisenhower, *Public Papers of the President* (Washington, D.C.: Government Printing Office, 1960), p. 115.

32. Herbert Stein, chairman of Nixon's Council of Economic Advisors, gives a surprisingly candid account of the planning and motivation of the NEP in chapter 5 of his *Presidential Economics* (New York: Simon and Schuster, 1984).

33. Cited in Alan Blinder, *Economic Policy and the Great Stagflation* (New York: Academic Press, 1979), p. 149.

34. The president advertised this proposal as a matched reduction of taxes and expenditure, with 28 billion dollars being the sum of the new 10-billion-dollar tax-cut proposal and the estimated 18-billion-dollar value of the extended 1975 cuts. Some viewed the proposal as election-cycle policy (the proposed spending reductions were to come largely after the 1976 election);

others worried about contractive effects (the spending reduction would have exceeded the new tax cuts). A report of contemporaneous political reactions appeared in Eileen Shanahan, "Senators Assail Ford Budget Aide on Economic Plan," *New York Times*, October 22, 1975, pp. 1, 4. For an economic analysis of this and other fiscal policy episodes during the 1970s, see Blinder, *Economic Policy*, chap. 7.

35. The Democratic view was well presented in the majority report of the Joint Economic Committee early in 1976. See the account by Edwin Dale, "Democrats Urge Spurs to Economy," *New York Times*, March 11, 1976.

36. See the press reports of Philip Shabecoff, "Ford Denounces Congress on Its Economic Policies," *New York Times*, April 27, 1976, p. 20; and James Naughton, "President Vetoes Jobs Bill; Calls Program Giveaway," *New York Times*, July 7, 1976, p. 1. The Democratic congressional majority, with help from Republicans from high-unemployment states, overrode Ford's veto of a scaled-down, 4-billion-dollar jobs bill on July 22, 1976.

37. Otto Eckstein, *The Great Recession* (Amsterdam: North Holland, 1978), p. 40.

38. Quoted in Vartanig G. Vartan, "Seidman Expects Leveling in Leading Economic Index: Ford Advisor Says Pause Is Now Lull," *New York Times*, October 26, 1976, p. 51.

39. Murray Weidenbaum, chairman of the President's Council of Economic Advisors, and Donald Regan, secretary of the Treasury, had complained much earlier about low money supply growth rates, which had helped produce extremely high interest rates. At one point in late 1981, the Republican congressional leadership—Howard Baker in the Senate and Robert Michel in the House—actually threatened "Wall Street" with credit controls and windfall taxes on interest if the financial community did not show more confidence in the president's program by lowering interest rates. The ignorance of the workings of financial markets displayed by this episode aside, it was amusing indeed to observe leading Republican lawmakers threatening to impose punitive restrictions on private credit institutions. Accounts of these events appeared in Steven Roberts, "2 Republican Legislators Threaten Wall Street with Tighter Controls," *New York Times*, October 10, 1981, pp. 1, B15; Thomas Friedman and Edward Cowan, "Wall St. Asks New Budget Trims and Changes in Reagan Program," *New York Times*, September 15, 1981, pp. 1, D13; and Jonathan Fuerbringer, "Fed Policy Too Tight for Regan," *New York Times*, October 7, 1981.

40. Because one can argue plausibly, as Tufte does, that all that is required to generate short-run movements in disposable income is control of fiscal policy (especially control of the short-term flow of transfers), the 1948 election year has been included in the analysis. Remember, however, that the favorable real income growth rate of 1948 owed much to the tax cut passed over Truman's veto by the Republican-controlled Congress.

41. Empirical work indicates that fourth-quarter-to-fourth-quarter changes in real disposable income may be a better predictor of election outcomes than are annual changes. See, for example, Robert F. Wescott and Miriam Gold-

berg, "The Economy and the 1984 Presidential Election," *Wharton Quarterly Model Outlook* (January 1984), 69–72. The behavior of fourth-quarter growth rates gives about the same degree of support to the election cycle hypothesis as does the pattern reviewed for annual growth rates, however. Comparison of median growth rates, rather than means, also yields about the same degree of support for the political business cycle thesis. The median rates are 2.2 percent for nonelection years, 1.1 percent for presidential years without incumbents running, 2.6 percent for mid-term years, and 2.8 percent for presidential years with incumbents in the race.

42. For a discussion of other factors that may inhibit election-period manipulation of the economy, see Tufte, *Political Control of the Economy*, pp. 62–64.

9. Macroeconomic and Distributional Outcomes during Reagan's First Four Years

1. Quoted by Hedrick Smith, "Reagan's Effort to Change Course of Government," *New York Times*, October 23, 1984, p. A26.

2. The systematic bias in presidential projections of macroeconomic performance, however, has been rather modest. See Mark Kamlet and David Mowery, "Economic, Political and Institutional Influences on Executive and Congressional Budgetary Priorities, 1953–1981," unpublished paper, Carnegie-Mellon University, September 1985; and Victor Zarnovitz, "On the Accuracy of Recent Macroeconomic Forecasts," *American Economic Review* 68 (May 1978), 313–319.

3. It is worth noting here that real output growth rates and other indicators of American economic performance were not nearly as poor during the 1970s as is sometimes assumed. In fact, output grew by about the same amount (36 percent) over the 1970s as over the 1950s, and after-tax income per person grew significantly more over the latter decade than over the former (23 percent versus 15 percent). The special problems of the 1970s were the escalation of inflation and the slowdown of productivity growth (output per hour worked), which owed much to the oil supply shocks and the large influx of young workers and inexperienced female workers into the labor force. A useful corrective to overly pessimistic accounts of the 1970s is John Schwarz and Thomas Volgy, "The Myth of America's Economic Decline," *Harvard Business Review* 63 (September-October 1985), 98–107.

4. A good account of the evidence written for a general audience may be found in Robert J. Gordon, "Why Stopping Inflation May Be Costly," in Robert E. Hall, ed., *Inflation.: Causes and Effects* (Chicago: University of Chicago Press, 1982), chap. 1. A more technical analysis appears in Gordon and S. J. King, "The Output Cost of Disinflation in Traditional and Vector Autoregressive Models," *Brookings Papers on Economic Activity*, 1982 (1), 205–244. See also the analysis later in this chapter of disinflation under Reagan.

5. James Tobin, "Reaganomics and Economics," *New York Review of Books*, December 3, 1981, p. 13.

6. Two well-known volumes making the supply-side case are Arthur Laffer and Jan Seymour, *The Economics of the Tax Revolt* (New York: Harcourt Brace Jovanovich, 1979); and Jude Wanniski, *The Way the World Works* (New York: Basic Books, 1978).

7. The Kemp-Roth tax bill first introduced in Congress in 1977 by Congressman Jack Kemp (R-N.Y.) and Senator William Roth (R-Del.). called for an across-the-board 30-percent decrease in personal tax rates. Later versions of the bill spread the cut over three years (thereby reducing the final reduction of rates from 30 percent to 27 percent) and included indexing of tax rates to inflation. The Kemp-Roth proposals were made part of the 1980 Republican platform and became the centerpiece of President Reagan's fiscal program. See the discussion later in this chapter.

8. Professional analyses of these ideas include Alan Blinder, "Thoughts on the Laffer Curve," in Laurence H. Meyer, ed., *The Supply-Side Effects of Economic Policy* (St. Louis, Mo.: Center for the Study of American Business, 1981); and Don Fullerton, "On the Possibility of an Inverse Relationship between Tax Rates and Government Revenues," *Journal of Public Economics* (October 1982), 3–22.

9. Vehicles and some light machinery and equipment fell under the three-year depreciation schedule; some light structures and most new equipment and machinery fell into the five-year class; business buildings and structures fell under the ten- and fifteen-year schedules. One-time investment tax credits of 6 and 10 percent (for vehicles and other investment assets, respectively) were also legislated by ERTA.

10. In addition to official government publications, good sources of information on the details of ERTA, TEFRA, and other aspects of fiscal policy during the Reagan years include annual volumes on the budget edited by Joseph Pechman, *Setting National Priorities* (Washington, D.C.: Brookings, various years). Also see a series of volumes sponsored and/or published by the Urban Institute, including John Palmer and Isabel Sawhill, eds., *The Reagan Experiment* (Washington, D.C.: Urban Institute Press, 1982); John Palmer and Isabel Sawhill, eds., *The Reagan Record* (Cambridge, Mass.: Ballinger, 1984); and Charles Stone and Isabel Sawhill, eds., *Economic Policy in the Reagan Years* (Washington, D.C.: Urban Institute Press, 1984).

11. Shortly after enactment of his fiscal package, in the face of soaring federal deficit projections, the president felt compelled to request an additional 13 billion dollars' worth of spending cuts along with 3 billion dollars' worth of tax increases ("revenue enhancements"). But the proposals were rebuffed by Congress. In the end the president got only 4 billion dollars of new spending reductions for FY 1982. Budgetary politics are discussed in more detail later in this chapter.

12. Cited in Thomas Edsall, *The New Politics of Inequality* (New York: Norton, 1984), p. 17. Moynihan made this remark on March 18 as the budget package sailed through the Senate Budget Committee.

13. Quoted in Martin Tolchin, "The Federal Budget and How It Was Finally Cut," *New York Times*, December 13, 1981, p. 40.

14. Table 9.11 includes data on actual fiscal year 1984 spending as a percentage of GNP.

15. The magnitude of the raw numbers in the president's defense spending requests prompted many alarming accounts of the scale of the projected defense budgets. In fact, Reagan's plan merely called for restoring defense spending as a fraction of GNP to the level prevailing in the early 1970s, and the rate of increase relative to GNP was much lower than that of the 1950–1953 Korean War buildup and only slightly higher than that of the 1965–1968 Vietnam buildup.

16. The money supply targets, which are shown along with actual money growth rates in the last part of Table 9.1, were announced in February 1981 and repeated in Beryl Sprinkel's July 23, 1981 *Statement before the House Committee on Banking, Finance and Urban Affairs.*

17. Recall from Chapter 8, Political Business Cycles, that the coordination of monetary policy and fiscal policy in an expansive direction during the last half of President Reagan's first term made possible a dramatic recovery from the 1981–1982 recession that peaked in the 1984 presidential election year.

18. For example, in "Tax Rules and the Mismanagement of Monetary Policy," *American Economic Review: Papers and Proceedings* (May 1980), 182–186, Feldstein wrote: "A more appropriate policy mix [than the traditional prescription of easy money and a tight fiscal position] for achieving the dual goals of balanced demand and increased business investment would combine a tight-money policy and fiscal incentives [tax cuts] for investment and saving" (p. 184). Ironically, in the same issue of the *Review*, in an article entitled "Stabilization Policy and Capital Formation," Robert Hall of Stanford University, appointed by Feldstein to head the Business Fluctuations program at the National Bureau of Economic Research, concluded: "Stimulus of aggregate demand through government expenditures appears to discourage investment, while stimulus through monetary expansion encourages investment" (p. 159). See Section 3.6 for more discussion of Feldstein's views on monetary policy and saving and investment.

19. A technical demonstration of how monetary policy can offset fiscal policy is given in Ray C. Fair, "The Sensitivity of Fiscal Policy Effects to Assumptions about the Behavior of the Federal Reserve," *Econometrica* 46 (September 1978), 1165–80.

20. The performance of 1984 did not carry over into 1985, however. In the first quarter of 1985, the annual real GNP growth rate slumped to 0.3 percent. Real output growth was about 2.2 percent for the year as a whole.

21. In 1985 the GNP gap rose again with the slump in growth rates from the election-year high.

22. See Iver Peterson, "Homeless Crisscross U.S., Until Their Cars and Their Dreams Break Down," *New York Times*, December 15, 1982, p. A16; and the stories carried on the front page of the *Wall Street Journal*, November 12, 1982. An unusually small fraction of the unemployed received jobless benefits during the 1981–1982 contraction: only about 45 percent, as compared to 78 percent during the 1975 recession. The main reason was the tightened

coverage requirements embodied in the administration's 1981 fiscal package. See Gary Burtless, "Why Is Insured Unemployment So Low?" *Brookings Papers on Economic Activity*, 1983 (1), 225–249.

23. As I edit this chapter in April 1986, the recovery from the 1981–1982 contraction has now lasted nearly four years, thanks in part to very favorable energy price developments. Yet unemployment remains just above 7 percent.

24. See the regression results in Table 3.13 on the response of investment to contractions and expansions.

25. An analysis of the decline in the CPI inflation rate during Reagan's first term appears in Charles Stone and Elizabeth Sawhill, *Economic Policy in the Reagan Years* (Washington, D.C.: Urban Institute Press, 1984), chap. 1.

26. It is sometimes argued that transitory changes in inflation are produced by changes in the unemployment gap and therefore the first difference of $(U - U^N)$ should also appear in rule-of-thumb equations such as (9.1) and (9.2). See, for example, Jeffrey Sachs's comments on Buiter and Miller in *Brookings Papers on Economic Activity*, 1983 (2), 366–372. Equations including a first difference term (or a lagged unemployment gap term, which amounts to the same thing) did not yield significant results or change appreciably the coefficients reported in equation (9.2), however.

27. Analyses reaching the same conclusion about the costs of disinflation during the first two years of the Reagan administration include Benjamin M. Friedman, "Lessons from the 1979–82 Monetary Policy Experiment," *American Economic Review, Papers and Proceedings* 74 (May 1984), 382–387; and, in a more popular form, William Nordhaus, "What's Behind Today's Disinflation," *New York Times*, October 31, 1982, pp. D1–D2.

28. Quoted in *Business Week*, April 13, 1981, p. 136.

29. Quoted in Steven R. Weisman, "Reaganomics and the President's Men," *New York Times Magazine*, October 24, 1982, p. 36.

30. Quoted in Caroline Atkinson, "Democrats Outline One-Year Tax Cut," *Washington Post*, April 10, 1981, p. 1.

31. *Congressional Quarterly Almanac*, 97th Congress, 1st Session, 1981 (Washington, D.C.: Congressional Quarterly, 1981), p. 97.

32. The data in the table do not include the 29-percent tax cut on unearned income from capital that was ultimately enacted.

33. It is also informative to compare the tax relief scheme proposed by President Carter in 1980 with President Reagan's 1981 plan. As was noted earlier, Carter proposed using income tax credits to offset Social Security payroll tax increases and inflation-induced bracket creep. To implement the Carter plan Democratic members of the House Ways and Means Committee favored a tax credit equal to 10 percent of each taxpayer's Social Security tax liabilities.

Under pre-ERTA tax law, the share of total federal income tax payments borne by those falling in the $20,000-and-below income classes was 16 percent. Under the 1981 Reagan plan, they receive 12 percent of the tax reduction benefits; under the 1980 Democratic plan, they would have received 31 percent of the benefits. Those with incomes of $50,000 and below bore 66 percent of the pre-ERTA federal income tax burden. Under Reagan's plan they receive 64 percent of the tax savings, as opposed to 90 percent under the Democrats' 1980 plan. Taxpayers with incomes above $50,000, who carried 34 percent of the pre-ERTA tax load, therefore enjoy 36 percent of the Reagan plan's benefits, but would have had to settle for only 10 percent of the benefits if the Carter plan had been implemented.

The data for these comparisons came from the Joint Economic Committee and the Congressional Budget Office and were reported in the *New York Times*, April 20, 1981, p. D3.

34. Although President Reagan supported indexing in principle, he wanted to defer it to a later tax bill, and so it was not part of the proposal submitted by the administration to Congress. After indexing passed on the Senate floor, however, the administration supported its incorporation into the Republican-sponsored bill in the House.

35. A similiar proposal made by Senator Hollings (D-S.C.) was rejected five days later by pretty much the same margin and partisan division of the vote.

36. *Congressional Quarterly Almanac*, 1981, p. 262.

37. As punishment for working so closely with the Republicans on the 1981 budget struggles (which included supplying the White House with Democratic budget strategy), the Democratic Steering and Policy Committee voted on January 3, 1982 to kick Congressman Gramm (D-Tex.) off the Budget Committee. Gramm resigned from the House on January 5 and, running as a Republican, won a special election for the seat on February 12. He rejoined the Budget Committee as a minority member on February 22.

38. According to the ABC News/*Washington Post* polls, the fraction of the public believing that "Reagan is going too far in attempting to cut back or eliminate government social programs" rose from just under 35 percent in April 1981 to over 50 percent in April 1982. The data are reported in John L. Goodman, Jr., *Public Opinion during the Reagan Administration* (Washington, D.C.: Urban Institute Press, 1983), fig. 8, p. 35.

39. Congressional Budget Office, "Effects of Major Changes in Individual Income and Excise Taxes Enacted in 1981 and 1982 for Households of Different Income Categories," staff memorandum, March 1984, table 1 (calendar years); and Congressional Budget Office, "Major Legislative Changes in Human Resources Programs since January 1981," special study, August 1983, summary table (fiscal years).

40. To conserve space I report Minarik's data only at five-year intervals for the years prior to 1980. Omitting the intervening years in no way distorts the basic pattern. In 1984 the median family income was about $25,000.

41. Between 1955 and 1980 the income tax code was modified ten times.

42. The Bureau of the Census publishes data on median incomes of all families, but not four-person families specifically. The four-person family data used as the basis for Table 9.6 and the associated discussion were assembled by Joseph Minarik from census source material. See Joseph Minarik,

"Income Distribution Effects of the 1981 Tax Cuts," paper presented at the annual meeting of the National Tax Association, Nashville, Tennessee, November 26, 1984, p. 15.

43. Alternatively, this may be thought of as a process of "real bracket creep." As real economic growth raised standards of living, "ability" to pay increased and real tax burdens rose commensurately.

44. Measuring the progression of an income tax system can become a rather technical matter—see, for example, the seminal article by Richard Musgrave and Tun Thin, "Income Tax Progression, 1928–48," *Journal of Political Economy* 56 (December 1948), 498–514—but in the examples ahead I take a rather casual approach.

45. The tax rates for the highest income classes in Table 9.6 are probably exaggerated a bit, because the computations did not factor in tax shelters and other preferences that some rich households employ. See the discussion in Minarik, "Income Distribution Effects."

46. The Tax Reduction Act of 1975 provided for a credit equal to 10 percent of the first $4000 of earned income (up to a maximum of $400). The Revenue Act of 1978 raised the earned income ceiling to $5000 and the maximum credit to $500, beginning in 1979. The credit falls to 0 as earned income rises from $5000 to $10,000. Families with income tax liabilities less than the credit receive a lump-sum payment equal to the difference. The credit is restricted to families with dependents, which was Congress's blunt way of excluding students and pensioners from the tax benefits. Of course this also meant that low-income working people without children were also excluded.

47. Appendix A of Joseph Pechman, *Federal Tax Policy* (Washington, D.C.: Brookings, 1983), gives a convenient historical summary of major changes in the federal income tax code.

48. The source of the data in Table 9.7—John Karl Scholz, "Individual Income Tax Provisions of the 1981 Tax Act," in Joseph Pechman, ed., *Setting National Priorities: The 1983 Budget* (Washington, D.C.: Brookings, 1983), pp. 251–262—also gives estimates for 1982 and 1983, before the full effects of ERTA were realized. It should be noted that the estimates of effective tax rates and tax reductions do not take into account the 1981 corporate tax cuts. If it were possible to accurately estimate the ultimate benefits to individuals of the corporate tax reductions, the relative gains of the highest income classes would undoubtedly be greater than those shown in Table 9.7

49. It should be noted that the distribution of taxpayers over income classes is not the same in Tables 9.6 and 9.7. Table 9.6 (as well as Table 9.3) pertains to four-person families, and the median family income in 1984 was about $25,000. Table 9.7 pertains to all people filing tax returns. When comparing effective tax rates on the lowest income classes in Tables 9.6 and 9.7, one should also remember that many more taxpayers in the latter table were without dependents and therefore were not eligible for the (negative tax) earned income credit.

50. If legislated increases in federal payroll (Social Security) taxes are factored in, only the upper half of the income distribution received any reduction in federal taxes between 1980 and 1984.

51. In dollar terms, the most important change made in the Social Security program by the amendments was a six-month delay (from July to January) in the payment of annual cost-of-living adjustments, which are based on the increase in the CPI over the preceding year. Because of the size of the Social Security program, this change reduced outlays by almost 10 billion dollars between FY 1983 and FY 1985.

52. For the same reason, spending on Food Stamps declined by a smaller percentage of the pre-Reagan policy base in FY 1983 than in FY 1984.

53. For discretionary programs, the Reagan "budget proposals" or "budget plans" were based on the lowest outlays proposed in the administration's FY 1982, FY 1983, or FY 1984 budgets. For entitlement programs, the Reagan proposals were based on the sum of all nonoverlapping program changes proposed in the administration's FY 1982 to FY 1984 budgets. The administration numbers were then compared with CBO estimates of outlays for FY 1985 under pre-Reagan policies to calculate the percentage reductions shown in the second column of Table 9.8. Enacted outlays were compared with the CBO estimates to calculate the percentage reductions shown in the third column of the table.

54. The president's remarks, along with pertinent statements by other administration officials, were reported in David Rosenbaum, "Reagan's 'Safety Net' Proposal: Who Will Land, Who Will Fall," *New York Times*, March 18, 1981, p. 1.

55. Murray Weidenbaum, one of President Reagan's chief economic advisers at that time, admitted years later that the "unstated criterion" for the safety net was "which were the politically vulnerable programs and which weren't." Weidenbaum was quoted by Paul Blustein in "Reagan's Record," *Wall Street Journal*, October 25, 1985, p. 2.

56. The 1983 Social Security Amendments cannot be tied to the Reagan administration. The measure had strong bipartisan support. Acting alone, the administration proposed cuts to Social Security on May 12, 1981, but the plan was greeted with a public furor and the Senate unanimously rejected it.

57. At the option of the states, AFDC benefits may also go to two-parent families with an unemployed head of household. Approximately 7 percent of families receiving benefits fall in this category.

58. As Table 7.4 indicated, in the mid-1970s the percentages of the outlays for these programs going to those with pretransfer incomes below the poverty line were as follows: 92 percent for AFDC, 78 percent for SSI, 83 percent for Food Stamps, and 73 percent for Medicaid.

59. Because AFDC is a joint federal-state program, with the federal government carrying about 55 percent of the cost and the states setting payment levels, benefits vary by state. For example, in California, a state with very high benefits, the average monthly disposable income in 1981 for working AFDC mothers (earnings plus benefit payments) under pre-OBRA law was $721. For nonworking AFDC recipients in California, average monthly disposable income (benefit payments only) was $533. AFDC mothers who worked in California therefore improved their standard of living by about 35 percent. In Texas, which has among the lowest benefits, working AFDC

mothers had average incomes of $371 per month and nonworking recipients had average incomes of $290 a month, a difference of 27 percent. Estimates of the returns to working for AFDC mothers in ten representative states appear in "The Poor: Profiles of Families in Poverty," University of Chicago Center for the Study of Welfare Policy, Washington, D.C., March 20, 1981).

60. The estimates of the numbers of households affected by the changes to the AFDC program are from the Congressional Budget Office, "Major Changes in Human Resources Programs," pp. 38–39.

61. Also, the estimates of the benefit changes are based on the cost of the programs to the government. Except in the case of Food Stamps, where benefits may for practical purposes be regarded as cash, estimates of changes in the value of benefits from in-kind programs are likely to exaggerate somewhat the value of the losses to individuals.

62. If $80,000 seems low as the threshold for the top 1.7 percent of the income distribution, remember that the categories are based on the concept of *adjusted* gross income under federal tax law. On average, adjusted gross incomes must be raised by a factor of about 25 percent to obtain personal incomes.

63. Changes in taxes are shown with positive signs because the tax reductions raised household incomes. The tax changes for the higher income classes in Table 9.9 are larger than those implied by the administration numbers shown in Table 9.3 because the latter table did not include the tax cut on unearned income and capital gains.

64. The distributional pattern for 1982 and 1983, not reported here but available in the CBO source memoranda, is essentially the same as that for 1984.

65. Earlier in this chapter I pointed out that aggregate personal tax cuts amounted to almost three times as much as aggregate social spending cuts. Further, only about six-tenths of the spending cuts can be allocated to individuals and families. The tax cuts, therefore, have four to five times the weight of the spending cuts in determining the change in the net income position of the average household in Table 9.9.

66. Remember, too, that as a computational matter the all-household average percentage change (3.4 percent) is income weighted. This means that the experience of each high-income household contributes more heavily to the average than does that of each low-income household.

67. Unfortunately, the federal government does not produce data on personal disposable income disaggregated by income class. The Census Bureau produces data on incomes of families and "unrelated" individuals by quintiles of the distribution, but the income concept is before tax and inclusive of cash transfers (see Table 3.2). Inasmuch as redistribution of tax burdens was a key feature of Reagan fiscal policy, the census income data are not useful here. The family disposable income data in Table 9.10 were compiled by the Urban Institute from government source materials, using the Census Bureau's quintile share data as the starting point. The Urban Institute data are net of personal taxes, are adjusted for inflation, and include cash transfers

and Food Stamps. See the source referenced at the bottom of Table 9.10 for more details.

68. The fact that the average actual percentage change in Table 9.10 is almost exactly equal to the average percentage change in net income positions (due to the changes in tax-and-transfer policies under Reagan relative to the pre-Reagan base) shown in Table 9.9 is coincidental.

69. As one might expect in view of this and related statistics, the official poverty rate also increased substantially during these years. For empirical analyses of the connection between Reagan policies and trends in poverty and inequality, see Committee on Ways and Means, U.S. House of Representatives, *Effects of the Omnibus Budget Reconciliation Act of 1981 (OBRA), Welfare Changes and the Recession on Poverty* (Washington, D.C.: Government Printing Office, July 25, 1984); Sheldon Danziger and Peter Gottschalk, "The Effects of Unemployment and Policy Changes on America's Poor," University of Wisconsin-Madison, Institute for Research on Poverty Discussion Paper 770-84; and Sheldon Danziger, "Poverty and Inequality under Reaganomics," *Journal of Contemporary Studies* 5 (Summer 1982), 17–30.

70. Mondale's remark is reported in Peter Kilborn, "4 Years Later: Who Is Better Off?" *New York Times*, October 9, 1984, p. 1.

71. The administration made small reductions ("recisions") in Carter's fiscal 1981 budget, but the significant tax and spending changes did not come until Reagan's first full budget year, fiscal 1982. Therefore I have used the average of fiscal 1980–1981 federal budget data as the benchmark for the Reagan shifts. Only estimates of FY 1985 budget data were available to me at the time of writing, and so fiscal 1984 is the last year shown in Table 9.11.

72. The dollar amount is much larger if expressed relative to projected spending under pre-Reagan policies, as in Tables 9.8 and 9.9.

73. The Social Security system payroll tax is a proportional tax on wages up to a ceiling. In 1983 the ceiling was raised from $29,700 to $35,700 and indexed to wage inflation. The payroll tax rate is 13.4 percent (with increases scheduled for the future) and is shared equally by employees and employers. Because the payroll tax falls to 0 on earnings above the wage ceiling, the Social Security tax structure is regressive for above-ceiling wages and proportional below the ceiling.

74. William Greider, *The Education of David Stockman* (New York: Dutton, 1982).

75. Quoted in Karen Arenson, "Critics Assail Supply-Side Results on Eve of President's 2nd Tax Cut," *New York Times*, June 30, 1982, p. 1.

76. Quoted in Hedrick Smith, "Conservative Shift Created in 190 Days," *New York Times*, July 30, 1981, p. 1.

77. Quoted in Tom Wicker, "The Deficit Looks Deliberate," *International Herald Tribune*, July 20–21, 1985, p. 4.

Index

Abortion issue, 200, 369
Accelerated Cost Recovery System, 285, 296
Administration-Gramm-Latta plan, 304
AFL-CIO, 217
Afghanistan invasion, 129, 174, 181
After-tax income equality, 234
Aid for Families with Dependent Children (AFDC), 48, 61, 234–235, 236, 314, 315; Unemployed Parent Program, 59
Anderson, John, 205
Anti-inflation policies, 122, 123, 253
Armstrong, William, 302

Bach, G. L., 267
Baily, Martin Neal, 32
Baker, Howard, 288, 386
Barber, James David, 280
Bay of Pigs fiasco, 128
Berlin blockade, 128
Big business, 216, 217. *See also* Income tax, corporate
Bolling, Royal, 306
Bracket creep, 92, 285, 296, 308
Bradley, Bill, 303
Brenner, M. Harvey, 50
Brookings Institution, 87
Bumpers, Dale, 303
Bureau of Labor Statistics, 65, 69
Burns, Arthur, 72–73, 264
Bush, George, 284
Business cycles, 100, 109, 255

Caldeira, Greg, 169
Capacity utilization, 292
Capital stock, 293–294
Carter, Jimmy: in 1980 election, 6, 175, 187, 197, 205, 206–207, 209, 273, 296–297; economic policy and perfor-
mance, 9, 74–75, 76, 124, 186, 191, 193, 195, 196, 198, 199–200, 205, 207–208, 236, 265, 273, 279, 286, 287, 293, 319; monetary policy, 76, 191; -induced recessions, 98, 218, 281, 289; and inflation, 124, 193, 195; crisis events during presidency, 129, 174–175, 200; and unemployment, 133, 153–154, 191, 265, 281, 292; approval ratings, 174–175, 180, 181, 195, 196, 203; and OPEC price shocks, 181, 226, 281; welfare policy, 186; fiscal policy, 191; in 1976 election, 208; tax policy, 390–391
Center for International Affairs (Harvard University), 217
Central bank, 328–329
Civil rights acts, 129
Commerce Department, 247–248
Commodity Credit Corporation Export-Import Bank, 28
Commodity substitutions, 70
Conable, Barber, 300
Conference Board, The, 216
Congressional Budget Office (CBO), 286, 312, 314, 315
Connolly, John, 221
Consumer expenditures, 66–67
Consumer Expenditure Survey, 66, 83
Consumer Price Index, 63, 67, 87, 302; defined, 19; inflation rate, 22, 23, 69, 70, 75, 76, 82–83, 90, 96, 97, 119, 135, 160, 193; revised, 63; and standard of living, 69; and food prices, 83; and cost-of-living measures, 90
Consumer prices. *See* Prices
Core inflation rate, 72, 73, 74, 75, 252. *See also* Inflation, rates
Cost-of-living adjustments (COLAs), 65
Cost-of-living wage escalators, 65